NAPOLEON
AND HIS PARENTS

NAPOLEON
AND HIS PARENTS

ON THE
THRESHOLD OF HISTORY

DOROTHY CARRINGTON

DUTTON NEW YORK

DUTTON
Published by the Penguin Group
Penguin Books USA Inc., 375 Hudson Street,
New York, New York 10014, U.S.A.
Penguin Books Ltd, 27 Wrights Lane,
London W8 5TZ, England
Penguin Books Australia Ltd, Ringwood,
Victoria, Australia
Penguin Books Canada Ltd, 2801 John Street,
Markham, Ontario, Canada L3R 1B4
Penguin Books (N.Z.) Ltd, 182–190 Wairau Road,
Auckland 10, New Zealand

Penguin Books Ltd, Registered Offices:
Harmondsworth, Middlesex, England

First published in the United States in 1990 by Dutton,
an imprint of Penguin Books USA Inc.

Originally published in Great Britain by Viking.

First printing, May, 1990

1 3 5 7 9 10 8 6 4 2

Library of Congress Cataloging-in-Publication Data

Carrington, Dorothy.
Napoleon and his parents : on the threshold of history / Dorothy
Carrington.
p.   cm.
Includes bibliographical references.
ISBN 0-525-24833-1
1. Napoleon I, Emperor of the French, 1769–1821—Family.
2. Napoleon I, Emperor of the French, 1769–1821—Childhood and
youth.   3. Bonaparte family.   4. France—Kings and rulers—
Biography.   I. Title.
DC205.C37   1990
944.05'092'2—dc20
[B]   90-2816
                                                          CIP

Printed in the United States of America

For His Imperial Highness
The Prince Napoleon

CONTENTS

❖ ❁ ❖

LIST OF ILLUSTRATIONS

AUTHOR'S NOTE

Before the French conquest the official, written language in Corsica was Italian, although Corsican, distantly derived from Latin, was also spoken. Priests or scribes sometimes wrote in Latin, as can be seen in the baptismal act of Joseph Bonaparte, and Latin was also the language in which were dispensed certain courses at the univesity of Corte, as can be judged by Carlo Bonaparte's academic essay,

The Christian names of Corsicans who became adult before the French conquest are given in this book in their Italian form, and double Christian names of eighteenth-century Corsicans are not linked by hyphens. The spelling of surnames, being not standardized at the period, has presented certain problems. When several spellings appear I have chosen that given in the source closest to my text, while indicating other versions. For simplification I have used one spelling only for members of a same family. Thus having chosen Paravisino for Carlo's brother-in-law, I have followed the same spelling for the maiden name of his kinswoman, Carlo's mother, although Paravisini is as often found in contemporary texts. In accordance with the practice of historians writing in English I have omitted accents from the names of Napoleon, Jerome and Josephine, except in titles of books and articles written in French.

The spelling of Corsican place-names, affected by Italian, French and Corsican usage, is at present a subject of debate. I have adopted a spelling that has become traditional since the French conquest and is employed in the *Guide Bleu* (1983 edn), but without accents.

✣()✣

ACKNOWLEDGEMENTS

I am deeply grateful to HIH The Prince Napoleon who graciously gave me access to his family archives before their recent cession to the Archives de France, and permission to reproduce pictures in his possession. By the kindness of the Prince and Princess I was thus able to examine, in ideal conditions, an assemblage of documents, for the most part unpublished, that throw an altogether new light on the parents and the early life of Napoleon.

I express my gratitude to the late François Flori, Corsican bibliographer, and to General Pascal-P. Santini, Corsican historian, who generously communicated to me rare or unpublished documents from their private collections.

I offer my warm thanks to Mr and Mrs Jonathan Gatty, and to Mrs Pamela Bulmer, who have allowed me to reproduce their unpublished portraits of Napoleon.

To M. Pierre Lamotte, Conservateur en Chef des Archives de la Région Corse et Directeur des Services d'Archives de la Corse du Sud, I express my grateful appreciation of his unfailing assistance. His erudition has made an important contribution to this book.

I give my thanks to the following who have facilitated my researches: P. André-Marie, O F M, Secrétaire de l'Association Franciscorsa; Mr Ian Greenlees, former Director of the British Institute of Florence; M. Gérard Hubert, Inspecteur-général des Musées chargé de la Conservation du Musée National des Châteaux de Malmaison et de Bois-Préau, de la Maison Bonaparte d'Ajaccio et du Musée de l'Île d'Aix; M. F. Jenn, Directeur des Services d'Archives des Yvelines; M. Alexis Peretti, Conservateur Régional des Monuments Historiques de Corse; Prof. Amando Saitta, Presidente dell' Istituto Storico per l'Età Moderna e Contemporanea, Rome; to the directors and staffs of:

The Public Record Office, the British Library, the London Library; the British Council, Paris, les Archives de France, la Bibliothèque Nationale, l'Institut Catholique, le Musée Carnavalet, la Documentation Photographique de la Réunion des Musées Nationaux (Paris); le Musée Napoléon Ier (Brienne-le-Château); les Archives Départementales de la Corse du Sud, Les Archives Communales d'Ajaccio; Les Archives Communales de Corte, l'Institut d'Études Corses, Université Pascal Paoli (Corte); la Biblioteca Mediciea Laurenziana (Florence).

I wish to thank the friends who in various ways have helped and encouraged me in this task and given me the benefit of their expert knowledge: M. René Durando, professeur d'Italien; Mme J. Charon, Archives de France; Mlle F. Ciccoli, professeur d'Italien, Marie-Rose Colonna de Cinarca, professeur de lettres classiques Maître Germain, Mrs E. Gotch, Mme R. Judais, Secrétaire générale de l'Association des Amis du Parc Naturel Régional de Corse, M. G. Oberti, correspondent de l'Institut de France, Cécile Pozzo di Borgo, Conservateur d'Archives au Ministère des Affaires Étrangères: Mlle M.-D. Roche, Conservateur des Musées de la ville d'Ajaccio et d'Objets d'Art de la Corse du Sud; Mlle C. Rocchi, Conseiller d'Orientation; Mme J. Serafini-Costoli, Conservateur du Musée d'Ethnographie Corse; M. Jacques Stuart.

Such a book can hardly be written without particular material aid. I wish to acknowledge my debt of gratitude to the British Academy, the Arts Council and the Royal Literary Fund for their timely and welcome assistance.

✣()✣

CHRONOLOGY

	Events within Bonaparte family	*Events outside Bonaparte family*
1729		Corsicans rebel against Genoa (Dec.).
1730		Corsican nationalists control interior.
1731		Greek immigrants driven from settlement in Paomia.
1731–2		Intervention of troops of Emperor Charles VI supporting Genoa.
1735		Three elected 'Generals of the nation', including Giacinto Paoli, call *consulta* in Corte at which national independence and a system of government are proclaimed (Jan.).
1736		Theodor von Neuhof lands in Corsica, is crowned king (15 April), leaves island (Nov.).
1738–41		Intervention of French troops supporting Genoa. Nationalists defeated; Giacinto Paoli retires to Naples taking Pasquale (b. 1725). Creation of French regiment, Royal Corse (1739).

	Events within Bonaparte family	*Events outside Bonaparte family*
1741	Giuseppe Maria Bonaparte (grandfather of Napoleon) marries Maria Saveria Paravisino.	
1743	Giovan' Geronimo Ramolino (father of Letizia) appointed commander of forces in Ajaccio.	
1745	Napoleone Bonaparte marries Maria Rosa Bozzi.	Intervention of Anglo-Sardinian forces supporting nationalists. Bastia captured (Nov.).
1746	Birth of Carlo Maria, father of Napoleon (27 March).	Bastia lost (Feb.).
1748		Publication of Montesquieu's *De l'esprit des lois*. Intervention of French troops commanded by marquis de Cursay, who administers Corsica until 1752.
1749	Giuseppe Maria Bonaparte represents Ajaccio at *consulta* in Corte convoked by marquis de Cursay (Jan.); welcomes him in Ajaccio with Paravisino (Feb.).	
1750	Giovan' Geronimo Ramolino appointed chancellor of jurisdiction of Bocognano.	
1752		Nationalists adopt system of government with General Gaffori as head of state (Oct.). De Cursay recalled (Dec.).
1753		General Gaffori assassinated (Oct.).

Events within Bonaparte family	*Events outside Bonaparte family*
1755	Return of Pasquale Paoli, elected General of the Nation (14 July); proclaims national constitution (16–18 Nov.).
1756	First Traité de Compiègne (Aug.), by which French troops occupy Genoese coastal towns.
1757 Angela Maria (Letizia's widowed mother) marries François Fesch.	
1758	Paoli founds L'Île-Rousse; establishes printing press.
1759 Giuseppe Maria and Luciano Bonaparte obtain recognition of kinship from Buonaparte of Tuscany.	French troops withdrawn from coastal towns.
1760	Apostolic visitor sent to Paoli by Pope Clement XIII.
1762	Publication of J.-J. Rousseau's *Du contrat social*.
1763 Birth of Joseph Fesch (3 Jan.). Marriage of Geltrude Bonaparte and Nicolò Paravisino (15 June). Death of Giuseppe Maria Bonaparte (13 Dec.).	
1764 Signing of dotal act of marriage between Carlo Bonaparte and Letizia Ramolino (31 May). Religious marriage ceremony (?). Carlo Bonaparte visits Leghorn, Rome, Florence (Sept. 1765). Birth and death of daughter to Letizia.	Matteo Buttafoco corresponds with Rousseau (1764–5). Second Traité de Compiègne (Aug. 1764) by which French troops (commanded by comte de Marbeuf) undertake to garrison Genoese ports for four years.

	Events within Bonaparte family	*Events outside Bonaparte family*
1765	Maria Rosa Bonaparte plans to marry daughter, Isabella, to Spoturno with Bozzi house as dowry. Carlo approaches Paoli and Marbeuf (Nov.), enrols in university in Corte (Dec.).	University opens in Corte (Jan.). James Boswell lands in Cap Corse (13 Oct.), stays with Paoli at Sollacaro (21–28 Oct.), with Marbeuf in Bastia (9–20 Nov.).
1766	Isabella Bonaparte marries Ludovico Ornano (16 Jan.), Luciano having induced her mother to exchange Bozzi house for one of his vineyards. Separation of Geltrude and Nicolò Paravisino.	
1767	Letizia, Napoleone Bonaparte and Geltrude Paravisino join Carlo in Corte (spring). Death of Napoleone (17 Aug.). Carlo visits Ajaccio as agent for Paoli while acting as his secretary.	Corsican nationalists capture Capraja (Feb.).
1768	Birth of Joseph Nabulion in Corte (7 Jan.), in house of Tommaseo and Maria Arrighi, his godparents. Letizia shines at reception of Tunisian envoy (spring). Speech urging Corsicans to resist invasion, made by Carlo? Carlo enrols in volunteer force to guard Paoli (23 Aug.–3 Sept.). Giuseppe Maria Pietrasanta appointed to Conseil Supérieur (Sept.). Geltrude and Nicolò Paravisino reconciled.	Publication of Boswell's *An Account of Corsica* (Feb.). Paoli entertains Tunisian envoy (spring). Breakdown of Paoli's negotiations with duc de Choiseul. Traité de Versailles (15 May) by which Genoa cedes Corsica to France. Chardon appointed *intendant*. *Consulta* in Corte (May). Conseil Supérieur established in Bastia (June). Paoli's proclamation to nation (Aug.). French troops defeated at Borgo (8–9 Nov.). French solicit armistice (Nov.).

Events within Bonaparte family	*Events outside Bonaparte family*
1769	Carlo receives remuneration for war service from Paoli (Jan.). Letizia orders clothes from Bastia (March). Carlo accompanies Paoli to Porto Vecchio; returns to Corte, takes Letizia and Joseph, via Niolo (?), to Ajaccio. Carlo dines with comte de Narbonne (7 July). Napoleon born in Ajaccio (15 Aug.). Carlo practises as *procureur* in court of Ajaccio (from 20 Sept.). Carlo awarded doctorate by university of Pisa (27–30 Nov.). Registered as lawyer by Conseil Supérieur (11 Dec.).	Comte de Vaux lands heavy reinforcements (spring). *Consulta* (March) mobilizes all men from 16 to 60 to national militia. De Vaux orders Corsicans to surrender. Delegation of city of Ajaccio, including Luciano Bonaparte, submits to French authorities (18 April). Corsicans defeated at Ponte Novo (8 May). French occupy Corte (21 May). Paoli reaches Porto Vecchio, sets sail in British vessel (13 June), reaches Leghorn (16 June). Comte de Marbeuf leaves Corsica (Aug.). Paoli lands in England (19 Sept.). Nationalists maintain resistance in interior, among them the Bonelli, cousins of Bonaparte. Publication of Voltaire's *Précis du siècle de Louis XV*, 2nd edition, with account of Corsican resistance to French invasion.
1770	Death of François Fesch (Jan.). Isabella and Ludovico Ornano bring suit against Luciano Bonaparte to recover Bozzi house (May).	Census of population of Corsica. Order of nobility created in Corsica (April). Marbeuf returns to Corsica as commander-in-chief (May). First meeting of Assemblée des États de Corse (15–27 Sept.).
1771	Napoleon baptized (21 July) with Maria Anna (b. 14 July).	Colla de Pradine succeeds Chardon as *intendant* (June).

	Events within Bonaparte family	*Events outside Bonaparte family*
1771 contd	Marbeuf visits Bonaparte (Aug.). Carlo and Luciano Bonaparte obtain recognition of nobility (13 Sept.). Carlo elected to Corsican Estates, a representative of nobility of Ajaccio (29 Sept.). Carlo appointed *assesseur* at court of Ajaccio (22 Nov.). Death of Maria Anna (23 Nov.).	Decision to re-establish Greek immigrants at Cargese (July).
1772	Carlo sits in Corsican Estates, elected to *Nobles Douze*. Lawsuit between Luciano Bonaparte and Ornano heard in court of Ajaccio (Aug.).	Publication of Guibert's *Essai général de tactique*. Assemblée des États de Corse (1–20 May, 15 July, 15–16 Nov.). Marquis de Monteynard appointed governor of Corsica (3 July).
1773	Ornano boast of imminent victory (April); Carlo begs Marbeuf's intervention; case settled, leaving Bonaparte in possession of Bozzi house (12 Sept.). Death of Giuseppe Maria Pietrasanta.	Order of Jesuits abolished.
1774	Carlo completes construction of terrace added to house (March).	Nicodemo Pasqualini lands in Corsica inciting revolt (March); meeting of 60 rebel leaders; revolt breaks out (June); severely repressed in Niolo: 11 executed, flocks slaughtered. Death of Louis XV (10 May). Marbeuf goes to Paris (Aug.). Corsican resistance drastically repressed by Narbonne and Sionville (Aug.–Nov.).
1775	Carlo sues Ramolino for full payment of Letizia's dowry; wins	Marbeuf returns to Corsica (May) with de Boucheporn, appointed

Events within Bonaparte family	*Events outside Bonaparte family*
1775 *contd* case (March); Ramolino's goods sold by auction (May).	*intendant* in succession to Colla de Pradine. Assemblée des États de Corse (25 May–22 June). Rivalry between Marbeuf and Narbonne. Narbonne leaves Corsica (June).
1776	Delegates of Estates to Louis XVI bring complaints against Marbeuf (Aug.). Amnesty granted to Corsican political prisoners and exiles. Benedetti meets Paoli, who refuses amnesty in London (3–5 Oct.).
1777 Birth of Maria Anna (Elisa) (13 Jan). With aid of Marbeuf Carlo is elected to Corsican Estates, and deputy for nobility to Versailles (2 June). His claim to Salines accepted with subsidy for draining site. Letizia entertained in Bastia by Marbeuf (winter 1777–8).	Assemblée des États de Corse (14 May–13 July). Scholarships offered to sons of nobles in French military colleges.
1778 Birth of Louis (2 Sept.), baptized with Marbeuf and Mme de Boucheporn godparents (24 Sept.). Carlo prepares claim to Odone heritage (Oct.–Nov.). Carlo and Letizia with comte Colchen visit Marbeuf in Cargese (Dec.). Carlo leaves Ajaccio with Letizia, Joseph and Napoleon (12 Dec.), sails from Bastia with his sons (15 Dec.), leaving Letizia with Marbeuf? Napoleon granted scholarship (31 Dec.).	Marbeuf in Ajaccio (spring); his devotion to Letizia notorious. Marbeuf granted land with marquisate at Cargese (17 June). He sponsors application for scholarship for Napoleon (July, Oct.).

	Events within Bonaparte family	*Events outside Bonaparte family*
1779	Napoleon's nomination to scholarship communicated by prince de Montbarey to Boucheporn (30 Jan.), who informs Carlo in Versailles (Feb.).	Assemblée des États de Corse (25 May–24 June). Publication of F.R.J. de Pommereul's *Histoire de l'Isle de Corse*, with eye-witness account of French invasion.
	Royal heraldist d'Hozier de Serigny delivers certificate of nobility for Napoleon while sending questionnaire to Carlo (8 March).	
	Carlo received with co-deputies by Louis XVI (10 March); answers questionnaire (15 March); is informed that Napoleon has been accepted at Brienne (28 March).	
	Napoleon leaves Autun (20–21 April); stays with Champeaux.	
	Carlo at Brienne (25 April).	
	Napoleon leaves for Brienne (12 May).	
	Carlo sits in Corsican Estates replacing Abbatucci.	Assemblée des États de Corse (25 May–24 June).
	Joseph Fesch elected to scholarship at seminary in Aix-en-Provence (22 June).	
	Ristori reports that Letizia, in presence of Marbeuf, gives birth to still-born son (Aug.).	
	Luciano appointed archdeacon of cathedral of Ajaccio (3 Sept.); baptizes Lucien and Maria-Anna (Elisa) (4 Sept.).	
	Carlo assembles 117 documents to prove his title to Odone heritage (Sept.).	
1780	Carlo receives legacy from Giuseppe Moccio Buonaparte of San Miniato.	

	Events within Bonaparte family	*Events outside Bonaparte family*
1780 contd	Napoleon takes part in *Exercices publics* at Brienne (Sept.). Birth of Paola Maria (Pauline) Bonaparte (20 Oct.). Carlo and Letizia visit Marbeuf in Cargese (12 Dec.).	
1781	Carlo and Letizia return to Ajaccio from Cargese (31 Jan.). Carlo sits in Corsican Estates, is elected to *Nobles Douze*; submits petition, which is accepted, to establish mulberry plantation in Salines. Carlo and Letizia visit Marbeuf in Cargese (15 Aug.–Oct.). Napoleon receives first communion at Brienne; takes part in *Exercices publics*; receives prize for mathematics from duc d'Orléans ?	Assemblée des États de Corse (1–27 June). Festivities given by Loménie de Brienne to honour visit of duc d'Orléans and Mme de Montesson.
1782	Birth of Maria Annunziata (Caroline) Bonaparte (24 March). Carlo and Letizia visit Marbeuf in Cargese (May). Carlo's government contract for mulberry plantation signed (19 June). Carlo and Letizia leave for Bourbonne-les-Bains (June). Visit Autun, Brienne, Paris; in Ajaccio 5 Sept. Napoleon, noticed by sub-inspector Keralio, plans to enter navy; takes part in *Exercices publics* (Sept.); shares prize in mathematics with Fauvelet de Bourrienne ? Joseph wins prizes at Autun; acts in *Les Fâcheux*. Lucien goes to Autun (autumn?). Elisa granted scholarship at Saint-Cyr (24 Nov.).	

Events within Bonaparte family	Events outside Bonaparte family
1782 Carlo quarrels with Maria *contd* Giustina.	
1783 Carlo wins case against Maria Giustina (Jan.). Bonaparte children visit Cargese (Feb.). Joseph announces intention to enter army (summer prize giving). Inspection of Salines unfavourable to Carlo; failure of mulberry seedlings (28 Oct.). Napoleon organizes snow-battle at Brienne.	Marbeuf marries Mlle Gaillardon de Fenoyl (Sept.).
1784 Inspection of mulberry plantation in Salines favourable to Carlo (June). Carlo leaves for France with Maria Anna (Elisa) and Mlle Casabianca (June); collects Lucien at Autun, reaches Brienne 21 June, Saint-Cyr 22 (?) June. Napoleon writes to Fesch (?) about Joseph's future (25 (?) June). Carlo in Paris, writes to maréchal de Ségur, minister of war (30 June); solicits entry of Napoleon to École Militaire, Joseph to army, scholarship for Lucien at Brienne, possession of Milelli (Odone heritage), renewed subsidy for Salines. Napoleon writes to Carlo in Corsica (12–13 Sept.). Lucien takes part in *Exercices* *publics* at Brienne (Sept.). Napoleon, selected for promotion to École Militaire, leaves Brienne (30 (?) Oct.), reaches Paris (3 (?) Nov.).	Attempt to send up balloon from Champs de Mars frustrated by monk and cadet (2 March). Birth of Alexandrine, daughter of Marbeuf (24 Dec.).

Events within Bonaparte family	*Events outside Bonaparte family*
1784 contd — Birth of Jerome Bonaparte (15 Nov.).	
1785 — Carlo and Joseph leave for France, land at Saint-Tropez (7 Jan.), reach Montpellier via Aix-en-Provence (14 Jan.). Carlo seriously ill; joined by Joseph Fesch (early Feb.). Death of Carlo Bonaparte (24 Feb.). Napoleon confirmed at École Militaire (15 May). Napoleon sits for entrance exam to artillery (Aug.), passes 42nd of 58 successful candidates; receives commission in regiment La Fère stationed in Valence (1 Sept.). Lucien takes part in *Exercices publics* at Brienne (Sept.).	De la Guillaumye succeeds de Boucheporn as *intendant* (Sept.).
1786 — Lucien leaves Brienne for seminary at Aix-en-Provence. Napoleon on leave in Corsica (from 15 Sept.).	Birth of Laurent, son of Marbeuf (26 May). Death of Marbeuf (20 Sept.).

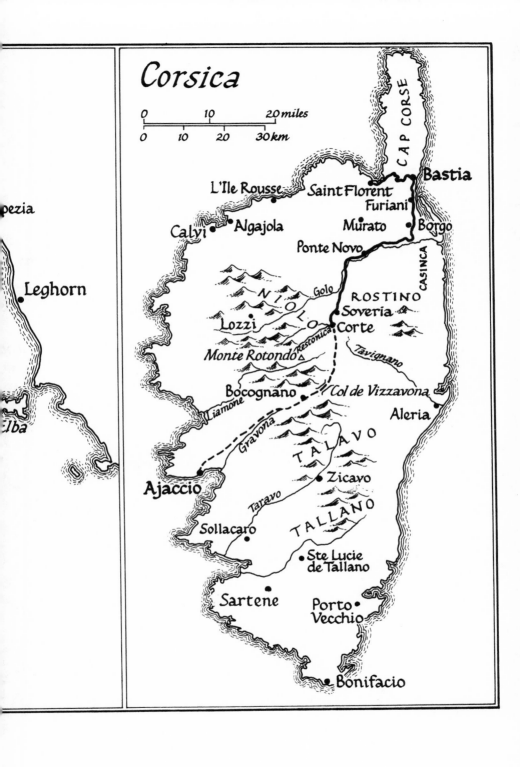

FOREWORD

Two stories are related in this book. One is the traditional tale, largely derived from chroniclers who relied as much on hearsay as nearly contemporary evidence and, combining the two, created a legend that rises at times into the realm of myth. Passages from memoirs of the Bonaparte family and their reported sayings have contributed further legendary items, designed to edify posterity. The resulting tale has been repeated by successive historians with minor variations and additions, and shifts of emphasis often dictated by moralistic or political views.

The other story is based on the hitherto unexploited archives of the Bonaparte family and scattered documents, mostly in Corsica, that have remained neglected or ignored. It is very different from the traditional tale, approaching closer to a truth that can never be entirely known. In the following pages the two stories are distinguished, confronted and compared. The early years of the two versions are however so widely divergent that they cannot be juxtaposed in a single narrative. They are therefore told separately: in Chapter 1 the traditional tale, veiled yet glowing in the aura of legend, and in Chapter 2 the more realistic one I have traced, which is nevertheless not devoid of the elements of drama that characterized the lives of Napoleon's parents as well as his own.

BIRTH OF THE AVENGER

The riders advanced in single file at the fast walking pace of their mules. No one spoke, except, now and then, a muttered interjection to urge a mule over a rough spot in the track, or a sharp warning to a child when it shifted its seat on a pack-saddle. One of the women was visibly pregnant, and in a basket tied below her saddle a baby was lying, wrapped in a dark lambskin.

Nearly all these people had a haggard appearance, their naturally long, angular features being accentuated by anxiety and fatigue. A few of the men wore scarlet coats, violently ripped and stained; but the majority were dressed in a coarse brownish homespun that showed less that they had come straight from the battlefields. Most had covered long distances; some had hardly slept for days.

Though whole families were on the move, they travelled light. The men carried only their water gourds and their weapons: muskets slung over their shoulders, and long pistols stuck into belts beside the leather bags that held the precious gunpowder, and the dagger for use in last-ditch, hand-to-hand fighting, when the munition was spent. The women, sitting sideways on wooden saddles padded with homewoven blankets, transported bags holding rye and barley bread, baked biscuit-hard. Few had much chestnut flour for making the heartwarming polenta, for the year's supply was running low now, in mid-May.[1]

The group was heading up a ravine that drove deep into a phalanx of high mountains. Snow still lay in the topmost crevasses and in the northern combs of Monte Rotondo, towering, majestic, to the left. It gleamed very white in the evening sun, dropping straight ahead towards the western peaks. Blotches of pine forest in the recesses were already sinking into shadow. The scene was enormous, monumental, and immobile save for the travellers threading their way along the track like a line of ants, and the Restonica roaring implacably in the bed of the ravine.

These people were not admiring the landscape; but neither were they indifferent to it. This savage world of mountain and torrent and rock and forest represented safety, freedom, their ultimate refuge. They could hold out there for months, for years even, as their ancestors had done in past invasions with the complicity of the roving shepherds, patriots to a man. And the news would spread, carried by shepherds moving singly, almost invisibly, across the mountains, that here, in the heart of the island, a band of chiefs had refused to surrender. Others would join the camp: the General's brother, Clemente, the monkish guerrilla who never wasted a bullet and prayed for his enemies' souls as he shot them down,[2] and the tough herdsmen he had gone to recruit in the Niolo, and the dark wiry men from the south, from beyond the ranges, who had not yet borne the brunt of the war.

The General himself, the *babbo*, the Father of the Nation, surely he would come to them: but where was he? Since the battle at Ponte Novo on that fatal 8 May all had been disaster and confusion. Hundreds had fallen on the bridge, others had jumped into the churning river and been dashed to death by its current. Since then the national militia had been dispersed, on the run, while the enemy marched from one cowed village to another offering the dire alternatives of immediate submission or the galleys. The conch shells that served the patriots as bugles no longer sounded their anguished call to war, and there was disgust and shame in the faces of men seen slinking back to their homes.

Such were the thoughts of the patriots riding up into the mountains with their women and children: the diehards, the last-standers. For one of them, one of the youngest, the defeat weighed particularly heavy because he had a responsibility for the war. Exactly a year ago, when the enemy's hostile intentions first became apparent, he had summoned the nation's youth to arms. The head of state, General Pasquale Paoli, had made a measured speech, presenting the facts to the *consulta*, the national assembly, inviting it to deliberate. But this young man, the General's twenty-two-year-old secretary, had spoken up boldly: 'Valorous youth, this is the fatal hour. If we fail to master the impending storm it will be the end at once of our reputation and our glory.' He had reminded them that liberty, greatest of all blessings, was only to be won by a virtue superior to every trial. He had called on the youth of Corsica to show themselves worthy of their ancestors who had shed their blood on so many fields of battle to free the island from the vile tyranny of the Genoese. For their hard-won independence was threatened at this very hour; and by whom? By the king of France, hitherto trusted mediator between Corsicans and Genoese, but who now, apparently, had leagued himself with the Genoese to reinstate their execrable rule by force of arms. But the Corsicans would pit force against force, and he, Carlo Maria Bonaparte, knew they would draw strength from the very inequality of the struggle: '. . . if it be written in heaven that the greatest monarch on earth shall measure himself with the smallest people in the world, then we have just reason to be proud and we are certain to live and die with glory'. The speech struck home; men were not lacking to take the solemn, momentous, suicidal vow: 'We will fight as men in despair who have resolved to overcome or to die . . . until our strength is completely broken and our weapons fall from our hands.'[3] And this was precisely what many of them had done.

It was not of course the first time the Corsicans had known defeat: all through their history they had been repeatedly conquered and colonized by foreigners, beginning with the ancient Romans. If their ferocious resistance to those first civilized invaders was known only to a few scholars, everyone was grievously familiar with their four-centuries-long opposition to the Genoese. The rebellions of the great feudal lords were celebrated in chronicles, popular tales and ballads. Some had won temporary victories, and ruled the island as independent princes; all had ended in tragedy, assassinated or imprisoned or executed by the Genoese. Later in time Sampiero Corso had emerged from a poor shepherd's family to lead his people to war against Genoa, first in alliance with Henry II of France, and then unaided by any foreign power, fighting year after year, ageing, yet always at the head of his troops until Vittolu, his dearest friend, betrayed him and he was hacked to pieces in the maquis.

After which Corsica, drained of men and hope and resources, had sunk under the unchallenged rule of Genoa for more than a hundred and fifty years. The people had endured the tyranny, without ever accepting it, until just four decades ago they had risen yet again, exasperated past bearing by the arrogance and cupidity of their colonial overlords. Carlo Bonaparte belonged to the second generation of militant patriots; but some of his companions retreating into the mountains had seen the whole forty years' struggle. They had fought under Giacinto Paoli, father of Pasquale, now ending his life in exile in

Naples, and under Gaffori, he who displayed 'the resolution of a Roman' until he was treacherously murdered. They had taken part in the marches and sieges and triumphs and reverses of the interminable, intermittent war, represented their villages in the national assemblies, the *consulte* that hammered out the organization and strategy of the liberated territory (comprising the greater part of the interior). They had tolerated two uneasy pacifications imposed by France on behalf of Genoa, had acclaimed a brave, popular German adventurer, Theodor von Neuhof, who had persuaded them to crown him constitutional monarch before he left, at the end of seven months, in search of funds. Later, during the War of the Austrian succession, they had taken, then lost heart during the bungling interventions of their British, Sardinian and Austrian allies. Finally they had witnessed the historic *consulte* of 1755 that elected Pasquale General-in-chief and adopted his national constitution. For them the rebellion had been all life, its aim and meaning; those who were coming of age when it erupted in December 1729, now, in May 1769, were worn old men whose survival seemed something of a miracle.[4]

With Paoli the immemorial dream of independence had at last come true: for a time at least: for the past fourteen years. This inspiring young man in his thirties, who had received an enlightened education in Naples, had given Corsica the status of a nation. A nation, moreover, admired by the foremost thinkers of the day. Had not the great philosopher Rousseau himself written: 'There is still one country in Europe capable of legislation, and that is the island of Corsica.'[5] And indeed, Paoli's constitution, pivoting on an elected national assembly, had set Europe an example in representative government. Some had called him a despot, but in the eyes of his many supporters this was unjust, for his powers were 'properly limited' by a coherent constitution. His overwhelming influence stemmed essentially from his popularity with the mass of the people.[6]

For his admirers he was a statesman in the style of the heroes of antiquity. Austere in his habits, 'avoiding every kind of luxury', celibate, morally irreproachable, he was wholly dedicated to his country's cause. Soldier and legislator, he was also philosopher, a man of learning; after consolidating the nation's military position he had introduced some of the refinements of civilization: a printing press that issued a gazette; a university at Corte, the mountain capital, where the élite of Corsican youth could study such subjects as mathematics, philosophy and law instead of becoming vagabond scholars abroad.[7]

True, this was only a beginning: the country was still poor and incompletely liberated. The patriots, with their home-manufactured or captured weapons, their cannon salvaged from wrecked ships, had never succeeded in taking the six main ports, fortified cities occupied by the Genoese, reinforced from 1764 by French garrisons. Yet though encircled by the enemy the Corsicans remained confident. The French commander, the comte de Marbeuf, had professed peaceful intentions; Paoli had entered into diplomatic negotiations with the French minister, the duc de Choiseul, and the patriots had convinced themselves that France intended to guarantee a settlement with Genoa that would acknowledge their independence. Britain, they believed, would tolerate no other solution. A gorgeously dressed gentleman by the name of Boswell had even come to visit Paoli, who had received him with every mark of deference: the Corsicans had no doubt but that he was an envoy from the British crown.[8]

It was therefore with consternation that in May 1768 they saw the landing of fresh French troops. Paoli's negotiations with Choiseul had broken down; France, so the rumour ran, had come to a secret understanding with Genoa. Young Carlo Bonaparte was among the first to grasp the seriousness of the situation; his resounding speech had spurred the nation to prepare for war. War came, in July. It was undeclared: Marbeuf simply shifted his troops inland. Soon afterwards the marquis de Chauvelin landed yet more troops and a bundle of edicts which informed the Corsicans that Genoa had ceded their country to the king of France. The Corsicans promptly burned the edicts and declared war. What else could they do? They had never been consulted about this deal that disposed of their country and their persons. Were they, in the words of Paoli, to be treated like Roman slaves, like inanimate objects, bought and sold? Even if Genoa had possessed any rights on Corsica, he argued, how could she now transfer the country to another power without the consent of its population? 'The true basis of sovereignty,' he declared, 'is the consent of the people . . .'

So the Corsicans had demonstrated in a forty years' anti-colonial struggle; so Paoli, versed in the doctrines of the Enlightenment, had taught them to believe. But the powers of Europe did not think on those lines. The king of France, for one, held to the principle that the cession of one country to another could only be validated by the consent of its legitimate ruler. And the legitimate ruler of Corsica was Genoa, even if she had lost control of the island nearly half a century before. In the eyes of the French monarch and his ministers Paoli and

the patriots were outlaws, mere brigands without political rights. Had
Louis XV consulted the Corsicans, European opinion would have
been just as much shocked as if France, today, were to annex a small
country *without* consulting its inhabitants. The Corsicans were thinking
two centuries ahead of their time.[9]

Like the French, they fought to defend a principle. 'War with blood
and fire until we shall be heard,' were the desperate words of their
national declaration in September 1768. Not 'War till victory shall be
ours'.[10] They were fighting, with small hope of success, to state their
case, to defend their right to determine their political status, their form
of government, to assert their national identity: they were waging an
ideological war. No one came to their rescue. Rousseau, bitterly
affronted, was too distressed to make any useful protest; indeed he
supposed that Choiseul had undertaken the 'iniquitous and ridiculous'
campaign for the sole purpose of humiliating him, he who first had
discerned in the Corsicans a free people capable of organization
whereas all Europe had seen in them only a horde of bandits.[11] Boswell
too was indignant, but he was powerless to change the course of
events. His book, appearing a few months before the outbreak of
hostilities, may have 'fanaticized the English for Corsica' (to quote
Paoli); but the attitude of the British government was summed up in
the words of Lord Holland: 'Foolish as we are, we cannot be so
foolish as to go to war because Mr Boswell has been in Corsica.' True,
Boswell and his pro-Corsican fans contrived to send the patriots some
money and arms; but this aid amounted to no more than a dribble that
could do nothing to affect the outcome of the struggle.[12]

Yet the French learnt, as others have since, that it is not so easy for a
large, rich, well-armed nation to conquer a small, poor, weakly armed
people when that people is fighting for its liberty, on its own soil. The
crowd of young courtiers who counted on a quick victory over a
rabble of peasants – *'cette canaille'* – before hurrying home for the
autumn at the Opera were in for a shock. Clemente Paoli, always
foremost in the ranks, drove the royal army from the wooded hills of
the Casinca in furious hand-to-hand fighting. French soldiers learned
to dread those little brown-clad men, agile as wild animals, who darted
out of the rocks and undergrowth to overwhelm isolated detachments
and vanished as suddenly to attack from another quarter. Their guile
was as unnerving as their courage. Peasants invited troops to occupy
their village, only to set on them at nightfall, firing and hurling missiles
from every house. 'The Corsicans loved liberty; we came to conquer

them; they laid traps for us; they were right to do so,' wrote Dumouriez, future general of the French Revolution, who played an audacious role in the shattering Corsican campaign.[13]

It can be seen, now, as a rehearsal for the gigantic struggle that just over twenty years later was to pit revolutionary France against her foreign foes, with the French, in Corsica, fighting on the anti-revolutionary side. Yet some of their officers were already stirred by the Enlightenment, and they recognized a new spirit in the Corsicans and respected it. '*Patria e Libertà*' was the Corsicans' battlecry, 'the noblest any people at that time possessed', wrote Pommereul, later Napoleon's examiner for his entry to the artillery, and later still his director of censorship, a valuable eyewitness to the Corsican war. The slogan was new, and exalting: it was the voice of the future, charged with an incalculable potential. Dumouriez, too, knew where the strength of the Corsicans lay: 'Liberty,' he commented, 'doubles the valour and force of man.'[14]

In the autumn of 1768 the French were actually reduced to soliciting an armistice while they moved their troops into winter quarters, a request Paoli is said to have dismissed with the reply: 'For us it is a matter of indifference whether we die in one season or another.'[15] Sporadic fighting continued through the winter; in the spring of 1769 the French were pouring reinforcements into the island so that the Corsicans faced an army of over twenty thousand men. Paoli, after a call-up of all able-bodied males between sixteen and sixty, in theory could muster as many and more; but by his own admission he would never count on more than four thousand of them at any one time. Their weapons, moreover, were hopelessly inadequate and outdated, mostly shooting rifles, without bayonettes, an innovation that was put to deadly use by their enemies.

Many gave up; others changed sides, or simply surrendered. Yet some sections of this quaint amateurish rustic militia fought with a mad courage the French had never seen before. The courage of despair? What else could have induced some two thousand crack troops to make an open, frontal attack on the French army posted in the mountains overlooking the river Golo? Who gave the suicide order? Or was there perhaps a mistiming of operations that cancelled an intended pincer movement? But why did some Swiss and German mercenaries fighting for the Corsicans fire on the patriots as they tried to retreat over the bridge of Ponte Novo? And why was Paoli not present on the scene of battle? These questions have remained unanswered ever since 8 May 1769, when the flower of the national army, amid cries of 'Treachery! Treachery!', was slaughtered, drowned and dispersed. Some escaped; others set an example that has left its mark on Corsican history. Voltaire reports that the defenders of the bridge recharged their muskets behind a barricade built with the corpses of their fallen comrades while the wounded voluntarily added their own bodies to the pile: 'Everywhere one sees valour,' he wrote, 'but one only sees such actions among free people.'

Their sacrifice did not however inspire further deeds of valour. On the contrary, the defeat of Ponte Novo 'spread consternation'; resistance collapsed; the French marched on Corte unopposed.[16] Paoli, reaching the capital just before them, could do nothing to defend it; deserted by his chief officer he disappeared into the southern mountains with a handful of partisans.

Other loyal survivors got away from Corte just ahead of the French army, escaping inland up the valley of the Restonica. Sold, betrayed and abandoned, they faced the alternatives of guerrilla war or exile. If resistance proved hopeless they would have to make their hazardous way to Italy, as many, all through Corsican history, had done before them. They would find friends in Tuscany, where Corsican expatriates had provided valued help all through the rebellion; but this would mean leaving their families and homes.[17] For Carlo Bonaparte the choice would be particularly painful. Every time he looked back at Letizia, riding uncomplainingly behind him, six months pregnant yet still beautiful, he shrank from the idea of their separation.

Her behaviour had been exemplary, worthy of the highest Corsican traditions, ever since he had married her, passionately in love, five years before. Her family, the Ramolino, people of noble Italian origin, had opposed the match; an heiress already famed for her beauty and not yet fourteen, she could afford to wait for a better offer. Carlo, it was true, also came from a distinguished Italian family that numbered among the founders of Ajaccio some two and a half centuries before; but the Bonaparte were poor. Yet the warmth and sincerity of his love had triumphed, and on a glorious day of early summer, on 2 June 1764, they had been married by Carlo's uncle, the archdeacon Luciano Bonaparte, under the great dome of the cathedral of Ajaccio, surrounded by their assembled relatives in a joyful ceremony accompanied by the customary showering of rice and chiming of bells.

They had not stayed in the city. A Genoese enclave, occupied by Genoese or French garrisons all through the rebellion, Ajaccio had remained aloof from the national liberation movement even though many of its inhabitants sympathized more or less openly with the patriots.[18] Carlo Bonaparte was one who had acted on his convictions: he had gone to Corte to offer his services to Paoli, taking with him his young bride, his sister Geltrude, and an uncle by the name of Napoleone.

Oppressed, now, by defeat and the desperate prospect of his future, Carlo could at least look back on that period of his life with pride. From the first the General had recognized his talents, appreciated his ardent love of liberty, his devotion to the national cause. Noting his brilliant studies at the newly founded university, he had made him his private secretary, then appointed him secretary of state. As a member of the national *consulta* Carlo had made good use of his natural eloquence in his appeal to the nation's youth to take to arms. And when war came he had proved his worth: as commander of the volunteers of the *pieve* (district) of Talavo, as aide-de-camp to Paoli at the victorious battle of Borgo, and finally at Ponte Novo where his uncle Napoleone, fighting gallantly beside him, had died in the holocaust on the bridge.

Letizia, too, had seen that fatal struggle; for though gentle and submissive she had a masculine courage, and her pregnancies had not prevented her following her husband to the battlefields and succouring the wounded while the bullets whistled past her ears. Contemptuous of social pleasures and feminine frivolities, she incarnated the austere virtues of antiquity, combining in herself the dignity of a Roman matron with the grace of a young girl. In time of defeat her loyalty had never wavered. Though after Ponte Novo her maternal grandfather, Pietrasanta, had offered her a safe-conduct to Bastia where he was already engaged as member of the French supreme tribunal, the Conseil Supérieur, she had chosen to stand by her husband, even though she was pregnant and caring for Joseph, her year-old child. She had already endured the deaths of two children with stoic fortitude: a boy named Napoleone, and then a girl.

The refugees were climbing the slopes of Monte Rotondo through a forest of tall pines. Though accustomed to such untamed, overwhelming scenes, they felt very vulnerable, very much alone. Isolation, exhaustion and hunger were beginning to undermine their resolution: was this flight not, after all, a folly? Could they hold out in those empty places very long? Eventually they found a shelter for the night: a cave made by an overhanging rock. The men unloaded and hobbled the mules; the women, encamped in the cave, breast-fed the younger children; the hard, dark bread was passed from hand to hand. Resting, they gave way. Children sobbed and were not scolded; women rocked their babies with little sounds between moaning and chanting; old men sprawled against the rocks, in lethal silence, 'with death in their eyes'. Meanwhile the younger men engaged in a discussion that grew increasingly emphatic. Were they to die in a cave like hunted animals? Would it not be better to emigrate? To surrender?

It was Letizia Bonaparte who pulled them together. Just as her husband, a year earlier, had exhorted his countrymen to resist invasion, so now she spoke her mind. Were they not ashamed of such weak, unmanly talk? She personally would rather give birth to her child here, in this cave, than abandon the struggle so long as the enemy occupied a single foot of Corsican soil.[19] She spoke boldly for a woman, but only half her thought. Secretly she was convinced that this child would redeem their defeat and humiliation; he – for she knew it would be a boy – would live to rehabilitate their nation, reconquer their liberty. Often, during the past weeks, as she rode to the scenes of war she had felt him stir in her womb, as though responding to the howl of the conch shells, the crack of gunfire; and that same day, as she retreated up the mountain, he had moved convulsively; in protest, so it seemed. She had no fear for his life, nor for her own. Strong in a simple religious faith, she had entrusted him to the blessed Virgin; she knew he would be born, vigorous and healthy, at the appointed hour, the avenger of them all.

Letizia had stated her opinion in no uncertain language; but she knew better than to insist on it. When, after a perishing cold, almost sleepless night a party of French officers appeared, waving white handkerchiefs in token of peace and armed only with their swords, she did nothing to discourage Carlo from returning with them to Corte. The war, they said, was over; all Corsica had surrendered, the General and his brother had left the island. If the patriots continued resisting they would be punished without mercy; but the comte de Vaux, commander-in-chief of the royal army, was prepared to receive a delegation and grant them honourable terms of surrender. The patriots knew the game was up. They lost no time in selecting delegates, a dozen or so representing the different localities from which they came. Carlo Bonaparte was chosen for Ajaccio, along with his brother-in-law, Nicolò Luigi Paravisino.

The sight of the capital swarming with French soldiers was no doubt humiliating, and the delegates must have kept their eyes averted from the fortress, crowning a spectacular rock peak, where the garrison had surrendered without a shot fired. And certainly they would have suffered acutely if they were received in the *palazzo nazionale*, just below the fortress, where Paoli had reigned during the past fourteen glorious years. But de Vaux, though a general with 'a terrible reputation of austerity', a 'hard, severe' man, 'taciturn and rigid', showed unexpected civility. 'Gentlemen, the Corsican affair is settled,' he told them, speaking bluntly as one soldier to another. Corsica had become part of France, and France would make Corsica prosperous and contented. 'My sovereign admires the Corsicans who have fought to defend their country, but now further resistance would be not only a folly but a crime.' The delegates thereupon swore loyalty to Louis XV and humbly thanked de Vaux for the safe-conducts he doled out to them. They had no choice.[20]

On reaching the cave on the slopes of Monte Rotondo, those who lived beyond the central range, in the region known as *dila dai monti*, had already covered some considerable distance in the direction of their homes. Rather than bring Letizia back to degraded Corte and follow the usual route to Ajaccio over the pass of Vizzavona and through Bocognano, where French troops were still engaged in mopping-up operations, Carlo decided to push on from the camp over the mountains to the west coast. They had a terrible journey. Rain storms – those brutal, slashing storms of the Corsican spring – made the stone-paved tracks so slippery that they had to lead their mules; to the end of her life Letizia would remember how she walked all one day along perilous paths carrying Joseph in her arms. Yet the worst ordeal came later, when they had reached the apparent safety of the chestnut woods on the western watershed and had to ford the Liamone. Swollen with rain and melted snow, the river was running abnormally high; Letizia's mule lost its foothold in midstream, and for a moment it looked as though mule, pregnant woman and child would be swept away on the current.

She must surely have felt deep triumphant gratitude to the mother of God when at last they caught sight of Ajaccio, the little white town on the shore of a vast, serene bay, with the dome and campanile of the cathedral, where they had been married five eventful years before, rising above the rooftops. Relations, friends and retainers were there to welcome them, the survivors, in the three-storeyed *casa* Bonaparte, one of the finest houses in the town. Saveria, Carlo's widowed mother, Luciano the archdeacon, Letizia's mother, with her second husband, a

Swiss officer, François Fesch, and their six-year-old boy, besides numerous aunts and uncles and cousins with their servants and dependants, surrounded the hard-driven husband, the exhausted pregnant woman, with all the loving tenderness a Corsican family, in such circumstances, will show.

The story now moves into the realm of myth and prodigy. On 15 August the townspeople were enjoying the first public holiday to take place in time of peace for as long as most of them could remember. They were celebrating the Assumption of the Virgin, the most joyous of Corsican festivals. Letizia, though heavily pregnant, went to mass at the cathedral to give thanks for the miraculous protection given to herself and her unborn child. The cathedral was only a few steps from the *casa* Bonaparte, along narrow streets shaded by the proximity of the house-fronts from the magnificent high-summer sun. And there, under the cool, painted vaults, while the priests chanted the liturgy, she felt her first labour pains. The women of her family helped her hurry home. Lying on a couch – she had no time to put herself to bed – she gave birth almost at once, almost without pain. The child was a boy with weak, spindly legs and an unusually large head. Caterina, the crusty, quarrelsome old servant who took charge of the delivery, laid him, screaming, on a carpet in which were woven scenes from the *Iliad* and the *Odyssey*.

That night a comet was seen streaming across the sky, tracing a shining arc above the bay of Ajaccio. The local inhabitants interpreted it as a sign of good fortune for the town; others said it presaged the birth of a great monarch; some connected it with the marriage of the French dauphin. Alone Letizia understood its true meaning: the avenger had been born.[21]

2

BIRTH OF NAPOLEON
BONAPARTE

The story just told has been handed down from one writer to another, with minor variations but few queries. It has been pieced together from chronicles, memoirs and word-of-mouth reminiscences. The objection to this evidence is that all of it was written, or uttered, by partisans of the Bonaparte, or by the Bonaparte themselves, well after Napoleon's achievement had shed a retrospective lustre on his parents' lives. The Corsican chroniclers, Rossi and Renucci, bear the chief responsibility, both of them writing soon after Napoleon's ascendancy. Ardent Bonapartists, they naturally sought to include his parents in his heroic aura, and to discern a premonitory, quasi-magical quality in the circumstances surrounding his birth. Subsequent historians repeated their narratives the more readily because various episodes were confirmed by Letizia in later life, by Napoleon at Saint Helena, and by his brothers in their memoirs. Few paused to consider how far the imperial family connived in the fabrication of its own legend.

Meanwhile documents that could have told another tale remained hidden away in Corsican homes and archives, too little known and too fragmentary to discredit the accepted story. And all this time, and till today, an essential source remained unexploited: the Bonaparte family papers, saved from the destruction of their home when they fled Corsica in 1793, and inherited by the present Prince Louis Napoleon. Access to this invaluable collection, for which I am deeply indebted to the prince and princess, has led me to a story very different from any hitherto presented; one which, if incomplete, and at moments obscure, is unquestionably closer to what really happened.

The most important testimony for the period preceding the birth of Napoleon is provided by Carlo Bonaparte's manuscript memoirs to the year 1780.[1] Seeing that he wrote this autobiography, as he explains, for the edification of his family, he cannot be expected to show himself in an unfavourable light. All the same, believing that his children could profit by knowledge of his youthful predicaments, he gives a remarkably frank, and at times humorous, self-portrait.

He begins by confessing that his marriage to Letizia was no love match. His first love, he asserts, was a young lady by the name of Forcioli.[2] Though she was without breeding or beauty, his heart 'knew no other flame than hers'. Driven by 'blind passion', he would have 'precipitated' himself into this marriage, disastrous for himself and his family, but for the 'strong hand' of his uncles, Luciano, the priest, and Napoleone. To prevent so unfortunate an alliance they induced him to marry Letizia Ramolino; Carlo admits that he 'gave in to reason' only after many disputes and discords of the kind inseparable from thwarted love.

Of Letizia's feelings about this forced marriage we know nothing; it is in fact unlikely that she had any say in the matter. She brought to her disenchanted and reluctant bridegroom, in his own words, 'real beauty' and 'irreproachable morals', besides property worth 7,000 Genoese lire. A notarial act nearly four pages long records that it consisted of three *lenze* of the vineyard called Torrevecchia; a public bread-oven in the suburb of Ajaccio with a flat above it, which was occupied by the baker-woman, and an adjoining room; a flat in a house near the abattoir, and as much of the vineyard called Vittolu as would be needed to complete the value of the 7,000 lire as estimated by the official public assessors. This dowry had been assigned to Letizia in the will of her great-uncle, Giovan' Andrea Ramolino, who was in fact still alive; her father had died nine years before. The contract was executed before a notary and witnesses on 31 May 1764 and confirmed in the office of the Genoese *commissario* of Ajaccio the following day. These details are highly important in view of what did and did not happen later.

A public bread-oven, a couple of flats in what were certainly poor, working-class houses, some strips of vineyards: this was no fortune. All the same it was by no means negligible in a country where dowries at that period seldom exceeded 11,000 lire.[3] Letizia's great-uncle seems to have acted generously, for contemporary evidence hardly suggests that the Ramolino were people of great means. They owned little land in a country where land was the chief source of revenue: according to a municipal register, considerably less than the Bonaparte, who were quite well provided with vineyards, then the most profitable form of agricultural property. The extreme poverty of the Bonaparte is a legend largely propagated by the Bonaparte themselves. True, they were small fry compared with a local magnate like Giuseppe Maria Peraldi, who controlled the coral-fishing fleet and possessed at least four times as much land, or the 'Croesus' Bacchiochi, whose property was estimated at 100,000 livres. The Bonaparte cried poverty because they were not as rich as they would have liked to be, and as a few of their neighbours in fact were.[4]

The Bonaparte property was obviously attractive to the Ramolino because it was all likely to be inherited by Carlo. He had what might be called excellent expectations. His only brother had died in childhood, his father in 1763. His uncle, the priest Luciano, who acted as his guardian, and with whom he shared his inheritance of vineyards and other lands, could be expected to leave him his own extensive properties: vineyards, pastures and olive groves in the hills above the town. Carlo would also come into the vineyards belonging to his widowed mother, Saveria. No one had a better claim; the family was small. His only sister, Geltrude, unhappily married to her first cousin, and childless, was already provided with a dowry, which in Corsican law deprived a daughter of any share in the family succession. His other uncle, Napoleone, who is not recorded as a landowner, had made money in trade and married an authentic Corsican aristocrat, Maria Rosa Bozzi. Though her family, like the rest of the Corsican nobility, had fallen on hard times, she still had means to dower her daughter Isabella, her only child. Carlo later found means of profiting by this dowry, as will be told.[5]

Tradition has it that the Ramolino were against his marriage to Letizia for political reasons: they supported the Genoese while the Bonaparte were Paolist. But this notion is no better founded than the belief that Carlo was romantically in love with his bride. Letizia's father, it is true, had been captain of the infantry and cavalry of the city of Ajaccio, and later inspector of roads and bridges and chancellor of the jurisdiction of Bocognano under Genoese rule; her maternal grandfather, Giuseppe Maria Pietrasanta, was a notary, who witnessed the cession of the fortress of Ajaccio by the Genoese *commissario* to the French military authorities in 1764. Four years later we find him appointed member of the supreme French tribunal, the Conseil Supérieur in Bastia.[6] The Bonaparte, too, had served both Genoa and France: Carlo's father, Giuseppe Maria, represented Ajaccio at a national *consulta* assembled in Corte in January 1749 by the marquis de Cursay, a French commander who administered the island for a time on behalf of Genoa; the following month he welcomed the marquis on his official visit to Ajaccio, together with his brother-in-law Paravisino, who held the post of French consul in the town, as did later his son Nicolò, married to Carlo's sister, Geltrude. In fact both families adhered to the usual policy of the Corsican upper class of siding with whoever was in power. Luciano, however, a man of stubborn originality, preferred the Genoese to the French even after the French conquest, perhaps because he had done his ecclesiastical studies at the Collegio del Bene in Genoa. Neither Carlo nor any of his relatives were Paolist at the time of his marriage to Letizia. But when he did attach himself to the Father of the Nation he was supported by both families, his decision, in their eyes, being justified by Paoli's growing power and prestige.[7]

If the Ramolino objected to the marriage it must have been on account of Carlo's previous 'blind passion'; but I have found no evidence that they did.[8] In so far as a Corsican marriage was an alliance between two families rather than two individuals, this one was suitable enough. The Bonaparte had comparable, perhaps slightly superior, means. They belonged to the same class, lived in the same respectable if mediocre style. They inhabited exactly the same kind of house. Contrary to common belief, the *casa* Bonaparte was nothing like the fairly imposing three-storeyed building one sees today. The house where every year thousands of tourists make their pilgrimage to Napoleon's birthplace represents the outcome of legal struggles, acquisitions and additions and restorations spaced over some twenty years, followed by extensive reconstruction after Napoleon's campaign of Italy and some later nineteenth-century modifications. At the time of his marriage Carlo's home consisted of a couple of three-roomed flats, one above the other. The *casa* Ramolino was almost identical. When French troops had to be billeted in Ajaccio both were classed as fit for lodging subaltern officers.[9]

The families had similar origins. Both descended from Italians, mercenaries in Genoese pay who settled in Corsica soon after the foundation of the town in 1490–92. Both were of patrician stock: that is to say their ancestors were not peasants or artisans. All the same they must have been in low water (if not disgrace) when they elected to seek their fortunes in this primitive, unpacified colony, which offered all too little to its indigenous inhabitants.

They were none the less proud of their ancestry. The Ramolino claimed that the founder of their line in Ajaccio was one Gabriele, a Florentine noble, officer in the guard of Charles V of Naples and son of Abramo, count of Coll'Alto of Venice. But the documents that give these and other impressive details about the early Ramolino in Corsica inspire small confidence and are dismissed by an eminent Corsican genealogist as crude fakes. The family's attempts to push back its origins to a Venetian count of the ninth century are no more convincing, and the Ramolino had to wait till the Second Empire before one of their members obtained the title of comte de Coll'Alto. All that is known for certain about Letizia's ancestors is that in the sixteenth century a certain Morgante Ramolino, after long service with the Genoese troops in Corsica, applied for the obscure appointment of guardian of a watchtower on the coast near Ajaccio.[10]

After this the Ramolino appear from time to time in local records as officials in the municipal administration. Though not so often as the Bonaparte, who were elected *anziani* – city councillors – in every generation from the late sixteenth century till the end of the Genoese regime. They too were descended from a soldier in Genoese pay, one Francesco, known as Il Mauro, presumably on account of his dark complexion; at all events no one, friend or foe, has used his name to attribute an Arab ancestry to Napoleon. He arrived soon after the building of the ramparts; his family belonged to Sarzana, a little town in Genoese territory. Two hundred and fifty years' residence in Ajaccio had not, however, brought the Bonaparte any higher distinctions until in 1759 Carlo's father and uncle Luciano prevailed on the Buonaparte of Tuscany to make formal acknowledgement of kinship with their ancestors. This was something of a social triumph: the Tuscan Buonaparte were much grander than the Bonaparte of insignificant Sarzana.[11]

There is reason to think that the two families were well satisfied when the negotiations between the uncles terminated in the signature of the dotal act in the *casa* Ramolino. Only the principal actors in the affair may have lacked enthusiasm. Yet outwardly, at least, they were well matched. Carlo, born on 27 March 1746, was eighteen, Letizia three or four years younger.[12] They made an unusually handsome pair. Contemporaries confirm Carlo's estimate of Letizia's beauty, and Napoleon often recalled it at Saint Helena with pride. She was 'ravishing', 'graceful', 'charming', 'one of the prettiest women in Corsica', one of her ladies-in-waiting esteems; 'the most agreeable and beautiful woman in the town', reports Las Cases, 'one of the most beautiful women of her time, her beauty was celebrated in the island . . .'. These appraisals, made after she had borne many children and endured domestic poverty and two civil wars, allow one only to imagine how she must have looked in the unimpaired freshness of adolescence. But how far can one rely on descriptions heavily coloured by hindsight? When they were written she was the mother of sovereigns. Her portraits hardly suggest a flawless beauty. They show the nearly classical features much admired in a period haunted by Graeco-Roman prototypes; but as often happens with Corsicans, the effect is marred by too tight a mouth, too long a nose, a certain 'severity in her physiognomy' which did not go unnoticed in her later years. Her remarkably large, deep-set eyes, however, lend a particular haunting quality to those asperities, giving her an enigmatic, hallucinating air: 'there is something of her soul in her expression', her lady-in-waiting, Laure d'Abrantès, observed. Undoubtedly Letizia was fascinating: this her story proves. Whether she was known in her youth as 'the little Madonna' as some writers maintain, and whether she matched the title, is nevertheless open to question. Her looks, in so far as we can judge, suggest, rather, a sibyl of the pagan world.[13]

Carlo's physique was equally striking. He was tall: a recommendation in itself among a people that tends to be short-legged; 'handsome and tall as Murat', Letizia recalled, comparing him with one of the best-looking men of his age. A French official who met him in Corsica depicts him as a 'man of tall stature, of handsome and noble countenance', as does his son Lucien, using almost the same words; the abbé Chardon, professor in Napoleon's first school in mainland France, describes him as 'superb'. All these images were of course drawn from memory at a time when he was known as the father of the ruler of Europe. There exists in Ajaccio an anonymous contemporary portrait likely to be nearer the hard truth. The typically Corsican almond-shaped eyes are sharp and humorous, the nose is salient and heavy, the lips are sensual: it is the alert, intelligent, not very refined face of a man who loved the good things of life and knew how to procure them.[14]

The dotal act signed on behalf of Carlo and Letizia constituted a true marriage contract, the first and essential undertaking whereby they engaged themselves to become man and wife. The marriage, one reads, had been negotiated, and concluded by the *verba de futuro* – the promise – of Carlo and Letizia; it was 'to be celebrated before the holy

Church' according to the regulations laid down by 'the sacred Council of Trent'.[15] These were accepted formulae; in the absence of any non-religious authority to register marriages the execution of the dotal act assumed the character of a civil wedding ceremony. It took place, habitually, in the home of the bride, in the presence of the assembled members of both families, and was followed by appropriate festivities.

The religious ceremony would normally be celebrated a day or two later. This is what Carlo Bonaparte is apparently referring to in his memoirs when he says he was married on 3 June 1764. His mention of the event is however surprisingly bald: 'The said marriage contracted and consummated, after a few months I left for Rome for the purpose of studying law, leaving my wife pregnant with a daughter who died.'[16] And what of the nuptial mass in the cathedral? Such an occurrence was unusual enough to be worth noting, for the municipal register of Ajaccio reveals that the Bonaparte – in common with many of their fellow-citizens – usually celebrated their marriages privately, in the house – the *casa* – of the bride. The Council of Trent had prescribed that marriages should be solemnized by a priest in the presence of witnesses, but not that the ceremony should take place in a church. In Corsica, particularly before the French conquest, very many weddings took place out of church. The ceremony was brief and to the point: the priest 'questioned' the bride and bridegroom, who thereupon gave their consent by *verba de presente* and were pronounced man and wife. Carlo's father, Giuseppe Maria, had been married in this way, and his uncle Napoleone, with Luciano officiating, and his sister Geltrude; on this latter occasion Letizia's uncle, Francesco Ramolino, had officiated and Carlo was one of the witnesses.[17]

One would therefore expect Carlo to have something to say about the celebration of his wedding. But no. He even avoids the word 'celebrated': the marriage is 'contracted' and 'consummated'; then he leaves for Rome.

The most likely reason for this omission is that no religious ceremony took place.

Historians have had to wait for Pierre Lamotte, most modest and unrecognized of scholars, to point out that in the municipal register of Ajaccio, in the record of marriages for the year 1764, one reads the words: 'May, June, July vacant'. That is to say that during those months no marriages occurred. The marriage of Carlo and Letizia is noted, but on another page, immediately below the last to be recorded in 1766. The notice is written in a hand totally unlike that which records the earlier marriages, and which appears to be that of Carlo Bonaparte; his small, clear, rounded handwriting is distinct from any one finds in Corsica at that time.

The date given is 1 June 1764; not the 2nd, as most writers affirm, nor the 3rd, as Carlo states in his memoirs. But could he be expected to remember the date of an event that had not taken place? The ceremony, one reads, was performed in the cathedral. The words are those generally used in this register, but they are placed differently, and written without the customary abbreviations. A close reading reveals another discordant detail: all the members of the Bonaparte family are designated 'di Bonaparte', instead of simply Bonaparte, as in other contemporary official documents. The prefix is extremely significant: it was not used in Corsica until after the French conquest, when it was adopted by people officially recognized as noble by the government. The Bonaparte obtained this recognition in September 1771. By this slip, which can be attributed to vanity combined with carelessness (the handwriting suggests haste), the author of the notice, who can hardly be other than Carlo Bonaparte, gives himself away.

There is no escaping the supposition, extraordinary as it may seem: Carlo and Letizia were not religiously married in 1764, if ever. At some moment after September 1771 Carlo, seeking to regularize his position, used a blank space in the parish register to insert a fraudulent act. It may not have been too hard for him to have access to this register. His uncle was archdeacon; while he himself, in his official capacity of *assesseur* – assistant judge – of the jurisdiction of Ajaccio, was required to sign and initial the record of baptisms, burials and marriages for the year 1774, in accordance with the French practice of supervising the municipal registers by members of the magistrature. It would have been tempting, and perhaps easy, while performing this task, to lay hands on an earlier register and slip in the notice of his own marriage.[18]

For an explanation we are left guessing. One that springs to mind after reading Carlo's memoirs is that having been pushed into marriage with Letizia, at the last moment he baulked at a religious ceremony. If so, one may wonder how he got so far as consummating the union. Unless, that is, one realizes that Corsican marriages were very often consummated immediately after the signing of the dotal act, after the family party, in the home of the bride. Though strenuously reproved by the clergy, the custom was widespread, whether or not a religious ceremony ensued. In fact the ceremony was often omitted, in spite of the injunctions of the Council of Trent. The Corsicans had always maintained a very independent attitude towards the Church. In this primitive island, old customs were tenaciously preserved, customs that had prevailed long before the Council of Trent and stemmed from immemorial notions of family relationships. To the Corsican way of thinking the authority of the male heads of the two families was sufficient to sanctify a marriage. The dotal act constituted a legal marriage contract; the publicity given to its execution validated the marriage in its social context; consummation made it a binding union.

Non-religious marriages were common enough in eighteenth-century Corsica, as recent research has shown; among the shepherds and peasants of remote rural areas they were almost the rule.[19] But Ajaccio, with nearly four thousand inhabitants, was the second town in the island, and the Bonaparte and the Ramolino were notables, proud of their urban Italian origins. Moreover there was a priest in either family: Luciano Bonaparte, and Letizia's uncle, Francesco Maria. Whatever the force of insular tradition they would hardly have agreed to a marriage unblessed by the Church, a union that in theory incurred drastic ecclesiastical penalties, including public excommunication. Such measures, it is true, were rarely put into practice; all the same, if the religious rite was omitted, some serious reason must surely have weighed against it.

The reason, I suggest, is to be found in Carlo's reluctance. Pressed by his uncles, he consented to marry Letizia; against his feelings, against his will. Her dowry was made over; the two families rejoiced; the union was consummated with their tacit approval. And then, perhaps the day after, Carlo refused to go through with the church ceremony. There is evidence to indicate that it had been planned. When in 1779 Carlo had to furnish details of his civil status to the royal heraldist of France, so as to get Napoleon admitted to a French military school, he sent, not a copy of his marriage act, but a permit to marry Letizia granted by the bishop of Ajaccio on 2 June 1764 (the date discredits, of course, the record of the marriage in the municipal register, dated 1 June).[20] Such permits were given in exceptional circumstances, to dispense, for instance, with the publication of the banns. We may suppose that in view of Carlo's attitude the banns had not been published, but that Luciano none the less secured permission for the marriage. But the ceremony was not performed: at the last moment Carlo refused it.

In so doing he threatened both families with scandal. To cancel the wedding at that juncture amounted to a public repudiation of Letizia, an insupportable affront to her and to all her family. But seeing that marriages could be solemnized privately it was possible to hush the matter up. Friends and neighbours could be allowed to think that the couple had been married by one of the priests of their families, in the home of the bride. Meanwhile the Ramolino could console themselves with the thought that Letizia was no worse married than hundreds of Corsican country girls. A religious ceremony might, after all, eventually take place. But even if it never did, and even if the truth leaked out, at least her children would be treated as legitimate: in Corsica the offspring of unblessed marriages could be baptized at the request of their parents and suffered no legal or ecclesiastical penalties. In their own interests, the Ramolino would be well advised to keep silence.

The alternative would mean legal action, mortifying in itself, followed by an application for the restitution of the dowry. The procedure might not succeed; contemporary records show that a bride's dowry was not easily recuperated, even when the husband was seriously at fault.[21] The Ramolino did not belong to that category of the population which settled its differences with a shot in the back fired from behind a rock in the maquis; among urban notables the approved weapon of retaliation was the law. Letizia's uncles must have known they were up against a tough trio: Luciano, who enjoyed nothing so much as lawsuits and nearly always won them; Napoleone, quarrelsome by nature, as we shall see; the headstrong Carlo. The Bonaparte would not willingly relinquish the dowry: after all it was what had recommended the marriage to them in the first place.

These are suppositions raised by the unexpected, baffling evidence that exists, and by the absence of the evidence one would expect. Should we suppose that Carlo consummated the union with the premeditated intention of securing Letizia's dowry and then refusing the religious ceremony, so as to leave himself a loophole of escape? We can only conjecture. Escape would anyhow be no easy matter. In the eyes of Corsican society he was married; he could only hope to recover his freedom by going abroad, for good, leaving the two families to fight over the dowry. Was this what he planned when he went to Rome, having got Letizia with child? Personally I find this hard to believe: had he been capable of so Machiavellian a scheme, he surely would have carried it through. At all events Luciano must have sponsored the journey, for he held the purse-strings. To me Carlo's behaviour seems rather that of a wilful, capricious young man, whose education at the Jesuits' college in Ajaccio had left him with the Voltairian scorn of the Church that became apparent in his later years. Perhaps he was already composing the anti-religious verses Napoleon recalled at Saint Helena.

Carlo had a gift for poetry, which he cultivated, so his sons recalled. In his memoirs he confides that he showed a marked talent for writing love poems while at school with the Jesuits in Ajaccio.[22] His uncle may well have thought that a lawyer would be more useful to the family than a poet. To me it seems likely that Luciano, satisfied that Carlo had contracted a union with Letizia, happily in control of her dowry, offered him this educational trip to Rome as a reward for his obedience, hoping he would come home reconciled to his marriage as well as qualified to earn a living. As for the Ramolino, they could only acquiesce, secretly wondering whether Carlo would return.

He did, though not before he had run out of money and invited scandal, as we shall see. But one scandal at least was avoided, then and later: the absence of a religious marriage was never suspected; never, that is, until Pierre Lamotte published his article on the subject in 1961. Had the fact, or even a suspicion of it, come out earlier, it would have certainly been used by enemies of the Bonaparte during the lifetime of Carlo and of his children, and later. Yet no hint of it appears in the innumerable criticisms that have been hurled against the family. Not one of Napoleon's most savage detractors has ever suggested that he was born out of wedlock. And that, certainly, was something Napoleon himself never suspected. On the contrary, he imagined his parents' marriage as a spectacular event in the traditional Corsican style: 'My mother went to her wedding accompanied by her fifty first cousins, all strong, handsome men,' he told Bertrand; cousins, as he explained to Las Cases, such as constituted a most valued part of the dowry of a bride.[23]

Carlo's visit to Rome has been regarded as something of a mystery. Historians have offered fanciful reasons for it, and one of the most serious, Frédéric Masson, denies it altogether. Carlo himself says nothing on the subject in his memoirs except that it lasted 'about two years'; an exaggeration, for in fact he was away only about half that length of time. He did not, it seems, study law: his name is not listed in the university register in Rome. In view of what has been said of his behaviour, an examination of the police records would seem more appropriate; but there too a blank has been drawn.[24]

The Corsican writer Marcaggi, one of the best-informed historians of Napoleon's early years, first provided material to fill this gap in Carlo's life story by publishing the revelations of a certain abbé Celli, made in a letter written to Letizia's grandfather, Pietrasanta, on 30 October 1765. Celli reports that Carlo had committed all kinds of follies and faults in Rome, including seducing a virgin and getting her with child; that he had to bolt, by night, to escape the vengeance of her family, after borrowing money from a fellow Corsican, the loan being guaranteed by another compatriot, Saliceti, doctor to the Pope.[25]

These accusations are supported by another contemporary document, a colourful, extravagant document of great interest: an anonymous open letter written by a Corsican in Corte on 1 April 1766. No doubt it was circulated with a view to blackening the reputation of Carlo and his family, who were doing just well enough at the time to excite jealousy. Until very recently anonymous letters were a preferred weapon in Corsican political and social rivalries. The author, who ranks as the earliest known articulate enemy of the Bonaparte, went to great lengths to collect injurious gossip from Corsicans and perhaps others Carlo had met in Italy. He also managed to lay hands on some self-condemnatory letters, or copies of letters, written by Carlo during his stay. These items are strung together on a note of ponderous, self-righteous irony.[26]

Carlo's bad behaviour, according to this writer, began from the time he landed in Leghorn. Welcomed by a Corsican family, the Costa, he abused their hospitality by speaking slightingly of their daughter (she was hideous, he remarked), squandered money recklessly and paid court to the local ladies, passing himself off as an unmarried man (as he may well in fact have been). The accusations are plausible. One is not altogether incredulous, either, when one reads that Carlo introduced himself in Rome as a noble Buonaparte of Florence with feudal estates in Corsica. We know that his father and uncle, five years earlier, had obtained recognition of their affiliation with the Tuscan Buonaparte. Carlo naturally made the most of this flattering connection. Too much of it: apparently it went to his head and inspired some mythomanic masquerading. Carlo had a theatrical streak in his nature that manifested itself all through his life.

Some of the anecdotes retailed by his accuser may seem to us merely comic, or even disarming: Carlo boasting of his fortune but too poor to buy summer clothes; driving his own coach through the streets of the eternal city by night to theatres, princely receptions, rendezvous of love. How did he pay for all this *dolce vita*? After racing through the money he had brought with him and that deposited with a Corsican notable in Rome for his keep, he then appropriated some intended for another student from Ajaccio, besides sponging on his compatriots. Eventually he struck lucky in a love-affair with a married woman who gave him four hundred crowns: enough to pay for elegant clothes, 'superb suppers' and 'magnificent receptions'.

When love and money dwindled he begged from all and sundry, and it was then that he confessed to seducing a virgin with promise of marriage and getting her pregnant. His need of cash was now urgent: menaced by her family he had to leave Rome without a minute's delay. Celli, the Jesuit priest in whom he confided, refused help; later, as we know, he repeated the whole story to Pietrasanta. But Saliceti, 'struck with horror' and more humane, advanced him fifty crowns which enabled him to leave secretly, by night, on 31 August 1765 (the anonymous letter writer goes so far as to give the date).

Did Carlo really seduce a girl, promising marriage? Perhaps. But is it not also conceivable that he invented this dreadful tale in a last, frantic, fantastical manoeuvre to raise funds? While his accuser gives plenty of circumstantial details about the rest of his deeds and misdeeds, quoting conversations and even names, he has nothing to add to Carlo's own account of an episode that would surely have made news in Rome. Carlo's self-accusation is the only evidence offered for the crime. Intoxicated by the glamour and grandeur of Italy, rejoicing in his temporary release from a forced marriage and his frugal Corsican home, was he prepared to expose himself to the odium of his friends and compatriots in the hope of extending his holiday a while longer? Perhaps. Had he really seduced a girl and been menaced by her parents surely he would have fled, as soon as he had the means to do so, and hurried straight back to Corsica. But no. He lingered in Rome long enough, we are told, to fit himself out with an expensive new wig and clothes before travelling not to Corsica, but to Florence, where he stayed to enjoy further social pleasures. This is hardly the behaviour of a man on the run.

His visit to Florence coincided with the arrival of the new ruler of Tuscany, the Austrian Grand-duke Leopold. Carlo lost no time in calling on one of the Tuscan Buonaparte with whom he proudly claimed kinship, an uncle, a priest at Prato (cathedral city near Florence), so he wrote to Count Rivarola, a Corsican acting as Sardinian consul in Leghorn in whom he apparently confided his adventures and problems at this time. The uncle was in all probability the canon Filippo Buonaparte who had procured the precious recognition of kinship of the Tuscan with the Corsican Bonaparte. He will appear again in this story. He was not in fact a member of the Florentine branch of the family, which had died out nearly two hundred years before, but belonged to the Buonaparte of San Miniato where a Ghibelline Buonaparte is said to have taken refuge in the thirteenth century, banished from Florence by the Guelphs. This is however unproved, and the affiliation of the Buonaparte of Florence and San Miniato has never been conclusively established.[27]

Carlo was not inclined to look into such details; his object was to secure official recognition of his nobility that would admit him to the inaugural audience of the grand-duke, the ceremony known as 'the kissing of the hand'. He did not, it seems, succeed; but at least he witnessed the state procession when the grand-duke and duchess entered the city on 13 September; at least he squeezed himself into the Palazzo Pitti (against regulations) and caught sight of them dining with the Count and Countess of Thurn, grand-chamberlain and first lady-in-waiting. This glimpse of the gorgeous glittering world of the great justified, in his eyes, a succession of begging letters to Rivarola; he had refrained, he wrote naïvely, from asking his Tuscan relations for money. His stay at the Locando del Centauro (The Inn of the Centaur), and the hire of a coach and a lackey had put him to heavy expense, he explained. He was also bothered about some lessons in dancing and flute-playing he had left unpaid when he had departed hurriedly from Rome, taking the flute with him. If we are to believe his anonymous accuser these were the only subjects he had studied there.[28]

The writer's venom increases as he relates Carlo's return journey, gossip presumably becoming more plentiful and circumstantial as he approached his home. In Capraja, the little Genoese island where he had to break the voyage, he made himself conspicuous by again posing as a Buonaparte of Tuscany. His valet was instructed to address him as count, a title the Corsican Bonaparte hoped to find in the annals of their ancestors but which they were never able to prove, even by investigation of the Florentine archives. Undeterred, Carlo let it be known that he was travelling to Corsica to chastise some vassals who had the impudence to assume the name of Buonaparte. Did he really go to such lengths of imposture? Was this his last, outrageous fling of play-acting before returning to the narrow realities of his homeland?[29]

The anecdote at all events provokes an explosion of rage from the anonymous narrator, in which he betrays his basic motive for composing the letter. Furiously he asserts that the Corsican Bonaparte had not come from Tuscany, that the Tuscan Buonaparte had never been noble, that the Bonaparte of Ajaccio had never been regarded as noble by the Genoese, that Carlo's father had been a cattle thief, that the ancestor who bore his name, Carlo Maria (his great-great-grandfather) had also been a thief, one so notorious that comic rhymes on the subject were still in circulation. The recent small successes of the Bonaparte were evidently insupportable to their rivals. Kinship with a family as distinguished as the Tuscan Buonaparte (who were in fact no longer very illustrious) implied a social status few of them could pretend to; Carlo's trip to Rome was a privilege few of them had enjoyed. All this was provoking enough. And then, to crown all, at the time the letter was written in the spring of 1766, Carlo, the spendthrift impostor, was well established in Corte, an outstanding university student on the way to becoming a favourite of Pasquale Paoli, Father of the Nation.[30]

How did this happen? What brought about this transformation of the impossible Carlo, some six months after he returned to Corsica, penniless and disgraced? His memoirs provide a clue. Here he gives his own reasons for leaving Rome. Not, of course, that he had run out of money and seduced a girl, but that 'inflamed with love of the nation then labouring to throw off the yoke of the Genoese', and hearing of the foundation of a university in Corte, he decided to join the Corsican patriots.[31] The explanation may be a half-truth; but it carries conviction. In Rome, besides meeting the rich and glamorous, Carlo must have come across Corsican students and expatriates more alive to the national struggle than were the stuffy notables of Ajaccio. The situation has parallels: the present Corsican nationalist movement was originally stimulated by Corsican students living outside the island. And Pasquale Paoli, formed by the *illuminismo* in Naples, was not alone among patriot leaders in having been educated abroad.

Carlo came home, then, with serious intentions. Perhaps they protected him, to a point, from the wrath of his uncle Luciano, which must have been terrible after he learnt the contents of the letter from the abbé Celli. Whatever the truth of the accusations brought against him, Carlo's behaviour had been irresponsible, to say the least. Yet his underlying motive was not. He was one of those Corsicans – and there have been some in all periods – who was simply unable to endure the obscure condition to which he was born. His shocking record in Italy, boasting, posing, lying, scrounging, borrowing, spending and over-spending, was a first act of rebellion, an explosive, ill-considered protest against his cramping, mediocre circumstances. It exposed him to some vicious criticism. But in the long run the whole experience proved salutary, for it cured him of many youthful cravings, enabled him to work them out of his system. Extravagant he was to remain; but not futile. After his return to Corsica he settled down to make a career, shackled himself to his chosen task of rising in society, pushing and dragging his family towards the same goal. The dimensions and difficulties of the programme consumed his superabundant energy, broke his health and killed him young: Carlo was as ambitious, in his way, as was his son Napoleon. And like Napoleon, he had the faculty of being able to stand back and see himself acting his life-drama, comparing it to a 'romance' or tale of adventure. 'My adventures could provide material for a complete romance,' he had written to Rivarola on reaching Florence; words that recall Napoleon's celebrated saying: 'What a romance . . . my life!'

Carlo had returned to Corsica resolved to throw in his lot with Paoli. He first attempted to approach him, it seems, from Bastia. A letter from one of Paoli's officers, Gio' Battista Ristori, from Furiani, a nationalist stronghold to the south of Bastia, dated 1 November 1765, introduces him to the head of state as a recommendable person desirous of serving the nation. The letter asks for help to be given him to find lodging, presumably in Corte, and a mount (horse or mule) if he had to continue his journey beyond the mountains to reach the General. Paoli's duties kept him constantly on the move: Boswell, visiting him the previous month, had to travel to the deep south-west where he was presiding over an itinerant court of appeal.[32]

It seems unlikely that Carlo met Paoli on this journey. The next hint we have of his activities is a letter from the comte de Marbeuf, the French military commander in Bastia, dated 5 November. He thanks Carlo for his letter written 'on the occasion of a journey into the interior'; its contents do not however concern him but the Genoese Republic. What news had Carlo given Marbeuf? Searching for Paoli, no doubt visiting Corte, had he picked up some information which he thought could interest the commander of the French forces? One may hazard a guess that Carlo was seizing a small opportunity of bringing himself to Marbeuf's notice; apparently with poor success, for Marbeuf's reply is dismissive. The French general was by no means cut off from the interior; people came and went freely between the

rebel-controlled territory and the coastal towns; he himself corresponded continuously with Paoli.[33] But Carlo, with his gambler's
temperament, must have thought it worth writing to him in the hope
that some favour might be forthcoming. This was to be his technique
through life, and he set the example for his sons. Neither he nor they
had the least hesitation in approaching the great and powerful, soliciting the attention of people they knew only slightly or not at all. And in
spite of some snubs and setbacks the method worked: it was what first
levered the family out of the rut of Corsican obscurity. This was
probably Carlo's first contact with Marbeuf, and though apparently
fruitless at the time it created a link with the man who was to promote
his fortune and that of his elder sons.

To give him his due, he may have been introduced to Marbeuf by
Pietrasanta, a wily man of influence who managed to keep on good
terms at once with the French authorities and the rebel leader. At all
events it was Pietrasanta who entrusted him the following month with
a personal letter to Paoli, the contents of which are unknown to us.
When Carlo delivered it to him in Corte on 16 December he took the
opportunity of writing a covering note in which he declares his devotion to Paoli, his 'great and sincere love' of the nation and his
willingness to place 'his life and substance' at their disposal.[34] As a
result of which Paoli received him with such kindness, so Carlo relates
in his memoirs, that he thereupon decided to join the university.

The atmosphere was surely exhilarating, for he found himself in a
crowd of young patriots, some of whom had actually abandoned Italian
universities so as to pursue their studies in their liberated homeland.
Inaugurated in January of that year, the university was one of the
successes of Paoli's regime, a visible justification of his confidence in
attempting important things with small means. Its purpose was to
form an élite to man the Corsican state: the magistrature, administration
and clergy. The Corsican Church financed it, and nearly all the professors were Franciscan monks. Father Mariani, originally of Corbara,
in Corsica, gave up a chair at the university of Alcalá, in Spain, to
assume the rectorship; the others were found on the spot.

Given this personnel the university had to keep to a rather limited
curriculum: mathematics and natural science were taught, but not
economics or medicine. All the same a real effort was made to give
traditional subjects a modern bias. The teaching of law was to demonstrate, echoing Montesquieu, 'the origin and true spirit of laws,
and the best uses of the same'; philosophy was to be taught 'according

to the most plausible systems of the modern philosophers'. This latter aim was apparently achieved: Pommereul, who probably took part in the looting of Corte during the French conquest, observes that he saw the works of Locke, Montesquieu, Hume and Rousseau in the libraries of the professor-monks.[35]

Carlo evidently went to work with a will. Making up for lost time in Rome he enrolled, in December 1765, in the rector's course in ethics. According to the original curriculum laid down for the university this usually daunting subject was to be taught on extremely modern lines for the express purpose of forming worthy citizens of the new nation-state. Ethics was defined as 'a science most useful for learning the rules of good beaviour, and the proper manner of acting in the different employments of civil society, and also of acquiring a knowledge of the law of nature and of men'. By January of the following year Carlo was sufficiently well-versed in this subject to publish 'Academic Exercises' in Latin on the second part of the course. A brochure of ten pages, beautifully printed in the recently established press in Corte, it is dedicated by 'Carolus Bonaparte patritius adjacensis' (Carlo never lost sight of his upper-class origin) to 'Paschali de Paoli, supreme chief of the kingdom of Corsica, after God, the author of public felicity.' His aim being to attract Paoli's attention, the dedicatory preface is packed with flattering phrases. Yet behind the stilted language one can discern something of the enthusiasm of a young man, working with others, to create a nation. The university, he writes, was 'worth more than one could hope for or believe'; the subject treated was 'of the greatest utility to one engaged in forming and perfecting a society'.

The 'exercises' were to be the subject of a public debate on 21 January. The university regularly organized activities for the benefit of the population, thus offering aspects of its learning to those charged with affairs of state. Given the nature of the publication we cannot hope to find any original thoughts of Carlo Bonaparte. But the text is in itself of very great interest for the light it throws on the teaching dispensed at Corte. Leading concepts of the Enlightenment, breathing optimism and generosity, take first place: law is a science designed to ensure the happiness of men living in society; man is endowed with reason; nature leads him to procure his own happiness. Natural law exists, and man can apprehend it, guided by nature. But the traditional teaching of the Church intervenes to curb the full implications of these ideas: the principle of law resides in God's will; man can achieve happiness only with the aid of God, who wishes it; natural law is given by God;

its essence is love. And, in a firm stand against a bold new concept of the day: the human race never existed in a state of nature; the best man can attain is 'the state of revelation'. In the course of these arguments some distinguished philosophers come in for condemnation: Hobbes, chiefly, then Spinoza. But in spite of the denial of the state of nature, the mighty voice (though unnamed) of Rousseau, then at the height of his contested career, seems to ring through the pious precepts: man 'is free'; 'all men are naturally equal'.

Such were the exalting prospects of Paoli's revolution. Hardly surprisingly, in practice it had contradictory facets. Another text surviving from the university, a law student's notes on a course in criminal procedure, tells us that the use of torture was authorized. This too Carlo must have learned at Corte; but the practice was in accordance with that of the time.[36]

While Carlo was discovering the Enlightenment in the heart of the Corsican mountains Letizia was left in Ajaccio. She can hardly have failed to hear something about his misdeeds in Rome. The news, though probably less shattering than to a young wife today (women were then trained to accept the worst men could do) must surely have added to her accumulating disappointment. The prettiest girl in Corsica could have hoped for a happier life. She had no children to console her. The child born during Carlo's absence in Rome – a girl so he tells us – had died; there is no contemporary evidence to support the contention of certain writers that it was a boy called Napoleon, and Carlo would hardly forget so important an event to a Corsican as the birth of his eldest son. We have no evidence, either, as to when, exactly, he visited Ajaccio after his return from Rome; but on such an occasion he may have got her pregnant again, perhaps with another girl, who also died in 1766 or early the following year. For this there is only tradition to go on; but Letizia said she gave birth to thirteen children and an examination of the dates suggests that one of them may have been born at this time.[37]

Those accustomed to the familiar image of Letizia as the high-minded young matron austerely dedicated to her household duties will be surprised to learn how she reacted to her misfortunes: by over-spending on clothes. Luciano, controlling her dowry, had to foot the bills, and he was furious. There was a new dress to be paid for, so he complained in a letter to Pietrasanta on 16 March 1767, besides bodices, mantillas, a flowered petticoat in the latest fashion and several pairs of shoes. He had remonstrated with her mother, who was encouraging her; but her mother had merely retorted that his money troubles were no concern of hers and that Letizia was anyhow deprived of her husband's company. By such feminine tactics the mother tried to punish the Bonaparte for Carlo's unfeeling treatment of her daughter. Meanwhile all Ajaccio, according to Luciano, was aghast at their extravagance. He hoped Letizia would improve when separated from her mother; but if she went on as at present nothing short of 'marriage to a prince' would satisfy her. This letter was written on the eve of great changes for Letizia. Carlo had at last decided to keep house with her: he was taking her to live in Corte at the invitation of Paoli. Luciano was of course notoriously stingy; Letizia was no doubt laying in a suitable wardrobe for the Corsican capital, where clothes were appallingly expensive, as Luciano himself admits.[38]

Geltrude and Napoleone were to join in the move, again at Paoli's suggestion. Both were now unattached, their marriages having broken down within the last year. We do not know why Geltrude, who was childless, fell out with her husband, her cousin Nicolò Luigi Paravisino; only that in July 1766 she recuperated her dowry. Their separation was however temporary; another document shows them reconciled in December 1768. They fought side by side, it seems, against the French invasion and eventually returned to live together in Ajaccio.[39]

The breach between Napoleone and his wife, Maria Rosa, née Bozzi, was more serious, and was to have extremely troublesome consequences. Maria Rosa had betrothed her daughter Isabella to a local notable, one Spoturno; the dotal act was drawn up in May 1765. But the chief item of Isabella's dowry was the *casa* Bozzi, which was situated next door to the *casa* Bonaparte, and the Bonaparte were most unwilling to see a house pass into the hands of another family when it could be so conveniently joined to their own. Napoleone opposed the match; Isabella sided with her father; eventually another, grander marriage was arranged for her with a Corsican aristocrat, Ludovico Ornano, descendant of one of the great feudal families. Luciano married them himself on 16 January 1766, in his own home; but not before he had persuaded Isabella and her mother to exchange the Bozzi house for one of his vineyards, which was now included in Isabella's dowry, while the much-coveted *casa* Bozzi became the property of the Bonaparte. The arrangement was to give rise to prolonged and bitter conflict.[40]

To attract families of notables to Corte from the coastal towns was obviously good policy for Paoli: if he failed to capture the Genoese enclaves at least he could rob them of their more distinguished citizens.

The collective conversion of the Bonaparte was something of a triumph, seeing that they had always been conservative in their allegiances: pro-Genoese and then pro-French. Geltrude's husband was actually French consul in Ajaccio; perhaps she welcomed this opportunity of getting away from him while contradicting his political views, just as Napoleone jumped at the chance of leaving his wife and daughter. Yet one must suppose that something even more compelling than domestic conflict was at work when the Bonaparte decided to uproot themselves; something more compelling, too, than Carlo's young enthusiasm and the gracious solicitations of the rebel chief. The national regime must have seemed to them stable enough to offer worldly advantages; even Luciano, most cautious of men, actually contemplated abandoning his vineyards and cattle, not to mention his religious functions, so as to set up a family home in Corte, he confided to Pietrasanta. The only misgivings he and his brother (Napoleone) entertained concerned the expenses of the move. Napoleone confessed his anxieties to Paoli; but the General brushed them aside: he would see to everything; Carlo's patriotism would be rewarded; Napoleone and the ladies would always be welcome at his table. All this was flattering but vague. Financial responsibility as usual fell on Luciano. How, he complained, was he to provide for four people and a servant 'in a foreign land'? But the General was not to be gainsaid: 'The counsels of princes are precepts,' Luciano sourly observes.

Until then Carlo had been lodging in a large house belonging to the Rossi, which had been made available to university students; but on the arrival of his family other accommodation had to be found. The Bonaparte were first welcomed to the house of Giovan' Tommaseo Arrighi, a notable married to a cousin of Letizia's, Maria, née Biadelli. Tall and stark as a fortress, it stands close to the walls of the citadel, a real patriot's stronghold that was seven times burned, so Napoleon relates, in the Corsican wars. There Carlo's eldest son, Joseph, was born, as he himself recalled. And there his uncle Napoleone died a natural death on 17 August 1767, and not, as has been said, at Ponte Novo; his death certificate can be seen in the municipal archives of Corte.[41]

Historians could have avoided this misapprehension, and others more serious, had they made the journey to that town. Born on 7 January 1768, Joseph was christened 'Joseph Nabulion' the following day: his baptismal act appears in the proper place in the municipal register, written in the same hand as those placed immediately after and before. One needs to insist on the authenticity of this document in view of the questions raised by historians unacquainted with it. Doubt and confusion were first aroused by a copy of the document made in Corte on 19 July 1782; it must have been required by Joseph's boarding-school at Autun, in mainland France, where Carlo and Letizia visited him that year. It is a virtually faithful copy of the original except in one, disturbing particular: the name Joseph is left out. This document eventually found its way to the archives of the French Ministry of War, and there it was read, just over a century ago, by Theodore Iung, an incautious and inexperienced scholar. Not having seen the original baptismal act in Corte he jumped to conclusions: this was Napoleon's baptismal act, not Joseph's; Napoleon, not Joseph, was the first born; their father concealed the fact for some crooked purpose of his own, faking or altering the relevant documents so as to make the world believe that Napoleon was the younger son. None of Iung's arguments stand up to serious examination; nor do those of the later writers who from time to time have revived his thesis. Carlo was not above faking documents: this we know. But he was innocent in regard to the baptismal acts of his sons. The worst he can be accused of is persuading the copyist at Corte to leave out Joseph's first name—Joseph—in the copy of 1782. Perhaps he thought that a baptismal certificate that could be used by either son might come in handy. It did: Napoleon confessed to using it for his marriage to Josephine, thus presenting his age as a year closer to hers. Any lingering doubts in the matter are dispelled by the unquestionable authenticity of his own baptismal act, which exists, in two examples, in Ajaccio.[42]

The brothers, as was the custom, were called after close relations. The name Napoleon (then written indifferently Nabulione, Napulione, Napolione, Napoleone) was given in memory of Carlo's recently deceased uncle. Though uncommon it was not outlandish; nor was it, in the romantic words of one writer 'the name of a fantastic prince of ancient Greek legend'. Carlo's grandfather had a godparent by that name, and it appears from time to time in the genealogy of the Bozzi, with whom the Bonaparte had intermarried in several generations. Joseph was simply the French form of Giuseppe, a name carried both by Carlo's father and Letizia's maternal grandfather, Pietrasanta. But why was the French form used? Why was Napoleon's elder brother christened Joseph and not Giuseppe? Historians have used this fact to argue that he must have been born after the French conquest, thus supporting Iung's theory of the faked documents. The explanation is simpler: Joseph's original baptismal act was written in Latin, and not in Italian as was then usual in Corsica. The erudite priest of Corte did his best to Latinize, or at least de-Italianize the Christian names. So Carlo became 'Carolo' and we find 'Joseph Nabulion' where we would expect 'Giuseppe Nabulione', or 'Napoleone'.[43]

His godparents were Giovan' Tommaseo Arrighi and his wife. The intimacy developing between the two families in this stirring period led to closer ties: the Arrighi's son, Giacinto, married Letizia's first cousin, Maria Antoinetta Benielli, and their son, Jean-Thomas, was an outstanding general in the wars of Napoleon, who created him duke of Padua. But at the time of Joseph's birth the Arrighi were staunchly pro-Paolist and anti-French, so that in the spring of 1768 their house became so crowded with partisans assembling to face the French invasion that the Bonaparte had to leave. They moved into a larger house, another patriot's fortress, home of Paoli's predecessor, the murdered General Gaffori. The old mansion, close by the church in the main square, is still pitted with cannonballs fired by the Genoese when they besieged it in 1750. A statue of the general, over life-size, stands outside; a bas-relief on its pedestal recalls how his wife, in his absence, forced her retainers to resist by threatening to blow up the lot of them if they spoke of surrender. The General arrived to relieve them just in time.[44]

In Joseph's baptismal act Carlo is described as being in Corte for purposes of study: '*ratione studiorum*'; evidently he was still following courses at the university. But he was also, at the same time, working for Paoli. Historians have however grossly over-estimated his role. He was not, as has been asserted, secretary of state (there was no such appointment in the Corsican government). Nor was he ever elected to the national *consulta*, the members of which had to be over twenty-five. Had he held any post of importance he would surely have said so in his memoirs, where he makes much of his patriotic activities; yet he never so much as mentions that Paoli engaged his services at this time. The chronicler Rossi, less flattering than usual when speaking of a Bonaparte, was probably telling the truth when he wrote: 'Carlo Bonaparte had no employment, but he enjoyed the confidence of the General: that is why it was said he was secretary, and it is true that many things were written by him, for he was not lacking in talent and zeal.' Among his qualifications were a neat, clear handwriting, and anyone who has set about reading contemporary Corsican documents will realize how rare an accomplishment that was. He must also have had some knowledge of French, which was already useful and was to prove a major asset after the conquest. Of the 'many things written by him' we are left to judge by the 'academic exercises'. His signature below Paoli's on a letter of marque issued to a Corsican sea-captain on 19 November 1768 at least proves that he did undertake some secretarial chores. We have reason to think, too, that on his visits to Ajaccio he made himself useful to Paoli in other ways. Jadart, the French commissioner of war, strongly suspected he was staying there to spy for Paoli, so he wrote to Marbeuf on 11 September 1767, and the following month he reiterated his complaints with increased irritation: Bonaparte, with a couple of companions, was 'turning the heads' of the population in private conversations; he would like to see them out of town. Carlo was evidently developing those abilities of go-between and propagandist that proved so valuable to him in later years.[45]

He might be without official status; but he had the confidence of Paoli, and this was a privilege, the first great chance of his life. At the threshold of his career he had the immense good fortune of associating with a man of high culture and advanced ideas, at once a skilled politician and one of the truly creative statesmen of his day. Though no more than forty when Carlo first knew him, Paoli had a capacity for guiding and inspiring younger men. Boswell, whose irresponsibility often rivalled Carlo's, bears memorable witness to the impact of Paoli's personality, at once sobering and uplifting, when he met him, a little before Carlo, in the south of the island in October 1765. 'The contemplation of such a character really existing was of more service to me than all I had been able to draw from books, from conversation, or from the exertions of my own mind . . . I saw my highest idea realized in Paoli.' It is strange to think how close ran the paths of those two young men who had so much in common: enthusiasm, naïvety, vanity, unexploited gifts, an intense desire to enter into the intimacy of important men and an ability to do so. They might well have met; and perhaps they did indeed see each other, without knowing it, in Bastia, where Boswell was staying with Marbeuf early in November 1765.

One is tempted to think that it was Paoli, who advised Boswell to marry, who also persuaded Carlo to live with his young wife, to make a home. In so doing he reconciled Carlo to his lot, showed him how to make the most of himself, and incidentally of Letizia. The example of his manners, admired even by the exacting standards of the eighteenth century, and of his conversation that 'dazzled' Boswell, must have done much to transform Carlo from the cocksure poseur of his Roman days into the astute, engaging man of the world who was the father of Napoleon. The most convincing criticism that emerges from the anonymous letter written about him is that he was insufferably bumptious at that time. Paoli, surely, showed him how to behave.[46]

It seems that Carlo spent considerable sums in Corte furnishing his lodgings, so that he could entertain there in style. These expenses were investments: the young Bonaparte were making their way. Letizia's outlay on clothes was no doubt proving of value. She was often invited to play cards with the General, so her children remembered, and usually won. Paoli admired her, though not as much, she admitted, as her sister-in-law, the handsome spirited Geltrude who was an accomplished horsewoman. As favourites of the head of state the Bonaparte were naturally drawn into a worldly style of life. In spite of much that has been said Paoli's court was not really so very austere, except in comparison with others of his time. Boswell, certainly, was struck by his frugality; but he stayed with him in a small country village in the dilapidated house of impoverished nobles. Moreover he had reached Corsica fresh from a tour of the German princes: the contrast must have been extreme. He does however note that Paoli received him dressed in green and gold, and that since the establishment of the French in the coastal towns he had given up wearing the monkish Corsican homespun so as 'to make the government appear in a more respectable light'. Pommereul reports that Paoli's wardrobe was magnificent, as were his horses, and that his table was well provided and well served: his description gives a picture of him living in the handsomely furnished *palazzo* in Corte like a country gentleman keeping open house to his supporters.[47]

This so-called palace was the old residence of the Genoese provincial governors, a massive edifice without architectural pretensions. 'Less beautiful than solid', according to the same observer, it is built and roofed in the dark local schist used for all the houses in the old town of Corte as well as for the paving-stones of the stepped streets converging on the citadel. The décor was dour; but Paoli did what he could with it. He imported chandeliers, mirrors and furniture from Italy, including a set of armchairs upholstered in crimson and gold, with a couple of larger ones. These latter infuriated the notables, who referred to them indignantly as 'thrones' and accused him of aspiring to kingship. All the furniture was looted by French troops when they took possession of the town in May 1769.

Such scraps of alien luxury could hardly change the character of

Corte, a cluster of dark houses on the slopes of a dark rock crowned by a medieval fortress, itself overshadowed by enormous mountain masses where dark rock is hatched with darker forest. Even today the whole scene is so forbidding as to make the dazzling Mediterranean sun seem irrelevant. Yet this sombre little capital, which struck a French officer as 'a horrible village', appeared to the young Carlo Bonaparte as a city embellished by the arts of letters and of arms.[48] He and Letizia must surely have delighted in the rudimentary glamour of Paoli's court, so different from their cramped childhood homes. Not for a moment could they imagine that they would come to know other palaces and rulers, incomparably grander. How could Carlo foresee his reception by Louis XVI at Versailles in the last days of its doomed splendour, or Letizia suppose that she would spend much of her life in courtly surroundings, mother of six sovereigns?

A faint, very faint, foretaste of her future was given to her in the spring of 1768, when she enjoyed a veritable social triumph at an official function. Paoli's policy was to seize every occasion to mask the fundamental weakness of the rebel state: that it was unrecognized by other states and had no allies to count on. Boswell's providential visit had enabled him to convince the simpler Corsicans, at least, that he had the support of Britain. Now, in 1768, came a chance to play a similar game of bluff. A Tunisian ship was wrecked on the coast, and the Corsicans, recalling gruesome raids by Barbary pirates, stole its cargo and captured its crew. Paoli promptly intervened, freed the crew, restored the cargo and had the ship repaired so that it could set sail. In due course the Bey sent an envoy to thank him, bringing exotic gifts: an Arab horse, a tiger and a couple of ostriches. Paoli received him at Corte with the honours due to an ambassador. At a party in the *palazzo* (where the gilded 'thrones' must have come in useful) he assembled the prettiest women in rebel society, with Letizia, resplendent, well in view. Her rivals, it is said, criticized her coquetry; but the visitor from the Maghreb was impressed, and Letizia learnt what she did not forget: that her beauty could be of use to men. The tiger lived to be looted by the French army; what happened to the ostriches is unsaid.[49]

The birth of a son, the visit of the Tunisian envoy: these were the last festive occasions the Bonaparte were to enjoy for a year and more. In May 1768 Genoa sold them to Louis XVI, along with their countrymen, and the patriots determined to resist by force of arms. According to the chronicler Rossi, Carlo was responsible for this heroic decision. Heroic, and also suicidal: that independent Corsica, a peasant nation of some hundred thousand inhabitants, should go to war with a nation of some twenty-two million, the richest and most civilized in the world, was as though Cuba, unaided, should challenge the armed might of the United States.

'Passionately' attached to Paoli and the nation, Carlo, when the representatives met at the *consulta* in May, knew just what to say to fire their resolution. The speech has the tone of an inspired anti-colonialist tract or a hymn to national liberty: 'All the nations that have aspired to the conquest of liberty have been exposed to the great vicissitudes that determine the triumphs of peoples. There have been peoples less valiant, less powerful, who none the less, by virtue of their constancy, have achieved the great object at which they aimed.' Napoleon, at Saint Helena, recalled a particularly trenchant passage, noted by two of his companions in exile: 'If, to be free, it were enough to desire freedom, then all peoples would be free.' It was the kind of statement Napoleon himself might have made as a young man.

The quotation is accurate: presumably Napoleon had a copy of the speech made at the time his father pronounced it half a century before. He cannot have taken it from Rossi, whose text was not published till 1902. But strangely, no such document has been found among Napoleon's papers, nor those of Joseph, who was also familiar with the speech. Stranger still, the text is not among the numerous documents kept by Carlo Bonaparte and inherited by his descendants. Stranger still, one finds no mention of it in his memoirs: not a word to recall the exalting moment when as spokesman of his generation he swayed the destiny of his country. Yet he never conceals his devotion to Paoli and the Corsican nation. Nor, be it said, any incident that could redound to his credit. The pompous address professor Vannucchi delivered in Latin when granting him his doctorate at the university of Pisa in 1769, is quoted in his memoirs in full. Why, one may well ask, did Carlo omit an incident so much to his honour?

The speech was first published four years after it was made, in 1772, by Cambiaggi, an Italian historian of Corsica. Cambiaggi states that it was made by a student of the university of Corte, but without mentioning Carlo. The university professors, he explains, had the 'laudable custom' of giving speeches in the intervals between debates at the *consulte*. The historic *consulta* of May 1768 of course provoked a series of pronouncements on the impending war. Another historian, the Corsican Renucci, relates that the rector, father Mariani, who first took the floor, counselled prudence in face of the military might of

France, but that father Leonardo Grimaldi, professor of mathematics and the advanced philosophy taught at Corte, appealed to the Corsicans to resist and so rival the Athenians at Marathon. Carlo's speech, in the same vein, may have come afterwards. But the historian says nothing about it.

One may suppose that such a speech was made, and recorded in the version transcribed by Cambiaggi, and still ask the question: was Carlo really its author? When Cambiaggi published his history in 1772 Carlo's name was no doubt too obscure to be worth mentioning. Did Cambiaggi even know who the author was? Did Rossi, copying Cambiaggi or his source (some document now lost), writing after the death of Carlo and the rise of Napoleon, attribute the speech to Carlo as part of his campaign of glorifying the parents of the Emperor?[50] And did not Napoleon simply lift it from Cambiaggi to add it to his self-created legend, at a time when he was striving to build up his own image as a champion of liberty?[51]

But whether Carlo did, or did not, make the speech is, I think, less important to history than that Napoleon chose to say that he did. Though he had small patience with his father's failings – extravagance, addiction to pleasure – he took pride in him as a faithful partisan of Paoli. As a young man, no less than his father, he idolized the Father of the Corsican Nation. Paoli's ideals predisposed him in favour of the French Revolution, and held some place in his own regime, even after it had become despotic. Freedom from feudal servitude and equality before the law were tenets Paoli and Napoleon shared. Carlo the lightweight, the clever climber, can also be seen as a hyphen between two great political innovators.

One may of course wonder how far he really shared Paoli's ideals. Was his attachment to the Corsican leader motivated by anything but self-interest? His principal aim in life, before meeting him, had been to get himself recognized as noble. Later, having obtained this recognition from Paoli's enemies, he was to exploit it in an unremitting struggle to scale the heights of French society. With such inclinations could he value or even comprehend Paoli's vision, so audacious in its day: that of the sovereign people, equal and free, shaping its own history?

Napoleon and Joseph both declare that he could and did. 'He was a friend of liberty,' wrote Joseph, and Napoleon went so far as to say that 'he loved liberty with fanaticism'. In Napoleon's words: 'He was strongly attached to the nobility and the aristocracy, on the other hand he was very enthusiastic for generous and liberal ideas.' This ambivalent attitude was after all not unknown to eighteenth-century gentlemen, and Carlo was well placed to maintain it. He might imbibe the idea in his course in ethics that all men are naturally equal; but he was not obliged to experience it in daily life. The Genoese government had excluded Corsicans from positions of authority; now Carlo found himself on intimate terms with the head of the independent nation and looking forward to an influential career. Paoli might have instituted a form of government described by Boswell as 'the best model that hath ever existed in the democratical form', but in fact the Corsican revolution, like the French, was manipulated by notables in their own interests. It was they who controlled the village elections, who sat in the *consulte*, who held executive office. In fact Paoli encouraged them to take the lead: they were people of education and means on whom the success of his government depended. It is true that he had allowed no significant privileges to the nobles or to the big landowners who aspired to be considered as such, and that their frustrated ambitions eventually brought the regime crashing. But Carlo, though harbouring similar ambitions, issued from a less exalted stratum of society; that of the minor notables, to whom Paoli had much to offer. Moreover he was young, ardent and somewhat superficial. For him liberty meant national independence rather than an exacting set of precepts; Paoli must have appeared to him not so much a revolutionary statesman as a chief; his chief. With a spontaneous loyalty that runs deep in Corsican tradition he had no hesitation in taking up arms for him, faithful in adversity as in good fortune, so his memoirs underline.[52]

Not all followed his example. The apparent unity of the Corsican nation masked deep cleavages of opinion such as often become apparent in colonial and ideological wars. The dissidents were the nobles and notables who felt slighted by Paoli's doctrine of egality, and certain members of the Royal Corse, a regiment stationed in France that had been formed for Corsicans back in 1739. Matteo Buttafoco, one of the officers, who had acted as Paoli's intermediary with the French foreign minister, the duc de Choiseul, had for some time been secretly serving France; when hostilities broke out he returned to Corsica with the invading army (which did not, however, include the Royal Corse) and went to work with a will to undermine national morale. The patriots branded him as a Vittolu (recalling the Judas of Sampiero), and sacked and burnt his home. None the less the French managed to raise a Corsican legion which went straight into battle after a brilliant crash training by the comte de Guibert, future author of an epoch-making work on military strategy that became the inspiration of the young Napoleon. These unashamed traitors had been won over by prospects of money and preferment. They duly received their rewards after the conquest and enjoyed them till the French Revolution twenty years later.[53]

Carlo Bonaparte's war record can be roughly pieced together from documents that have recently come to light. Paoli's regular paid army was no more than a token force of two regiments, each of three hundred men, who guarded the capital and head of state. The bulk of the fighting force was constituted by the call-up, as circumstances demanded, of able-bodied men in each parish. When war threatened in May 1768 the *consulta* voted that the paid troops be increased as far as funds allowed. An appeal was made for volunteers. Carlo was one who responded; his name appears on rolls of volunteers engaged for three consecutive four-day periods between 23 August and 3 September. They were paid 2 lire a head for each period.

Carlo's assignment was to guard the General, and he had difficulty in living on half a lira a day. This is what emerges from the letter Paoli wrote on 28 August 1768 from the scene of battle in Cap Corse to one of his officers in the south. He urges him to help Luciano Bonaparte to send his oxen to the butcher so as to provide for his nephew 'who is still with me'. Such were the problems, despairingly petty, of the Corsican war. Later, during the truce in January 1769, Paoli wrote to his treasury: 'I have never given anything to Bonaparte who has served with such punctuality and devotion all through the war . . .' and ordered that he should be paid 200 lire. Carlo's loyalty was certainly not inspired by hope of material gain, and we have no reason to doubt him when he states that he took part in all the engagements of the war, so confirming the tradition that he was present in the battles of Borgo and Ponte Novo.[54]

But if he acted as Paoli's bodyguard, or aide-de-camp, as seems probable, he cannot have seen much fighting. According to a French officer Paoli never appeared at the head of his troops; a disappointing observation, confirmed by Rossi: the General always stayed well in the background crying 'Don't abandon my brother', the intrepid Clemente. Contemporary French witnesses, including those who most respected Corsican valour, agree in criticizing Paoli's military performance. Dumouriez considered that he showed genius and character rather than military talent; Pommereul defines him as a statesman 'born to shine in the cabinets [chancelleries] rather than in the camps [battle-fields]'. Paoli's letter of 28 August, already quoted, exactly illustrates this latter judgement. France, he wrote, might well win the war; but she would never be allowed to remain 'mistress of Corsica'; the other powers would oblige her to restore her conquest to Genoa. If the Corsicans, he argued, now gave in tamely, they would be in no position, when this happened, to bargain for 'privileges' or 'guarantees'. They would have thrown away their liberty, they would not be listened to. But if, on the contrary, they put up a stiff resistance, they would at least demonstrate that they rejected the French treaty with Genoa and could only be deprived of their liberty by force of arms. In short their object, in Paoli's view, was not to fight to the last man but to state their political case on the battlefield. His calculation, uninspiring in itself, was also mistaken.[55]

Attending on such a leader it is unlikely that Carlo was much exposed to the violence of close combat. He had served, in Paoli's words, with 'punctuality and devotion', not with 'outstanding valour'. The role of the female Bonaparte has also, it seems, been somewhat exaggerated. Lucien Bonaparte recalls that Geltrude earned such a reputation for courage that the shepherds, chanting, as was their wont, verses from Tasso's *Jerusalem Delivered*, never failed to substitute her name for that of the gallant Clorinda. The portrait is attractive, and makes one regret that Lucien's memoirs are so often fanciful. As for Letizia, she enjoyed recounting her amazonian experiences, and no doubt they lost nothing in the telling: '. . . our good and valiant mother,' writes Lucien, 'spoke rather willingly of her exploits in our war of independence . . .'. Her reminiscences have come to us through those of Lucien, of Napoleon and of her ladies-in-waiting. But how reliable were they, even at first hand?

The one contemporary document I have found about her at this period shows her in a very different light. What was this national heroine doing in the spring of 1769, that desperate period when the French were crowding the ports with fresh troops and Paoli was calling on every man and boy able to hold a gun? What was Letizia doing in March 1769, then four months' pregnant with Napoleon? Buying clothes. This was the subject of a letter she wrote to her grandfather Pietrasanta in Bastia on the 13th of the month: there was a 'dress of nobility' to be wrapped in a white cloth, a roll of Lyons silk to be made into a dress with basques similar to those of the 'dress of nobility'; she would send for and pay for them both. War or no war,

Letizia's dresses would somehow be conveyed by a long day's rough riding from Bastia to Corte. In fairness it should be said that Carlo was encouraging her; the letter is written in his hand (her own was barely legible). Perhaps keeping up appearances was part of national policy in this sombre hour; it was anyhow Letizia's usual reaction to misfortune.[56]

But the days for dressing up in Corte were numbered: on 8 May the Corsican nation perished with the men on the bridge of Ponte Novo. If Carlo was with Paoli he can only have seen the battle from the top of a hill more than two miles away. Paoli's behaviour in the last stages of the war has embarrassed his firmest admirers. Why was he not at hand to prevent the débâcle of Ponte Novo? Or share in it? Was it true, as the Corsican chroniclers insist, that he had posted foreign mercenaries at the end of the bridge with orders to fire on any Corsican who tried to retreat? And why, after the battle, did he make no attempt to rally his troops? To stop the enemy marching on Corte? To defend the capital? The noble Plutarchian image hallowed by tradition disintegrates under close scrutiny. Father of the Nation, he was not prepared to defend it to the death. Nor, let it be said, were the majority of his officers. They had been deserting, covertly, all through the French offensive of the spring; after Ponte Novo they simply surrendered.

Until now the disillusion cast by revelations about Paoli and his collaborators has been in great measure redeemed by the episode of Ponte Novo. Paoli was cowardly, calculating, irresolute, his officers cowardly, self-interested, treacherous; but at least on the bridge the Corsicans proved their worth, gave a historic example of the heroism of a free people defending its liberty. Voltaire's tale of how the patriots fought behind a barricade built with the bodies of their own dead and wounded has stirred generations of readers, Corsican and others. But now, just before I write these lines, a document has surfaced in the Corsican archives: a letter from Paoli to Carli, the *intendant* of the mint, dated 9 May. It is a brief note dashed off the day after the battle; not an official communicaton to his government. The Corsicans, he states, were on the point of winning a great victory; but they advanced imprudently and were driven back in confusion to the bridge. There twenty died under French fire and a greater number were wounded. The rest, crowded together, lay down on the bridge to make the French think they were dead; the French abandoned the attack and the Corsicans, close to 'exploding with anguish', were relieved by a detachment of patriots at one in the morning. In these few lines the national myth crumbles. The hundreds of dead are reduced to a mere twenty; the pile of corpses and wounded used as a barricade by the survivors becomes a heap of frightened men shamming dead. Was Paoli, perhaps, minimizing the defeat, just as the French, announcing hundreds of casualties and 'a great carnage', were exaggerating their victory? The various accounts of the battle are obviously extremely subjective. Did the Corsican chroniclers, speaking of the soldiers posted at the end of the bridge with orders to fire on whoever crossed it, misinterpret Paoli's orders so as to leave him the blame for the failure of the operation? And did not Voltaire, whose source has never been traced, heighten hearsay to uphold his faith in the virtues of free men? His version, the most tragic, and also the least credible, is the one the public has preferred. Myth demands sacrificial victims.[57]

Carlo was among the few to keep faith with Paoli. He stayed with him, he writes, until he embarked; that is to say he accompanied him on the long trek over the mountains to Porto Vecchio on the southeast coast. There, on 13 June, Paoli and some three hundred partisans embarked in two British ships and set sail for Italy. Carlo confesses he would have joined them had Paoli not reminded him of his duty to his family. There was nothing for it: he had to retrace his steps to Corte, collect Letizia and Joseph, take them home to Ajaccio and submit to 'the yoke of the victor'. He had defended the liberty of his country, he writes, at the cost of his 'blood and fortune', and 'all the treasure on earth' would not have corrupted him. 'Now I serve the king of France,' he continues, 'I serve him faithfully and I would be incapable of betraying him on any pretext whatsoever.' An opportunist, Carlo was none the less loyal to his engagement; and that, no doubt, was why he attracted such valuable protectors.[58]

But what of the retreat to Monte Rotondo? The contemplated last stand in the mountains? The night in the cave? Carlo says not a word about any of this, and indeed the story is incompatible with his memoirs. It is, however, not the only tale about the supposed adventures of Carlo and Letizia after Ponte Novo. Rossi, leaving out Monte Rotondo, the cave, the delegation to de Vaux, relates that they accompanied Paoli's brother Clemente westwards across the high plateau of the Niolo in the hope of raising reinforcements among the shepherds. A house in the stony little village of Lozzi at over three thousand feet is shown as one where Letizia stayed on the way.

Legend, probably, has been grafted on to what was at first merely

the memory of a hard journey, coloured, certainly, by Letizia's reminiscences. Since fighting was still to be feared on the route from Corte
to Ajaccio by way of Vizzavona and Bocognano, the Bonaparte may
well have chosen the much rougher one, due west over the central
cluster of mountains. This meant two or three days' riding through an
outrageously rugged, barely inhabited country: a tough ordeal for a
woman six months' pregnant caring for a year-old child. Letizia's
contemporaries, including her lady-in-waiting, Laure d'Abrantès, recall
that she often spoke of the hardships of crossing the mountains, and
Napoleon remembered hearing her say that she had been prepared to
give birth to him in a cave. Perhaps she and Carlo did leave Corte by
the track leading up the valley of the Restonica under the shadow of
Monte Rotondo; perhaps they were joined by other refugees and had to
spend a night in a cave. The delegation to Corte seems to be a legend
designed to add to their posthumous prestige, and it is unlikely they
could have accompanied Clemente who set out in search of reinforcements immediately after Ponte Novo; but possibly they did make their
way through the Niolo to the west coast and so back to Ajaccio. And
very likely they were smitten and drenched by rain or even snow: a
French report speaks of violent freak storms in that mid-June causing
men and horses to die of cold. Perhaps too, Letizia really did risk
drowning in the swollen current of the Liamone after the dangers of
the expedition seemed to be past.[59]

Eventually the young couple rode into Ajaccio. Here the traditional
tale, and the more factual one I have traced, converge. Carlo and
Letizia reached their home: less glorious than the figures of legend but
more plausible, and all things considered, courageous enough. Letizia
no doubt went to mass on the feast of the Assumption: almost everyone
did. Napoleon was certainly born that day. He was delivered by the
old family retainer Caterina, though not on to a carpet: Letizia denied
this tale to some French visitors she received in Rome in 1833 with the
statement that there were no carpets to be seen in Ajaccio, let alone in
summer. 'I entered the world in the arms of Mammuccia Caterina,'
Napoleon related at Saint Helena. 'She was stubborn, difficult, continually at war with those around her.' But he never forgot the tears
she shed when he was taken away to school. The night after his birth a
comet was seen from Ajaccio. Another was seen from Saint Helena,
just before he died. 'A comet heralded the death of Caesar,' he
observed.[60]

3

THE STRUGGLES AND TRIALS
OF A CORSICAN FAMILY

'I was born when the nation was perishing. Thirty thousand Frenchmen spewed on to our coasts, engulfing the throne of liberty in seas of blood: such was the odious sight that first met my eyes. The cries of the dying, the groans of the oppressed, tears of despair surrounded my cradle from the hour of my birth.'[1] So Napoleon, at the age of twenty, began an unsolicited letter to Paoli, still in exile in England. If due allowance be made for the language of rhetoric, this shockingly written passage is closer to fact than most commentators have supposed.

To consolidate the French victory, de Vaux had ordered the Corsicans to give up their weapons to their municipal officers and swear fidelity to Louis XV. As had always happened in Corsica in like circumstances, the notables hastened to make submission. Those, on the other hand, who had less to gain or to lose, for whom liberty was their most valued possession, fought on. While Carlo Bonaparte was courting the favour of the new regime his less genteel cousin, Angelo Matteo Bonelli, nicknamed Zampaglino, was killing French grenadiers in the mountains near his native Bocognano at the head of some twenty desperadoes. He got out of Corsica in time to save his skin and lived to boost his cousin's career: Napoleon owed his first political victory to his disreputable aid. The head of the patriots' 'league', Domenico Leca, more intransigent, earned the title of 'chief of the martyrs of liberty of the nation' while he kept up the fight till he died of his wounds in a cave. Known as Circinello, he was a priest of noble lineage who had never hesitated to interrupt the celebration of mass to hurl abuse at the invaders.[2]

When all the military leaders had surrendered, the national movement was kept alive by the clergy. Parish priests preached guerrilla war from the pulpit and hoarded arms under cover of the capacious baroque altars. There were several of them in every village, de Vaux complained, more like bandits than ministers of religion. The Franciscans, over a thousand of them, who had never acknowledged any authority but Rome, put heart into the resistants by announcing the imminent return of Paoli. Their sixty-three monasteries served as arsenals and hideouts for the patriots, as they had all through the rebellion.[3]

Simple people responded to their appeal. Shepherds and peasants roamed the mountains in groups thirty to forty strong, taking pride in every Frenchman they killed. Andrea Anfosi, of the remote Niolo, caught and sentenced to death, asked for a priest to whom he proposed confessing all his faults except the killing of a French soldier, for which he had been condemned. Execution meant having legs, thighs and arms broken, and then being exposed on the 'wheel' in the gruesome words of the official formula, 'face to the sky', for as long as it pleased God to preserve life. This was the penalty, until then unknown in Corsica, for any act that could be construed as rebellion. The corpses were exhibited along the mule tracks, and at crossroads, hanging from trees or stretched on wheels; all over the island the tortured rotting bodies reminded the Corsicans that they were a beaten people.

Yet the repression was insufficient to prevent a large-scale rebellion in 1774, of which more will be said. In the meantime the resistance was kept alive by scattered bands of patriots, nourished on dark, suicidal passions of revenge. Denying them the dignity of political status, the French classed them as bandits, along with the outlaws who had always hung out in the mountains, men evading the law or pursuing private feuds. Hounded by special troops, sold and betrayed, sometimes by their own countrymen, they went to their horrible deaths unrepentant, uttering the same single word: *pazienza. Pazienza* was also what many apparently law-abiding people said when speaking in private of the French regime, while devising elaborate subterfuges to send the so-called bandits supplies.[4]

This, then, was the environment Napoleon was born into, that determined the emotional climate of his first years. Defeat, resistance, betrayal, heroism, torture, execution and conspiracy were the topics of the first conversations he overheard. Conversations that left a permanent imprint on his mind. As he told Bertrand at Saint Helena, many of his ideas about conquered peoples were derived from his

memories of the Corsicans' struggles against the French. The Bonaparte appear as good patriots in his recollections, or rather, perhaps, in
what he chose to recall. The bandits 'were esteemed and honoured as
defenders of their liberties,' he told Bertrand, 'one sent food to them
every day'. Was he speaking of his own family? Perhaps, for after all
the Bonaparte were related to Zampaglino and through him to nearly
everyone in the 'terrible village of Bocognano'; 'they were all my
cousins,' Napoleon declared. Connected as they were, both with the
brigands of Bocognano and with Pietrasanta, member of the Conseil
Supérieur, the Bonaparte were in an awkward position, with divided
loyalties, as were many Corsican families at that time. Luciano detested
the French, Napoleon remembered, while his father supported them,
but not without reservations.[5]

His indication of Carlo's half-heartedness is of interest, because
Carlo kept it well hidden outside his family and it is something historians
have generally ignored. Nearly all underline his prompt allegiance to
the French and interpret it as the sign of a deplorably unprincipled,
self-seeking disposition. Yet Carlo merely did what almost everyone
did in his social category, and later than the majority. Most of the
officers and notables who had not already betrayed Paoli surrendered
to the French after they entered Corte on 21 May 1769, including
Francesco Gaffori, his second in command. Carlo, according to his
own account, stayed with Paoli till he embarked on 13 June. His
submission was one of the last to come in from a leading patriot, but
was not, for that, he observes, ill received. Enemies, he concludes,
respect integrity; they encourage treason but despise traitors.[6]

His next step was to try to ingratiate himself with the new
government. In this, too, he merely behaved like others of his kind;
his career has come under fire simply because it was exceptionally
successful, and that of his second son even more so. Luciano, albeit
anti-French, had paved the way for him in Ajaccio when in April 1769
he had taken part in a deputation to pronounce the vow of fidelity to
Louis XV on behalf of the town. On his return there Carlo lost no
time in paying his respects to the military commander, whose authority
extended over all western and southern Corsica (the *'dila dai monti'*,
'delà des monts'). 'Yesterday I dined with the comte de Narbonne', he
wrote to Pietrasanta on 8 July. 'I shall visit him as often as is necessary
to show my gratitude and devotion, he himself not caring for greater
familiarity . . .' The reception must have been cold. Narbonne was a
high-born aristocrat, a soldier of outstanding bravura who had earned

the right to style himself Narbonne-Fritzlar in recognition of his gallantry in defending a town of that name during the Seven Years' War.
After fighting through the Corsican campaign at the head of the forces
in the *delà des monts* he had become a person of importance in the
island, a possible successor to de Vaux. It seems that he and Carlo
were out of sympathy from the start. The situation eventually turned
to Carlo's advantage; but for the time being he was discouraged. The
public was kept in ignorance of French intentions, he complained to
Pietrasanta; the king of France apparently meant to stay in the island
eternally; Corsica could have hoped for a better fate.[7]

To make matters worse the comte de Marbeuf left the island in
August. An indifferent soldier, he had twice been passed over for the
supreme command during the Corsican campaign. Now it looked as if
he were gone for good. Marbeuf had known the free Corsica; he had
met and corresponded with Paoli; he had written, at least, to Carlo;
now he might conceivably have helped him. But Carlo had little to
expect from those two hard-headed military men, de Vaux and Narbonne. According to the new system, the commander-in-chief of the
French forces and the *intendant* governed the island as despots with the
aid of their French subordinates; Corsicans were excluded from the
upper ranks of the administration, as in the bad old days of the
Genoese. Luckily Carlo had a sense of humour. He consoled himself
composing satirical ditties. In one that became popular, Paoli, personified as a shepherd, lamented the infidelity of Corsica, his beloved
shepherdess, *pastorella infida*. It never occurred to Carlo, so unques-
tioning was his devotion, that the shepherd might be thought to have
abandoned his flock.[8]

But the time for idealistic sentiments was over: Carlo had to set to
work to rebuild his career. And in very unfavourable circumstances.
Defeat had obliterated the world he had lived in, of which he had been
a part. The head of state he had served was now an outlaw, an exile.
The state no longer existed, nor was it allowed by the conquerors ever
to have had an existence. His own record had become a handicap,
something to hide. His future, which had seemed full of exalting
possibilities, was reduced to earning a living in Ajaccio; the second
town in the island, it is true, but in relation to France a small poor
backward provincial spot far from the seats of power. Since the
conquest everything in Corsica had lost value and meaning.

Ajaccio had not grown up as a result of any natural development; it
was an alien colonial establishment planted there by the Genoese for

the double purpose of protecting the seaboard and policing the interior. The same was true of the other coastal towns. The survival of their populations, originally Genoese soldiers and settlers, represented real feats of adaptation to environment. Saint-Florent and Algajola had never expanded much beyond their initial fortified citadels. But Bonifacio, isolated on the southern tip of the island, had prospered in the Middle Ages by trading with Sardinia (now it was in decline), and Calvi had traded in the oil of the hinterland as well as sending some of its citizens to re-emigrate to Spain and the New World. Meanwhile Bastia, the capital, exporting wine and chestnuts and cereals to neighbouring Italy, dignified by the presence of the Genoese governor and several bishops who habitually resided there, had become quite a handsome city with over five thousand inhabitants. Ajaccio had less than four thousand. Some, like the Bonaparte, the Ramolino, the Paravisino, descended from the original Genoese colonists; others, the Pozzo di Borgo, the Bozzi, the Ornano, had moved in from the surrounding country to escape the Barbary pirate raids. The city offered the protection of walls (now demolished) and a small fortified citadel, or rather 'a little fort decorated with the name of citadel' in Pommereul's scornful words. Yet he esteemed the town the most beautiful in the island; perhaps because he had the eighteenth-century dislike of the irregular and the rugged (he loathed Corte), and Ajaccio had been laid out from scratch on a flat tongue of land with a network of straight streets, rare in Corsica. It certainly had nothing to boast of in the way of architecture. Whereas the houses of Bastia, rising six and seven storeys on the Genoese model, were embellished with vaulted stairways and ceilings, colonnaded galleries and elaborate baroque doorways, the existence in Ajaccio of a totally plain three-storeyed building, the *palazzo pubblico* (seat of the Genoese *commissario*) was exceptional.

To add a third storey to one's home was a sign of success; the Bonaparte did not achieve this prestige symbol until well after the birth of Napoleon. Nothing in the situation of Ajaccio encouraged the accumulation of wealth. Bastia could drain the produce of a fertile hinterland to Italy, just out of sight beyond the visible Tuscan isles; the panorama of the Sardinian coast on the horizon of Bonifacio was a permanent incitement to trading ventures, not to mention piracy. But in Ajaccio, looking back across the bay, a vast, little-used harbour, into empty, infertile blue hills, no one except the coral merchants made fortunes in trade.[9]

Generalized poverty was reflected in the absence of monuments, of style. Only the cathedral, built in the late sixteenth century, has any distinction. Though one may doubt the tradition that attributes it to Giacomo della Porta, a Roman architect who took a hand in designing the dome of St Peter's, it none the less bears the stamp of a grand tradition. True, in the period of Napoleon's youth it smelt so bad as to make worshippers faint, due to the custom of burying corpses just under the paving stones. How did Letizia, one wonders, get through even part of the mass on 15 August, in the heat of midsummer? According to a contemporary visitor the prevailing stench was increased by that of the animals slaughtered in the streets outside the butchers' shops, and the hides stretched to tan in the sun. No doubt the other Corsican towns were no more hygienic; but the situation in Ajaccio was aggravated by the stifling summer climate and an acute shortage of water. 'Ajaccio shouldn't be there, it lacks water,' Napoleon observed. Was his addiction to lying in hot baths a compensation for a childhood deprivation? [10]

His family's position was in fact quite privileged in a place that offered so few advantages. Like the rest of the upper class, the Bonaparte lived from the land they owned outside the town. The vineyards seem to have been directly exploited, the rest rented, probably on a share-cropping basis. Napoleon recalled a rustic, feudal style of abundance maintained by a system of exchange and barter and present-giving that has remained a harmonious feature of Corsican life into the present age. The peasants brought the family milk and cheese and kid and lamb; they came on Sundays, which were days of feasting. Relations arrived to lay in stocks of oil and wine after the olive and grape harvests; they were given presents of perishable products. The country people paid with fish and flour for the use of a mill owned by the Bonaparte. The 'Genoese cherries' from a family orchard were one of Napoleon's happy memories: 'I can't remember ever eating anything better,' he recalled.

The one snag to this idyllic existence was the lack of ready money. 'In my family the principle was not to spend,' Napoleon explained to Bertrand. 'Never to spend money except on things that were absolutely necessary, such as clothes, furniture . . .' and groceries. Little can have been spent in his childhood, or he would hardly have remembered eating off the local black earthenware; but no doubt there was porcelain for special occasions, when Carlo and Letizia entertained. In this they were exceptional; according to a contemporary French observer the notables of Ajaccio were characterized by 'the most sordid avarice'.

Carlo, on the contrary, was always aware – too much aware – of the benefits to be gained by an outlay on entertaining and clothes, and his view was shared by Letizia, at least for as long as he was alive.[11]

For a man in his position the means of earning money in Ajaccio were limited. The family properties did not yield any great surplus; shopkeeping and manual trades entailed loss of status. Only professional activities were acceptable: official functions, the Church, the army, the law. Luciano had chosen the Church, although he seems to have been more interested in farming and legislation; but he made his way and was appointed archdeacon in 1779 (he did not, as historians have asserted, occupy this post at the time of the union of Carlo and Letizia, or of the baptism of Napoleon). For Carlo the obvious choice was the law. He had no time to lose. When he first returned to Ajaccio he was completely dependent on Luciano, even for the purchase of a book: writing to Pietrasanta on 8 July he begged him to send him a book on French law 'which is absolutely necessary to me. My uncle will immediately pay you the price you mention to him.' The book was *Nouveau commentaire sur l'ordonnance civile du mois d'avril 1767*; it concerned the civil code the French government intended to apply to Corsica.[12]

From 20 September 1769 his name appears in the register of the provincial court of Ajaccio (seat of one of the ten jurisdictions established by the French), acting as *procureur*. This did not mean '*procureur du roi*' – public prosecutor – but a minor function roughly equivalent to that of solicitor, for which no particular qualifications were required. The post was in fact incompatible with noble status in eighteenth-century France. A *procureur* advised clients but did not plead in court. Most of Carlo's clients were his relations, whose liking for litigation must have been of great help to him, supposing they paid him (but did they?). His first case was to defend Luciano in a suit against two Pozzo di Borgo, members of a powerful landowning family in the hinterland, which also had a place in the legal world of Ajaccio. His next appearance was on behalf of his mother, Saveria, claiming an overdue payment of 48 livres for some corn; later he also represented Antonio Tusoli, one of his more respectable cousins of Bocognano. After 21 October, when he finally obtained his mother's payment, he disappears from the register till January of the following year.[13] He was much more agreeably occupied during this interval, getting himself a doctorate in law in Pisa.

Very likely he was acting on the advice of Pietrasanta, who knew the value of this qualification, having been himself obliged to acquire it to satisfy official regulations when he was appointed to the Conseil Supérieur.[14] Carlo was not required to stay any length of time at the university, or to undertake further studies. The Pisan faculty of law dispensed doctorates with a readiness that seems positively irre-sponsible: they were given to almost anyone who applied, including innkeepers, so it was said. At all events Carlo, and later his son Joseph, received theirs after the briefest visits. Their name, it is true, carried weight there. During the past two centuries no less than fifteen Buonaparte, all patricians of San Miniato, had taken doctorates at the university, where the last of them, Giovan' Battista Buonaparte, was then a professor of medicine. Carlo's name is absent from the register of students. It was enough for him to swear 'hand on heart', on 27 November 1769, that he had completed the necessary studies, for him to be admitted to present his thesis two days later before a panel that included the distinguished jurist Vannucchi as examiner, and his kinsman Giovan' Battista among the witnesses. On the 30th he was awarded his doctorate by Vannucchi and the chancellor of the univer-sity, who was also vicar of the archbishop of Pisa; in the relevant docu-ment he is described as 'Signor Carlo son of the late Signor Giuseppe Buonaparte noble Florentine patrician of San Miniato and Ajaccio'.

Nothing is said of Carlo's thesis in these documents, which are preserved in the state archives of Pisa. Yet a recent historian, who has received rather little attention, describes it, without, most regrettably, giving his source. His information is however too intriguing to be ignored. Carlo's thesis, he asserts, consisted of a few pages only, on a subject of canon law: the conditions of validity of religious marriage. What subject could have been of greater concern to a young man who had omitted the religious celebration of his own marriage at the time of the consummation of the union, and perhaps altogether? Was his choice of thesis prompted by guilt? Or a need for self-justification? Or was it perhaps not really a thesis as we understand the term today, but merely an exposé of a course given in the university, as the indication of only a few pages suggests? It is unlikely we will ever know more on this matter, for the historian in question is deceased.[15]

There is no reference to any thesis in the speech Vannucchi made when granting Carlo his doctorate, no indication whatever of the scope of his knowledge of law. In this ancient university, lineage, it seems, was fully as important as learning. Carlo's stays at the 'camps of Minerva' (universities) of Rome and Corsica are indeed mentioned;

but most of this fulsome Latin eulogy is devoted to praise of his ancestors: noble, courageous, rich and powerful through the centuries in Florence and San Miniato; senators, soldiers, statesmen, magnates, men eminent in the arts of music and letters. A celebrated historian is included, apparently Jacopo Buonaparte of San Miniato, supposed author of an eyewitness account of the sack of Rome in 1527. Later his connection with the Bonaparte of Ajaccio was to be publicly accepted: Napoleon recalls that when he was marching on Rome an emissary from the Pope at Tolentino reminded him that this ancestor had described the exploit he himself was about to perform.[16]

But Jacopo's authorship has been questioned; there was better justification for Vannucchi's flattering portrait of a certain Niccolò Buonaparte who founded a course of law at the university and so 'offered the flame of his enlightenment to other eminent jurists'.[17] A philosopher and a theologian are also mentioned, and finally Carlo's living relatives: the doctor Giovan' Battista, and the canon Filippo of San Miniato, he who had procured for his father and uncle recognition of their kinship with the Buonaparte of Florence and whom Carlo had probably visited on his first wild trip to Italy. One may suppose that it was Giovan' Battista who did the research for this oration; he too, perhaps, who obtained for Carlo what was surely the crowning triumph of this memorable day: an authorization from the archbishop of Pisa to use the title 'noble patrician' of Tuscany.[18] Decked with these honours, Carlo returned to Corsica to be sworn in as a qualified lawyer – *avocat* – on 11 December by the Conseil Supérieur in Bastia.[19]

The journey had been a spectacular success; one of those that punctuated his uphill struggle. A success – and this was also in keeping with the pattern of his life – that was in part illusion. The doctorate did not count for much with people of real learning; moreover Carlo was to make only a limited use of his qualification as lawyer and of his legal career as a whole. As for the recognition of nobility, in spite of all the gratifying phrases, in spite, even, of the archbishop's authorization, it was no more than a gesture of courtesy that left his affiliation with the Tuscan branches of the family unproved. The Buonaparte of Florence had in fact died out in 1570 in the person of one Giovanni, a gentleman attached to the house of Orsini, or according to another author their line had become extinct in 1620. The Buonaparte of San Miniato liked to think they descended from a Ghibelline captain Niccolò Buonaparte, banished from Florence in 1265, who had settled in the city, then a miniature republic under imperial protection. But this had never been conclusively proved, while the second emigration of the Buonaparte from San Miniato to Sarzana, the authentic place of origin of the Corsican Bonaparte, was pure supposition. Vannucchi, jumbling up the three families in a collective adulation, had added not a grain of evidence to show they were related.[20] If Carlo was later able to use the archbishop's authorization to his advantage, as will be told, it was because by then he had other powerful protection. But now, in Pisa, in his days of obscurity, impressed and elated, he naturally felt bound to celebrate the occasion by giving an expensive party. His family never forgot it. It cost six thousand francs, a sum equivalent to his revenue for two years, so Napoleon complained to Montholon nearly half a century later: 'my father consumed his patrimony in Pisa'.[21]

From such censorious statements, mostly pronounced by Napoleon in his latter days, is derived the familiar image of Letizia, the long-suffering victim of a feckless, ever-absent husband, reduced to penury in her home. Yet this is not what the available evidence suggests, at least for the years she spent with Carlo. There came a time, after his death, when she had six children to provide for and dreaded paying a servant's wages; but in 1770 she had two children only, and – according to a census taken that year – two servants, Francesca and Mariantonia, aged twenty-nine and forty-seven. True, they were paid a mere pittance of some four to six francs a month, but their presence alone points to a ladylike style of living.[22] She also had the services of Caterina, who had acted as midwife at the birth of Napoleon, besides a wet-nurse (an unusual luxury in Corsica), Camilla Ilari, wife of a local seaman.

In those anxious days after the French conquest there was no lack of loving care and attention for the two small boys in the *casa* Bonaparte, brothers already distinct in temperament: the one placid and sunny, the other irresponsibly combative. Conditions might be desperate outside the home, but within its walls the women generated the warm collective emotion that in Corsica serves to insulate a family from the violence of local life. Both brothers, in their different ways, were permanently marked by the dichotomy of their first years. An early consciousness of national disaster gave to each a sense of patriotic vocation, of being called upon to play a role in public affairs. And both were endowed with a boundless self-assurance derived from being a centre of admiring interest in infancy, treated like little kings.

The house must have been crowded with women: not only those who lived there, but the female relatives and dependants who came and went, clustering in the Corsican manner round the family's youngest generation. Napoleon remembered them with affection when he later wrote home from school: *minana* (grandmama) Saveria (Carlo's mother), *zia* (aunt) Geltrude (Carlo's sister), *zia* Touta (probably Letizia's cousin Antoinetta Benielli, who married Giacinto Arrighi), *minana* Francesca (presumably Letizia's mother, the wife of François Fesch), Giovanna, Camilla Ilari's daughter. 'Please take care of them,' he wrote to his father, 'give me their news and let me know if they are well.' [23]

The personalities of these women who sheltered his early childhood can be glimpsed in scattered records, each sharply defined. Camilla Ilari appears as sentimental, bold and shrewd. She adored Napoleon as a child; years afterwards he remembered the delicacies she gave him in secret when Letizia punished him with a diet of dry bread. In later life she clung to him; her devotion amounted to 'a kind of cult', so that she and her family had their share of the extraordinary experiences that befell almost everyone connected with his career. She was among the first to welcome him when he visited Ajaccio in 1799 on his return from Egypt. She went to Paris for his coronation, amused him and Josephine, amused the Pope; she witnessed the fabulous ceremony his real mother sourly avoided. The Pope gave her holy images and blessings, Josephine diamonds, Napoleon money and land. He would have given her the family home in Ajaccio as well had not Letizia, encouraged by Joseph Fesch, insisted it should go to her cousin, André Ramolino; but Napoleon obliged him to give her his own house in exchange. Even so, faced with Ramolino's opposition, Camilla would never have got possession of it had she not sent her beautiful granddaughter, Faustina, to Paris to plead with the Emperor, who was also her godfather. Faustina's husband, Bernard Poli, gave spectacular proof of the family's gratitude when after Waterloo he resisted the Bourbon governor of Corsica and waged a forgotten war of rebellion in the mountains till May 1816 at the head of a thousand or so Bonapartist partisans.[24]

The female relations, too, doted on the little boys. Geltrude, the dashing Geltrude, Paoli's favourite and the shepherds' heroine, on her return to Ajaccio at the age of twenty-nine had settled down; reconciled with her husband, but childless, she devoted herself to her brother's children: she 'was a second mother to us', Joseph recalled.[25] Saveria was also devoted to the children and spoilt them outrageously, running to cuddle them at their least cry (as also, incidentally, did their wayward father). Living in a realm of simple, uncritical piety, she thought it her duty to hear a mass a day for every child, so that according to Letizia she ended by hearing nine daily; she must have included one for the little Maria Anna who was baptized with Napoleon and died soon afterwards, as well as for the eight who survived. But Letizia was surely exaggerating; perhaps to justify her admission that having little time herself for church-going she could rely on her mother-in-law for prayers.[26]

Her own mother, Angela Maria, was a very different type of woman. Spirited and determined, she had defended her daughter in the first bad years of her marriage and set her an example in buying costly clothes. Evidently she knew how to get her own way. Refusing the doleful constraints of Corsican widowhood she had remarried, in 1757, François Fesch, a Swiss officer in the French garrison forces in Ajaccio. Her family had been scandalized because he was a protestant; it was as bad as marrying a Turk, Napoleon remembered, and Saveria the bigot had declared that she was damned. But Fesch consented to undergo a conversion at the hands of Luciano and all Angela Maria had to suffer on religious grounds was the loss of a desirable legacy when her husband was disinherited by his father, a banker in Basle. For a woman of expensive tastes the situation must have been galling. All the same, she agreed that their only son, Joseph, should enter the Church so as to minimize the risk of his reverting to his grandfather's wicked faith with a view to recovering his heritage. Meanwhile her husband had to be satisfied with her meagre dowry of 4,000 lire. Resigning from the army, perhaps because he feared political strife with his Corsican family, he settled down to running her properties. Lucien Bonaparte allows us to imagine what he was like through his lively portrait of the son who much resembled him: 'always fresh, if not as a rose at least as a beetroot of fine quality, with an excellent appetite, a true son of Switzerland, drinking cool and neat without ever feeling the least effects, what one would call today a rather agreeable bon vivant'.[27]

It is sad to think that the attractive, enterprising Angela Maria ended her life crippled with rheumatism; but this is what the evidence suggests. She seems to have been the grandmother Napoleon described as walking bent over a stick, 'like an old fairy', a butt for the cruel mimicry of the children, so that she rounded on Letizia, accusing her of bringing them up without respect for age, and Letizia dealt out appropriate punishments. The story is rather confused; but we know

for certain that in 1784, when Angela Maria attended Jerome Bonaparte's baptism as his godmother, she declared herself unable to write:
unable, not illiterate, presumably because of a deformation of her
hands.[28]

After her husband's death in 1770 she went to live with her sister,
mother of Antoinetta Arrighi. Contrary to Corsican custom, the
widowed mothers did not share the Bonaparte home; Saveria also had
her own lodging in another part of the town. The Bonaparte were
exceptional in not living huddled together in one house. If a contemporary French doctor's account of families of eight and ten
crammed into a single airless room certainly applied specifically to
the poor, the records show that even the notables lived in cramped
quarters, with seldom as much as a room a head. The Bonaparte, on
the other hand, possessed not only their six-roomed house in the
Contrada . . . Malerba, but had recently more than doubled their living
space by annexing the adjoining *casa* Bozzi.

Both these properties they owed to what had hitherto been their
principal means of social ascension: advantageous marriages. Their
original home had been close to the ramparts of the citadel where their
ancestors from Sarzana had done garrison service. It was apparently
demolished in the sixteenth century when the French, temporarily
controlling Corsica, had enlarged the fortress. Where the Bonaparte
lived after that is unknown until they won possession of the historic
casa Bonaparte (or rather part of it) by the marriage in 1703, of
Giuseppe, Carlo's great-grandfather, to a certain Maria Bozzi, daughter
of a noble Corsican family, who brought the house with her dowry. In
fact she can have brought only half the house standing on the site,
which was divided vertically, to give her a dowry, as often happens in
Corsica. The Bonaparte lived next door to the other half, still owned
by the Bozzi, until they married their way into it by a second alliance
with that family, when in 1743 Napoleone took for wife Maria Rosa
Bozzi, with the house as her dowry, as has been told.

The acquisition of the second Bozzi house was a stroke of great
good fortune or good management. Though it was not yet joined to
the *casa* Bonaparte by a unified facade, it was treated as part of the
family home. Luciano, manager of the family fortunes, lost no time
in laying hands on it by engaging in 'grandiose expenses' for its restoration. The Bozzi, he declared, had let it fall into ruin; not only had
he to repair windows and roof, but build a garret, and a staircase to
replace a wooden ladder. In so doing he added two habitable rooms to

the house, which had formerly consisted of two three-roomed flats, like that of the Bonaparte, with a ground-floor store-room or cellar. A scheme, in 1765, to arrange a marriage for Isabella, daughter of Maria Rosa and Napoleone, giving her the *casa* Bozzi as her dowry, had caused Luciano some concern; but he had astutely settled the matter, as will be remembered, by prevailing on Maria Rosa to exchange the house for one of his own vineyards, which became Isabella's dowry when a year later she married another man of his choosing. These arrangements were not concluded without breaking up her parents' marriage: Maria Rosa had gone to live with her family, while Napoleone had accompanied Carlo to Corte, where he had died in 1767.

At the time of Napoleon's birth the Bozzi had thus been completely ousted from their former home, and the Bonaparte could spread themselves over fourteen rooms in the adjoining houses: more than enough for Luciano and Carlo and Letizia and their children and dependants. Tradition may not be at fault in locating the room where Napoleon was born as the first to the back on the first floor, in the right-hand corner of the house overlooking the former Strada del Pevero (now rue Letizia). The *casa* Bozzi, it can be ascertained, stood at the corner of that street and the Contrada ... Malerba, and it would have been natural for Luciano to install Carlo there with his family while he, as is recorded, occupied three or four rooms in the original *casa* Bonaparte.[29]

The young couple would have lived in agreeable, almost privileged surroundings, had Luciano not been such a terrible neighbour. Until Carlo came to earn an adequate income he was at the mercy of his uncle's parsimony, which could be tyrannical. Returning from a journey at the end of April 1770 he wrote to Pietrasanta, his guide and friend, entreating him to reason with Luciano, whose behaviour was driving him to 'despair', so that he risked losing patience. Luciano had dismissed him on his arrival without a meal or even a piece of bread; he had removed his writing desk and the lamp he used 'for study'; he had reduced his household to famine rations of flour and wine, quite insufficient for him and Letizia, a maid, a nurse, two children and 'a third on the way'. Of this child I have found no trace; it must have been one of those who died at birth or just afterwards. Letizia was certainly being victimized at this period, but by Luciano rather than by her husband.[30]

In fairness to Luciano it must be said that serious trouble was coming his way, and if he already had wind of it his bad temper is understandable. Mortified, no doubt, by the sight of the dilapidated old *casa* Bozzi transformed into a commodious residence for the Bonaparte, Isabella and her husband, Ludovico Ornano, four years after the exchange with Luciano, attacked him in law. Their contention was that the arrangement had been no better than a swindle, that Napoleone had forced his wife to accept it under threat of violence, that Luciano's vineyard was valueless. The case came up on 31 May 1770, with Carlo acting as Luciano's *procureur*.

This legal battle was to drag on through the next four years, a source of excruciating anxiety to the Bonaparte. Its implications went far beyond any considerations of domestic comfort: not only was their living space at stake but their social position, their prestige, the possibility, even, of continued residence in their homeland. The very word 'house' was synonymous with family, lineage: the *casa* Bonaparte was not just a building but a symbol of all the Bonaparte, living and dead, in Corsica, Sarzana, San Miniato and Florence, back to the Middle Ages and perhaps beyond. If they lost the lawsuit they would be utterly ruined in public esteem and obliged to leave the country, so Luciano wrote in torment to Pietrasanta on 17 August 1770. And they risked losing it, he insisted, because of the judge's inexcusable 'precipitation'. Precipitation is not, however, what strikes one today when tracing the course of this affair. The following year the case was transferred to the Conseil Supérieur in Bastia. Luciano protested; the case was sent back to Ajaccio; examination of the evidence began only in August 1772.[31]

While Luciano was fighting to protect the family honour, Carlo was endeavouring to build up a practice in the law. In 1770 he was constantly in court; between 8 January and 13 December he appeared in ninety-eight out of 184 hearings. In each case he acted, as formerly, as *procureur*; this low-paid work was easier to get than that of *avocat* (barrister), which was reserved for criminal or important civil cases. Most of those he handled were petty to a degree; payments for rent, wages, the sale of livestock and produce were the usual subjects of dispute, sharply contested even when the sums involved were insignificant. His clients, as before, were often relations: Luciano, whom he represented in the preliminary stages of his struggle with the Ornano, members of Letizia's family, the Ramolino, the Pietrasanta, the Benielli, and connections of the Bonaparte, the Paravisino, the Tusoli, the Costa, the Ternano. They had no shame whatever in going for each other; a Ramolino against a Pietrasanta, or a Paravisino, a Costa against Luciano

Bonaparte, one Tusoli against another. In August he represented Pierre Ilari, presumably Camilla's husband, and obtained 13 livres 12 sols for him in wages for his services aboard the boat of a certain Matteo Moresco.

It must have been a dreary grind for one who had glimpsed the world of the great and dreamt of entering it. His client Theresa d'Aragon, in spite of her illustrious name, thought fit to sue a Mademoiselle Grignon for the payment for ten livres of coffee. Some of his cases brought him face to face with the grimy essence of local squalor, as when he defended an innkeeper with the ironical name of Beau, accused by the *directeur des domaines du roi* (director of crown property) of throwing refuse and filth out of a window on to his roof, which was thereby practically destroyed. Beau, in his defence, stated that the window in question was never opened, as could be judged by the quantity of 'ancient cobwebs' that entirely covered it.[32]

Towards the end of the year Carlo found more congenial work as occasional substitute for the *procureur du roi*, Lorenzo Giubega; though he had no appointment to justify the exercise of this function, the arrangement was tolerated. The first criminal case concerned a certain Elisabetta Tassi, who was seduced in the house of her father, a leather merchant of Manosque, by an employee, a tailor of leather trousers, formerly a pastrycook in Rome. Pregnant, Elisabetta ran away to join her Italian lover in Fréjus; the two of them wandered a while around France before landing in Corsica, where Feretti gave satisfaction for a time as nurse in the military hospital in Corte but was later accused, with Elisabetta, of stealing some clothes in Ajaccio. The theft was unproved; but Elisabetta allowed herself to be abducted by an innkeeper who lodged her in a private house and offered her marriage. Today she would be regarded as a victim, and the marriage as a lucky way out of her misfortunes; but Carlo recommended that she should be condemned for life to a '*maison de force*', and Feretti for life to the galleys, while the innkeeper was to be permanently exiled from Corsica. It is true that Elisabetta's own father had asked that she should be sent to prison. Such heartless punishments were in accordance with contemporary practice. Yet the judge, Cuneo, more humane, sentenced Elisabetta to only three years and Feretti to nine, and reduced the innkeeper's term of exile to a decade.[33]

In February 1771 Carlo saw new opportunities opening out for him. A post of *assesseur* – assistant judge – was created in each of the provincial courts of Corsica, and at about the same time Giubega was appointed secretary to the Corsican Estates, an assembly instituted by the French for the purpose of giving the Corsicans a semblance of political liberty. This meant that he would soon give up his function of *procureur du roi*, leaving a place accessible to Carlo. Carlo's letters to Pietrasanta show him eager to snatch possession of it, so incurring Pietrasanta's displeasure, while running down rival candidates whose success, he maintains, would dishonour him. A certain Orto was at all costs to be excluded: he would prefer a *'coglione'* unable to make the sign of the cross; better the devil in Ajaccio, he wrote explosively. Meanwhile he was also angling for the post of *assesseur*, for preference in Bastia so as to avoid working with Cuneo, who, he contended, would be a 'permanent obstacle' to his career.[34]

By the middle of September his problems were solved. Cuneo, he heard, was to be superseded and he himself would be appointed *assesseur* in Ajaccio. He was however perturbed by the absence of any official notification; communications between Corsica and the capital were exasperatingly slow. His nomination had in fact been made in Versailles on 10 May; it reached him, according to his memoirs, on 4 October, and was inscribed on the register of the Conseil Supérieur on the 22nd of the following month. It brought him a salary of 1,200 livres a year. A Frenchman would have received 1,500; but Corsicans were paid less for the same work on the grounds that they were living in their own homes and were anyhow used to poverty. All the same, the appointment gave Carlo a modicum of financial independence, besides something fully as valuable: public position, influence in local affairs.[35]

He had other reasons for satisfaction at this time. On 13 September he had received official recognition, with Luciano, of his noble status, and on the 29th he had been elected deputy to the Corsican Estates for the nobility of the province of Ajaccio. He had emerged from the pit of humiliating poverty and obscurity. Frustration and anxiety, it is true, lay ahead: he was not officially admitted to his function of *assesseur* until June 1772,[36] and the lawsuit with the Ornano was to drag on for another two years after that. But he faced these difficulties with a new and efficient means of defence. The summer of 1771 was a turning-point in the fortunes of Carlo and his family: he had acquired what was indispensable for any noteworthy success in the France of the Ancien Régime, and particularly in Corsica: a powerful protector.

✳(4)✳

THE TRIUMPHS OF A CORSICAN FAMILY

We do not know exactly when the friendship between the Bonaparte and the comte de Marbeuf began. Carlo had probably met him before he attached himself as part-time secretary to Paoli; at all events they had exchanged letters as early as November 1765. In May 1770, after nearly a year's absence, Marbeuf returned to Corsica with the title of commander-in-chief. How soon after that did he start visiting the Bonaparte's home? Unpublished letters from Carlo and Luciano in the Archives Napoléon reveal that he was doing so in the summer of 1771. They do not indicate that he had never been there before, but their tone does suggest that his interest in the Bonaparte was sufficiently recent for them to regard it as a matter for self-congratulation.[1]

The first letter, dated 24 July, is from Luciano to Pietrasanta. It refers to an event of some importance in this story: the christening of Napoleon on the 21st of the month, together with Maria Anna, the little sister born only a week before who died the following November. Baptizing two children at a time was a common practice in large Corsican families until recent years, one that allowed parents to economize on the number of expensive parties social custom demanded. It was therefore in no way unusual that Napoleon was kept waiting for the ceremony for nearly two years: Lucien and Elisa, born in 1775 and 1777, were baptized, together, as late as September 1779.

The day chosen for Napoleon and Maria Anna was perhaps prompted by the news that Marbeuf, normally resident in Bastia, was coming to Ajaccio that day. He evidently meant to go to the christening party; but he was overwhelmed by his obligations, so he explained. He spent only six hours in town, writes Luciano; he had hoped to visit the *casa* Bonaparte 'before dinner'; but at eight in the evening, seeing his own reception room crowded with 'the whole town and the officials' he had sprung on to his horse and made off, leaving his major-domo to convey his apologies to Letizia. He also, Luciano tells Pietrasanta, discreetly dispatched Lorenzo Giubega to be godfather to the two children, apparently instead of himself.[2]

Luciano here demolishes assumptions repeated by almost everyone who has written on the subject. He shows us that Marbeuf was already a family friend, whereas it is generally supposed that the relationship developed some years later. And he leads us to believe that Marbeuf had agreed to be Napoleon's godfather, and that Giubega replaced him at the last minute at his request. In this choice one must see proof of Marbeuf's solicitude, for if he was unable to officiate himself Giubega was no doubt the next best person available. Descendant of a distinguished Genoese family of Calvi, he was one of those Corsican notables who knew how to float to the top of successive regimes; a man 'with all the subtlety of the Italians and the best qualities of the Corsicans', in the opinion of a contemporary. Having studied law in Genoa, he had actively collaborated with Paoli; after the conquest he was elected to the Corsican Estates, appointed *procureur du roi*, then secretary to the Estates, in which capacity, earning 8,000 livres a year, he was to become one of the most prosperous and influential Corsicans of his day. Evidence for the repeated assertion that he was Carlo's comrade in arms during the French invasion is lacking; but as we know, he lent Carlo a hand when he was *procureur du roi* in Ajaccio, and later proved a valuable ally in his legal tussle with the Ornano. The two men evidently became warm friends: in a letter Carlo wrote to him on 18 May 1776 he addresses him as '*Amatissimo signor compare*'.[3]

It is invariably said that Napoleon was baptized in the cathedral, where a font is shown to tourists as the one used. Luciano however says nothing about the cathedral in his letter; on the contrary he states that the baptism of Napoleon that took place on 21 July was a substitute for the Church ceremony; in other words that he was baptized at home. And this is precisely what is indicated by an unbiased reading of the text of the baptismal act. The cathedral is not mentioned in this document. The words that have been taken to mean that Luciano had previously anointed Napoleon *in casa* – at home – on birth (on the assumption that he was a delicate child unlikely to survive) can just as well be taken to mean that Luciano baptized him *in casa* on 21 July

1771. The parish register of Ajaccio reveals that many children were baptized *in casa*, the practice being no doubt facilitated in families that counted a priest among their members. Both Lucien and Elisa Bonaparte were baptized in the *casa* Bonaparte, and the formula used in these entries is similar to that in the baptismal act of Napoleon. If, on the other hand, a baptism took place in church, then the church is always named: Louis Bonaparte, as is noted in his baptismal act, was christened in the oratory of San Gerolamo.[4]

So much for this item of Napoleonic legend. But Luciano's letter raises other, more exciting questions. Why had Marbeuf taken such a fancy to the Bonaparte? What were his feelings for Letizia? And hers for him?

Letters from Luciano and Carlo to Pietrasanta written soon after the baptism add explosive fuel to a debate that has been argued on and off ever since Napoleon made his name. It was the period of midsummer sociability that culminated in the festival of the Assumption of the Virgin on 15 August. Marbeuf had arrived in Ajaccio that day, and his first visit, the day after, had been to the Bonaparte: 'he went for a walk with Letizia and came back to the house where he stayed till one in the morning,' Luciano writes on the 17th of the month. '*Passegiata*' is the word he uses for 'walk', meaning a ceremonious and conspicuous evening stroll, or rather parade in the main street such as still takes place in some Italian provincial towns and could be seen in Ajaccio until recent years. The outing was repeated, so Carlo wrote in triumph to Pietrasanta on the 25th of the month. Marbeuf in his goodness was showing much favour to the family; for the past eight days he had taken Letizia for a walk every evening and sat up late in the *casa* Bonaparte, to the 'anger and envy' of their 'rivals'. Whatever the nature of the relationship no attempt was made to hide its existence.[5]

The question none the less remains: was their intimacy limited to the *passegiata*? In other words: was Letizia Marbeuf's mistress? Was Marbeuf the father of Napoleon?

So rumour ran, and was believed by many of Napoleon's contemporaries, and not only his avowed enemies. It seemed to explain why Marbeuf had protected Carlo and procured Napoleon a scholarship in a French military school. Napoleon himself was aware of it and dismissed it with suitable disdain. His mother, so he told Las Cases, was 'the most agreeable, the most beautiful woman in town'; nothing could be more 'natural' than that Marbeuf should show a preference for her. As for the thesis of his paternity, product of public 'malignity': 'the simple verification of dates is enough to make it absurd'. The argument is unanswerable: born on 15 August 1769, Napoleon was therefore conceived around 4 November of the preceding year. This was precisely the time when Marbeuf was settling his troops into winter quarters in the Nebbio between skirmishes with the Paolists. It is not to be imagined that Letizia, living in Corte with her husband, could or would have paid him a visit. Nor that he would have visited Corte without the event being on record. Of all Letizia's children Napoleon is the one who definitely could not have been fathered by Marbeuf. One may reflect that had Marbeuf been able to accept the role of godfather the rumour would have become even more insistent.[6]

The comte Colchen, arriving in Corsica in 1779 as secretary to the *intendant*, dismisses the supposition with the assurance of his first-hand knowledge of the insular scene. Marbeuf, he writes, was not seeing Letizia at the period of Napoleon's conception and birth because he was then living with a certain Madame Varese. But he was convinced, like everyone else, that she later became his mistress and that Louis, born in 1778, was Marbeuf's son. Marbeuf was then wildly, '*éperdument*', in love with her. This was eight years after the baptism of Napoleon: Marbeuf's feelings for her were evidently neither passing nor superficial. Though Colchen wrote his memoirs decades later, they are of exceptional value because he witnessed what he describes. Other memoir writers relied on hearsay. Claire de Rémusat repeats the story of Marbeuf's paternity of Napoleon as a possibility, without comment. Chaptal, Napoleon's minister of the interior, ignores it but notes as an established fact that Napoleon owed his education to Letizia's liaison with Marbeuf; the colonel de Romain, a hostile Royalist, states that she prevailed on Marbeuf to grant Carlo his recognition of nobility.[7]

It is easy to understand how these tales originated, spread and became generally accepted after reading the letters of Carlo and Luciano of July 1771. Far from being embarrassed by Marbeuf's admiration of Letizia they were proud of it, delighted when it became the talk of the town. Every time she paraded on his arm through the narrow streets of Ajaccio she was scoring a triumph for her husband and family. The Bonaparte could make light of local gossip because they were flying high.

All blessings and honours flowed from Marbeuf; he virtually ruled the island, together with the *intendant*. But while the *intendants* came

and went – four between the French conquest and the Revolution –
Marbeuf, as commander-in-chief, reigned in Corsica from 1770 till his
death in 1786. He wielded powers that made a mockery of apparent
French concessions to Corsican notions of liberty. He could and did
annul elections at all levels and substitute men of his choice. He
dictated his will to the Assembly of Estates, could influence the course
of justice, make and break careers, eliminate his enemies by *lettres de
cachet*. He was also able to procure honours, concessions, functions,
and to dispense money. He was wealthy; by Corsican standards im-
mensely so. His income from his various appointments as courtier,
soldier and administrator amounted to some 80,000 livres, half of
which came from his former attendance on Stanislas Leczinsky, duke
of Lorraine (ex-king of Poland and father-in-law to Louis XV). This
was not including revenues from his marriage to a grandly-connected
widow, older than he, who had brought him the enjoyment of properties and a couple of castles in Brittany. Their union was so far from
being a love match that she stipulated in their marriage contract that
she had the right to reside in places of her choice and could not be
obliged to keep house for him in any others. Corsica was not one she
chose, and she never joined him there, though it was said in Paris that
she offered ostentatious prayers on his behalf when he was taken ill in
Ajaccio. They had no children.[8]

The Corsicans had a traditional technique for dealing with foreign
rulers; they knew how to take advantage of their weaknesses.
Marbeuf's bachelor status and his obvious liking for women could be
exploited. From the time of his first arrival in 1764 he was bewitched,
'entirely led', according to Dumouriez, by Madame Varese, the ageing
Corsican 'Cleopatra' who had seduced most of the influential
Frenchmen who had come to the island within the last three decades:
the marquis de Contades, the marquis de Cursay, the son of the marquis
de Maillebois, as well as Paoli according to her almost certainly un-
truthful boasting. Already around fifty when Marbeuf came to know
her, handsome but 'dressed like a courtesan', she was notoriously,
unashamedly grasping; yet Marbeuf adored her for ten years or more.
This did not prevent him from 'tenderly' loving the wife of the
intendant Chardon, while at the same time conniving in her affair with
the duc de Lauzun and so doubly humiliating a rival colleague.[9]

Letizia was the woman he preferred in Ajaccio. Their attachment
began while he was still linked with Madame Varese and lasted at least
till 1783, when as a seventy-one-year-old widower he married the

eighteen-year-old daughter of a noble French family in the hope (which came true) of an heir. During all those years he was fascinated by Letizia. Her young beauty, which before her features settled into the mould of a Roman matron had a haunting, slightly fey quality, surely enchanted him, as well as a simplicity that contrasted with Cleopatra's wiles and the frivolity of Madame Chardon. Carlo must also have counted in his choice for more than has generally been allowed. Marbeuf was less irresponsible in love than he appeared; according to a contemporary observer he put up with much from Cleopatra for the sake of the information she gave him on local ambitions and intrigues. Letizia may have accidentally let slip items of interest of local gossip; but in Carlo Marbeuf found a valuable informer who had already proved his abilities as such in the service of Paoli. He was later to develop this skill to Marbeuf's advantage in high circles.[10]

Marbeuf needed allies in spite of all his powers. Even in so un-democratic a regime the Corsicans could make themselves heard: at the Assembly of Estates, where they could air grievances though not take decisions, in the *cahiers de doléances* their deputies carried to the throne after each session, in memoirs presented to ministers and men of influence in the capital, and in the last resort by blind, bloody revolt (and indeed all these methods were tried). The commander-in-chief and the *intendant*, '*commissaires du roi*', so superb in their treatment of the conquered people, were also scheming anxious functionaries travel-ling backwards and forwards to Paris to secure their jobs with ministers who were themselves the scheming anxious servants of the king. By such manoeuvres Marbeuf had managed to unseat de Vaux; but when he returned to Corsica in 1770 he had to contend with Narbonne, who had hoped to replace de Vaux, and soon afterwards with the new *intendant*, Colla de Pradine, who became Narbonne's ally.[11]

Corsicans could be mobilized in these struggles. In Ajaccio, centre of Narbonne's sphere of influence, Marbeuf was endeavouring to build up a party. When he persuaded Giubega to stand godfather to Carlo's children he was consolidating a link in a network of supporters. He could make use of Carlo's abilities, as informer, propagandist, go-between. Fluency in French, knowledge of the law, eloquence in speech and writing and an experience of public life were by no means common assets to find united in one person in Corsica at that time. Carlo's humour and sociability were probably even more rare. Marbeuf enjoyed his company. The Corsicans as a whole appeared a forbidding lot to the French: suspicious, secretive, vindictive, deceitful, arrogant, sombre, melancholy are among the adjectives with which the dismayed conquerors described this needy, war-hardened disenchanted people. The inhabitants of Ajaccio, it was complained, were vain and avaricious and rude, and though the peasants held to a traditional code of hospitality they were incurably joyless: all their festivals were like funerals. Nor were the French officers stationed in the island much better company. Most regarded their service in Corsica as a punishment and endured it in a mood of resentful depression.[12]

Marbeuf had small patience with all this gloom. Nobleman and courtier, he practised the art of living with a magnificence that earned him the title of 'luxurious pasha' in the sterner days of the French Revolution. He lodged in the finest house on the island, a vast monastery in Bastia built in the Genoese style, with a loggia overlooking the sea, and so close to it that it appeared, when approaching the coast by ship, to rise straight out of the waves. It was known as 'Les Missionnaires' from the name of the monks who owned it, more properly termed Lazarists. In fact only five inhabited the monastery, where they did good business renting apartments to French officials and overcharging them for their home-grown vegetables, which were as expensive as in Paris. Finding no theatre in Bastia, Marbeuf built himself one up against a window of the parish church, to the indignation of the bishop. He also enjoyed a country retreat, a garden outside the town bought at prohibitive cost from Cleopatra, where he erected a pavilion 'in the Italian style' and sumptuously furnished its rooms. This was no doubt the spot where he 'entertained himself' (in the words of Boswell) 'laying out several pieces of pleasure ground'. Eventually he designed and built for himself a veritable palace on his domain in the marquisate of Cargese.[13]

He was cordial and 'open-hearted', so Boswell, who just missed meeting Carlo, discovered when he called on him in Bastia, shaking with fever, in November 1765. 'Gay without levity, and judicious without severity', Marbeuf was at pains to 'amuse' his ailing guest, and 'made merry' with him about the rumour of his being a British ambassador, a matter another man might have taken less lightly. Exceedingly arrogant if crossed, Marbeuf was inclined to paternalistic indulgence with those who shared his tastes and fell in with his views. In Carlo he must have discerned qualities of enthusiasm and vivacity such as had charmed him in Boswell. Like Boswell, like Marbeuf, Carlo appreciated pleasure; 'too fond of pleasure', Napoleon censoriously declared, a connoisseur of women, liqueurs and good food: the characteristics that helped his father give him a start in life were precisely those Napoleon disapproved of. The chronicler Rossi, on the other hand, attributes his advancement to a high moral quality: his scrupulous, unswerving loyalty to whoever he served. Admirer of the Bonaparte, he has nothing to say about Letizia's supposed contribution to his success.[14]

Other writers have been less discreet. The exact nature of Letizia's relationship with Marbeuf being unknown, they have imagined it according to their historico-political and personal views, some presenting her as a blameless victim of calumny, others as no better than a tart.[15] In the light of the letters of Carlo and Luciano, the arguments in both camps need to be revised. We now know that in accepting Marbeuf's attentions Letizia was doing no more than what was expected of her, by her husband and also by her uncle-in-law – a churchman be it remembered. The limits of their long, public connection can only be surmised. Would Letizia have 'yielded' to Marbeuf if Carlo's interests were at stake? Or her childrens'? The answer depends, surely, less on her character than on his. Was Marbeuf chivalrous enough to resist exploiting his hold over her during a period of at least twelve years? The question will be examined as this story unfolds.

In their drive for social advancement the Bonaparte acted as a team, each contributing his assets: Luciano his peasant's thrift and tenacity, Carlo his skills as lawyer and flair as man of the world, Letizia her looks and charm. And in spite of some divergencies of opinion between Carlo and Luciano as to the strategy to adopt, their collaboration worked well. From the time they captured Marbeuf's interest in the summer of 1771 they began to receive a succession of benefits and favours, to move up in the world.

Carlo's appointment as *assesseur* was an indispensable first step. His other, equally urgent preoccupation at this time was to obtain official recognition of his family's noble status. Nothing the French monarchy did in Corsica pleased so many people as the creation of an 'order of nobility'. Being a noble in Corsica had never implied the powers, privileges and dignities known to nobles elsewhere. Feudal lords, sometimes recognized as such by foreign princes, as well as land-grabbing chieftains, self-appointed and self-made, had fought their way to eminence in the Middle Ages, been massacred, ruined and dispossessed in the unending insular wars, Corsicans versus Corsicans and foreign powers. Their survivors had been battered between Corsican popular factions (predominant in the fourteenth century in the north of the island) and the Genoese government, which progressively stripped them of any significant powers. To recover their privileges – real or supposed – had been the great hope of such families at the time of the national rebellion; but they had been disappointed by Paoli and betrayed him accordingly. Now, at long last, the French sovereign offered them the possibility of reasserting their rank and assuming what they thought to be their proper place in society. Not that the feudal system was re-established in Corsica: the newly recognized nobles were granted no fiefs (in the exact sense of the term), could levy no dues; they did not even enjoy tax exemptions like their peers in mainland France. But they did have the satisfaction (in Corsica beyond price) of social prestige, besides the right to carry arms. Eventually they were also allowed to propose their children for scholarships in mainland schools. The avowed aim of the French government was to create, by these means, a caste loyal to the Crown. Half a dozen titles (only) of count and viscount, and one of prince, were distributed to favourites of the regime along with concessions of crown property in the island.

The measure concerning ennoblement was announced in April 1770; acts of recognition began to be delivered in February of the following year. The qualifications required were not in themselves too severe, but had to be substantiated by documentary proof which was often far from easy to assemble. Candidates had to show that their families had been regarded as noble for the past two hundred years. Evidence not only of privileges accorded by the Genoese government, of participation in municipal or insular administrations, of titles or dignities or functions, but even of forms of address, which were in fact merely courtesy titles, such as *magnifico, illustrissimo, egregio,* were considered adequate. Applications were judged by the Conseil Supérieur: the work kept the court busy until it was swept away by the French Revolution, together with the nobility. Acts of recognition for eighty-six families or branches of families have been found; fewer, in all probability, than were granted. The number of nobles anyhow far exceeded the number of noble families, for recognition was given not to heads of families but to individuals. In this way forty-three Pietri of Sartene got themselves ennobled simultaneously, and no less than fifty-six Ortoli who, with their households, made up the entire population of the little village of Olmiccia.[16]

Luciano and Carlo applied jointly for recognition. That it was of extreme importance to them can be judged by the excessive nature of their reactions, as expressed in their letters. In March 1771 we find Carlo impatiently complaining to Pietrasanta that Luciano is trying to delay taking steps as long as possible. On 25 August he begs him to put in hand the examination of their claim before the court's summer recess, and 'to make capital on every occasion' of Marbeuf's partiality for the family. Yet he would have been mortified had Marbeuf's support become public knowledge. A few days before he had incurred Luciano's fury when Marbeuf, visiting their home, offered to help them with their claim, speaking *sotto voce* to Carlo in the presence of Letizia, and Carlo had refused, saying that he had submitted his documents and they were in order. Luciano was furious: 'There's the pride of a man who wants to play the grand seigneur,' he expostulated to Pietrasanta; the whole matter, he had told Carlo, would have been settled with Marbeuf's protection. 'I think that man will never get ahead,' raged Luciano. Carlo, to our way of thinking, rather often swallowed his pride in order to get ahead; but there was evidently one thing he could not have endured: to have it said that he owed his noble status to Marbeuf, Letizia aiding.[17]

The act was delivered on 13 September: a family triumph. 'Ajaccio is stupefied and filled with jealousy by the news of the nobility conferred on the Bonaparte family,' Carlo wrote jubilantly to Pietrasanta on the 18th of the month. They were in fact the fourth family in the town to be ennobled, and this constituted a victory over all the others kept waiting. Luciano, writing to Pietrasanta the following day, asks for two extra copies of the act to send to 'a Buonaparte of Florence' (the canon of San Miniato?) and a Lomellino in his nineties who was their last surviving kinsman in Genoa. He hopes Pietrasanta will insert in the act that the Bonaparte had 'two hundred years of nobility'; the Cuneo, he had heard, were forty years short.[18]

To produce documents of the required antiquity was for most candidates a problem. The Colonna d'Istria and the Gentile, authentic descendants of the feudal nobility, could send in printed volumes confidently tracing their ancestry to the Middle Ages; but they were the exceptions. Many of the old feudal families were extinct; others had become too poor and obscure to assert themselves; the opportunity of ennoblement appealed mainly to ambitious rural and urban notables. Particular consideration was shown to those who had already rendered services to the monarch; Matteo Buttafoco, the Judas of Paoli, based his claim on nothing better than a will (in the fifteenth century it is true) by which an ancestor had made a bequest to the local clergy; but in view of his exemplary political record no questions were raised. Others, less well-placed, resorted to a certain Bernadino Delfino who did good business fabricating family documents dating from the sixteenth century: notarial acts written in black and red ink on parchment for which he charged up to 240 livres. Denounced in 1786, he escaped before his house was ransacked by the police, without betraying the families who had been his dupes or accomplices; the majority, it has been said, of those ennobled before that date. No retroactive measures were taken against them, and some have preserved their fraudulent documents to this day. Described in a census taken the year of his arrest as 'bandito fugitivo', Delfino, it seems, was prudently allowed to disappear.

A catalogue of some hundred noble Corsican families, compiled in the fifteenth century and said to have belonged to him, has recently come to light.[19] The Bonaparte are included; but they do not appear to have been his clients. Perhaps it was Delfino's work of reference rather than a record of his victims. Yet the Bonaparte's claim is not above suspicion. The acts of recognition give inventories of the documents submitted, the documents being returned to the families. The Bonaparte's act has nothing to say about their first ancestor in Ajaccio, Francesco Il Mauro. The earliest documents they produced name his grandson Geronimo, and concern his role in municipal affairs in 1536 and 1554. The municipal archives, however, make no mention of him before 1572, when he appears as spokesman to the Genoese senate on behalf of the city, making various requests, one of which is for the edification of a cathedral. That year, 1572, was one, but only one short of the two hundred required to prove noble status. Taking no risks, the Bonaparte avoided quoting the document.

Pinoteau, distinguished genealogist of the family, rejects the documents of 1536 and 1554 as forgeries, pointing out that Geronimo's career took place after 1560. The argument is confirmed by contemporary records. Moreover new evidence is now available to support Pinoteau's view: documents relative to Geronimo in the Archives Napoléon, dated 1536 and 1554. They are presented as copies of originals, authenticated by the clerk of the court of the jurisdiction of Ajaccio. There can be no doubt that they were those submitted to the Conseil Supérieur: the copy of that of 1536 is dated Ajaccio, 14 May 1771: the moment when the Bonaparte would have been preparing their claim. It treats the same subject as is summarized in the 1536 document in the act of recognition: the municipal councillors, among whom is Geronimo Bonaparte, appeal to a Genoese edict prohibiting Corsicans (as opposed to Genoese colonists) from residing in the town. The source of the document is noted: the Libro Grosso. This volume still exists: a massive register of municipal edicts. But the Bonaparte's document cannot be verified, for the early pages of the volume are missing, so that its first entry is in 1596. At what date did it begin when Carlo and Luciano were trying to prove their nobility? Did they really make use of it? Or did they not rather filch material from a genuine entry of 1577 in the municipal archives, where Geronimo is cited as spokesman for the city, making a request that Corsicans be forbidden to live there? It is hard to resist this conclusion in view of the document of 1554 in the Archives Napoléon. Here Geronimo makes an elaborate plea to the Genoese Republic for the building of a cathedral. The source mentioned is again the Libro Rosso, where it cannot be verified. But another source exists: the authentic archival document of 1572 mentioned above. Carlo and Luciano had no need of Delfino, and indeed neither of their suspect documents bear the mark of his workmanship. Their procedure was safer and more subtle: to present material from genuine documents, affixing dates several decades earlier. The clerk of the court must have accepted their so-called copies on trust.

After Geronimo the Bonaparte were on firmer ground, and their act of recognition traces their lineage accurately enough from his son through five generations to Carlo. There is no mention, oddly enough, of the archbishop of Pisa's authorization to use the title of noble patrician which Carlo had proudly brought back with his doctorate. Nor is included a certificate from the 'principal nobles' of Ajaccio attesting that the Bonaparte had always been considered noble by virtue of their marriages into noble families. Dated 10 August 1771, it perhaps came to hand too late to be used. Both were submitted in the revised claim to nobility supplied by Carlo on behalf of Napoleon in 1779. In the meantime the examiners in the Conseil Supérieur were satisfied and pronounced the evidence produced as 'good, sufficient and valid'.[20]

This achievement meant a lot to Luciano; but it was not good enough for his great-nephew's biographers. It did not even content Carlo when his worldly position improved, nor his son Joseph when he carried the weight of his family's ambitions after his father had died and before Napoleon made his name. It is fascinating to see how the Bonaparte's family tree was progressively expanded with their expanding prestige. Carlo corrected and extended his genealogy when he had to supply a version to get Napoleon into a French gentleman's school. Joseph, student in Pisa a decade later, vainly laboured to obtain proof of the affiliation of the Tuscan Buonaparte with his ancestors in Sarzana.[21] Napoleon had no such problems: as he fought his way from city to city at the head of the army of Italy he was hailed as descendant of all the Buonaparte of the peninsula.[22]

Later his genealogy was to be stretched and twisted to include a selection of the ruling dynasties of Europe, operative and defunct: the Paleologi of Byzantium, the Comnenos, emperors of Byzantium and Trebizond,[23] the 'old kings of the north', the Brunswicks, the English royal family, and of course the Bourbons, through a complex web of relationship to Henri IV, not to mention 'the man in the iron mask'.[24] George Sand had the originality to propose forbears in Mallorca.[25] Napoleon treated these fables as they deserved: 'My titles are in my sword'; 'the house of Bonaparte dates from the 18 Brumaire'; 'permit me to be the Rudolph of my line'. Yet he had to allow that a proved descent from Clovis king of the Franks would have helped justify his crown, and so no doubt would have approved of the erudite genealogy by which the Corsican historian, Cesari Rocca, traces his descent from Charlemagne.[26]

Cesari Rocca begins by demolishing almost everything that had been said about Napoleon's ancestry, beginning with the belief that the Bonaparte of Ajaccio and Sarzana were related to those of San Miniato and Florence and elsewhere in Italy where the name was known: Bologna, Trevisa, Sienna, Ascoli. In his view (shared by most serious genealogists), the name, common in northern Italy from the thirteenth century, was originally no more than a nickname meaning 'good party', given to partisans in the struggles between Guelphs and Ghibellines. Eventually various unrelated families called Buonaparte came to suppose a common origin and adopted the same coat of arms, so that the Buonaparte of San Miniato were sincerely convinced that they were related to those of Florence, and also to those of Sarzana and Ajaccio.[27]

Having thus reduced Napoleon's possibilities of illustrious lineage to a single obscure family in obscure Sarzana, Cesari Rocca proceeds to show that Cesare Bonaparte, grandfather of Franceso Il Mauro, first of the family to settle in Ajaccio, in 1440 married one Apollonia, a daughter of the noble house of Malaspina. True, she was illegitimate, but Cesari Rocca is able to trace her lineage through twenty generations to no less a person than Charlemagne. The performance invites respect, even though it has far less interest today than when it was published in 1905. Few people now believe that a noble pedigree necessarily produces outstanding gifts, or that outstanding gifts are inherited from one particular outstanding ancestor, so that it matters little to us whether Napoleon was among the thousands of people descended from Charlemagne.[28]

Nor, on the other hand, need we be surprised to learn from Cesari Rocca that the rest of his forbears were insignificant. In Sarzana, as in Ajaccio, the top-rankers were municipal officers sometimes sent on missions to represent their cities with the grand title of orator, deputy or ambassador, or else minor ecclesiastics or notaries. Others were merchants, merchants of all kinds: one sold dogs in Genoa. When Napoleon described his ancestors, with an affectation of modesty, as '*condottieri*' or 'little gentleman adventurers' he was still hitting slightly above the mark. Luckily for his self-esteem Carlo was unaware of the mediocrity of his heritage when he set out to make himself a place in the world, armed with dubious proof of his minimal nobility.[29]

It came just in time for him to stand for election to the Corsican Estates as one of the five nobles representing the province of Ajaccio. The primary election took place on 24 September 1771; the severest test for noble candidates in the extremely complex electoral system devised by the French government. The forty-four nobles of the *pieve* (district) of Ajaccio met to elect one of their number to represent them in the assembly of the province, which comprised eight *pieves*.[30] In fact many of the forty-four had not yet received official recognition of their nobility; but they were allowed to participate on the assumption that their claims would be granted. Each had to vote for or against every other. The contest was between Carlo and a certain Fozzani (or Fozzano, perhaps one of the rival *procureurs* whose name frequently appears in proceedings of the court of Ajaccio). A marginal note in the electoral record tells us exactly what happened. Fozzani got twenty-six votes, Carlo twenty-seven, with seventeen against, a score incomprehensible if, as he asserts, he had abstained from voting for himself (as had Fozzani). The president of the meeting evidently thought he was lying, for he removed the twenty-seventh vote from his count, assumed that the two candidates had equal scores, and ordered the election to be repeated. Fozzani got most votes in the second round; but Carlo opposed his victory on the grounds that since he was officially recognized as noble, whereas Fozzani was not, he ought to be considered the winner in the case of a tie. Fozzani was nevertheless declared elected. Whereupon Carlo, so we learn from a letter to Pietrasanta of 11 October, promptly appealed to Marbeuf, who cancelled Fozzani's election in favour of Carlo's. We may suppose that his influence was also brought to bear in the secondary election at the provincial assembly on the 29th of the month; but this was a less exacting test. The province of Ajaccio returned five nobles to the Estates, and were elected from eight, representing the eight *pieves* of the provinces, so that only three had to be eliminated. Once again Carlo was successful.[31]

His victory had been won by means that were far from unusual. The electoral system in Corsica under the French monarchy was little more than a blind. Every election had to be confirmed by the commander-in-chief and the *intendant*, who quite often cancelled the result and substituted men of their choice. So little did they believe in the virtues of democracy that they tended to regard the winner of an election with suspicion, as someone who had got his way by base intrigue.[32] Their choices, ostensibly made in the interests of Corsica, in fact served their own. Marbeuf needed Carlo at this time; he was busy mobilizing his supporters in the *delà des monts*, where Narbonne was setting himself up like a feudal princeling with folkloric trappings.

The two men used contrary methods to attract a following. Marbeuf, more diplomat than soldier, self-indulgent, yet shrewd and resourceful, lived among the Corsicans as a luxurious French nobleman prepared to admit them into his charmed circle provided they bent to his will. Narbonne, of superior birth, dashing hero of the Seven Years' War, played the Corsican chieftain. He claimed relationship with the family of the historic patriot Sampiero Corso (no less); he wore the local costume of rough goats' hair (like Boswell's); he gave a ball in the bandits' village, Bocognano, where the guests appeared in national dress and the illumination was by flaring pinewood torches instead of degenerate candles. Lending his authority to Corsican grievances, he accused Marbeuf of harshness and arrogance. This was in fact precisely what Marbeuf's supporters said of Narbonne: Marbeuf was 'gentle', Narbonne 'haughty and violent', Napoleon told Las Cases; a French officer serving in Corsica considered Marbeuf mild to the point of weakness.[33] Yet in the light of hindsight there seems little to choose between them for haughtiness and a severity that sometimes verged on inhumanity, even if both made much of certain Corsicans with a view to ensuring their personal success.

The Assembly of Estates opened on 1 May 1772. Carlo reached Bastia in the suite of the *intendant*, Colla de Pradine, after escorting him on a tour of the south. So we learn from an unpublished letter from Luciano to Pietrasanta, which reveals that Carlo had succeeded in winning his good graces no less than Marbeuf's, and had constantly entertained him in the *casa* Bonaparte during his stay in Ajaccio. This was a diplomatic triumph, though of a dangerous kind, for de Pradine was no friend to Marbeuf and later came out on the side of Narbonne. But Carlo was by nature a gambler. He thus appeared in Bastia as a person of high influence, intimate with both the *commissaires du roi* as well as with Giubega, now secretary to the Estates with the grand title of 'Chancellor'.

After attending mass in the vast bare marble baroque interior of the parish church, Saint Jean Baptiste, *commissaires* and deputies proceeded to the oratory of La Conception, where the Estates met: the five bishops, the elected members of the clergy, and the nobles and commoners, twenty-three of each. The oratory was sumptuous, the property of a wealthy religious fraternity; even today one is struck by the opulence of its vaulted painted ceiling and gilded stucco work. During meetings of the Estates it was further embellished with velvet and damask hangings lent by the neighbouring fraternity of Saint Roch.[34]

Yet surely there were some present to regret the *consulte* in bleak Corte in the exalting days of national independence. The Estates had been cynically designed to give the Corsicans a semblance of liberty, and its illusory character was to become increasingly obvious. The *commissaires du roi* presided over the meetings with an iron hand. Deputies could introduce subjects but not discuss them; they could deliberate and vote only on the invitation of the *commissaires*. The subject the *commissaires* most often brought to their attention was taxation. Paoli had levied a uniform hearth tax. The French government, with a concern for justice which was little appreciated, contended that it had been inequitable because weighing most heavily on the poor, and introduced a system of taxation by *vingtièmes* – twentieths – of agricultural production, to be imposed on all land-owners, nobles and clergy not excepted. This innovation, enlightened in comparison with the systems then prevailing in mainland France, met with such resistance that the *commissaires* agreed to convert the required two-twentieths into a fixed overall payment of 120,000 livres, to be levied from the whole population.[35]

The session of 1772 opened with pronouncements from the *commissaires* of the most embittering kind: the payment was to be stepped up to 180,000 livres, and a further 64,000 was to be found for billeting the army of occupation. In addition – and this was evidently felt to be the last straw – the expenses, previously paid by the Crown, of the three deputies (a bishop, a noble and a commoner) who carried the *cahier de doléances* to the king in Versailles at the end of the session, were now to be covered by additional taxation.

The deputies fought back as best they could. They elected a committee to work out ways and means of raising extra taxes; Carlo was one of its twenty-four members. They decided that, to save money, no delegation would be sent to Versailles; Marbeuf would represent them before the king. This austere proposal was their way of stating their case: if they were to be so highly taxed they could no longer afford the privilege of sending a delegation to their sovereign; if Marbeuf was to rule despotically, then let him represent them. Louis XV must have felt the sharp edge of their gesture, for his reply was intransigent: they must send their deputies and pay their expenses. The Estates thereupon voted what were obviously considered minimal allowances: 4,000 livres for the bishop, 3,000 for the noble and 2,500 for the representative of the Third Estate. When it came to electing them many deputies hastened to withdraw their candidature, appalled at the prospect of having to spend their own money on the trip: eight nobles and nineteen commoners backed out on pretexts of health.

Carlo stayed in the running: he was prepared to risk all he had to reach the throne. But his day was yet to come. For the time being he had to make do with a lesser dignity: election as one of the *Nobles Douze*, the twelve nobles who advised the *commissaires* until the next session of the Estates, in principle in two years' time. They had to reside in Bastia, two at a time, turn by turn, for periods of two months allocated by the drawing of lots. Carlo, conveniently, was assigned the period immediately following the session of the Estates. During this time he received, like his colleague, an expense allowance of 150 livres a month. It must have been welcome, even if he lodged with Pietrasanta or with Giubega, for being a member of the Estates was a costly honour that year. The assembly was re-summoned in July and November to be informed of decisions made in Versailles; priests and nobles received no more than 2 livres a day during their attendance, commoners a mere 30 sous. And since the French conquest Bastia had become almost as expensive as Paris.[36]

While Carlo was striving to lay the foundations of a public career he was also, with Luciano, fighting the Ornano for possession of the *casa* Bozzi. Sent up to the Conseil Supérieur the previous year, the case on Luciano's plea was now sent back to the court of Ajaccio. On 6 August 1772 the parties were ordered to produce their evidence; it was stipulated that Carlo, who was acting as one of Luciano's two legal advisors, would not be able to officiate as assistant judge. Experts were called in by both sides to estimate the value of the vineyard Luciano had given to Isabella's mother in exchange for the house, and which had become Isabella's dowry. Luciano's witnesses, who had pruned it in the past, maintained that Isabella had neglected it; worth 500 livres when it was first made over to her, it was now worth barely 300. In the autumn Isabella was trying to prove that her father had bullied her mother into accepting the exchange. Witnesses argued over the deceased Napoleone's character: kindly, pacific and honourable according to Luciano's, violent, irrascible and unprincipled according to those of his daughter. The witnesses themselves came under scrutiny: Isabella's were described by Luciano's as public beggars and sworn enemies of the Bonaparte; one was reported to have fired a pistol both at Luciano and Napoleone. The condition of the house was assessed, Luciano insisting on the expenses of building the staircase. Finally, on 9 November, judgement was given in favour of the Bonaparte.[37]

They barely had time to celebrate before Isabella and her husband again appealed to the Conseil Supérieur. Luciano lodged his defence on 21 November. The battle was now desperate: 'I fear the year '73 will be the fatal epoque,' Luciano wrote ominously to Pietrasanta. Perhaps the Ornano had friends at court; at all events Luciano's letters betray an anxiety verging on hysteria. The family, he exclaimed, would be 'lost' if the Ornano were allowed to give further evidence. He was 'crucified' not, it seems by the Ornano but by Carlo, who had once again incurred his wrath, perhaps because he was already seeking a compromise, something dishonourable in Luciano's eyes. He wept, he declared, for his two nephews (Carlo's sons), 'little stars', 'poor orphans', for orphans they were with such a father. And now he himself was about to abandon them to seek a spot on foreign soil where he could die in peace (he was then fifty-five). If the Ornano won the case he, who had always bought property, would be obliged to sell so as to settle the legal expenses. For Luciano, this was the very abyss of shame: he implores Pietrasanta in the name of 'charity' to save the family from 'destruction' and 'shipwreck'.

This was in April 1773; in June he was practically raving about the 'master stroke of vengeance' of the Ornano, who were now boasting they would be living in the house within a month. 'No doubt it is the expiation of my sins,' he wrote piteously to Pietrasanta; he had no choice but to beg his bread under 'another sky' to avoid being 'trampled underfoot' by the pride of the Ornano (he is speaking of two nephews) who had taken to climbing the stairs – his staircase – to shout insults at him at two and three in the morning. Less perturbed, Carlo wrote calmly to Pietrasanta on 8 July to tell him that the Ornano had raised further difficulties but that Marbeuf was paying 'a thousand attentions' to Letizia. He was martialling his assets with the self-assurance of a man who knew their value. He enlisted Giubega's cooperation in drawing up a defence of forty-seven pages. He addressed a memoir to Marbeuf entreating him to bring about an accommodation. The case, he explained, had lasted six years and had already cost the Bonaparte 1,000 écus (3,000 livres); the family was threatened with ruin; his uncle wanted to leave the island; he himself was prepared to 'buy his peace with money' and he had heard from Giubega and others that the Ornano were prepared to drop the case for 3,500 Genoese lire. Marbeuf intervened as requested. On 12 September he witnessed a notarial act by which Luciano made peace with Isabella for the sum of 4,500 lire; some bargaining had taken place but the deal was esteemed, in the words of the notary 'an honest and amicable agreement'. The Bonaparte could triumph; the house was theirs, though at a cost that must have handicapped them for some time to come.[38]

To choose this moment to enlarge and improve their home was perhaps a gesture necessary to their prestige, though it must have put an added strain on their resources. An entry in Carlo's commonplace book (the 'Livre de Raison' that succeeds his memoirs as an intimate revelation of his daily life) notes that on 19 May 1774 he completed the construction of a terrace at the cost of about 600 francs on a 'site' acquired from a certain Ponte. The 'site' was the forty-foot-long flat roof over a vaulted ground floor belonging to the Ponte, running at right angles to the former *casa* Bozzi. Years later, in 1797, after the Bonaparte's home had been lost and looted and occupied and re-covered, and Napoleon had become famous commanding the army of Italy, Letizia built a splendid reception room covering about half the width of the terrace; later still, Napoleon III bought out the owners of the ground-floor room below. But for the time being this ample first-floor space between street and courtyard, open to the sky, was a luxury in the stifling Ajaccio summers, an airy retreat for sitting out and entertaining friends such as one can still find attached to some of the old houses of the town. Did the Bonaparte, at this time, also add another storey to their home? It existed when the house was looted in 1793, and one may suppose that it was built before Carlo died in 1785 and stringent economy became the rule; but evidence on the subject is lacking. To add a storey to one's home was a status symbol, a sign of success, and the moment was certainly ripe for such a gesture.[39]

✠〔 5 〕✠

THE WAY TO THE THRONE

While the Bonaparte triumphed, spent, built and entertained, others were desperate and hungry. These were lesser, country people; people too insignificant to receive any benefits from the French government, personified in their eyes by the contemptuous, sometimes brutal soldiers sent to their homes to collect arrears in taxes. Two harvests in succession had failed; famine threatened.

During the grim winter of '73 and the following spring unfamiliar figures could be seen on the mule tracks, weaving their way from village to village through the snow. Often they appeared as strangers, but not as foreigners; in fact they were Corsicans returned from Tuscany where they had been living in exile since the conquest. Now, perhaps urged on by Clemente, Pasquale Paoli's brother, they had judged the moment ripe for rebellion. Scores of militant patriots were secretly returning to the island, where a multitude of small creeks encased in vegetation allowed for secret landings. In March came a certain Nicodemo Pasqualini, bringing a message, a plan. The Father of the Nation had not forgotten his people; he was about to deliver them from their servitude; British battleships would seize the port of Saint Florent; Russian ships would bring weapons and supplies; arms, munitions and fighting men would be landed on the east coast from Tuscany; they would advance inland, join forces with the shepherds of the Niolo, march on Corte. The national capital would be seized, the conch shells would sound again and the mountain re-echo with cries of '*Patria! Libertà!*' Paoli, aided by the king of England, would come to complete the national liberation.

So people said and hoped and dreamed by the smoking fires of poor homes while the snow melted; but how much of this was anything but dreaming? There is no evidence that Paoli supported the project, let alone the tsar of Russia or the king of England. Yet Pasqualini felt sufficiently confident to summon a *consulta* on Easter Sunday on the heights of Monte Stello, and at least sixty Corsican chiefs were bold enough to attend. Though their conspiracy was soon reported to Marbeuf, and several were arrested, the remainder went ahead with their doomed scheme as though hypnotized by Paoli's magic name. There was no sign of British or Russian ships; but men and supplies were landed on the east coast as arranged. Armed bands moved inland; Albertini, a priest of the Niolo, wrote an incendiary circular letter inciting the shepherds to revolt. Cervoni, chief of a little mountain village, Soveria, mobilized partisans; the insurgents began to march towards Corte.

Warned in good time, French forces converged on the rebels, from Bastia, led by Marbeuf, from Ajaccio by Narbonne, seconded by a general Sionville who became the scapegoat for what followed. The Provincial Corse, a regiment formed for collaborators and commanded by Paoli's one-time right-hand man, Francesco Gaffori, was there to complete the discomfiture of the rebels. Some pleaded with him, vainly, to procure a general amnesty; others panicked, scattered, fled. French troops entered the rock-embattled Niolo in pursuit of the fugitives, only to find most of the villages abandoned. There was no real fighting. Few shots were fired except on livestock, when the great herds were systematically slaughtered by the invading soldiers, who, in the scornful words of the French officer comte Roux de Laric, 'made a prodigious mess'. Some forty men were caught, and to serve as an example eleven were condemned after rapid trials to be broken on the wheel. Their bodies were hung on trees outside their homes, and that night, by fire and torchlight, women gathered to wail their dead, kissing their feet and hailing them as 'martyrs of liberty'. Others were sent to slow deaths in the galleys or the Great Tower of Toulon. Pasqualini contrived to escape to Tuscany; but Albertini got a life-sentence in the galleys and another patriot priest committed suicide.

Louis XV had died in May; in August Marbeuf went to the capital to present himself to his new sovereign and render account of a job well done. Narbonne was left to deal with the remaining resistants. He began, it is said, by suggesting that all the Corsican males should be transported to the continent or to the East Indies (though not to the same place) and that a number of worthy citizens should then be imported to marry the Corsican women. According to the chronicler Rossi, the proposal was included in a memoir addressed to the minister of war which came to light during the French Revolution; however it has not been seen since. What is certain is that Narbonne acted with extreme ruthlessness. Resistants were summoned to surrender, and if they so much as hesitated were pursued and shot at sight, their houses were sacked and burned, their women raped, their livestock killed, their vines uprooted, their chestnuts and olives cut down. Women and children were driven from the ruins of their homes on the assumption (which proved correct) that they would go to join their men who had taken refuge in the maquis and so reveal their hiding places. In the course of the summer and autumn hundreds were disposed of by these means, killed on the spot or condemned to die of hunger and exposure. Others were sent to meet their fellow-countrymen in the prisons of Toulon or the galleys. By November Corsica was at peace; there was no more thought of rebellion for the next fifteen years.[1]

The episode struck public imagination, became part of the black national myth. The eleven victims of the Niolo entered history; the mass executions of men and beasts, the rotting broken corpses and the blood of the slaughtered herds, the wailing of bereaved women and the wandering bands of homeless, hungry children became confused in a frightful picture of atrocities; worse, even, than the reality. Blame was heaped on Sionville, who had no following like Marbeuf and Narbonne. Tales of his barbarities were circulated all over the island and revived with added grisly details during the French Revolution. The old general, then in his nineties, was burnt in effigy by a jeering crowd in Sartene, and after witnessing this hideous celebration died, it is said, of shock and grief.[2]

His crimes real or supposed were known to Napoleon from what he had heard in childhood, and later, and they inspired him, as a young artillery officer, to write a romantic horror story in which one assertion at least corresponds with fact: the rebellion was started by sixty men. Entitled 'Nouvelle Corse' – 'Corsican Novella' – it ends abruptly after eight printed pages, as though incomplete; but one may wonder how much longer the author could have maintained the uninterrupted sequence of ghastly happenings. It begins with the shipwreck of an English traveller on Gorgona, the little island one can see from northern Corsica on a clear day, here depicted as a precipitous rock constantly lashed by furious seas, a grave of ships and men. Assuming this 'sterile' spot to be uninhabited, the Englishman, comparing himself to Robinson Crusoe, pitches his tent in the shelter of some ancient ivy-clad ruins in the true romantic tradition; but let us remember that when Napoleon was writing, probably in 1789, the tradition was undeveloped. He wakes to see his tent burning and hear the cry 'Thus all men perish' above the howling of the waves. His tent has been set on fire by an aged Corsican and his daughter. Later, suspecting that his victim may be English and therefore his country's ally, the old Corsican is seized with a paroxysm of remorse and threatens to cast himself into the purifying flames while enjoining his daughter to live on to revenge him on the tyrants of his native land.

The Englishman thereupon falls to the feet of the 'virtuous old man', who welcomes him to the 'cavern' where he lives with his daughter and pours out his fearful tale. Partisan of Paoli, he kept up the resistance after the conquest, saw forty comrades captured and executed and joined a band of sixty conspirators pledged to drive out the French, 'enemies of free men'. After some engagements, in which a hundred Frenchmen are taken prisoner, he reaches his village to find his father lying in his own blood, his mother mutilated and naked 'in the most revolting posture' and his wife and seven sons hanging from trees. His daughter has disappeared. Soon he sets sail with some fellow rebels from 'the accursed isle where tigers reigned'. They call at Gorgona; he decides to stay on there alone while they continue their voyage. He finds water by the ruins of an ancient monastery and learns to live on the products of nature. His home is the cave which he leaves only by night, his misfortunes having rendered odious the light of day. His daughter is eventually brought to the island by Turkish pirates, apparently unharmed (the infidels, it is implied, are more humane than the French). French ships are from time to time wrecked on the shore; after some unhappy encounters with the crews, which the old Corsican is at first inclined to treat with humanity, he and his daughter make a point of killing the survivors. But on one occasion he is captured with his daughter by a French ship anchored offshore; freed on his promise to bring water, he stabs a sailor to death and frees his daughter with whom he assassinates the rest. They burn their bodies on a funeral pyre, the incense of which is pleasing 'to the divinity'. Here the story stops short.

Various influences are apparent: obviously of Defoe, faintly of Ossian, which Napoleon had read at school, unmistakably of Bernardin de Saint-Pierre whose *Paul et Virginie* had appeared in 1788, and overwhelmingly of Rousseau whose influence on Napoleon was paramount at this period of his life. 'He was a passionate admirer of Jean Jacques,' writes Joseph, describing his first return to Corsica on leave from his regiment; this, he adds 'was what we called being the inhabitant of the ideal world'. And indeed the voice of Rousseau rings through the tale, in the long, emotional declamatory speeches, and in the observations on the human condition and invocations to natural law that give a philosophical dimension to Rousseau's fiction at the expense of the individuation of character. When the English traveller perceives the ruins surrounding his tent by the light of the flames that consume it, he reflects that 'all perishes in nature' and he too must perish; the old man welcomes him with the words: 'Virtue has the right to be everywhere respected'; the dying Corsican calls on his son to avenge him: 'That is the first law of nature.'

Gorgona, scene of so much distress, is none the less also the magic isle of pre-Romantic imagination; in such a place Paul and Virginie might have loved in undefiled innocence; it is Rousseau's ideal world, uncorrupted and unimpaired, where one might live, so the shipwrecked visitor esteems, 'sheltered from the seductions of mankind, their ambitious deceits, their ephemeral passions'. Nature, as in the Île-de-France of Bernardin de Saint-Pierre, is generous, in spite of mournful undertones that recall Ossian; the old Corsican can survive on acorns and seafood in an honest existence of rigorous simplicity; the pine-wood torch that illuminates his nightly fishing 'shines only on just actions'.

'Just' in Napoleon's definition; for this is Rousseau's ideal world seen through Corsican eyes. Vengeance, the 'first law of nature', is the guiding principle of the 'virtuous old man', lifted to the status of a religion: 'I have sworn on my altars by the gods they [the French] have outraged, to massacre all those who fall within my power.' He indeed massacres some; but not enough. When he is captured by the French ship he has no doubt but that this misfortune is a punishment for the inadequacy of his revenge: 'my ancestors avenged themselves for my betrayal of the vengeance due to their spirits'. Duty to the murdered dead; the essence of the Corsican code of honour, of justice: injury and death must be avenged by death, and death by death, not only to satisfy the living but to appease the spirits of those who have been killed. The compulsive obligation to the ancestors which held sway in Corsican society until very recently has never been more clearly formulated. The theme gives force and originality to what would otherwise be no more than a rather insignificant reflection of contemporary writers.[3]

It is easy to understand how Napoleon absorbed this code, even if his parents thought themselves civilized enough to live above it (but Luciano certainly heeded its commands although his weapon was the law). The mingling of people of all classes that traditionally takes place in a Corsican home, the nurses and servants, the peasants and fishermen delivering their products, the people of all kinds bringing their grain to the mill, would have made Napoleon early and vividly aware of the code that dictated so much Corsican behaviour. The wonder is that he discarded it: in adult life he was not personally vindictive even though he had all power to be so. The Corsican traits in his character which his years at school served only to reinforce, were progressively shed between 1789 and 1793, under the impact of the French Revolution, which showed him aspects of the French he could admire and which seemed likely to give the Corsicans a better deal. The rub of active life, his political and military enterprises, mostly unsuccessful, completed the process during those extremely formative years. Napoleon simply grew out of certain Corsican values as of constricting clothes. Other insular characteristics, more estimable ones, stayed with him to the end: generosity, gratitude, fidelity to family and friends. Yet one may wonder if his neglect of Corsica in the years of his supremacy was not motivated by vindictive resentment of having been driven out of the island in 1793.

Stendhal, in a strong imaginative reconstruction of Napoleon's youth, dwells on the noble tone of the conversation he was exposed to in childhood, all charged with a sense of patriotic endeavour, and contrasts it with the petty gossip characteristic of a family of analogous social status in mainland France.[4] Passionate and dramatic are perhaps more appropriate terms for describing the talk that must have gone on in the *casa* Bonaparte, about Paoli, father and founder of the nation, the war with Genoa, the war with France, the desperate last stand at Ponte Novo, the resistance and the patriot-bandits and the reprisals and betrayals and tortures and executions, and the final disastrous uprising. Passionate and dramatic, too, must have been the discussions of family affairs, with Luciano fulminating against Carlo's extravagance, Letizia's outlay on clothes and the perfidy of the Ornano, and Carlo denouncing Luciano's meanness and the abysmal incapacity of his rivals, while each of the women had her say and the Ornano shouted insults on the staircase in the small hours. Life was lived at a constant high pitch in this family of wilful, intransigent, ambitious individuals. It is much easier to understand the formation of Napoleon's character in this environment than Joseph's.

Far from being crushed or oppressed by hearing of so many horrors and conflicts, Napoleon was evidently stimulated by what he heard. To judge by his own reminiscences he enjoyed his Corsican childhood and was more than equal to its challenges. At the time of the rebellion he was going to a little mixed school run by nuns. His recollections of the experience, and Letizia's, are of considerable importance in showing what some writers have questioned: that his original sexual instincts were entirely normal. At school he fell in love with 'a charming child' called Giacominetta, and went around holding her hand. Careless of his appearance, as in later years, he was always letting his socks slide on to his shoes, so that his rivals chanted tauntingly in the streets: '*Napoleone di mezza calzetta, fa l'amore a Giacominetta*' (Napoleon of the half-socks makes love to Giacominetta). But Napoleon knew how to strike back, hurling himself on his tormentors with sticks and stones, undismayed by their numbers. Letizia recalls the same anecdote in her 'Souvenirs', with more accent on the sloppy socks than on love. But she also tells us that he made up shamelessly to the nuns, who petted him with sweets and jam.[5]

He was a bold, brave, turbulent child. He gave Joseph a terrible time: 'he was beaten, bitten, scolded and I was already picking another quarrel with him before he recovered'. Letizia tried to master him with the whip, as was the custom in Corsican homes; spoiling in infancy being followed by a long period of rigorous discipline. According to Saveria, a family servant who stayed with Letizia in the days of her grandeur, Napoleon never whimpered or cried under the lash. Carlo, on the other hand, pampered the children whenever he was with them, which was seldom. And this too was in keeping with Corsican custom; something Napoleon forgot when he told Antommarchi that his father was 'too fond of pleasure' to bother about their upbringing. In fact Carlo behaved much like any other father in a country where the men were habitually away from home engaged in politics and war, leaving the women to rule their households unchallenged. Letizia had nothing against an arrangement that allowed her to satisfy a natural taste for authority. This woman, described by Napoleon as being 'more of a masculine than a feminine nature', regarded herself (as any other wife) as the head of the family: mothers, she states in her 'Souvenirs', should beware of going to church too often, for many things could go wrong in a family 'in the absence of its chief'.[6]

She was formidable in her role. Loved, respected and above all feared, she watched over her children with an inquisitorial eye, punishing the least fault, for this was her way of loving; her tenderness, said Napoleon, was 'severe'. Until he left for school at the end of 1778 he had a large share of attention, for Joseph was a quiet, obedient little boy, and the younger children, Lucien, Elisa, Louis, born in 1775, 1777 and 1778, were still babies who could be handed over to nurses and servants. During the first nine years of his life Letizia strove to mould his character, driving him to mass with slaps and blows, beating him after he misbehaved in church, stole fruit or laughed at a crippled grandmother: tales of his childhood naughtiness are numerous. Reading Napoleon's reminiscences of Letizia and hers of him, one has the impression of a constant duel between them. At the end of his life he paid her the highest tribute, when he told his companions at Saint Helena that he owed his success, his 'elevation' to her upbringing. Yet some of her lessons went unheeded. Letizia set great store by truthfulness, Napoleon remembered; but we know he was deficient in this virtue, and apparently from childhood. Later he boasted to Claire de Rémusat and to O'Meara that his uncle (presumably Luciano) predicted he would 'govern the world' because he was an habitual liar.[7]

Letizia was more successful in imparting her particular cult of austerity because he had natural leanings in that direction. When she gave him white bread for his school lunch and he exchanged it with a soldier in the garrison for the dark bread dealt out to the army she reproved him, but only because he was letting down family appearances. Appearances were supremely important in her scale of values, worth any sacrifice. At home he must learn to live on bread and bread alone if he wanted to get on in the world, she told him; better to have an elegant drawing-room, a fine costume and a good horse than spend money on food. She drummed in this precept by methods he never forgot: 'She sometimes made me go to bed without supper, not only as a punishment, but also as though there were nothing to eat in the house. One had to learn to suffer and not let others see it.' In this way he acquired a self-discipline that Letizia hoped would help him shine in Ajaccio, and in fact helped him win an empire.

None of her other children responded so well to her teaching; on the contrary they became notorious for their self-indulgence. Napoleon was her masterpiece, fashioned in the nine years' loving intimacy between the proud, spirited, handsome young mother and her intrepid little son. Yet their relationship was not altogether unclouded. The adoration of his mother he proclaimed to inferiors like Antommarchi and O'Meara was flawed by grudges he only admitted to a tried friend like Bertrand. As a child Napoleon had also loved his father, and respected him, and he had been deeply shocked when Letizia, giving way to a deplorably mean habit of Corsican wives, sent him to spy on Carlo in a café where the city notables met to talk and play cards. 'Go and see if your father's gambling,' she ordered him. Napoleon was revolted by this procedure; he never forgave her for it, he told Bertrand, nor for another act of meanness. A priest had taken him to serve mass, and Napoleon performed his duties carelessly. Letizia contained her anger through the rest of the day. The day after she told Napoleon that his uncle had invited him to lunch in the country to taste his cherries. Napoleon went happily to his room to change his clothes. He had barely taken down his pants before Letizia, who had been concealed in some corner, pounced on him and gave him a hiding. He never forgot it, he told Bertrand; he reproached her for it years later when they were together in Elba; how could anyone deceive a child?[8]

These are the kind of grievances that arise in childhood, and are none the less serious for being trivial; grievances that can work through a lifetime, deform a character. How far Napoleon's ambivalent feelings for Letizia affected his future relations with women is a subject worthy of study. Were the older women who fascinated him at the start of his adult life, Madame Permon, Madame de Colombier, substitutes for his beautiful, domineering mother? Was his marriage to Josephine, who combined all the traits of character Letizia deplored, his masterstroke against the adored mother who had deceived him?

As often happens with couples, Letizia and Carlo aggravated each other's faults, Carlo, with his optimistic extravagance encouraging Letizia's hardness and meanness. Yet Carlo too could be hard and mean when he needed money badly. It will be remembered that Letizia had brought him a dowry consisting of property supposedly worth 7,000 lire. A clause in the dotal act stipulated that if its value was shown to be less, her great-uncle, Andrea Ramolino, or his successor, would be obliged to pay the difference. Now, in 1775, nearly eleven years later, Carlo sued Andrea's heir, his brother Giovanni, Letizia's eighty-four-year-old grandfather, on the grounds that the property was several hundred lire short of the stated seven thousand. In March he won his case; in May Ramolino, being apparently without the means to pay, saw his belongings sold by auction in the market place, the poor agricultural equipment of a small wine producer, such as 'two little barrels in bad condition' and 'two wooden bowls for carrying grapes'. The whole fetched 323 livres and 10 sous. It is true that suing for wives' dowries was a common practice in Ajaccio; yet one can hardly believe that Letizia was not grieved by this public humiliation of her impoverished old grandfather. She certainly remained loyal to her family, seeing that she later insisted that her cousin, André Ramolino, should be given the Bonaparte's home. His shabby treatment of Camilla Ilari can be seen as an act of family revenge.[9]

It was perhaps money shortage that prevented Carlo presenting himself for election to the Estates of May 1775, besides, more certainly, the absence of his protector. Marbeuf reached Corsica just before the assembly after an absence of nearly a year. He brought with him a new *intendant*, Bertrand de Boucheporn, to replace Colla de Pradine who had turned 'narbonniste' and already been recalled. The two of them, working in harmony, were to govern Corsica, successfully according to their lights, for the next decade.

But first they had to get the better of the powerful faction backing Narbonne. When Narbonne arrived in Bastia for the opening of the Estates he got an enthusiastic welcome, with songs improvised in his honour, while Marbeuf, mockingly hailed as 'Caporal Galletta', met with jeers. The Estates then voted Narbonne the thanks of the Corsican nation, with the request that he and his eldest male descendants be granted, in perpetuity, the title of 'first-class noble' with the right to attend meetings of the assembly. Marbeuf, presiding over the session, appeared unmoved by this bizarre petition; but his nerves must have been on edge, for he insulted several deputies without good reason, including Cesar Petriconi, who had manifested pro-French sympathies at an early age by enlisting as an adolescent in the Royal Corse. In view of his scorched-earth tactics, Narbonne's popularity is hard to understand; but his victims were after all humble people who had no voice in public affairs, while his supporters were notables delighted to see order restored. According to a French officer then serving in Corsica Narbonne's forthright character, combining severity with a sense of justice, endeared him to the army, whereas Marbeuf, never a military man, failed to earn its respect. But underlying such considerations was there not also a deep, instinctive hostility in all classes to the representative of French power? So that while the acts of repression committed by the commander-in-chief were regarded as brutal tyranny, those of Narbonne, in fact no less brutal, were excused. Ironically, he became the champion of the Corsican patriots whose humbler fellows he had murdered and ruined.

His supporters in the assembly pressed Marbeuf to procure an amnesty not only for the many prisoners dying on the galleys and in dungeons, but for the Paolist exiles as well. The deputies elected to go to Versailles were all '*narbonisti*', hostile to Marbeuf: the bishop, de Guernes, who, though French, identified himself with the Corsicans and was campaigning to rescue the priest Albertini from the galleys, Benedetti, an ardent Paolist who had done a term of transportation in America for his part in the post-conquest resistance, and the now furiously offended Petriconi. Yet Marbeuf could still make himself feared, if not liked, for before the end of the session he too obtained a vote of thanks from the assembly, while contriving the recall of Narbonne, who left Corsica in June 1775; it was however said that for many months he had been craving to go.[10]

Led by de Guernes, the deputies were bolder in formulating grievances than the previous delegations; but it was the speech made by the bishop when they were presented to the king that brought about their disgrace. Instead of keeping to the servile expressions of gratitude appropriate to the occasion, he made an impassioned plea for a better understanding of the Corsicans, 'a new people' (new to civilization), while deploring the 'acts of arbitrary authority' to which they had been subjected. The words got back to Marbeuf, who was then in Paris, apprehensive of trouble. He promptly complained to the king's ministers; the bishop was asked to explain himself and came out with twenty-nine accusations against Marbeuf. Some of them must have seemed trivial or childish in Versailles. What did the ministers care if Marbeuf had been rude to some barbarous Corsicans? Were they really much shocked if he were responsible for some unjust arrests and imprisonments in a province that was after all barely pacified? And surely they must have laughed at the bishop's righteous condemnation of his liaison with the Cleopatra of Bastia, accused of keeping a public gaming-house as well as a shop where she brazenly sold the gifts she had received from people soliciting his favours.

She must indeed have been very fascinating, or very useful to Marbeuf, for him to put up with this kind of thing. But one can also understand why he was drawn to Letizia, who was singularly innocent of corruption. In fact only one anecdote has come down to us to show that she ever begged favours, and it is so naïve as to be comical. An old aunt, on her deathbed, entreated her to obtain Marbeuf's permission for her to be buried in the vault of the cathedral, a traditional privilege that the French had forbidden so as to spare the population the resulting noxious smells. Letizia was much embarassed by the request. Not so Marbeuf, who refused it, but told Letizia to tell her aunt it had been granted, because once dead she would no longer care where she was buried.[11]

The deputies at Versailles fought a losing battle with Marbeuf; yet far better than other, more submissive delegations, they made the voice of their people heard. Two of their most important requests met with royal approval: the granting of scholarships to the children of poor nobles in French military schools, and the pardon of political prisoners and exiles. And they had the courage to raise the burning, hitherto unspoken question: if a general amnesty were given, what would happen to Pasquale Paoli? How could he be excluded?

Saint-Germain, minister of war, was surprisingly sympathetic. While dismissing the idea of an official approach to Paoli he gave Benedetti a passport to England, so that he could visit the General and sound his views. The historic meeting between them took place in London between the 3rd and the 5th of October 1776; their conversations are recorded in a journal by Benedetti and a memoir dictated by Paoli. The gist of Paoli's arguments was that he refused to return to France while his countrymen were enslaved, in his eyes, to a tyrannical regime; that he was convinced that only a protectorate status would satisfy them, in which they would control all except military and foreign affairs. His words can hardly have left Benedetti unmoved; but he made, or at least recorded, a prudent reply: the Corsicans were perfectly happy to be French and only wanted some administrative reforms. Yet he did let slip in his journal that Paoli, while denying any part in the recent revolt, spoke of a possible future 'revolution' in Corsica. When the time came, he confided, he would advise the population to keep clear of the fighting between the French and the foreign troops who would be landed in the island and quietly await the outcome of the battle. Was he hoping for a British intervention?

One might think that the equivocal nature of their talk would have cast official suspicion on Benedetti, with unhappy consequences for his career. But no. The plots Paoli might have communicated to his visitor, and so to all Corsica, mattered less to Marbeuf and the ministers than the criticism of the government made by the other deputies. So while Benedetti was actually ennobled for his services to the Crown, his colleagues were sanctioned by *lettres de cachet*, the bishop being confined to his diocese and Petriconi relegated to Toulon. This happened to them, at the instigation of Marbeuf, after they had given a triumphant and indiscreet account of their mission at the opening of the Corsican Estates in May 1777. Marbeuf was now victorious. The *narbonisti* were crushed; his own supporters filled the assembly, Carlo among them. At their request a marble tablet was set up in Bastia on which was inscribed a testimony of 'the sentiments of love that had long been engraved in their hearts'.[12]

All the same, Marbeuf was leaving nothing to chance. His reputation had been badly jolted; this time he handpicked the deputies to Versailles. Carlo was to be the spokesman for the nobility: the imprudence of Petriconi had opened his way to the throne. But why was he selected, when so many older, more experienced men were available? It is not indispensable to postulate a love-affair between Marbeuf and Letizia to explain the choice. Carlo's fluency in French, his natural charm and eloquence, fitted him for a role which mainly consisted in saying what Marbeuf instructed him to say. And also, no doubt, in observing what was going on and reporting it back to Marbeuf. De Roux, who disliked Carlo, describes him as Marbeuf's 'base and servile spy'. In other words he used his powers of observations in Marbeuf's interests, as he had once done in Paoli's. Rossi's opinion is that he was the obedient executor of Marbeuf's commands and someone he could rely on for 'maximum loyalty'. Once an unconditional Paolist, he was now an equally firm supporter of the French Crown. And he was sincerely grateful to his protector, Rossi insists; the post of *assesseur* ensured his lifelong devotion to Marbeuf (Rossi did not know of the equally important benefit he had received in the settlement of the lawsuit with the Ornano).

The value Marbeuf attached to Carlo's cooperation is proved by the lengths he went to for ensuring his election to the Estates. The system of ennoblement in Corsica, by which recognition was granted to individuals, not heads of families, had given noble families with numerous adult males a controlling voice in the primary elections of the *pievi*. Carlo's handicap was his lack of noble relatives. To overcome the difficulty Marbeuf went to Ajaccio and arranged a formal treaty of assistance between the Bonaparte and the Pozzo di Borgo, a family with no less than thirteen nobles in its ranks. Landowners in the neighbouring mountains, of ancient Corsican stock, the Pozzo di Borgo had gained a foothold in Ajaccio some two centuries earlier. Stable, so far, rather than brilliant, they had held municipal office alongside the Bonaparte under Genoese rule and produced more than their quota of men of law. Their professional activities had led to conflict as well as intimacy with the Bonaparte; while Innocenzo Pozzo di Borgo acted as the Bonaparte's notary, two of his kinsmen often pleaded against Carlo in the court of Ajaccio; Luciano owned property jointly with several members of the family, which did not prevent him going to law with them on small pretexts.

None of these minor frictions counted, however, when it came to Carlo's election. Marbeuf knew how to make the deal attractive. While Carlo was to be elected for the nobility of the province of Ajaccio, Geronimo Pozzo di Borgo was to represent the Third Estate, for nobles were allowed to sit among the commoners and often did. He was moreover to receive 'advantages in the country' in return for giving Carlo his family's massive support. The author of this information is Charles-André Pozzo di Borgo, a contemporary of Napoleon's who, like him, lifted his family from Corsican obscurity into the limelight of the European stage. His recollections, contained in his unpublished memoirs, of the importance Marbeuf attached to Carlo's services, are of particular interest in coming from one who had become Napoleon's arch-enemy. Friends in their youth, Charles-André and Napoleon fell out at an early stage of their careers and engaged in a lifelong feud with Europe as its scene. Diplomatic adviser to Tsar Alexander I, Charles-André ended as Russian ambassador to the court of Louis XVIII. Naturally enough Napoleon had a good many disparaging things to say about him to his companions at Saint Helena. All the same, with his amazing memory for figures, he did recall that long ago in Corsica the Pozzo di Borgo had 'thirteen voices in the Estates of the nobility' and that these had been very useful to his father. He was seven years old when Carlo stood for election, and he evidently never forgot the tense calculations and predictions that must have filled family conversation at this crucial time.

Everything went according to Marbeuf's plan. Carlo and Geronimo won the primary and secondary elections and took their seats in the Estates. On 2 July 1777 Carlo was elected to represent the nobility in the deputation to Versailles, with thirty votes, well ahead of his closest rival, who got only twenty-one. According to Charles-André Pozzo di Borgo, his family used their influence to ensure this success; but Marbeuf must have manipulated the whole election. De Roux, a carping *narbonniste*, reports that the votes were bought and practically forced from the members of the Estates. The Pozzo di Borgo, at all events, got their reward: a concession of land from the royal domain at Verdana, which though not very large was apparently valuable. This was the period when the French government was distributing concessions of land, sometimes accompanied by titles, to its supporters,

Corsican and French. These properties were carved out of the royal domain that had been inherited, with numerous disputes, from that held by the Genoese Republic. Since these lands were mostly in coastal areas that had been abandoned by their populations in times of Barbary pirate raids, they were often fertile, if unhealthy. Big prizes went to the favourites of the regime: Matteo Buttafoco, the original Corsican collaborator, got an inland bay or lagoon of Biguglia that supplied fish to Bastia, besides rich tracts of surrounding country and the title of count, while Marbeuf eventually became marquis with a handsome stretch of land near the new settlement of the Greek immigrants.[13]

Carlo's share in the handout, offered in anticipation of a satisfactory performance at Versailles, was Marbeuf's support of his application for a free place for his second son in a French military school. Such patronage was invaluable, even though Carlo was exactly the kind of person for whose benefit these scholarships were intended. A royal circular issued in February 1776, when twelve provincial military colleges were made available, specifies seven categories of children eligible for scholarships, all of them sons of officers in the French army, and an eighth category consisting of children of the 'indigent nobility'. The 'certificate of indigence' Carlo procured for himself, guaranteed by two fellow nobles of Ajaccio, often cited as evidence of shameless parasitism, was simply one of the documents that had to be forwarded with the *intendant*'s recommendation to the minister of war. Other qualifications for candidates were that they should be between seven and twelve years old, well built, able to read and write, and that their fathers should furnish proof of four generations of nobility.

The free places were the object of ruthless competition and intrigue, for there were only six hundred or so for the whole of France, and indigence was as common among the French provincial nobles as the Corsican. Though only the recommendation of the *intendant* was officially required, in fact the intervention of highly placed persons was indispensable; most of the little scholars were sponsored by great names. During the year 1778, when Carlo was waiting to be summoned to court, Marbeuf twice wrote to the minister of war to insist on Napoleon's admission; the favourable answer, dated 31 December, was not received in Corsica till mid-January, when Carlo was already on his way to Versailles. He had reason to feel privileged; yet once again it is not necessary to suppose a love-affair between Marbeuf and his wife: Marbeuf did as much for at least two other little boys in Corsica, Marius Matra and Élie Balathier de Bragelonne, whose subsequent careers were too obscure to cast doubt on their mothers' morals.[14]

Where Marbeuf showed exceptional kindness, which must surely have encouraged gossip, was in the interest he took in the Bonaparte family as a whole. Not only Napoleon, but his brother Joseph, and Letizia's half-brother, Joseph Fesch, and her cousin, Aurele Varese, were all indebted to him for their start in life. Marbeuf was well placed to help them because all three were seeking careers in the Church, and his nephew, bishop of Autun, controlled nomination to the ecclesiastical benefices. One can hardly fail to think that the Bonaparte obtained more from Marbeuf, and more easily, than they would have done had Letizia been indifferent to him.[15]

When distributing these advantages it was obvious that Napoleon was the one who should be given facilities for a military career. He had in fact already chosen it. He made friends with the soldiers in the garrison, shocked Letizia by enjoying their dark bread; he dressed up as a soldier with sword and drum, covered the nursery walls with drawings of soldiers; he alarmed the household by staying out one night in a violent thunderstorm on the pretext that a future soldier should harden himself against bad weather. These and other more or less reliable anecdotes, coming to us through Letizia and her contemporaries, compose a plausible portrait of Napoleon as a child, though one less significant than its authors seem to have assumed. How many little boys have dreamed of becoming soldiers? How many have grown up to win forty battles?[16]

Since Napoleon was obviously cut out for the army, it was concluded, on less good grounds, that the gentle-natured Joseph must be suited to the Church. It need hardly be said that entering the Church was not at that period thought to demand any marked vocation: Luciano Bonaparte never gives the impression of caring much about religion; Joseph, and later his younger brother Lucien, though destined for a time to ecclesiastical careers, obviously did not, while Aurele Varese seized the opportunity to leave the Church provided by the French Revolution.

There was a college at Autun, one of the oldest and best in France, and Marbeuf arranged for Joseph to be admitted there with the idea that his nephew would keep an eye on him and eventually patronize his ecclesiastical career. Napoleon, again on Marbeuf's advice, was to be left with his brother at the same school, where he could learn to read and write French, while his father went to Paris and there completed the remaining formalities for his entry to a military college. Aurele Varese, already an ordained priest, was to accompany the Bonaparte children to Autun, and be immediately taken under the bishop's protection. This kind of counsel was precious to Carlo in his Corsican isolation, even though he had to pay for his sons' school fees at Autun. Joseph certainly reaped advantages from his years there, even though his ecclesiastical career came to nothing, as was also the case with Aurele Varese. Joseph Fesch, who won a scholarship to the seminary in Aix-en-Provence the following year, however did what was expected of him, and later very much more, with Napoleon's colossal aid.[17]

Without these educational advantages, would any of these young men have ever been heard of outside Corsica, Napoleon included? One may wonder. Napoleon always showed gratitude for his French education, insisted that his years at school had fundamentally changed his outlook on life, and generously rewarded everyone concerned, including Marbeuf's widow and son. Education in Corsica, always inadequate, had actually deteriorated since the French conquest. One of the first acts of the government had been to expel the Jesuits, who had run colleges in Bastia and Ajaccio. The seminaries had been occupied by troops; Paoli's university had collapsed with his regime. Corsican requests to revive it, to recuperate the seminaries, and to found colleges at key points in the island, repeated in almost every assembly of the Estates, met with a lukewarm reception from the French authorities, who held to the colonial principle that too much learning would drain away labour from the land. It was cheaper and safer to provide scholarships in mainland schools for a few young nobles who in this way, it was calculated, would become loyally attached to their king. Only two colleges came into existence in Corsica, after long delays, in the towns; the resurrection of the university had to wait till the present day. Meanwhile the clergy, though under-financed and always suspect to the French, kept alive such schools as existed. In the villages they limited themselves to the traditional teaching, narrow but not uninspiring, of the catechism and Italian poetry. Tasso's *Jerusalem Delivered*, which had become almost a war-song during the French invasion, and Dante's *Divine Comedy* remained the basic culture of the country people for generations to come, so that shepherds could still be heard reciting their verses, with grave relish, until a few years ago. In the towns teaching was focused on the classics. Joseph Bonaparte was sent to the former Jesuit school in Ajaccio, then run by a certain abbé Recco, where the pupils seem to have enjoyed themselves absorbing rudiments of ancient history. They sat facing each other in two groups, representing the Carthaginians and the Romans, each with a huge banner hanging overhead. When Napoleon, after leaving the nuns, joined his elder brother there, he refused to sit among the Carthaginians because they had been defeated.[18]

The year 1778 must have been an exceptionally happy one for the Bonaparte, as they saw their ambitions taking shape with Carlo's grand mission and the privileged education of their sons. Marbeuf was often in Ajaccio, for he had much business to attend to in Cargese, some thirty miles up the coast. He had already supervised the establishment there of some five hundred descendants of the Greek refugees who had come to Corsica, a century earlier, from the Mani in the Peloponnese, to escape the servitudes of Turkish rule. The Genoese allotted them land, where they prospered, until they were driven off it during the national rebellion and had to find shelter in Ajaccio. In 1774, after many vicissitudes, the survivors were resettled in Cargese, near their former home, a seaport village built from scratch according to a spacious and pleasant official design. The leaders of the colony, the Stephanopoli, believed themselves to be no less than descendants of the Comnenos emperors of Byzantium and Trebizond. One induced Louis XVI to grant him the title of prince; another obtained a concession of crown land near Ajaccio. A daughter of this doubtful house, married to a French financier, Permon, comforted Carlo Bonaparte on his deathbed, and befriended Joseph, Joseph Fesch and Napoleon in their youth. Her daughter, Laure, married Junot, one of Napoleon's generals, and became duchesse d'Abrantès. Napoleon appointed her lady-in-waiting to Letizia, though he had no patience with her claim that they shared the same exalted lineage, nor with her belief in her own. He was however unnecessarily unkind when he pretended to Bertrand that her mother had started life as Letizia's housemaid.[19]

Now, in 1778, Marbeuf was rewarded for his services to Corsica and the Crown by the grant of a large property in the neighbourhood of Cargese that carried the title of marquis. As usually happened in connection with these arrogant royal gifts, small people saw their lands, traditional rights and usages impinged on, and being Corsicans, protested fiercely; the pro-French Greeks themselves complained of Marbeuf's feudal status, even though the grant gave him no seigneurial prerogatives. Yet the disagreements and protests, the wrangling and haggling and bargaining and rectification of boundaries and exchanges of land in no way prevented Marbeuf from sailing ahead with his private plans. He built himself a house such as had never been seen in Corsica before, soberly, imposingly French in its architecture, but Italian in the disposition of its grounds, complete with pavilions and orange groves, fountains and cascades, a pleasure palace where he entertained Carlo and Letizia and their children for weeks on end.[20]

His passion for Letizia was now at its peak. Count Colchen, recently arrived in Corsica as secretary to Boucheporn, the new *intendant*, observes that Marbeuf had been paying her court – a 'cult' – for the past two years. We have seen, from the family correspondence in the Archives Napoléon, that he had been attracted to her for much longer, at least since 1771. But during the early years of their friendship she had a powerful rival in the person of Madame Varese, the Cleopatra of Bastia. Now she had his undivided attention, for as Colchen notes, he had dropped Cleopatra in 1775 or 1776. No doubt the trouble their liaison had cost him in public gossip and the bishop's indiscretions in Versailles had outweighed her worn, disreputable charm.

Now, in Colchen's words, he was 'wildly' (*éperdument*) in love with Letizia. In her late twenties, she looked wonderful: 'The elegance of her figure, the radiance of her complexion, the regularity and delicacy of her features made her a perfect beauty.' This was no small tribute to a woman who had known the stresses of war and domestic insecurity, besides giving birth to at least six children. Her only defect, in the eyes of Colchen, was an excessive timidity that gave a certain awkwardness to her bearing. Laure d'Abrantès makes the same observation: Letizia was never at ease in high society, and her experience of it in Corsica had only increased a natural shyness which she masked under a cold exterior. Yet perhaps her very aloofness, her reticence, were pleasing to Marbeuf after the overwhelming effrontery of Madame Varese.

No one could ignore their relationship. The French officer de Roux relates that Marbeuf took her to Bastia during the winter of 1777–8, 'kept her with him [in his home] as long as he could' and gave every reception [every '*fête*'] in her honour. All the ladies, he writes, had to pay court to her, the 'reigning sultana', including the *intendant*'s wife, Madame de Boucheporn, whose position should have placed her above any such obligation. But Marbeuf, he tells us, was totally obsessed, entirely absorbed by Letizia, to the point of neglecting official business. There was nothing to be got out of him; he refused to see anyone; never had anything like it been known before; the very children mocked at his servile devotion to his 'idol'. When he visited Ajaccio in the spring of 1778 his sole object was to be with her; he had an apartment made for himself adjoining her home; he stayed on into August, 'and with reason', so de Roux pointedly observes.

Much of this was no doubt exaggeration or pure calumny, for de Roux was hostile to the Marbeuf and the Bonaparte, being a protégé of de Pradine and Narbonne. Need one suppose that Letizia stayed with Marbeuf in Bastia without her husband? Or think ill of her, wife of a man in the public eye, for accepting official invitations in one of the few periods of her young life when she was not pregnant (Elisa had been born in January 1777)? One cannot believe, either, that Marbeuf lodged any closer to the *casa* Bonaparte than he usually did in a nearby street, in the old *palazzo* of the Genoese *commissario*.

But did he, as de Roux hints, prolong his stay in Ajaccio because she was again pregnant and he believed, rightly or not, that he was the father of the child? Undoubtedly the situation, exalting to a man in his sixties without an heir, would account for an excessive concern for her at this time. Born on 2 September, Louis was baptized on the 24th of the month in the oratory of San Gerolamo, with Marbeuf and Madame de Boucheporn as godparents. This is of course no proof of Marbeuf's paternity; but it may be remembered that while Louis was baptized in a church with these powerful sponsors in 1778, Lucien, born in 1775, and Elisa in 1777 were still awaiting the ceremony which eventually took place in 1779 with undistinguished godparents, and at home. Everyone, according to Colchen, believed Louis to be Marbeuf's son. He himself had no doubt about it, then or later; Louis, he insists, was quite unlike the other Bonaparte children in looks and character, while his brusque, irascible manners recalled Marbeuf. This was written around 1811, and it is strange that Colchen should have been blind to the family resemblance apparent in all the portraits of the Bonaparte children, that Roman look Louis shared with his brothers and sisters as though – to quote Laure d'Abrantès – they had been 'stamped with the same coin'. And was the occasional irascibility of Marbeuf, by all accounts usually social and urbane, in any way comparable to Louis's constantly morose manner? One may moreover suppose that had Louis been his son, Marbeuf would have remembered him in his will. Whereas Louis, whose repeated applications for a scholarship were turned down, was the least well provided for of all the Bonaparte brothers. Or did Marbeuf lose interest in him after his remarriage, and especially after his young wife, shortly before his death, gave him a legitimate son and heir?[21]

If Marbeuf was never more drawn to Letizia than during the period before and after Louis's birth, it may be noted that the Bonaparte never had greater need of him than then. Carlo's worldly ambition was for the time being satisfied, and the prospect of Napoleon's scholarship offered hope for the future; yet he had more than ever cause for anxiety. His salary, and the revenues from the properties he shared with Luciano or which had come to him with Letizia's dowry, were proving less and less adequate to the style of life he had assumed and intended to improve. In this predicament, Carlo shrewdly marshalled his rather meagre resources. To increase his personal income he put in hand two schemes connected with the properties known as Les Milelli and Les Salines. Both, need it be said, have been misunderstood and derided with scraps of documents quoted out of context to show Carlo, incorrigibly feckless, plunging headlong into hopeless ventures to the ruin of himself and his family. Yet anyone prepared to wade through the enormous correspondence on these subjects (some, but not all in the Archives Napoléon), must be struck by the ingenuity and patience with which he set about exploiting these enterprises. The Milelli scheme was in fact entirely successful, but as it involved negotiations with the government it made snail's pace progress and was not completed till after Carlo's death. The other undertaking, at the Salines, certainly turned to disappointment, but for this Carlo was less to blame than the government, which had sponsored it. In both he relied heavily on Marbeuf; his assets were too fragile to be developed without powerful backing.

His title of ownership to both of these properties rested on shaky foundations. His claim to the Salines was that his ancestor Geronimo, the man of law who in the sixteenth century had made the family noteworthy, had been granted some land by the city of Ajaccio including a swamp or pool by the sea, which he had drained and cultivated and protected from pirate incursions by the building of a tower. The spot was known as the Saline on account of saltpans that had once existed there. Such a donation was in keeping with the practice of the city under the Genoese regime, and Carlo was able to produce a document, dated 1584, stating that the community of Ajaccio had passed an act before the notary Gabrielo Staglione, granting the '*Stagno delle Saline*' and adjoining land to Geronimo and his descendants.

Unfortunately the document was damaged and some of the text missing; even more unfortunately the copy inscribed in the notary's register had perished, so Carlo asserted, by fire. But he was able to find three notaries to vouch for the authenticity of his own copy by comparing its handwriting with that of authentic documents in the city archives that Staglione had written and signed.

It must be admitted that Carlo's document, like some others he produced, such as the early items in his initial act of nobility, is somewhat unconvincing. So indeed thought a high-ranking official in the ministry of finance in Versailles, when he considered his claim in December 1776 after it had worked its way through the hands of the royal judge in Ajaccio, the *intendant*'s geometer, the *intendant*'s *subdélégué* and the *intendant* Boucheporn himself. The title-deed, he observed, was 'in a very equivocal state', and the gaps in the text came exactly where one would expect to find precise information about the limits of the donation. Moreover was the land really the property of the town or not, rather, of the Genoese Republic? In other words was the donation valid? Searches in the city archives proved 'useless'; but the oldest inhabitants of Ajaccio agreed that the Bonaparte had always been considered owners of the tower and adjoining land. And they were not mistaken. A map recently found in the Genoese archives, apparently of the seventeenth century, shows the name Bonaparte written below the tower. Carlo cannot have known of this document or he would have used it; he had summoned all his ingenuity to prove what was in fact true.[22]

His application was the more easily granted because no one else was interested in the site. The pond 'infected the air', in other words was a source of fever lethal to the inhabitants, and, as the French administrators underlined, the garrison of the town. Carlo insisted that his ancestors had kept it drained and cultivated until French troops, during the conquest, had destroyed the drainage system and crops. Now he put in for a compensation of 6,000 livres to enable him to re-drain and re-cultivate the area in the interests of public health, thus presenting himself at once as the victim of the French army and its potential benefactor. His request was accepted at the end of 1776, after a suggestion to cut the subsidy to 4,500 livres had been dismissed; for as the *subdélégué* pointed out to the minister, no one else in Ajaccio would have agreed to take on the job for so small a sum. The geometer had actually estimated its cost at 10,000 livres.

Carlo had got his way by running a risk, and he was soon made to realize that the odds were against him. Luckily the undertaking had official approval. For labour he was assigned troops, in accordance with the eighteenth-century practice of employing the army on public works in time of peace. The drainage scheme was drawn up by Vuillier, an official geometer. But he had underrated the violence of the Corsican winter storms. The work, according to Carlo, was totally wasted, and though he was paid 2,400 livres in December 1777 as a first instalment of his subsidy, he was out of pocket to the tune of over a thousand. 'Appalled' by the expense, he would have thrown up the whole enterprise but for Marbeuf, who had it 'at heart' and urged him to continue with the support of 'his protection and his purse'. Things later took a turn for the better when in 1782 Carlo came to benefit from a government scheme for planting mulberries; but for the time being he was dependent on Marbeuf's generosity and obliged to spend a vast amount of money at the moment when he could least afford it.[23]

The scheme connected with the Milelli was more costly in frustration than in cash, and though it might seem the less realistic of the two, or indeed quite fantastical, it eventually worked out to the family's advantage. Carlo's great-great-grandfather, that Carlo Maria Bonaparte whose propensity to theft had been immortalized in comic rhymes, and who was also remembered as a skilful merchant, shipowner and moneylender, had married Virginea, daughter of Pietro Odone, a well-off landowner. Pietro stipulated in his will that if his son and heir, or his son's son, died without issue, his property was to go to Virginea and her descendants. It so happened that Pietro's grandson, Paolo Francesco, did die childless. His property should therefore have reverted to the Bonaparte. But Paolo Francesco, in Carlo's words, 'thinking to perform a worthy action', bequeathed his property to the Jesuits of Ajaccio, who took possession of it in 1711. And such was the power of the Jesuits, who refused the Bonaparte access to the relevant documents, not to mention the feebleness of the Genoese government, assailed by rebellion during the following decades, that the Bonaparte, 'reduced to indigence' (an expression Carlo was frequently to use in the coming years), had never been able to reclaim their heritage.

They might have given up hope of doing so, had the Jesuits not been expelled from France in 1764 and from Corsica in 1768, and their property made over to a fund for public education. (Their order was abolished by Pope Clement XIV in 1773.) Carlo decided to appeal to the French government. Not for the total restitution of the heritage: this would have involved him in prolonged, ruinous litigation, for the Jesuits had sold some of the properties left to them and transformed – 'denatured' – others. Well-advised by Marbeuf, Carlo applied for only two items: the house known as La Badina in the same street as the *casa* Bonaparte, which he could use for storing his wine, and the land just outside the town known as Les Milelli, most suitable for the cultivation of olives. Nor did he solicit possession; he would be satisfied with a long lease from the government.

His petition was eventually granted; but not before many memoranda had been composed and documents assembled and delays endured and opposition from various quarters overcome. The first problem was to procure a copy of Pietro Odone's will, which was inscribed in the register of the notary Spoturno. Acting for the expelled Jesuits, Spoturno caused every possible delay. For over a month he and Carlo haggled over the price of providing a copy, which Carlo finally obtained on 27 November for 120 livres, having beaten down Spoturno from two hundred. It came just in time for him to take it to Versailles to present to the prince de Montbarey, the minister in charge of Corsican affairs.[24]

Before leaving, he and Letizia enjoyed a farewell visit to Marbeuf's fine house at Cargese in the company of Colchen and the Boucheporn. According to an entry in his 'Livre de Raison' Carlo started on his journey on 12 December 1778. Napoleon, in a youthful manuscript, notes the day of departure as the 15th. The discrepancy is easily explained by the fact Napoleon related to Bertrand: the travellers sailed from Bastia. The journey over the mountains between the two towns then took the best part of three days, with nights spent, usually, at Bocognano and Corte. 'I was with Joseph,' Napoleon recalled; 'Madame Letizia was in the carriage of M. de Marbeuf. It was a procession that struck me.' This must have been on the last stage of the journey, on the recently built carriage road between Corte and Bastia; the longer distance from Ajaccio to Corte had to be covered by horse or mule.[25]

The party must have reached Bastia on the 14th, on the evening before Carlo and his children set sail. And naturally enough they stayed with Marbeuf in his apartment in Les Missionnaires, the vast monastery of the Lazarists overlooking the sea. This is confirmed by a certain Ristori in a letter that has been taken as sufficient proof of Letizia's liaison with their host. The author is not the patriot of the same name who served Paoli, but a dislikeable officer in the Régiment Provincial Corse who was pestering Marbeuf for some favour, perhaps the Croix de Saint Louis, a decoration given at the close of a military career. While Marbeuf avoided him, Ristori poured out his grievances.

to his protector, the former *intendant* Colla de Pradine, who was then in Paris. Marbeuf had spent a long time in Ajaccio, he complains, and now he had at last returned to Bastia he was 'nearly all the time shut up with Madame Bonaparte in his apartment in the Missionnaires'. A tradition repeated by several historians relates that Letizia had her children blessed by the Lazarists before their journey. If Ristori had gained admittance to Marbeuf's apartment before they sailed he would most likely have interrupted a solemn religious family gathering rather than the amorous tête-à-tête he imagined.

But Ristori wrote his letter on 16 December, and the ship had sailed the day before, and Marbeuf was still, apparently, 'shut up' with Letizia in the Missionnaires. Evidently she had stayed on in Bastia as his guest. But did this prove she was his mistress? Could Ristori deduce as much from an arrangement obviously in her interests and which her husband must have agreed to, if not instigated? It would have been impossible for her to leave Bastia immediately: a long and hazardous journey had to be organized, to Corte by carriage (there was as yet no public coach service), and then a two days' ride over the mountains to Ajaccio. Or she might have travelled home by sea, round the north of the island and down the west coast; when and if a ship were available. Marbeuf was certainly the person to take charge of these arrangements, and to look after Letizia until they were made. In the meantime he could hardly send her to an inn, a place, then, of ill fame as well as discomfort. And she no longer had her grandfather to give her hospitality, for Pietrasanta had died in 1773, a heavy loss to the Bonaparte of which I have found no echo in their correspondence. Nor could she stay with Madame de Boucheporn because, as we know from Ristori's letter, the *intendant* and his wife were then on holiday in Italy.[26]

But we know nothing more. We cannot say what went on between Letizia and Marbeuf in the Missionnaires, nor even if they were much alone together. His apartment was not, after all, a bedsitting room, but a very grand and vast establishment where he entertained officially and housed his servants and suite. Boswell describes him holding court at a public levee that delighted him by its 'brilliancy'; 'it was like passing . . . from the mountains of Corsica to the banks of the Seine'; de Roux notes that during sessions of the Estates he habitually sat down with eighty guests to dinner. We can only speculate as to what happened to Letizia after her husband and children went to sea leaving her in the hands of their benefactor. Undoubtedly Marbeuf held her at his mercy. How chivalrous was he? How strong-minded? How strong-minded was she?[27]

{ 6 }

EFFORTS AND REWARDS

'I'm not Corsican. I was brought up in France, therefore I'm French; my brothers too.'[1] With this statement, firmly in line with the modern faith in the pre-eminence of nurture over nature, Napoleon insisted on the transformation he and his brothers underwent in their French schools. Born just before and after a bitter conquest he and Joseph, at least, must have thought of themselves in early childhood as the involuntary subjects of an alien king. Their years at school in the land of the victor turned them into Frenchmen, proud of their new nationality, French in their behaviour, attitudes and values. Or so Napoleon liked to say. In the light of hindsight they appear unmistakably marked by their Corsican origin. Their characters had already taken shape before they were thrust into the new environment, to be forced into a foreign mould. Each reacted according to temperament. Joseph adapted himself, not without unhappiness, by using his gift to please. Napoleon's predicament was more painful: the impact of French civilization stirred a deep, resentful, vindictive love of his conquered homeland which lasted well into his early adult years.

Their first and cruel realization was that Corsica was a rather miserable place. According to Napoleon their father drummed this in before they had even set foot in France. 'You see what a stupid pride we take in our country!' he exclaimed, as they sailed past Villefranche, coasting towards Marseilles. 'We boast of the Grande Rue in Ajaccio, and there's a street in an ordinary French town quite as fine and wide.'[2]

The object lesson would have been less needed had Carlo and his sons travelled, as Napoleon maintains, by way of Florence; for if the Florentine streets are narrow they certainly have a magnificence unimagined in Ajaccio. Napoleon states that they were received there by the Grand-duke Leopold, who gave Carlo an introduction to his sister, Marie-Antoinette. But here Napoleon, wittingly or not, was adding an item to the Bonaparte legend. A detour via Florence seems unlikely, given the time spent on the journey; at all events research has shown that the grand-duke was not in Florence at that moment.[3] And had he been there, would he have done so much for Carlo, or even received him? In a period when lineage was of supreme importance, it was gratifying for an obscure Corsican to be accepted as kinsman by the Tuscan Buonaparte; but this by no means implied moving up into princely circles. Though a number of the Florentine Buonaparte – at least twenty according to an Italian author – had held eminent public office under the Medici, to whom they were apparently related, they seem never to have been granted a title of count or marquis. Moreover their line had died out, perhaps as long as two centuries before Carlo undertook his mission.[4] In San Miniato Buonaparte had distinguished themselves in learning and letters, but nothing in their record entitled them to court favours. By 1779 they were anyhow diminished, in numbers and in status. Giovan' Battista, the professor of medicine who had boosted Carlo's prestige when he took his doctorate in Pisa, had died in 1774, leaving as representatives of the family Giuseppe Moccio of Empoli, a lawyer, and the canon Filippo, he whom Carlo had probably called on during his first wild journey to Italy. Giuseppe Moccio, to quote Letizia, married his servant 'with one foot in the grave', and dying without issue, in 1780 made Carlo his heir; but family papers were about all he had to bequeath. Impoverished and *déclassé*, he none the less looked down on the canon who, so he assured Letizia, was a Buonaparte only through the female line.[5]

Yet whatever their shortcomings they were the Corsican Bonaparte's one link with the authentic European aristocracy, and they were valued as such. According to Letizia, Luciano several times visited the canon Filippo. In April 1778 Carlo did likewise and received a courteous letter from him, dated the 22nd of the month, together with some documents concerning his patrician origins. Carlo must have gone to Italy to seek further evidence of his affiliation with the Tuscan Buonaparte that might stand him in good stead in his coming visit to Versailles. This is presumably the journey Joseph refers to in his *Mémoires*, without affixing a date, but asserting, like Napoleon, that his father was received by the grand-duke.[6] It is safe to say that he was

not. Had he achieved so spectacular a social triumph we would expect
to find an echo of it in his memoirs, or in Letizia's; but neither of them
has a word to say on the subject.

How did Joseph and Napoleon get hold of the story? Did they
really believe it? What is surprising is that they went out of their way
to repeat it after Napoleon had become ruler of France. The store the
Bonaparte set by their possible Tuscan connection gives the measure
of their original social insecurity. Carlo never lost sight of it; Joseph,
after his father's death, though snubbed by the canon, pursued the
matter as one obsessed.[7] Letizia's contempt for the surviving Buonaparte of San Miniato was no doubt her way of getting even with a
family who in her youth had made her feel small. More astonishingly,
Napoleon, while pouring scorn on the 'musty old records of Florence'
where his ambassador Clarke endeavoured to trace his ancestry, could
not resist boasting of his father's princely frequentations. He also,
more truthfully, related how he himself had visited the canon Filippo
at the head of the army of Italy, and how the old man had given him
and his staff a magnificent reception with enough food and wine to
win the hearts of the anti-clerical officers. The canon then entreated
Napoleon to procure the canonization of an ancestor, Bonaventura
Bonaparte, a Capuchin monk of seventeenth-century Bologna. But
Napoleon was shrewd enough to steer clear of such family exhibi-
tionism and palm off his host with a decoration: the Order of San
Stefano (which Joseph had failed to obtain for himself in his student
days).[8]

It is a pity that neither Napoleon nor Joseph has left any more
trustworthy account of their journey to Autun, or any recollections of
their first view of the country that was to be the theatre of their lives.
One would like to know what they thought of Marseilles, where they
may well have spent Christmas, how they reacted to that scene of
strident activity which even today, when one arrives there from Corsica, makes one feel one has landed on another planet. Dazed and
stunned by the noise, the crowds, they must surely have enjoyed the
next lap of their journey, the new experience of rolling by coach along
straight, almost flat roads towards Autun, in southern Burgundy,
through a tamed landscape of vineyards and cultivated fields. Or did
they travel by water coach, then the cheapest conveyance, up the
stately reaches of the Rhône and Saône, with glimpses of castles on
their wooded shores?

They reached their destination on New Year's Day; Napoleon

notes the date in an early personal manuscript.[9] Autun is one of the
beautiful, historic French towns; not, perhaps, among the most
spectacular, but a place where discerning sightseers linger and reflect
that France has been civilized for some two thousand years. Its original name, Augustodunum, derives from the emperor who founded
it as a provincial capital in Roman Gaul; from the time of Tiberius
it was famed for its schools of learning, and it was also a centre of
gladiatorial training. The Romans have left a theatre and a couple
of handsome two-tiered gateways, still in use; towered ramparts en-
close the city and a medieval cathedral points skywards with a Gothic
spire.

The young Corsicans can hardly have seen much of these monuments
on their arrival; but no doubt they were impressed, and perhaps intimi-
dated, when they passed through the splendid wrought-iron gateway
into the courtyard of the austere eighteenth-century building that was
their school. Founded in 1341 by the cardinal Bertrand d'Annonay, it
was one of the highly considered colleges of the kingdom, the 'French
Eton', to borrow Vincent Cronin's words. The expulsion in 1764 of
the Jesuits, who had erected the existing edifice in the early years of
the century, had however somewhat lowered its prestige; when the
Bonaparte boys arrived there only thirty boarders occupied the huge
establishment, then run by Oratorian priests.[10]

We can be sure the Corsicans were received as privileged people, for
they came as protégés of Marbeuf's very influential nephew, the bishop
of Autun, who had promised to further the ecclesiastical careers of
Joseph and Aurele Varese. His protection, it is true, amounted to little
in the long run: Joseph refused to enter the Church, even though he
had been promised an appointment of *sous-diacre* with emoluments
amounting to 3,000 livres a year. As for Aurele Varese, after receiving
eminent appointments in the diocese (to his own astonishment, as the
abbé Chardon, one of the college professors, observed), he took advantage of the Revolution to marry and become, like Joseph Fesch,
commissioner of supplies to the army, an enviable and lucrative role.
He reappears in the context of Corsica in 1793 as author of an in-
flammatory anti-Paolist manifesto addressed to the Convention on
behalf of a patriotic club in Bastia. All the same, in 1779 the favour of
a bishop counted for much, particularly of one like Marbeuf who
controlled the allocation of ecclesiastical benefices. In fact he was more
often at court than in his diocese; one, incidentally, notoriously
occupied by worldly prelates (his successor was Talleyrand). When

Carlo arrived Marbeuf was actually at Versailles. Carlo was however equal to the situation. As deputy for the Corsican nobility on his way to court he appeared as a person of some importance in his own right, and he had the looks and manner that in the eighteenth century commanded respect: he was 'a superb man', the same college professor remarks.[11]

The journey was a turning-point for Carlo, no less than for his sons and Aurele Varese. It crowned a decade of relentless effort to scale the French social ladder; his mission was at once a victory and a test. If he gave good account of himself, defending Marbeuf's interests while at the same time making a favourable impression on the king's ministers, a crucial step in his career would be achieved. He could look forward to a new life; one perhaps no less wearing than the old, but lived on another level, sustained by a rising reputation as courtier-politician. Rewards might come his way: concessions of crown lands in Corsica where he could make profitable crops and plantations grow; a new official appointment, perhaps, a pension even and – why not? a title of count, viscount, marquis: all this must have seemed possible. The government was dealing generous handouts in Corsica to favourites of the regime, French and Corsican alike. Matteo Buttafoco, arch-collaborator in the conquest, had received the profitable fishing rights in the Étang de Biguglia as well as some rich surrounding land, not to mention the rank of colonel and a regiment bearing his name; two years later he was to be created count. Giuseppe Maria Casabianca, another military collaborator, had recently been granted a tract of land on the fertile east coast near Aleria with the title of viscount, while Georges Stephanopoli, leader of the family supposedly descended from the emperors of Byzantium and Trebizond which later claimed relationship with the Bonaparte, received some desirable land known as La Confina in the bay of Ajaccio in recognition of his aid in settling his fellow Greeks in Cargese. This did not prevent Marbeuf being simultaneously invested with a vast domain in Cargese that carried the title of marquis.

If these gains and dignities could be justified by services to the state, others seem to have depended as much on catching the eye and ear of persons in authority. Pietro Paolo Colonna de Cesari Rocca, beneficiary of a lease on a much-coveted area of crown land near Porto Vecchio, would seem to have had no better qualifications than Carlo: if his family was more illustrious his achievement was less. Captain in the Régiment Provincial Corse, like Carlo he was twice elected to represent the nobility of his province in the Corsican Estates. He was however never chosen as deputy to the court. From the time of his first election, in 1773, he was striving and scheming for a ninety-nine-year lease on crown land accompanied by a marquisate; but after a purposeful visit to Paris in 1785 he had to make do without the marquisate but with a lease for twenty-five years. Meanwhile, like Carlo, he had shaken down a government contract for exploiting a mulberry plantation, which, like Carlo's, proved unsatisfactory and was annulled five years later. His manoeuvres for the lease were apparently seconded by the de Roux, father and son, who were angling for concessions of land for themselves with a marquisate thrown in. Neither had any claim on royal bounty. The comte Roux de Laric, an obscure Provençal gentleman with a propensity to intrigue, based his petitions on a vague memory of an ancestor who had held property in Corsica in the Middle Ages. His son, Alexandre-Louis-Gabriel, author of scornful letters on Corsica and the Corsicans (the Bonaparte included) had taken no part in the conquest and was then an unpaid officer on Marbeuf's staff with no apparent activities beyond ingratiating himself with his superiors.[12]

If Carlo entertained dreams of lands and titles he could be excused. In the meantime he had the satisfaction of knowing that his children would be educated in keeping with an improving status. And not only the boys: Carlo nourished a plan, which he may or may not have put in hand during this journey, to obtain a scholarship for his daughter Maria Anna (the future Elisa) at Saint-Cyr, the elegant boarding-school founded by Madame de Maintenon.[13] His immediate task was however to secure Napoleon's scholarship in a military college.

Equipped with appropriate documents, buoyed up by promises and still more by ambition, but no doubt more than a little anxious, he set out from Autun to Paris, where he would join his co-deputies. The bishop, Santini, had won his election over the head of Doria, bishop of Ajaccio, because Doria's Genoese origin made him unpopular even though he had been born in Corsica. The most recently consecrated of the five Corsican bishops, presiding over the poorest of the dioceses, Santini returned home, according to an official document, 'sunk in debt', having been even more embarrassed by the expenses of the expedition than Carlo. De Roux refers to him as a windbag: *cabot*.[14] The other deputy, Paolo Casabianca, representing the Third Estate, came from a recently ennobled family of flamboyant military

notables who had fought for both French and Corsicans and eventually lent a dozen distinguished generals to the eighteenth-century
wars.[15] According to the chronicler Rossi, it was he, with his
'proud character', who had most difficulty in living down to the
submissive role prescribed by Marbeuf. All three were Marbeuf's
men and had been briefed by him before leaving Corsica: they were
not to deviate an iota from the *cahier* drawn up by the Estates, and
they were to present it 'with all possible modesty'. Rossi reports that
they played their parts so well – the naturally arrogant Casabianca
taking his cue from the two others – that the French believed they
had 'begun to tame the Corsicans' thanks to the punishments inflicted on Petriconi and de Guernes. Carlo, surprisingly, is described
as a model of discretion, who never gave himself airs: life, and his
own ambition had taught him a lot since he had first tried his luck
in Rome fifteen years before.

But there was more than this to the mission, at any rate for Carlo.
Besides putting on a show of subservience he had to defend Marbeuf
against his critics, the still-active *'narbonisti'*. Napoleon went so far as
to say that he obtained the recall of Narbonne, who in consequence
became 'a mortal enemy' of the Bonaparte and passed on the feud to
his daughter, Madame de Chevreuse, who bore Napoleon a personal
grudge for her father's dismissal. The story has gone unchallenged.
Yet one may wonder how a petty provincial magistrate managed to
disgrace the noble hero of the Seven Years' War. Nor did he. Narbonne,
it is on record, had left Corsica, willingly and by no means disgraced,
at the end of May or beginning of June 1775. Napoleon was merely
adding another touch to a family legend in which all the colours are
heightened, his father being invariably described as more powerful
and important, as well as more flighty and frivolous, than he really
was. Carlo's role in the capital was in fact inconspicuous but astute.
De Roux dismissed him as 'a base and servile spy' of Marbeuf, a
judgement that seems hypocritical from one who prided himself on his
assiduous sucking up to Marbeuf while remaining at heart among the
'narbonisti'. It would be fairer to describe Carlo as diplomat and observer. As such he made himself very useful to his protector. Manoeuvring
tactfully in ministerial circles, according to Rossi he was constantly
advised by the bishop of Autun and sent daily reports to Marbeuf.
We can only regret that this correspondence has never come to
light.[16]

We can however form some idea of how Carlo spent his time from the records of other Corsican missions to Versailles, in particular the colourful account of that of the Estates of 1785 by the bishop Santini, again representing the clergy. Written with a naïve concentration on detail, it conveys at once how marvellous was the experience and how exacting and costly. The administrative machine being even slower in the Ancien Régime than it is today, this deputation took over four months to get through its business; Carlo's took more than three. The deputies lodged in Versailles, then a miniature international city of princes known as 'the inn of Europe' where the innkeepers charged prices considered extortionate: up to 20 livres a day. Their first task was to obtain audiences with the ministers in charge of Corsican affairs: the minister of war and the all-powerful *contrôleur général* or minister of finance, besides the marquis de Monteynard, a minister of war soon after the conquest of Corsica, who had made himself so respected that the Corsicans, in their extreme need of a protector, had obtained for him the life appointment of governor-general. The audience with the King took place towards the end of their stay.

Monteynard lived in Paris, which meant travelling by hired coach to and from Versailles. Each official interview was enacted with the precision of a ballet, according to a meticulous etiquette, a language quite as significant as the stilted phrases exchanged. Primed in the ritual gestures, the Corsicans also had to scrutinize the reciprocal motions of their hosts. Whether one or both panels of the folding doors were opened for them, whether a minister stepped forward to welcome them or accompanied them back to the door when leaving, enabled them to gauge the impression they were making and their chances of success. Everywhere ushers, guards and gentlemen-in-waiting hovered to levy a toll for the services they could provide those seeking to approach their superiors. The Swiss guard in the royal ante-chamber extorted 48 livres for noting each name to be mentioned in the *Gazette de France*.

The presentation to the King was the culminating event, after the main business had been dealt with in the offices of the ministers. Elaborate preparations were involved. The deputies had to request the grand master of ceremonies to escort them (the occasion, no doubt, for a handsome tip), they had to order special coaches to take them to the palace entrance and sedan chairs to carry them about within its precincts. Each wore a prescribed dress: the bishop a purple robe, the deputy for the nobility a coloured costume, with a sword, while the representative of the Third Estate was dressed in black. Court dress for a noble might cost as much as 240 livres, with another 100 livres for the lace trimmings considered indispensable in such situations. One may be sure that Carlo, by all accounts a connoisseur of clothes, spared no expense in turning himself out well for the occasion.

Having proceeded to the hall of the ambassadors in their sedan chairs, the deputies, conducted by the master of ceremonies, entered the room where the King was seated, surrounded by his courtiers. Monteynard was there to introduce the Corsicans. They made a deep bow to their sovereign, took two steps forward and made another, then advanced two more steps and bowed yet again, and each time they bowed the King lifted his hat. Then came the moment for the bishop to deliver his speech, standing between his co-deputies, the representative of the Third Estate kneeling on one knee with the *cahier* in his hand. At the end of the speech he handed it to the bishop, who handed it to the monarch, who passed it on to Monteynard after addressing a few words to the bishop. Its contents had already been discussed in the less glamorous company of the acute, unobtrusive secretaries and clerks of the ministries. Representing the nobility, Carlo played only a passive role in the ceremony; but surely one he for ever remembered with pride.

This was not the end of the royal receptions. In the Ancien Régime a purely administrative operation like the presentation of a provincial *cahier* could assume a social and even personal character. After their audience with the sovereign the members of the 1785 deputation made a round of ceremonial visits to the Queen and all the near relatives of the royal family; had Carlo really been armed with a letter to Marie-Antoinette it would have been an asset beyond price. Yet even without it the experience of Versailles must have been one of those that wash away the pains of a lifetime. Here he touched the summit of the civilized world, entered the magic circle reserved to the élite of Europe; no environment more opulent or privileged was then known or imagined. Whether or not Carlo really cared for art, he had the Corsican love of the spectacular, and he cannot have been otherwise than deeply stirred by the prodigal displays of paintings and marble statuary in which grandiose mythological figures vied with the crowds of living courtiers, and by the suites of silver furniture and the silver chandeliers and candelabra where flickered so many candles that the whole palace seemed to be on fire. Here, for some unreal hours, Carlo lived as a noble among authentic nobles, men who felt themselves to

be so different from the rest of humanity as to belong to another
species. Surely he dreamed of winning a foothold for himself in that
glittering structure of power. What never occurred to him was that his
second son would rule over it, a monarch for a time more powerful
than the one he had bowed to, married to the niece of that monarch's
queen.[17]

This son took up much of Carlo's time during his stay in the capital.
Historians have assumed he stopped there longer than necessary,
indulging in extravagant pleasures; but in fact he cannot have stretched
his visit much beyond his obligations, if at all. The deputies were not
summoned to the royal presence till 10 March, and that may not have
been the last of their duties. Carlo, we know, was still busy with
Napoleon's affairs on the 28th, and later. He left Paris shortly before
the 25th of the following month. Meanwhile he had other family
business to attend to. Perhaps, as Joseph mentions, he took the preliminary steps to secure Elisa's scholarship at Saint-Cyr. True, she was
only two years old, but competition must have been fierce for the
places – two or three only – reserved for Corsican girls at this courtly
boarding-school. He certainly submitted his application for the Odone
heritage to the prince de Montbarey, who looked on it favourably, so
one learns. And he surely tackled the minister of finance in the hope of
squeezing out further subsidies for draining the exasperating Salines.

All this left little time for amusement; yet it would have been un-
natural had Carlo and his colleagues allowed themselves none at all.
We can judge of the attractive possibilities by the account of the 1785
mission, led by the same Bishop Santini, which shows the deputies
enjoying a spate of sightseeing expeditions and parties, a regular
Corsican spree. They began by collecting a suite of twenty-four friends,
mostly Corsicans living in Paris, who accompanied them, a band of
partisans, wherever they went, even, it seems, to their audience with
the King. 'Many ladies of their acquaintance' joined them after the
court ceremonies, and together they toured the gardens of Versailles,
where they arranged with the director of the royal buildings for the
fountains to be played; a delight to be had for a fee. Scattered about
the vast grounds, often hidden in groves of vegetation, the intricately
designed fountains consumed so much water that they were normally
only turned on when the King passed by. The jets then numbered
fifteen hundred, reduced to a mere overwhelming three hundred today.
This privileged vision was given to the Corsicans before they glided
along the canal to look at the two Trianon palaces in real gondolas, an

exotic amenity introduced by a present from the Venetian Republic a century before. Another day was spent at the royal menagerie, and yet another at Marly, with the royal fountains turned on for them once again. They wound up with a trip to Saint-Germain, where they saw the palace, after which a Corsican lady entertained them all to a splendid meal.

One may suppose that Santini, moving spirit in these outings, had learnt his way round on his previous visit in the company of Carlo and Casabianca. But did Carlo, the 'man of pleasure' who was 'inclined to like women' go in for less innocent distractions, as well as the opera and theatre and card-playing? Did he, as a biographer suggests, gamble away some of his money, in a place where gambling was a passion and plague, not only in the palace but in the adjoining town? Fortunes were nightly lost and won in Versailles, and Carlo, like many Corsicans an addicted player, no doubt counted on winning: gambling was something the ambitious provincial lawyer had in common with the reckless spendthrift courtiers, linked with them by a shared insecurity. But Carlo also, undoubtedly, laid out considerable sums for his personal advancement, and that of his family: his main gamble was not at the card-tables but in life.[18]

The news essential to his immediate project reached him in Versailles: a letter from the office of the *intendant* of Corsica, informing him that the prince de Montbarey, minister of war, had accepted Napoleon as a king's scholar in a military college, without specifying which. He was instructed to send proof of his nobility at once to the minister, who would forward the documents for verification to one of the royal heraldists, d'Hozier de Serigny.[19] Carlo had come well prepared; he had put in some hard work on his genealogy since presenting the makeshift one of 1771. The dubious, probably fraudulent acts of 1536 and 1554 concerning Geronimo Bonaparte are replaced by others, later in date, more credible, and which correspond with facts ascertainable from other sources; two genuine, earlier ancestors are introduced: Gabriel, Geronimo's father, and François, father of Gabriel, who is none other than Francesco '*il Mauro di Sarzana*'. The supposed Tuscan connection is underlined: the recognition of kinship given by the Tuscan Buonaparte in 1759 being presented alongside the patent whereby the archbishop of Pisa had granted Carlo the title of patrician ten years later. There is one document, however, which whether genuine or not, might have brought Carlo's ambitions crashing: a permit to marry Letizia from the bishop of Ajaccio delivered on 2 June 1764. Why did Carlo send it instead of a copy of his certificate of marriage? And why is it dated 2 June whereas the marriage act is dated 1 June? Had he perhaps not yet inserted the act, which is written in his own hand? Or was there perhaps no one he could trust in Ajaccio to copy and authenticate an act that was obviously a fraud? Was the bishop's permit faked as well? We cannot judge of this because the documents he submitted to d'Hozier have not come down to us, only a list of them.[20]

We do however know the impression they made on the royal heraldist from the questionnaire he addressed to Carlo on 8 March, two days before his presentation to the king. Luckily it never occurred to d'Hozier de Serigny to question Carlo's marriage. What worried him were the foreign names. Was Buonaparte or Bonaparte the correct spelling? Carlo plumped for Buonaparte in his reply. What was Letizia's family name and how should it be translated into French? That, Carlo answered, was hardly possible. Napoleone, surely, was an Italian name; what was the French equivalent? Again Carlo had no answer. As for the Bonaparte's arms, d'Hozier could make nothing of Carlo's description; he must send a painting immediately.[21]

This Carlo supplied, in exact conformity with his description. But he seems to have been indulging in some fashionable fancies. The escutcheon he presents is embellished with the letters B and P on either side, and an elegant rococo frame surmounted by a crown. These decorative features were in keeping with contemporary taste, but they do not appear in any previous representation of the Bonaparte's arms. They are notably absent from the austere stone-carved escutcheon on the facade of the *casa* Bonaparte. Presumably Carlo thought it unlikely that d'Hozier would ever compare the two. And he was no doubt guilty of another inaccuracy when he maintained to d'Hozier that it had been there 'since time immemorial', seeing that the Bonaparte had acquired the house only at the beginning of the century. It has even been suggested that they had adopted the coat of arms quite recently, when they obtained recognition of kinship with the Tuscan Buonaparte in 1759. Perhaps. Yet neither the arms presented by Carlo, nor those on the family home are identical with those known to have been carried by the Tuscan branches of the family. An escutcheon once to be seen on a tombstone in the cloisters of the church of Santo Spirito in Florence is crossed by two bands diagonally from top right to bottom left of the escutcheon, as is that on the memorial to Jacopo Buonaparte in the cathedral of San Miniato, whereas the escutcheon presented by Carlo, as well as that on the *casa* Bonaparte, is crossed by two bars from top left to bottom right. The Bonaparte may of course have copied another model, but this design has not been reported outside Corsica. Carlo assured d'Hozier that a representation of the Bonaparte's arms appeared in the palace of 'the ancient *podestà*s of Florence' – the Bargello – but here again he was inaccurate; the Bonaparte's arms are not to be found there. The subject is in no way elucidated by a conversation between Napoleon and Antommarchi about a house of the Bonaparte – 'a monument, a curiosity no one can ignore' – standing in the centre of Florence with the family arms 'perfectly intact' carved on its facade in stone. The house, if it ever existed, has disappeared with the rebuilding of the city centre in the last century.²²

Carlo sent his answers to d'Hozier, with a painting of his arms and a covering note on 15 March from his lodging in the rue Saint-Médéric in Versailles. In fact the whole procedure was no more than a formality, for we learn from Carlo's letter that d'Hozier had already sent Napoleon's certificate of nobility to the minister of war, for which Carlo thanked him with '*un million de grâces*'. Why he was favoured in this way we can only surmise. Was his connection with the two Marbeufs sufficient to ensure him exceptional treatment? Or did he have to spend money to hurry d'Hozier along? The fee for the certificate – 100–200 livres, was paid by the Crown through the École Royale Militaire in Paris; but it was the custom for anxious applicants to give presents to royal heraldists, especially when the future of a son was at stake. Though d'Hozier is said to have been above taking bribes, he was notoriously partial to gifts of luxury foods, and these Carlo would surely not have spared. The hoped-for result was not long in coming: on 28 March the minister of war informed him that Napoleon had been accepted at the military college of Brienne-le-Château in Champagne.

Carlo had by then moved to Paris, to the Hôtel de Hambourg, rue Jacob, no doubt for economy. Following the minister's instructions he had to make immediate arrangements for Napoleon to enter the school, equipped with the regulation trousseau.²³ This was as elaborate and no doubt as costly as in any upper-class boarding-school. The uniform seems to have been attractive: according to the specification of 1776 (when the college opened) it was in blue cloth with red facings and red breeches and jacket. Another specification – perhaps adopted later – mentions a blue cloth overcoat with a blue lining, a blue '*habit*' with a

'Jesuits' collar' and white buttons inscribed with the school's arms, a black 'jacket' lined with white, and black breeches. Carlo, who set such store by clothes, had the satisfaction of knowing that his son would be dressed in keeping with his rank. Hygiene was also a matter of concern at Brienne: pupils changed their linen twice a week and so had to bring stated numbers of shirts and collars, handkerchiefs, stockings and nightcaps, besides several pairs of shoes. Other requirements were sheets, a silver spoon and fork, a goblet and napkins. Parents had also to deposit a sum of 25 livres towards the cost of books and salaries to servants. These expenses, it is true, were not repeated; the college thereafter bore the cost of renewing uniform and books. All the same, the initial outlay must have been considerable, for clothes were expensive in eighteenth-century France. The four complete suits Carlo had to buy for Joseph at Autun cost 284 livres, and there is no reason to think that Napoleon's were any cheaper.[24]

While Carlo was straining all his assets to turn Napoleon into a conventional French nobleman, Napoleon was developing contrary tendencies: the immediate result of his French education was to increase his awareness of being Corsican. Joseph, we are told, took pains to disarm the foreigners by his cheerful, considerate ways, and though naturally lazy, learnt French in record time so as to endear himself to his master. Napoleon, so we learn from the same master, also learnt French very rapidly, but had already assumed the aloof, sombre manner that marked him all through his schooldays. A fellow-pupil, Jean-Baptiste de Grandchamp, as an old man drew the same picture of the two boys: Joseph, his special friend, was gentle and affectionate, Napoleon taciturn, distant (*rêveur*), irascible. Born of pride and the consciousness of being different, his attitude only excited the cruelty of the little French boys who, so his master recalls, missed no opportunity of taunting him with his origins. If Corsica had been conquered it was because the Corsicans were cowards, they declared as they sat round the classroom stove. To which Napoleon retorted that if they had been fighting one to four they would never have been defeated; but they were fighting one against ten. 'But you had a good general in Paoli,' the master soothingly interposed. 'Yes sir, and I should very much like to resemble him,' answered this strangely solemn child.

The anecdote, if true, is very interesting in showing the early age at which Napoleon began to plan his future. Not, of course, the future that really happened, but the one he imagined and tried, unsuccessfully, to bring true up to the age of twenty-three. The shock of being transplanted to France must have crystallized diffuse emotions generated by family fireside talk: tales of the Father of the Nation and the patriots' heroic resistance, aided by the gallant deeds of the Bonaparte and their relations. Now he had set his course, dedicated himself to following the example of Paoli, just as Letizia dreamed he would when she carried him in her womb. The decision, once taken, gathered strength, became his comfort and inspiration in an alien environment. It also directed and derailed the first years of his adult life, led him into unsuccessful Corsican ventures until in 1793 he and his family were hounded out of the beloved ill-starred island by the partisans of Paoli, who had become their political opponent. But until then Paoli was his idol, a father-figure who supplanted his natural father even while Carlo was still alive. His attitude to his father was in consequence uneasy, ambivalent, as became increasingly evident at Brienne. Champion of liberty, right-hand man to Paoli, Carlo had betrayed the national cause. Napoleon perhaps felt shame for him as one of those Corsicans who, so he wrote in a youthful outpouring, 'laden with chains, tremblingly kiss the hand that oppresses them', and feeling shame for his father logically should have felt shame for himself in accepting what his father provided. But this was nothing less than an education that influenced him so profoundly that he could say: 'In my mind, Brienne is my native country,' and 'I am more Champenois than Corsican.' Carlo, doing his level best for his son, burdened him with mental conflicts that could only be resolved after years of painful struggle.[25]

As a conscientious father, Carlo travelled from Paris to Brienne to supervise his son's entry to his new school; the date of a letter he wrote shows he was there on 25 April 1779. Napoleon left Autun on the 20th or 21st; the accounts' register notes that he had been at the school three months and twenty days. The parting was dramatic for the little brothers, who until then had been able to take refuge in an affectionate intimacy dating from their earliest years. Now each would be isolated among foreigners and strangers. Joseph never forgot the day; he wept copiously, so he later admitted, while Napoleon, stoical, shed only a single tear which he tried to hide. Abbé Simon, the perceptive under-principal, observed to Joseph that this single tear was as much a proof of his grief as Joseph's floods. Certainly it was Napoleon who had the most to suffer, because he was the one who less easily made friends.

Napoleon's journey to Brienne has been the subject of detailed research such as is often lacking for more significant episodes of his early life. According to the Abbé Chardon, and Napoleon himself, he was put in charge of a Monsieur de Champeaux who was taking his own son to Brienne; 'he treated me as his son', Napoleon recalled. They reached Brienne, states Chardon, on 25 April, where they found Carlo Bonaparte who had been there several days. A tradition in the Champeaux family maintains that Napoleon spent a few days on the way at their home at Thoisy-le-Désert. The house still stands, a charming small manor with a pentagonal tower overlooking the lush green countryside ('le Désert' was added to the name after the region was temporarily abandoned in a medieval plague).

So far so good: this version of the story agrees with established dates. But in his youthful manuscript, 'Époques de ma vie', Napoleon states that he left for Brienne (he does not say where from) on 12 May. Frédéric Masson, conscientious biographer of his youth, offers an explanation; M. de Champeaux was not taking a son to Brienne; he never had a son there, so Masson has ascertained. The bishop Marbeuf dispatched his *grand-vicaire* to accompany Napoleon, the abbé Hemey, known as Hemey d'Auberive, a writer on religious subjects who also had an interest in the occult sciences. If this evidence is to be trusted Napoleon must have spent some three weeks with the Champeaux before being entrusted to the literary, somewhat eccentric priest for the journey to Brienne.[26]

Carlo, then, must have missed seeing his son, for he was back in Corsica in time for the opening of the Estates on 25 May. He attended the assembly in a double capacity: as member of the deputation to court, which was to render an account of its mission, and also as the substitute for Giacomo Pietro Abbatucci, member for the nobility for the province of Ajaccio, who had just been thrown into a 'rat-infested dungeon' on the charge of suborning witnesses in a murder trial. His indictment cast a cloud over the Estates, particularly when this distinguished officer of the Régiment Provincial Corse (formerly an opponent, then partisan of Paoli) was condemned to the ruthless sentence of branding and nine years in the galleys.[27]

Meanwhile Carlo was riding the crest of a wave. He had further cause for satisfaction when on 22 June Joseph Fesch was elected by the Estates to a scholarship at the seminary of Aix-en-Provence. The king had granted twenty scholarships there to young Corsicans; on this occasion the Estates proceeded to elect ten from lists of four presented by each of the five bishops, two from each. Joseph was elected for the diocese of Ajaccio with thirty-one votes, just behind an Ornano with thirty-two.

The choice, it was stipulated, had to be approved by the *commissaires du roi*, Boucheporn and Marbeuf. Of course Marbeuf had ensured Joseph's success. This is made abundantly clear in an unpublished letter from the collection of the Prince Napoleon which Letizia wrote jointly to her mother and half-brother. 'Dear brother . . . Study if you hope to win any advantage. He who fails to study gains nothing. I hope that the inspector has given some information about our family, or simply written that '*il signor conte*' [Marbeuf] will do something for us' (she evidently refers to some preliminary official investigation). The letter is undated; Carlo was still away: 'I have no news from France,' she writes. But where was Letizia? Apparently with Marbeuf. 'Don't sell our wine,' she begs her mother, 'which *il signor conte* wants to take to Cargese, if it keeps well, as I hope.' She ends the letter by sending her mother Marbeuf's compliments.[28]

What had happened to Letizia since Carlo left her, the guest of Marbeuf in his palatial residence in Bastia on 15 December of the previous year? Another undated letter to her mother, again from the collection of the Prince Napoleon, was written in March: 'I have heard from Carlo who was presented to the king on the 10th of this month, and I think he will leave Paris after Easter.' It was not yet known, she adds, if the 'gratification' was obtained (the royal grant to the deputies which was in fact accorded the following month). The letter runs on with news from Carlo about her sons. Their master was so pleased with them that he frequently wrote about them to the general's nephew in Paris (Marbeuf's nephew, bishop of Autun); he (the master) would be sorry to see Napoleon leave. She then speaks of a personal grief (a death, it seems) and, predictably, of clothes. She has made herself a smart black silk dress (for mourning?), but with difficulty, because she was short of money. But where was she, one may ask? With Marbeuf? In Bastia? Cargese? And on what terms? The disarmingly homely letters give no clue, except that if she really were Marbeuf's mistress he would hardly have left her without the means of paying for a black silk dress. But was Letizia prepared to face public scandal to further her husband's career and the education of her half-brother and sons, and yet too proud to beg a small sum for herself from their benefactor? It seems not impossible.

Unfortunately Marbeuf has left no self-incriminating journal such as reveals, for certain, that Boswell seduced Thérèse Le Vasseur on his way home from Corsica to England. Apart from Letizia's two letters we have only one item of evidence on her behaviour in Carlo's absence: a letter the ill-natured Ristori sent to de Pradine on 17 August from Bastia. This last fact needs to be underlined because he describes events that had taken place in Ajaccio and that he can only have learnt by long-distance gossip. Madame Bonaparte, he writes, went for a walk with Marbeuf near the Chapelle des Grecs (a mile or so along the flowering coastline to the west of the town), and there she was delivered of a stillborn male child. Marbeuf, 'in the greatest anger', hailed a passing peasant and sent him to fetch a chair to carry Letizia home with the little dead boy. The accident, Ristori declares, brought her close to death, but she was recovering. The story, of which no echo is found elsewhere, smells of calumny. Yet supposing it to be true, how can one tell that Carlo was not the father, Carlo who had left Corsica only seven months before? Is Marbeuf's reported anger proof of his paternity? Hardly. Perhaps this was one of the two stillborn children Letizia mentions in her 'Souvenirs'. No trace of the child appears in the parish register because it records not every birth, but only those of the children who survived to be baptized.

All one can say is that the five months of Carlo's absence were the period when Letizia was exposed to the greatest temptation. Yet is temptation the proper word to use in this context? Carlo was aware of Marbeuf's adoration of his wife, was proud of it and encouraged their meetings; one can hardly suppose him unable to foresee the possible consequences. That Marbeuf was more than twice her age can only have acted on him as an incitement. Letizia may have found herself in a position in which refusal was virtually impossible.

One otherwise unconvincing writer makes a point when he argues that Marbeuf must have made love to her because her company would have bored him: 'her profound silences usually covered a fundamental ignorance'. It is true that no one has ever described Letizia's company as cultured or amusing, and that to judge by her letters her mind ran almost exclusively on her family, domestic topics, money and clothes. But was not this plain style in itself an attraction to an ageing man who had known too many women of wit?

Letizia's supporters have insisted on her rigid Corsican and Catholic morality; yet there is little to support this view. Far from being a benighted, sombre peasant woman whose infidelity could provoke a vendetta and a chain of murders, she was the elegant young wife of an

ambitious public man manoeuvring in the sophisticated French society
of the garrison towns. Renaud de la Greslaie, a French inspector of
forests who arrived in Corsica in 1776, draws a strong contrast between
the primitive, hospitable, ferocious men of the interior and their
dutiful, overworked wives, and the Corsicans of the towns who took
only a few months to become Frenchified (*'francisé'*). All were lovers
of luxury, gambling and adornment. The women were haughty
(*'hautes'*) and demanding, but sensitive to the attentions paid to them.
In the upper strata of society they had entirely abandoned the characteristic Corsican dress, with the head veil (*mezzaro*), and appeared decked
and beplumed in the French style. This is how one may imagine
Letizia.

There is small evidence of her piety at this period of her life. With
an irreligious husband and an ecclesiastical uncle-in-law more interested in stock-breeding and litigation than Christianity, she may not
have paid much attention to the Church beyond going to mass on
Sundays and feast days; as she admits in her 'Souvenirs' she counted
on her mother-in-law to do the praying for the family the rest of the
time. It is true that she named her daughters after the Virgin; they all
had Marie attached to their names. But did she ensure them a religious
upbringing? There is no proof of this. It never occurred to her, for
instance, to give Elisa a religious wedding, and Napoleon had to insist
on it for the sake of appearances. Perhaps Letizia had not so much
minded the delay or absence of the ceremony for herself. How much
importance did she attach to sexual morality? Did she perhaps share
the realistic view surprisingly common among Mediterranean Catholic
women? She is never known to have objected to her daughters'
notoriously free living; and indeed Pauline, the ravishing nympho-
maniac, was her favourite because, in Napoleon's words 'she was the
prettiest and most charming'.

On the other hand Letizia never forgave Caroline for betraying
Napoleon in his time of defeat. Loyalty was paramount in her scale of
values. She never, it seems, encouraged any suitor after Carlo's death;
not even in times of acute poverty, when her beauty was almost her
only asset. It is impossible, I think, to envisage her 'deceiving' or
'betraying' her husband. Her loyalty to him was absolute even if, for a
time, she may have ventured on to that perilous ground, for a woman,
where loyalty and betrayal are synonymous.

One may think of Letizia as an austere heroine, resolutely resisting
the advances of the most powerful man in Corsica year after year

(about a dozen in all); but the accumulated evidence may suggest another tale. Extremely attracted to her at least since 1771, Marbeuf perhaps allowed her to hold him at arm's length so long as he remained attached to Madame Varese. But after 1776, when he discarded his ageing mistress, he devoted himself wholly, passionately to Letizia. Their love-affair, one may surmise, flared up at the period when Carlo was elected to the Estates, to the deputation to the court, while he was launching the development of the Salines and visiting the capital; a period, be it noted, when he had a great need of money. The two children born to Letizia at this time, Louis in 1778, the stillborn boy the following year, may have been Marbeuf's sons. But would she, or Marbeuf, have been really sure of his paternity? It is hard to know how such matters were viewed in a pre-contraception age.[29]

At all events there are no signs of discord between Carlo and his wife. After the closure of the Estates of 1779 they were together again in Ajaccio, receiving family and friends on 4 September at the long-delayed christening of Lucien and Elisa in their home. They were in fact doubly celebrating, for the day before Luciano had been received as archdeacon at the cathedral of Ajaccio. Officiating at the baptism, and also acting as godfather to Lucien, he was able to sign himself in the register: *Lucianus archidiaconus de Bona Parte*. At the age of sixty-one he had not been forgotten in the handout that made this year memorable for the Bonaparte. A suitable favour had been granted to this irascible, unaccommodating old man, anti-French and, it seems, anti-religious: when on his deathbed thirteen years later Joseph Fesch, in surplice and stole, came to offer him the comforts of his faith, Luciano told him to clear out and leave him to die in peace.[30]

In January 1780 Letizia was pregnant once again. The child was Paola Maria, the loving and lovable Pauline whom no one has ever suspected of being Marbeuf's daughter. In fact she took after both her parents: pleasure-loving as Carlo and entertaining as he is said to have been; beautiful as Letizia and loyal in the same fundamental way; alone among the sisters she stood by Napoleon in his hour of defeat. She was born at half-past ten on the night of 20 October; a nurse (presumably a wet-nurse) entered the household that same day.[31]

By then the *casa* Bonaparte had lost any appearance of rusticity. Carlo, by his own account, had spent 896 francs improving it that year, as though its modest interior had become unbearable to him after the vision of Versailles. The decorations, luxurious in the context, were imported from Genoa – some being acquired with the aid of his friend

Lorenzo Giubega. A marble mantelpiece in his bedroom, which he did up entirely, may be the one carved with a graceful bas-relief of Cupid and Psyche that can be seen today. The crimson material that cost him 75 livres is reproduced in the present wall-coverings and in the damask upholstery of the Louis XV bed and cabriolet chairs which recall Napoleon's description of Letizia's bedroom. But it would be useless to look for any furniture of that period in a house twice emptied of its contents before it was restored in recent years. An inventory drawn up by Letizia in 1798 with a view to obtaining compensation for the looting of the house in 1793 gives some idea of its contents. Much of the furniture was in the sober provincial style one can still find in some of the old houses of Ajaccio and the homes of village notables: the walnut cupboards and *canapés* and the sets of cane-seated chairs. These were probably locally made, as were also, perhaps, the six walnut card-tables covered in green baize where the Bonaparte's guests gathered for the parties recalled by Colchen, the *intendant*'s secretary who was so struck by Letizia's beauty. But an air of foreign elegance must have been introduced with the marble chimneypieces (Letizia lists four) and the 'six large mirrors in crystal of France', not to mention the eighteen pairs of white muslin curtains, a refinement rare in Corsica then and later.[32]

Even more exceptional was the library of over a thousand volumes that gives proof of the extent of Carlo's culture. No catalogue has survived, and only two volumes, kept in the Fesch Museum in Ajaccio: the letters of Bernardo Tasso published in Venice in 1785, which Carlo must have bought just before he died, and a Latin treatise, *Descriptiones oratoriae*, which he acquired in 1761 when he was still a student with the Jesuits, perhaps as a prize. We also know from a letter of Napoleon's that he possessed a copy of Boswell's *Account of Corsica*, either in French or Italian.[33]

An inventory of his clothes in his 'Livre de Raison' suggests a costly and colourful wardrobe: suits in black silk and velvet, in satin, in blue material with braiding, in yellow, and a complete outfit in bronze-coloured cloth. We also know that he sometimes dressed up in a cerise jacket with puce breeches. He now habitually wore the powdered wig of the French aristocracy; payments to his wig-dresser are noted before important occasions: his departure to Bastia in May 1781 to attend the Estates (to which he had been elected for the third time); his visits to Marbeuf in Cargese. Of Letizia's wardrobe nothing is said in the 'Livre de Raison' except that he bought two pairs of shoes for himself

and one for her (a fact interpreted by historians as proof of her austerity). Yet as his wife and Marbeuf's reigning favourite she was surely
well turned-out when on 12 December 1780 they arrived at his splendid
mansion in Cargese, where they spent Christmas and the New Year,
staying on till the end of January. The visit was evidently a triumphant
success, to judge by the entry in Carlo's 'Livre de Raison' on New
Year's Day: '1 January 1781. I have given two cows to fatten to
Giovanni Greco, according to the custom of Ajaccio. He will keep
them in Cargese, marquisate of the comte de Marbeuf, benefactor of
our house, whose memory I hope will always be dear to my children
and their descendants.'[34]

The young couple had climbed to the summit of local society; or
rather seemed to have done so, for their means were unequal to appearances. Carlo, in his own words, had returned from Paris without a
penny—'senza un soldo'—having spent, again on his own admission,
9,400 livres since leaving home. He was never allowed to forget it; nor,
for that matter, have been the innumerable readers of biographies of his
son. The note Carlo unsuspectingly jotted into his commonplace book,
with humour, surely, rather than self-reproach, has been repeatedly
quoted against him while pages of meticulous entries are generally
ignored. The memoranda of payments to servants and labourers, the
lists of tools entrusted to workmen, the records of amounts of wine
stored, and sold, when and for how much and to whom, of debts to
members of his family and their repayment (Carlo scrupulously paid
back loans), all this surely tells us as much about his character as the
confession of his expenditure abroad. But Luciano had no use for
foreign travel and constantly declared that Carlo had ruined the family
by his journeys, and Napoleon repeated what he said, forgetting the
immense advantages those journeys had brought to him personally
and to his family. So Carlo went down to posterity: extravagant,
feckless, weak, vain, muddle-headed, irresolute, irresponsible (the
adjectives are lifted from history books), an altogether foolish and
worthless person.

To say that the whole family could have lived for at least a year on
what he had spent abroad in five months in 1779 is to forget that
almost three quarters of the money was given to him for precisely that
purpose. He had received an allowance of 'mille scudi' – 1,000 écus or
3,000 livres – from the Corsican Estates; another 4,000 were his share
of the royal bounty of 12,000 livres for the three deputies. It was given –
not very willingly – because they really needed it to accomplish their

1. Napoleon as First Consul. Portrait by L. Boilly, 1800

2. Carlo Bonaparte, handsome, shrewd and pleasure-loving. Contemporary portrait by
an unknown artist

3. Pasquale Paoli presented as an enlightened statesman. Lithograph by Doyen the younger, 1880, after an imaginary portrait by Masutti

4. A portrait that suggests the haunting quality of Letizia's beauty in her youth. Miniature by C. Bourgeois

5. Imaginary view of Napoleon and his brothers at play in front of the *casa* Bonaparte. The house is little changed today

6. Ajaccio, much as it was when Napoleon was a child

7. The room where Napoleon is said to have been born

8. Olive press on the ground floor of the Bonapartes' house, such as may have existed when they lived there

9. Supposed house of the Tusoli, cousins of the Bonaparte, in Poggiola, a hamlet of Bocognano. Now abandoned, it is dated 1666

10. Mountain landscape

11. The 'grotte des refugiés' where Carlo and Letizia are said to have sheltered when fleeing from the victorious French army

12. Valley of the Restonica, where Carlo and Letizia are said to have retreated with Paoli's partisans

13. House in the mountain village, Lozzi, where Letizia is said to have stayed on her way back to Ajaccio after the Corsican surrender. Built in 1735, it was less dour then than today

14. Letizia Bonaparte, idealized portrait. Anonymous alabaster statuette

15. Carlo Bonaparte, posthumous idealized portrait, marble bust, by J.-C. Marin

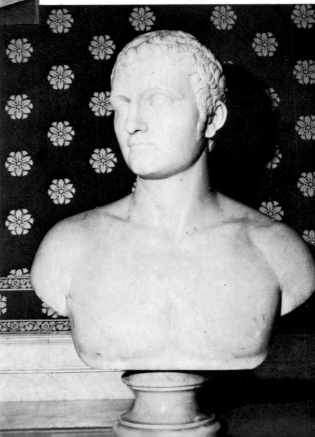

16. Anonymous portrait from memory of Napoleon as a
child. His bow and arrow are perhaps intended
as a symbol

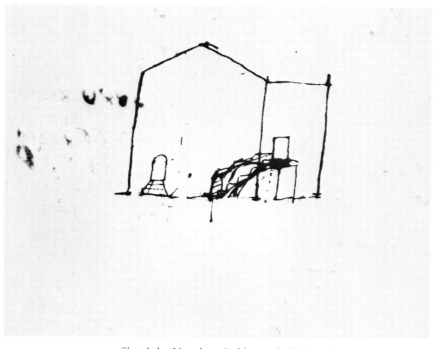

17. Sketch by Napoleon in his youth. Undated

né a 1769 le 15. du mois d'aoust
parti pour france le 15 Decembre 1778
arrivé a autun le 1 janvier 1779
partie pour brienne le 12 mai 1779
partie pour l'école de paris le 30 octobre 1784
partie pour le regiment de la fere en qualité d'
1iere ferrault en second le 30 octobre 1785
partie de valence pour semnes a ajaxio 1786,
je suis donc arrivé dans ma patrie 7 ans 9 mois après
mon depart agé de 17 ans 1 mois j'ai été
officier a l'age de 16 ans 15 jours.

arrivée le 15 septembre 1786 je su
suis parti le 12 sept 1787 pour paris d'ou
je suis reparti pour brise reste su
arrivé le 1 janvier 1788 d'ou je suis
parti le 1er juin pour auxonne

18. Note in the hand of Napoleon summarizing his life to 1788

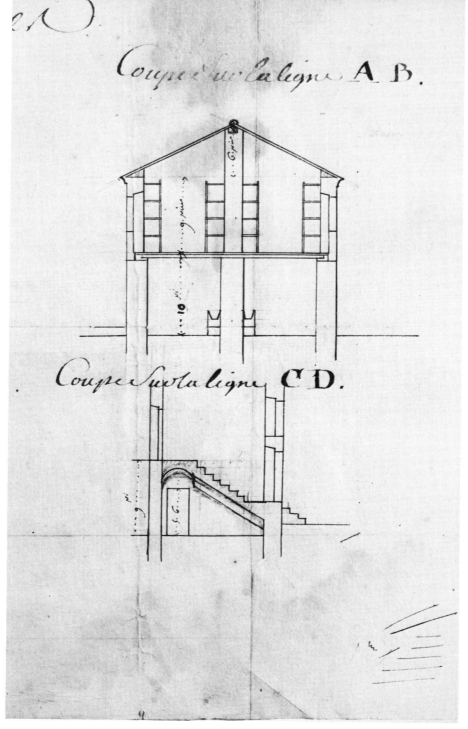

19. Plan by Carlo Bonaparte for a house to be built in the Salines

VUE DE CORTÉ, DEP^{mt} DE LA CORSE.

Dédié à Monsieur le Général Baron de Pommereul
Conseiller d'État, Directeur général de l'Imprimerie et de la Librairie

20. Corte, once the Corsican capital. View dedicated, *c.* 1811, to Baron Général de Pommereul, who took part in the French invasion

21. Battle of Ponte Novo, 8 May 1769, an imaginary view

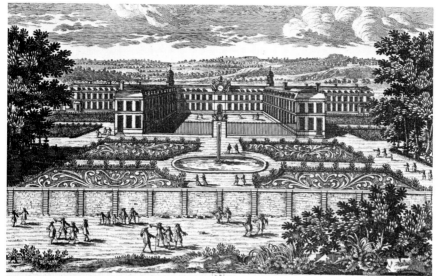

Veüe et perspectiue de la maison des Dames de St Cyr du côté du Jardin
Dessiné et Gravé par Aueline Auec Privilege du Roy

22. Saint-Cyr, the elegant boarding-school near Versailles where Elisa Bonaparte
spent eight years

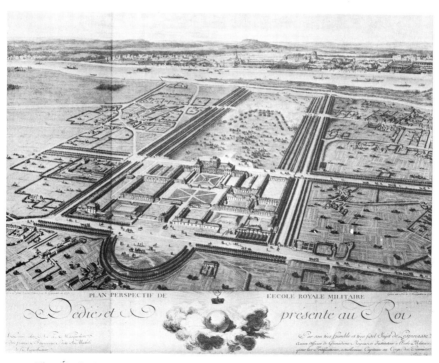

PLAN PERSPECTIF DE   L'ÉCOLE ROYALE MILITAIRE

Dedié et   presenté au Roi

23. The École Royale Militaire, Paris, magnificently designed by J.-A. Gabriel,
where Napoleon studied in 1784 and 1785

24. Designed by Jean-Louis Fontaine to replace a medieval castle, the residence of the Loménie de Brienne was finished shortly before Napoleon went to the neighbouring college of Brienne-le-Château

25. Imaginary view of Napoleon commanding his schoolfellows at Brienne in a snow battle

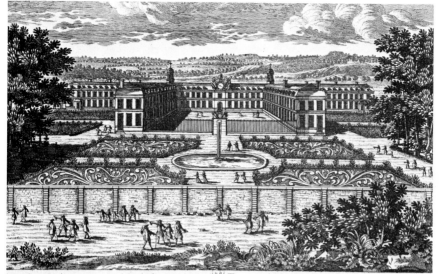

Veüe et perspectiue de la maison des Dames de St Cyr du côté du Jardin
dessiné et Gravé par Aveline suiv. Priuilege du Roy

22. Saint-Cyr, the elegant boarding-school near Versailles where Elisa Bonaparte spent eight years

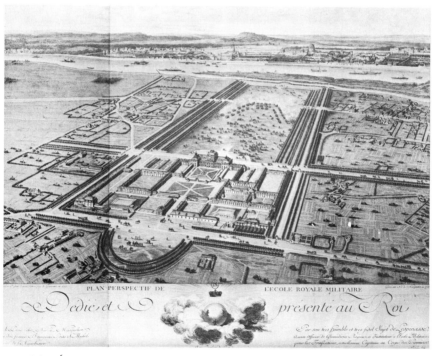

PLAN PERSPECTIF DE   L'ECOLE ROYALE MILITAIRE
Dedié et   presenté au Roi

23. The École Royale Militaire, Paris, magnificently designed by J.-A. Gabriel, where Napoleon studied in 1784 and 1785

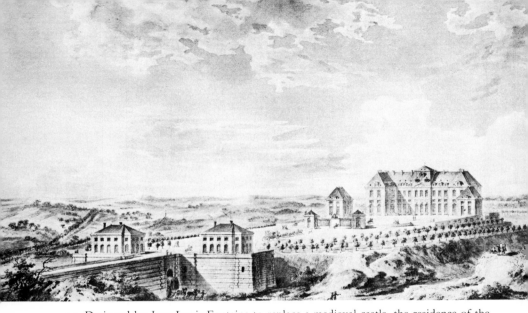

24. Designed by Jean-Louis Fontaine to replace a medieval castle, the residence of the Loménie de Brienne was finished shortly before Napoleon went to the neighbouring college of Brienne-le-Château

25. Imaginary view of Napoleon commanding his schoolfellows at Brienne in a snow battle

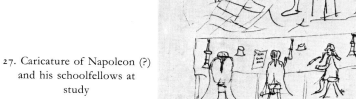

26. Napoleon prepared to defend Paoli, ineffectually restrained by a teacher, Caricature by a schoolfellow

27. Caricature of Napoleon (?) and his schoolfellows at study

28. Portrait of Napoleon as First Consul drawn from life in Paris by Thomas Phillips, RA. Once in the collection of Lord Byron

mission. Actually the minister of finance tried to fob them off with 6,000, but in April 1779 he agreed to double the sum in view of their good conduct and piteous pleas of poverty. This did not prevent them from presenting the Estates on their return with a bill for 1,815 livres for 'gratifications' they had been obliged to dole out during their stay in the capital.[35]

Only 2,400 livres of Carlo's own money (or rather that of his family) was therefore spent over and above the expense-money allocated to him. Out of this he had to pay for his journey with his three charges to Autun, Napoleon's trousseau for Brienne, his own costs in making a detour there, as well, probably, as entertainment or presents to d'Hozier de Serigny, not to mention 'gratifications' to other func-tionaries. Not much can have been left over for gambling and women.

On his return he immediately had to find 1,421 livres to send to the principal at Autun for the school fees of Joseph and Napoleon. The bishop Marbeuf had promised Joseph a stipend of 3,000 livres a year when he became *sous-diacre*, an office that could be held before ordi-nation. 'That was a great thing, a way to fortune that cost nothing,' Napoleon observed to Bertrand. He had forgotten Joseph's school bills, insignificant in view of the expected advantages but enough to embarrass his family. The basic fee at Autun was reasonable, working out at about a livre a day; but as in many superior boarding-schools it was more than doubled by extras: charges for games and laundry and the use of the library, for the retribution of a servant, a music master and a priest, besides clothes, that very costly item in eighteenth-century living: 57 livres were spent on Joseph's shoes alone.[36]

The expenses of Napoleon's education came to an end after he went to Brienne in April 1779, the school thereafter undertaking the upkeep and renewal of his clothes. But the bills from Autun were doubled after Lucien joined his brother at the college, for Carlo offered a French education to his third son. Lucien relates in his memoirs, rather pathetically, that he left Ajaccio in 1781 when he had just entered his seventh year; his father was away at the time and he never saw him again. Carlo was in fact in Bastia at the Estates all through June of that year and Lucien's sixth birthday fell on 21 May, so that the date he gives is credible. For the journey, he writes, he was put in charge of Joseph Fesch, who was going to take up his scholarship in Aix-en-Provence. The voyage lasted several days; he was seasick; but Joseph, the hearty, pink-faced, hard-drinking son of a Swiss kept a good appetite.

The story is lively and convincing; but like so many of Lucien's, untrue. According to a professor at the college he did not reach Autun till late in 1782, and he certainly saw his father again, when Carlo fetched him from Autun in the summer of 1784 to take him to Brienne. Lucien moreover gives himself away when he adds that he and Joseph made a detour to visit the bishop Marbeuf at Lyons (Talleyrand having succeeded him at Autun), and that Marbeuf treated him as a favourite and loaded him with holy pictures of saints and angels clustering round the Virgin. All this is fantasy: Marbeuf was not appointed to Lyons nor Talleyrand to Autun till 1788. If it seems likely that the eighteen-year-old Joseph Fesch did go to Aix in 1781 (for he would hardly have waited till the following year to take up his scholarship), he did not accompany Lucien, nor did he go to Lyons.

Lucien's charming inventions invite sympathy; one cannot help feeling sorry for the little boy heartlessly bundled off to school, whether at the age of six or seven (the treatment, incidentally, habitually meted out to the sons of the British aristocracy). But one also realizes that he was amazingly lucky. Had Carlo been the rigidly calculating father his uncle would have preferred, he would never have taken the risk of adding Lucien's school fees to Joseph's, even though he had hopes of getting him a scholarship later on at Brienne. In the meantime the fees for his two sons must have eaten up the greater part of his salary of 1,200 livres a year.[37]

The legacy from his supposed Tuscan cousin, Giuseppe Moccio, coming to him in 1780, can have been of small help or none. Carlo notes the event in his 'Livre de Raison', with a genealogy showing Giuseppe Moccio's descent from two ancestors, 'knights of the golden spur' nine and ten generations back, followed by his own family tree from Francesco (il Mauro) through eight generations to himself; the presence of several people by the name of Francesco perhaps encouraged his hope of identifying a common ancestor. But he makes no mention of money; either he received none or the sum was too disappointingly small to be mentioned.[38]

Naturally he pinned his hopes on the two money-making schemes he had set in motion: the Odone heritage and the Salines. Both demanded a huge amount of effort, and both were to prove frustrating, though for contrary reasons. The Odone heritage got stuck for years in the bureaucratic machine; the enterprise of the Salines jerked along between dramatic encouragements and setbacks.

Montbarey, minister of war, had looked not unfavourably on Carlo's claim to part of the succession that had fallen into the hands of the Jesuits thanks to the inconsiderate piety of his collateral ancestor, Paolo Francesco Odone. But his right to it had to be proved. To this end he went to work after his return from Paris with such zeal that in spite of his duties at the Estates in Bastia and in court in Ajaccio by September 1779 he had assembled a hundred and seventeen relevant documents; no less. These he presented to Marbeuf, who passed them on to the *intendant*, who passed them on to a pair of lawyers, whose work, as the *intendant*'s secretary tartly observed, would 'not be a matter of a quarter of an hour'. Even so, the main obstruction seems to have come from the *subdélégué*, Souiris, who as administrator of the Jesuits' former property (then assigned to public education) evidently drew enough profit from it not to want to see it escape his control. Carlo's request for a long lease on the olive grove, I Milelli, and the house, La Badina, was never refused; but neither was it granted, while year after year report followed report and appeal appeal, and the correspondence piled up between Carlo, the *commissaires du roi*, and successive ministers of war. In 1782, father of seven children, he was begging possession so as to have the means of giving them an education. Father of eight, he sent a tragic plea on the eve of his death; but Souiris saw to it that the lease was not drawn up till November 1785, when Carlo had been nine months in his tomb. The family did not enter into possession of the properties till May of the following year.[39]

But while the Odone heritage escaped his grasp, at certain moments after his return from Paris the Salines seemed to justify his highest expectations. At the Estates of 1779 the French government announced a scheme for promoting a silk industry in Corsica. It was one of those, adopted after somewhat hasty reports from proclaimed experts, that have from time to time captivated the habitually sceptical French administrators of the island – usually with disappointing results (the latest was a canning factory that sprang up and collapsed within five years in the 1970s). In 1779 the *commissaires du roi* were full of confidence. The deputies to the Estates were enjoined to cease moaning about bad harvests and apply their minds to this scheme that would make Corsica 'at last . . . useful and happy'. Mulberry trees would be distributed to landowners, a third of the price being borne by the government; better still, nursery gardens for mulberries would be created with government contracts and subsidies. Lorenzo Giubega, secretary to the Estates, undertook to drain a marsh near Calvi and supply 100,000 young trees over a period of fifteen years with government aid. Another, even larger plantation was to be created near Bastia. Proposals were invited for a similar enterprise in the province of Ajaccio.[40]

Naturally enough, Carlo, encouraged by Marbeuf, saw the scheme as a providential opportunity for exploiting the Salines. The example of his so far very successful friend Giubega was an added incitement; the existence of a competitor for the government contract in Ajaccio, a certain Colonna, acted as a challenge. Undeterred by his unhappy experience of the previous year, on 30 August 1779 he resumed draining operations. This time Bedigis, the official geometer of the *Plan Terrier* (the territorial survey) was put in charge, and again he had the use of troops for labour. In October, on the recommendation of Bedigis, he received 2,000 livres (a second instalment of the subsidy granted in 1776). As he estimated the cost of the undertaking since August 1777 at just over 2,974 livres, and had already received 4,400, he must have been in pocket.[41]

But not for long. If the work continued, intermittently, during the ensuing years it was thanks to the largesse of Marbeuf who 'helped him with a great deal of money', he wrote, with pride rather than embarrassment, when in June 1781 he submitted a petition to the Estates for a government contract for planting mulberry trees. As token of his good intentions he had already planted more than two thousand, to the admiration, he declared, of everyone in the neighbourhood. He had also imported a gardener from Tuscany, Alessandro Bacini of Girollo, one in a series of foreign gardeners he brought to this thankless task. Such experts were lacking in the archaic world of Corsican agriculture. Nor, for that matter, was there anyone who understood how to drain a marsh; Bedigis, for all his authority, failed.

Carlo might have taken warning from the wily, wealthy Lorenzo Giubega, who at this same session of the Estates admitted that the 8,500 livres he had received for draining his property near Calvi had been insufficient and pleaded for another 11,000 (he got 8,333). But Carlo remained blindly optimistic. He requested a contract on the same conditions as Giubega's and underlined his case by remarking that it was only justice to create a mulberry plantation in the south of the island, seeing that the two existing ones were in the north. His application was accepted, in preference to that of Colonna, his rival candidate in Ajaccio, while another similar contract was given to

Pietro Paolo Colonna de Cesari Rocca of Porto Vecchio. At this same session Carlo was elected a member of the Nobles Douze.[42]

Elated no doubt by success, or what he counted as such, on 15 August, Napoleon's birthday and the festival of the Assumption of the Virgin, having paid his wig-dresser, and accompanied, presumably, by Letizia, Carlo went to Cargese to enjoy his benefactor's hospitality. They stayed till October, when Carlo dispatched some clothes to Ajaccio, as well, it seems, as a dining-table for twenty people nine and a half *pieds* long by five and a half wide. Did he have it made on Marbeuf's estate? It illustrated, anyhow, the expansive scale of the Bonaparte's entertaining.[43]

In November Carlo had the minor satisfaction of receiving 1,600 livres, the balance of his subsidy for developing the Salines. On 1 May 1782 he imported another gardener, a skilled Tuscan nurseryman from a village near Prato (there where he had called on his kinsman the canon on his first journey to Italy).[44] The patronage of Marbeuf was now assured; having paid his wig-dresser up to date he enjoyed yet another visit with Letizia to Cargese.[45] On the fifteenth of the month the inspector of agriculture, accompanied by a member of the Nobles Douze, examined his property at the Salines and pronounced it fit for the cultivation of mulberries. His contract was signed on 19 June. Carlo undertook to supply 100,000 young mulberry trees over a period of fifteen years at the rate of 10,000 a year after the fifth year. During the first five years he would receive a total advance of 8,500 livres, as well as 600 livres a year for a gardener's salary. The *intendant* undertook to collect and distribute the trees, for which Carlo would be paid either by the government or private buyers at the rate of 3 sols each, plus one sol per tree for the expense of grafting. Carlo would reimburse the advances made during the first five years over the next ten, the sums being deducted from the payments due to him.[46]

Looked at closely the deal was not really very advantageous. All he could expect was an income, in five years' time, for ten years, of 2,000 livres a year, which would be more than halved by the repayment of the advances. Provided, always, that the trees could be grown in sufficient numbers and that the local farmers were keen on acquiring them, as no one among the office-bound functionaries and their aristocratic beneficiaries doubted. They had to learn that mulberry trees, until then a rarity in Corsica, do only moderately well there: the Bonaparte were never able to produce their quota; the Salines, now a municipal housing estate, never became a mulberry grove. And despite energetic efforts to promote a silk industry, then and again under the Restoration, farmers remained unenthusiastic; Corsican silk is an unknown commodity and mulberry trees are an unusual sight in the island, whereas the olive tree, introduced in classical times, covers miles and miles of the countryside with its silver forests.[47]

Carlo's situation, after signing the contract, demanded, surely, that he should concentrate on his new task in a spirit of sober economy. But no. Once again, as when he obtained his doctorate in Pisa, he indulged in an extravagant celebration of what he thought of as a victory. 'In June 1782 I left with Madame Letizia for the waters of Bourbonne-les-Bains, in Champagne,' he announces in his 'Livre de Raison', without explanation or comment. Bourbonne-les-Bains was then a fashionable health resort, the waters being considered an infallible remedy for postnatal indispositions. Letizia had given birth to her seventh child, Maria Annunziata (later known as Caroline) on 24 March; historians have therefore concluded that her health had suffered sufficiently to incite Carlo to offer her this holiday and cure. The gesture was unusual from a Corsican husband; moreover why did he choose Bourbonne-les-Bains when there were several health-giving waters at hand in Corsica? Why did he take her to this distant spot in north-eastern France, one of the most expensive in Europe? Precisely because it was expensive, one may surmise. There are no real holidays for those who strive to make their way up through worldly connections, and watering-places have always been good hunting grounds for adventurers and social climbers. It would be much easier to make or renew acquaintances with the great in this small town than in Paris or Versailles, where they were hidden in their own grand houses or hedged about with the etiquette of the court. Carlo, quite likely, knew people who might be useful to him whom he hoped to find there, and attract, Letizia's beauty aiding.

So the handsome aspiring provincial couple set off for the resort where the duc de Fitz-James thought nothing of renting a house for 1,224 livres for a season, where the local inhabitants, in the words of Diderot, viewed the visitors as the Jews the manna in the desert and extorted from them up to 150,000 livres for a stay. And all this in a dreary hole, Diderot insists, devoid of walks, public gardens or shade in summer. It is however unlikely that Carlo and Letizia minded these shortcomings; probably boredom rendered the great more approachable. They stayed perhaps a month; the whole journey, including detours to Autun and Brienne and Paris, may have taken about double that time. An entry in Carlo's 'Livre de Raison' shows that they were home by 5 September.[48]

How did they pay for the trip? It is hardly possible that Carlo could have met the cost from his own resources; unlikely that Luciano would have financed an expedition that he must have regarded as frivolous, even if family business could be dealt with on the way. Did Marbeuf foot the bill? As a gesture to Letizia? Evidence is lacking. Nor is there any trace of debts in connection with this journey, as there is with the next one, in 1784. Clothes alone for Carlo and Letizia must have cost a small fortune. Two witnesses both emphasize the elaboration of their dressing. One is Jean-Baptiste de Grandchamp, Joseph's friend at Autun. Though he was eighty-six when he communicated his souvenirs and some are inexact (the Bonaparte, he asserts, were on their way to Plombières) their appearance stuck in his mind. Carlo was tall, thin, dry ('*sec*') and bourgeois in style. He wore a horseshoe-shaped wig, a black suit with braid trimmings ('*branden-bourgs*') and carried a sword. Letizia, young and superb – 'Roman' – in her bearing, wore a dress with white silk panniers ornamented with green flowers; her chestnut-coloured hair was arranged in a chignon held by a lace veil.[49]

They went of course to see Joseph, and to discuss his progress with his masters, and it is also probable that Carlo made arrangements for Lucien's entry to the college later in the year. No trace of this however appears in his 'Livre de Raison' or any document, nor any indication of when exactly Lucien went to Autun or with whom. Lucien already appears as the odd man out of the family. We do know that he was a pupil at Autun, and at Brienne; but he did not apparently win a scholarship there and when Carlo died his fees in both schools were unpaid.

Napoleon kept a vivid memory of his parents' visit to Brienne. Letizia, he recalled, was 'beautiful as the nymphs of antiquity' ('*belle comme les amours*'). His father also cut a handsome figure with his well-curled wig, cerise jacket ('*habit*'), puce-coloured breeches and silver-buckled shoes. But his manners rather embarrassed him. 'He affected too much the ridiculous politeness of the age,' he observed to Bertrand, and recalled how this struck him in his father's behaviour to a monk at Brienne when it came to deciding who should first pass through the doors. That Carlo's manners were slightly caricatural is easy to believe. His supporter, Rossi, was of the opinion that he was generally 'more affable than necessary'.[50]

Letizia later gave her own somewhat fanciful version of this visit to Brienne to Napoleon's minister, Chaptal, one designed to demonstrate Napoleon's intelligence even though it no longer needed proving. She had gone to the school to remove him, she said, because she had heard he was ailing. But the master of mathematics advised her to take him away for another reason: he had been wasting his time for the past six months because no one had anything more to teach him. This, as we shall see, was inexact.[51]

Admired at Brienne, Letizia also, according to Napoleon, attracted attention in Paris, where she accompanied her husband on the same journey.[52] Unfortunately we know even less about this episode. The only relevant evidence is that on 24 November 1782 a place was granted to Maria-Anna (Elisa) at the school of Saint-Cyr. The achievement was surely a result of Carlo's visit to Paris that summer, though he may have taken preliminary steps during his previous stay in the capital. No other document has come to light to show how he procured this enormous privilege for his daughter. Only two or three places were available to Corsican girls in this elegant boarding-school. Conditions of admittance included proof of the nobility of the father's family for the past hundred and forty years (those unable to produce it were advised to abstain) and a memoir to show that the father or grandfather had served at least ten years in His Majesty's army or been killed or invalided in battle. Proof of nobility had however been simplified for Corsican candidates and the military qualifications waived; luckily for Carlo, seeing that his only fighting had been against his king.[53]

Founded by Madame de Maintenon in 1686 with the blessing of Louis XIV, Saint-Cyr offered, gratis, a refined and quite enlightened education to the daughters of the poor military nobility. The buildings, austerely harmonious, stood at the extremity of the park of Versailles, within the aura of the court. Madame de Maintenon, who ended her life there, was a frequent visitor, often accompanied by the King. There was room for two hundred and fifty pupils, admitted between the ages of seven and twelve on the understanding that they would stay there till the age of twenty, when they would receive dowries of 3,000 livres. It was not at first a convent school. The curriculum was designed to turn out young ladies equipped with a 'civilized piety' and the accomplishments proper to noblemen's wives. In the opinion of père La Chaise, who assisted in drawing up the original constitution, there were enough good nuns in France but not enough good mothers of families. The teachers were thirty-six lady professors (the *'dames'*) drawn from the same social background as the girls. They taught religion, music, decorative needlework, domestic skills and the lives of saints, as well as elements of French, history, geography and that beguiling subject common to eighteenth-century schools, mythology. Madame de Maintenon also gave occasional lessons in conversation and deportment. Attractive uniforms were designed both for *'dames'* and girls, who were encouraged to care for their appearance.

True, there was a severe timetable to be observed that meant getting up at 6 a.m., and by the time Elisa entered the school some of its worldly distractions had been abolished. Gone were the days when the pupils acted the plays of Corneille, or Racine, who actually wrote *Esther* for them. They had performed it in 1689 in costumes decked with real pearls and diamonds before an audience that included two kings: Louis XIV and the exiled James II. But soon afterwards stern reforms had been imposed. Theatricals were banned as immodest; no longer could the girls dream of Cinderella marriages with their admirers in the courtly audiences. Even poetry reading was forbidden. Plain dressing was to be the rule, and the *'dames'*, who had not previously taken irrevocable vows, were unwillingly inserted into the order of Saint Augustin.

Yet Saint-Cyr remained a place of refined culture. Horace Walpole, visiting it the year Napoleon was born, was charmed by the young girls in their pretty black dresses trimmed with coloured ribbons, and describes them playing chess, dancing minuets and singing the glorious choruses of Racine's *Athalie* which had several times been performed there. One of the nuns, Madame de Corbis, appeared to him beautiful as a Madonna. They ended by chanting vespers in the chapel where Madame de Maintenon was buried. In this select environment Elisa spent eight years of her young life, miraculously removed from the pervading roughness and violence of Corsica and the bitterness and intrigues on which was poised the precarious gentility of her home.[54]

We may assume that Carlo busied himself securing her place when he visited the capital in 1782. He probably also knocked on various doors in the hope of advancing his interests in the Odone heritage. But what were the pleasures of his visit? What did he show Letizia in the capital? Where was she seen and admired? And by who? Only one clue has come to us: an anecdote repeated by some of Letizia's biographers and apparently based on tradition. Carlo, it is said, took her to Versailles where she saw Marie-Antoinette and marvelled that she looked so sad. We may rule out any idea that the Bonaparte were personally entertained by the queen on the strength of a recommendation from the Grand-duke Leopold. Carlo in all probability was never received by the Grand-duke, and certainly not by Marie-Antoinette. Nor was he one of the small number of 'presented nobles' admitted to the royal circle who were included in court functions and went hunting with the King. But it is by no means impossible that he and Letizia slipped into the grounds of Versailles and caught sight of the unhappy queen. To enter the palace offered small difficulty to anyone who was adequately dressed and, if a man, carried a sword, which could be hired from a concierge for the occasion. And indeed all sorts of unsuitable people found their way into the courtyards and gardens to mingle with the hordes of courtiers and their hangers-on, while the more enterprising penetrated the building itself. Prostitutes lurked in corridors; Robert Damien posted himself at the foot of a staircase to stab Louis XV; the notorious Madame de La Motte wandered freely in and out of the palace and planted a prostitute to impersonate Marie-Antoinette in the garden in the execution of her attempted swindle of the 'Diamond Necklace'.[55] Carlo, who knew his way about Versailles, no doubt found getting into the palace precincts easier than his youthful exploit of gatecrashing the Palazzo Pitti.

That summer marked the limit of his social ascension. He, and Letizia as his wife, never climbed higher than during those enchanted days when they rubbed shoulders with the great at Bourbonne-les-Bains and Versailles. The three years between his mission to court in 1779 and his journey with Letizia encompass the summit of his career. After that his luck turned; or rather, he had exhausted his possibilities. And yet he had not accomplished much by standards other than Corsican. The well-born men he envied took for granted what he struggled to win: their children's education, a visit to a health resort, access to the royal palace. Anxiety, frustration and early death lay ahead of him, and for Letizia early widowhood, the collapse of her expectations and poverty that seemed likely to last for ever. Years and years were to go by before she saw any light on her horizon. And during this interminable dreary period she could never have dreamed of re-entering that lustrous world her husband had shown her. A respect-worthy position in Ajaccio for herself and her family was the most she could hope for. And even this modest, reasonable ambition seemed to be smashed for good when on 13 June 1793 she landed at Toulon with her children, refugees flying for their lives with little or nothing but the clothes they were wearing.

⋆⟨ 7 ⟩⋆

FORMATION OF A HERO

Letizia had been shocked by Napoleon's appearance when she visited him at Brienne: he was alarmingly thin and his features, she thought, had changed. This was the result of overwork, Napoleon told Montholon: he studied all through the recreation periods and even at night because he could never bear the idea of not being top of his class. Napoleon was boasting. He was not good at all subjects, only at history and geography and, above all, mathematics. If we are to believe his schoolfriend, Fauvelet de Bourrienne, he was not regarded as a very promising pupil: 'He had no taste for the study of languages, polite literature or the arts. As there were no indications of his ever becoming a scholar, the pedants of the establishment were inclined to think him stupid.' Only the master of mathematics, father Patrault, was pleased with him, though when Letizia told Chaptal that he had advised her to remove Napoleon from the school because he had nothing more to teach him she was boosting Napoleon's reputation at the expense of the monk's. It is enough to accept the judgement of Bourrienne, himself good at mathematics, that Napoleon was 'undoubtedly the cleverest lad in the college' in this subject.[1]

Bourrienne's memoirs are among the four accounts by Napoleon's schoolfellows that constitute the closest available evidence of his life at Brienne, apart from some scraps embedded in Napoleon's conversations at Saint Helena. All these texts have the weakness of being much posterior to the events and heavily coloured by personal feeling. Napoleon's contribution consists of humiliating incidents that had stuck in his mind mixed with some inaccurate observations designed to show him in a better light. None of the four schoolboy witnesses is innocent of embroidering on fact or slipping in doubtful anecdotes, while Bourrienne, the most questionable, left his memoirs to be ghosted by a journalist during the Restoration.[2] Yet in outline all four say the same thing, and it agrees with Napoleon's unhappier memories: at Brienne he was unadapted, unsociable, unpopular and aggressive. 'Gloomy and fierce to excess', like one 'newly issued from a forest, and until then, withdrawn from the sight of men', writes the fellow student who signs himself C.H., an English boy – perhaps a certain Cumming of Craigmillar – who seems the most trustworthy of the four. And Bourrienne comments on his 'piercing, scrutinizing glance', that inquisitorial Corsican look that had unnerved Boswell in the presence of Paoli.[3]

His sallow skin, too, set him apart from the other boys, as though his wet-nurse had suckled him on olive oil, so they liked to say. His name was another stigma: no one had ever heard of such a name as Napoleone, which he pronounced in the Italian way – Napoleone – accentuating the final e. It had already given rise to rude mirth at Autun; at Brienne it was transformed into *paille au nez*: 'straw in the nose'. Napoleon had not forgotten this affront at Saint Helena, nor the mockery he encountered when, seeing ice for the first time in his water jug one winter morning, he exclaimed: 'Who's put glass in my jug?'[4] The incident was trivial; but all this taunting and teasing carried the sting of contempt for a foreigner: a despised foreigner, moreover, a barbarous Corsican. The situation was the same as at Autun, but aggravated by numbers: Napoleon had at least three times as many potential tormentors at Brienne. His ordeal, to quote his biographer Norwood Young, was 'burial alive among his nation's enemies'. Small wonder if he declared to Bourrienne: 'I will do these French all the mischief I can.' And so he did, lashing out at them with counter-insults till they set on him in a body, and then driving them off single-handed with cold courage. He was too proud to complain to the masters of these assaults.[5]

Unluckily for Napoleon there was no other Corsican at Brienne who might have stood up for him. True, in 1782 Élie-Charles Balathier de Bragelonne of Bastia entered the school; but his father was the French military commander of that town. The royal scholarships were bestowed indifferently on the children of gentlemen living in Corsica, Corsican or not; a practice the Corsicans might have resented though I have no evidence that they complained. Élie Charles, like Napoleon, was a protégé of Marbeuf, who was one of his godparents, together with the scandalous Madame Varese. Far from welcoming him, Napoleon tried to tear him to pieces at sight. His comrades had played

a diabolical trick on the two boys. Napoleon was for ever telling them
how his countrymen abhorred their former rulers, the Genoese. When
Bragelonne arrived they told Napoleon he was Genoese and put
Bragelonne up to acting the part. Since his name was un-Corsican and
he came from the former Genoese capital (where many families of
Genoese origin had stayed on after the conquest), Napoleon believed
them, and without more ado flung himself on the unfortunate boy,
grabbing him by the hair. We know nothing of their subsequent relations at Brienne, nor why Élie Charles, who excelled in Bible studies,
German and geography besides music, dancing and singing and the
exercise of arms, was expelled in 1786. During the Revolution he
emigrated, served with the prince de Condé and then with the British,
but eventually changed sides and proved his worth as a general in
Napoleon's wars.[6]

Though Brienne offered Napoleon a new environment, the dramatic
impressions of his childhood still overclouded his mind. He blas-
phemed at the sight of a portrait of the duc de Choiseul, flared up if
anyone – master or pupil – spoke ill of Paoli; Bourrienne even asserts
that in the presence of the monks assembled at dinner he blamed his
father for rallying to the French instead of standing by Paoli to the
end. Joseph Bonaparte later refuted Bourrienne's statement as a double
calumny, of son and father.[7]

Napoleon's isolation turned in a vicious circle. His rejection was
particularly humiliating because it was provoked not so much because
he was a foreigner – the English boy, C.H., never complains on that
score – but because he belonged to a defeated people. His reaction was
defiance: as Harold T. Parker observes, he 'accepted the Corsican
identity thrust on him'. Not only accepted it, but gloried in it. Despised
as one of the conquered, he despised his conquerors; unjustly treated,
he assimilated the injustices he suffered with those inflicted on his
countrymen, brooding on their misfortunes as his own. Their hero,
Paoli, was 'his god', the leader he dreamed of succeeding: 'If Paoli
cannot break the shameful chains that bind Corsica, I shall go to help
him when I have sufficient strength,' he is quoted as saying, and
adding: 'Who knows? The destiny of an empire often depends on a
single man.' Prophetic words, pointing to exploits beyond the dream.
At the time, however, they merely inspired a fellow-student's caricature
of Napoleon, outsize, braced to defend Paoli with a diminutive old
professor like an insect hanging on to his pigtail to restrain him.
'*Bonaparte cours, vole, au secours de Paoli,*' one reads scrawled below.[8]

With such extreme behaviour, typical of Corsicans when their race is in any way disparaged, Napoleon aggravated his critics by accentuating everything they held against him. But beneath the rhetorical speeches and attitudes there was certainly a simple, heart-felt homesickness. Nostalgia for Corsica, where everything was better than elsewhere; the country one could recognize blindfold by its scent alone. Often he must have thought of it as he trudged across the mud-clogged fields of Champagne, picturing to himself the mountains and torrents and precipices he described at Saint Helena 'with strokes of fire'. And more intimately he must have missed the *casa* Bonaparte, full of loved, loving relatives and their dependants: cantankerous Luciano, adoring Camilla Ilari, Letizia, scolding and protecting, Carlo, remembered as the over-indulgent father rather than the traitor to his country, and Mammuccia Caterina whose tears when he left Corsica he recalled forty years later.[9]

It is ironical that Napoleon should have been bullied at Brienne on account of his Corsican origin, for the guiding principle of the military colleges, laid down by their founder, the comte de Saint-Germain, minister of war, was a suprisingly modern cult of equality, racial as well as social. Brienne was one of the ten (later twelve) schools scattered about the provinces to replace the École Royale Militaire in Paris in 1776, which was judged too costly by the minister. In the new colleges some six hundred king's scholars, sons of the poor nobility, were to mix on equal terms with paying pupils, including sons of foreign nobles living in France. Rich and poor, French and foreign, scholars and paying pupils (who were not always of noble extraction) shared the same, Spartan conditions. They were to dress themselves in the prescribed uniform without the help of servants (a trial for the children of some aristocratic homes), keep their hair short till the age of twelve and afterwards only powder it on Sundays and feast days. Each was to sleep in a separate, sparsely furnished room (the risk of homosexuality was not forgotten) in an uncurtained bed with one blanket only, even in winter, and wash daily in cold water.[10]

On the other hand corporal punishment was forbidden as damaging to body and soul; such punishments as were inflicted were to avoid humiliating the culprit. Injunctions necessary but apparently not always heeded. The comte de Vaublanc, who loathed his years at the college La Flèche, speaks of cruel and shaming punishments, including being forced to wear the coarse homespun monk's habit, a mortification so intolerable that one victim beat his head against a wall until his life was endangered. This was precisely the punishment inflicted on Napoleon by a brute of a master who forced him, wearing the homespun, to eat his lunch kneeling at the refectory door. Whereupon Napoleon was seized by a fit of nerves and vomiting until he was rescued with reproofs to his tormentor by father Patrault, the tall, red-faced 'rather ordinary' looking man who was the one master who cared for him. Napoleon was sufficiently scarred by the experience to recall it at Saint Helena. Can we have the same confidence in the tale about the monk who tried to bring Napoleon to order with the words: 'Who do you think you are?' To which Napoleon is said to have replied: 'A man'? If so, it indicates not so much Napoleon's awareness of growing up as a basic human dignity common to Corsicans of all ages and walks of life.[11]

The military colleges aimed at forming young men, in the words of Saint-Germain, with 'robust bodies, enlightened minds and honest hearts'. Time was to be given to outdoor recreation as well as to the worldly physical arts of fencing and dancing. If the curriculum was lacking in the exhilarating revolutionary ideology Napoleon's father had discovered at the university of Corte, it was modern for its period in being related to the students' future activities. Latin was to be studied with a view to reading the classical authors but without useless exercises in rhetoric; religion, morals and logic were to be taught without metaphysical superfluities. Importance was attached to the learning of German (for use in future wars), history and geography, and mathematics as applied to military topography and fortification.

This sensible, not very exalting teaching was entrusted to various orders and congregations of monks, including Benedictines, Oratorians and Doctrinaires, although not all the masters were churchmen. When Napoleon went to school, Brienne was the only college run by the Minimes, the Franciscans. Their order was not the most learned, nor did their school have a high reputation among the twelve. It was one of the smallest: the number of pupils seems never to have exceeded a hundred and fifty, whereas La Flèche had close on five hundred. It was also one of the poorest, and therefore unable to engage first-class teachers, so Bourrienne complained. The Loménie de Brienne, lords of the local manor, may have been largely to blame, for they appointed the masters and though very rich evidently failed to subsidize them adequately, if at all. Official inspections in 1785 and 1787 were disapproving: in 1785 carelessness was reported general and a repugnance to work common to students and professors; in 1787 disorder and indiscipline reigned. Even religious observance was perfunctory: the vice-principal regularly got through mass in nine or ten minutes. And in spite of the precaution of locking up the boys at night, each in his cell, the homosexual 'nymphs' of Brienne were notorious.[12]

Some twenty professors taught six classes under the authority of the principal and vice-principal, the Berton brothers, both of whom had started life in the army. Father Patrault, one of three professors of mathematics, and a professor of French, father Dupuy, evidently taught Napoleon something of value and were remembered by him with esteem. The rest seem to have been second-rate. Louis Berton had been appointed principal, soon after Napoleon entered the school, to restore discipline neglected by his predecessor, father Henri Lélue; but he too was judged incompetent as well as vulgar and pretentious. Napoleon, as First Consul, condemned him as 'too hard'; but he may have had bad memories of their first encounter, when Napoleon and his comrades welcomed him by chanting rude songs under his window until Berton seized 'the little Corsican' by the collar and punished him with three days confinement, or so the story goes. Napoleon none the less rescued him from the penury to which he had been reduced by the Revolution and enabled him to make a career as educational administrator; but again he proved unsatisfactory and he eventually died insane. His brother, he who gabbled mass, had a light, worldly disposition that became increasingly apparent after the Revolution released him from his vows. Earning his living, also thanks to Napoleon, as an administrator of hospitals, he was much given to daring jokes and bursting into song at wedding parties. A student-teacher who helped Napoleon with mathematics needed no rewarding: Pichegru, who conspired to assassinate him, with Cadoudal, in 1803, ended strangled in his prison cell.[13]

Napoleon spent over five uninterrupted years at Brienne. The boys were never allowed to visit their homes except in situations of extreme gravity like a serious illness or death in the family. They had no real holidays, though there was a yearly break between 21 August and 8 September when certain classes were cancelled and they were taken on long walks in the neighbourhood. The school stood at the entrance to the village, Brienne-le-Château, so-named on account of the residence of the Loménie de Brienne that overlooked it. The surrounding country is flat, agricultural, often waterlogged and spotted with rather lugubrious villages where one still finds dilapidated thatched or timbered hovels such as Napoleon must have seen and which appear in

Boucher's sentimental scenes of rustic poverty painted some decades earlier. Vast buildings had been added to the original monastery when it became a military college in 1776; but these were destroyed during the French Revolution, so that today only the original seventeenth-century monastic nucleus remains, a low L-shaped edifice (now a museum) at the end of an avenue of limes, knotted with much pruning, which Napoleon must have known.[14]

The days were regulated by a timetable covering the hours between 6 a.m., when the boys were woken in their cells, each sparsely furnished with camp-bed, jug and basin, to 10 p.m., when they were locked in them for the night. The morning was filled with the practice and instruction of religion and lessons in mathematics, Latin, German, history, geography and drawing; a two-hour break for lunch and recreation was followed by a lighter programme of fencing, dancing, music and writing (all subjects in which Napoleon made a poor showing). The food seems to have been wholesome if rather austere: only bread and water, with fruit, for breakfast and the afternoon '*goûter*'; but soup, '*bouilli*', roasts, salad and desserts at the two main meals. And there were treats on feast days: the menu for Epiphany (the day of '*les Rois*') was sufficiently appreciated for Napoleon to record it on the flyleaf of his atlas: chicken, cake, cauliflower, beetroot salad and a hot dessert with chestnuts which must have reminded him of his home. The scribbled note brings one strangely close to the lonely, homesick thirteen-year-old boy who had none the less kept a good appetite.[15]

Parker observes that the young Napoleon, living under the stress of disdain for years on end, never turned for comfort to sex or to religion. On the contrary he rejected both. His strict morality earned him enemies at Brienne, where he was regarded as a fault-finding 'pédagogue', in other words a prig. In Paris he held to the same severe principles which he retained well after his schooldays in an aloofness to sex in any form. As for his religious faith, alive when he went to Brienne, it crumbled under the impact of his studies, which stimulated passions vigorous enough to overcome his unhappiness.[16]

His ability in subjects that appealed to him soon became apparent. Towards the end of the school year, in late August or early September, the college opened its doors to give a display known as the '*exercices publics*'. During several days the masters questioned the best pupils in their best subjects in the presence of the local notables, the occasion being presided over by a dignitary of Church or state. Prize-giving closed the last day, usually followed by a theatrical performance by the pupils. Printed programmes of the proceedings were issued, which have survived; though they obviously do not mention the prize winners they do give the names of all the pupils questioned. Napoleon was among those questioned in 1780, probably in 1781, and certainly in 1782 and 1783; the absence of records prevents one from knowing whether he was chosen in his last year, 1784, as seems likely enough. In 1780, in the *exercices* presided over by the bishop of Troyes, he features among fourteen students questioned on 'the four principal miracles of Jesus Christ', the history of the New Testament, the fables of Phaedrus and French grammar, among twenty-two answering problems in mathematics and among six questioned on the geography of the world. He was not selected again for religious knowledge. The following year he is said to have been questioned in geometry and trigonometry and to have received a prize from no less a person than the duc d'Orléans, Louis-Philippe 'le Gros', father of Philippe Egalité, who was visiting the Loménie de Brienne with his mistress, Madame de Montesson. For this we have only the testimony of a writer who claims to have seen the printed programme, now disappeared: the anecdote seems to be true even though one may marvel at Napoleon's ability to solve problems of trigonometry at the age of twelve. The year after, in the presence of the duc de Châtelet, it is recorded that he was again questioned in mathematics, as well as on the history of the ancient Egyptians, Babylonians, Carthaginians and Greeks and on geography ancient and modern. Finally, in 1783, he appears in the programme as one of the top three mathematicians of the college together with Bourrienne and a certain Brizard de Martret, solving problems in arithmetic, algebra, spherical and rectilinear geometry and mathematics applied to such practical matters as the measurements of fortifications. Bourrienne asserts that he and Napoleon shared the prize. We do not know in what it consisted. Napoleon had already received a prize that year, in May: the *Histoire de Scipion l'Africain* in an edition of 1752 which can still be seen at Brienne; but it seems more likely that this volume was a reward for the other subject in which he distinguished himself: ancient history.[17]

Excellence in these subjects was the means by which Napoleon first earned respect, asserted his intellectual quality. Hedged in by the pettiness and spite and constraints of Brienne he found compensation in the grandeur of the ancient world and the pure, abstract realm of mathematics. A passion for antiquity was widespread among his contemporaries; a mastery of mathematics, equally in tune with the times, was more difficult and unusual. For Napoleon mathematics was an art, the highest: geometry was 'the sublime abstract, like great poetry'. His grasp of its discipline won him public applause, the esteem of father Patrault and the grudging admiration of his comrades. Mathematics remained a support throughout his career: 'I consider the study of mathematics very important,' he told Bertrand. 'Of all the things I know it is the one I would abandon most unwillingly . . . It is applicable to every need; everything has a dimension; one must calculate all through life.'

Here Napoleon was speaking as a man of his age, when mathematics had come to be regarded as the highest development of the human mind. Mathematics had always meant power over nature and so, simply, power. Now, in the post-Newtonian era, applied to the investigation of a measurable universe, mathematics appeared as the key to knowledge, the instrument for mastering and transforming the world. The mathematical spirit was the spirit of reason, the supreme faculty of man; mathematical knowledge was truth. This was made manifest in the works of the leading astronomers, physicians and philosophers, and this their disciples believed.

Napoleon's addiction to mathematics indicates the early age at which his mind was affected by the Enlightenment. Yet one may wonder how much he was exposed to its influence. The Franciscans of Brienne, though they paid their teachers in mathematics better than any others, avoided old-fashioned pedantry and made light, it seems, of the celebration of the mass, were far less modern in their ideas than the Franciscans of Paoli's university who had boldly proclaimed the equality of men. Napoleon's father had devoured their teaching at the time; but how much of it did he retain after defeat and conquest had driven him into the obscure ranks of the Ancien Régime? How much of the new ideal did he pass on to his sons while he wangled his way from favour to favour through local jealousies, lawsuits with cousins and framed elections? One may also wonder if Carlo Bonaparte had much taste or talent for the exact sciences. Were there any works on such subjects in his library of a thousand volumes? His education with the Jesuits in Ajaccio and later at Paoli's university seems to have been essentially literary and philosophical, with some legal studies thrown in. Certainly his domestic and agricultural accounts, covering pages of his 'Livre de Raison' and hardly ever confronting debits with credits are irrational and confused.

Yet Napoleon already showed an aptitude for mathematics before leaving Corsica. 'From his earliest years,' Letizia recalls in her 'Souvenirs', 'he showed a particular disposition for the study of numbers', so that the nuns who gave him his first lessons called him 'the mathematician' and rewarded him with treats of jam. By the age of eight he had taken such a liking to this form of study that a little plank shelter was built for him on the terrace of the *casa* Bonaparte (that terrace Carlo had recklessly constructed in 1774) where he could isolate himself from the other children. At this same period he astonished one of the Bonaparte's farmers by observing with great attention the functioning of a watermill. Having noted how much grain was milled in an hour he dumbfounded the farmer by calculating how much he could expect in a day and a week; a performance that shows the farmer to have been as backward as Napoleon was precocious. Rather than seek influences to explain his proficiency it seems more reasonable to suppose that he was endowed with gifts in line with the trends of his day; an aspect of his good fortune and a potent factor in his success.[18]

All the same, Napoleon never penetrated into the higher spheres of mathematics. When he referred to father Patrault as a 'great mathematician' he was overrating his abilities as much as Letizia underrated them. Napoleon's presence at Brienne has deformed retrospective judgements – his own included – of a school that was probably no better nor worse than moderately good, and certainly better than any to be found in Corsica. Castres quotes the director of studies at the École Militaire in Paris as saying that it was the best of the provincial colleges for mathematics. An exaggeration perhaps. But Bourrienne was surely also exaggerating when he wrote: 'The often repeated assertion of Bonaparte having received a *careful education* at Brienne is untrue. The monks were incapable of giving it to him . . . It is surprising that the establishment should have produced a single able man.' In his opinion, had the teaching been better Napoleon would have distinguished himself in other, more laudable directions: 'If we had any incitement to the study of chemistry, natural philosophy, astronomy etc., I am convinced that Bonaparte would have pursued these sciences with all the genius and spirit of investigation which he displayed in a career more brilliant . . . but less useful to mankind.' A notion intriguing, but prejudiced. It need hardly be said that Napoleon was above all a man of action, born to the domination of lands and men. The obscure dedication of the scientist, the scholar, was alien to his nature and to an intellect that impresses less by its profundity than by its scope.

Attracted to the exact sciences, he was equally, perhaps more attracted, to the study of history; his mind, as has often been pointed out, was at once rational and imaginative, classical and romantic. If Napoleon revered the mathematical spirit, he never developed it in himself to its logical extreme. When the astronomer Laplace presented him with his great work, *Mécanique céleste*, Napoleon actually reproved him for not mentioning God. To which Laplace made his celebrated reply: 'I have no need of this hypothesis.'[19]

Yet Napoleon's original religious faith, the beliefs instilled in Corsica when Letizia whipped him to church and the nuns petted him with jam, had by then long since crumbled under the impact of his education, leaving him with some uncertain, fluctuating notions about Christianity (good for women and the poor) but a steadfast belief in the Deity: 'All things proclaim the existence of a God, it is undeniable; but all our religions are the children of men.' And the cause, or at least pretext of his first doubts lay not in his study of mathematics but in the other subject that fascinated him: ancient history.[20]

The classical world filled a large place in French eighteenth-century education; so large that when the monks of Brienne issued a prospectus for their college they found it necessary to state: 'Teaching will not be limited to Latin.' They furthermore believed that 'history can become a young man's school of morality and virtue'. In consequence of this dual allegiance the pupils were nourished on Graeco-Roman history. The programme dated from 'the fabulous and heroic age', passed on to the republics of Sparta and Athens, and eventually, of course, to the rise and fall of the republic of Rome. In the original regulations of the military colleges, the reading of Plutarch was prescribed on moral as well as on cultural grounds. His *Parallel Lives*, a work that became something of a gospel in eighteenth-century culture, was read in Amyot's stately translation; the students were not made to learn Greek. But their reading of Latin texts, especially of the historical writers, was extensive: Caesar, Cornelius Nepos, Sallust and Livy, besides Virgil, Cicero and Horace. They also studied Eutropius, a fourth-century Latin compiler of the history of Rome. Courses in mythology completed their vision of antiquity: in the *exercises* of 1783 they were questioned on the first- and second-class gods, the marine, infernal, rural and domestic divinities, and the origin of the expression '*terreur panique*' (the alarm produced by the surprise appearance of the god Pan).

For Napoleon the discovery of these majestic figures, the legendary gods and heroes, the statesmen, lawgivers and conquerors, was no less than an illuminator. Not that he learned much about them in the original texts: the study of Latin was repugnant to him, Bourrienne observes. His knowledge of antiquity came through translations: Amyot's Plutarch, and the translations of Latin authors he found in the library then being formed in the college. The English boy, C.H., happily in charge of it, was often 'plagued', to use his own expression, by Napoleon's demands. But Napoleon was not to be put off. Reading had introduced him to the lives of the great scattered over some thousand years of ancient history; it had revealed to him a dimension where the hero – a type of being he had hitherto only apprehended in the person of Paoli – reigned. C.H. describes him, in the 'concealed retirement' of the garden, 'feasting on the example of those great men which he was preparing himself to surpass'; de Castres, on the other hand, relates how he was to be seen standing on table tops with Bourrienne acting scenes in the lives of their favourite heroes. In this way Napoleon's isolation was doubly breached, for his reading of the classics gave him at once familiarity with the illustrious men of the ancient world and a new relationship with his comrades.[21]

In all the pantheon of antiquity Caesar seems to have been the figure he most admired; indeed it is impossible to read Plutarch's account of him without being reminded of Napoleon. Caesar's example stood before him through life: the conqueror of huge tracts of Europe, architect of an empire; the general who overwhelmed his enemies with the speed of his strategy, who knew how to appeal to the pride of his men; the soldier who never shirked tasks or hardships yet dictated his letters from the battlefield. Caesar was surely his guide, the ruler who restored order out of chaos, generous in peace and magnanimous in war; the administrator who conceived public works too vast to be realized in his lifetime; the man who in the marvellous words of Plutarch was for ever 'competing with himself, as though he was someone else, and was struggling to make the future excel the past'. And when Napoleon knew his end was near and was told of the appearance of a comet, he recalled that a comet had announced the death of Caesar, dying like him in his fifties: this too he had read in the library at Brienne.[22]

Napoleon and his friends were by no means unusual in experiencing the intoxication of the ancient world and adopting its heroes as models. Such attitudes were general in the colleges where this generation of schoolboys equated antiquity with liberty. 'They [the masters] spoke to us unceasingly of the liberty of the ancient republics while we were real slaves,' Vaublanc bitterly observed. But others took heart from the vision of what seemed a nobler and freer world. The young men who propelled the French Revolution owed much of their idealism to the ample teaching of the classics innocently dispensed at school. They contrasted the liberty and austerity of the ancient republics with the decadent despotism of the monarchy, saw in the frugality and physical hardiness of the Spartans qualities fit to redeem contemporary society. For the young Napoleon the acceptance of republican principles came easily: had not Paoli established a democratic republic on the ruins of Genoese tyranny? His childhood memories seemed to give concrete illustrations of the highest achievements of antiquity. He was a 'born republican', a schoolfellow observes, dedicated to 'liberty and independence'. Nevertheless it was Caesar the dictator he admired, rather than Marcus Brutus, the murdering champion of freedom who became a deity of the Revolution, his bust enthroned in the hall of the Convention.

The professors of the colleges were not unaware of the threat to the established order that lurked in study of the classics. As a precaution they tried to play down the heroes of antiquity, encouraging pupils to admire their private virtues rather than their public deeds. The monks of Brienne sought to lower the prestige of the Roman heroes by insisting that they were pagans doomed to hell. Their tactics had the opposite effect on Napoleon: they alienated him from Christianity. His faith was badly jolted by a sermon that condemned Cato and Caesar: 'I was eleven years old. I was scandalized to hear that the most virtuous men of antiquity would burn eternally for not having followed a religion they did not know ... From that moment I had no more religion,' he told Bertrand. Speaking to Las Cases he places the break rather later: 'Consider the clumsiness of those who educate us; they bring us up amid the Greeks and Romans with their myriads of divinities ... I needed to believe, I believed; but my faith was shocked and uncertain from the time I began to learn and to reason, and that happened as early as my thirteenth year.'

The difference in date is unimportant: in the course of these formative years of his life Napoleon lost the certainties of his childhood religion, though without totally rejecting it. He duly received his first communion in 1781 or 1782 from the village priest whom he later treated with kindness, and he was subsequently confirmed in Paris at the École Militaire. All the same, he apparently attached so little importance to his prayer book that he gave it to a servant at Brienne,

Jeanne Colin, who cared for him when he was ill. It changed hands and was the object of a prolonged litigation during the Second Empire, before being recuperated by the Bonaparte.[23]

Napoleon looked back on his years at Brienne as a time of change in his character. To Las Cases he confided that at the age of puberty he became sombre and morose and took refuge in reading 'with a passion that became a rage'. This suggests, rather, that the process of growing up brought no real alteration, but an accentuation of traits already existing. Far from making him more flexible and conciliating, his education served to stiffen his self-confidence, taught him to assert himself as he was, at times only too well. Almost every day he quarrelled with his schoolmates and usually came to blows. He made many enemies by 'the austerity of his morals' among the 'dissipated youth', which must mean the 'nymphs', for no other form of dissipation was possible. His brother Lucien who joined him at school in 1784 observed that he was generally disliked because he inspired fear. Yet as ringleader of revolts he was compelling enough to overcome his unpopularity: 'I was conscious of my strength, I enjoyed my supremacy,' he told Antommarchi. He took the ensuing punishments without complaint. Years later he recalled how he egged on his comrades to throw their mattresses out of a window in order to bait a monk who excited ridicule by his great height and 'stentorian' voice: the newly appointed Berton, perhaps. But his voice alone sufficed to restore order. Impressed by his disciplinary technique, Napoleon subsequently appointed him director of a *lycée*.[24]

On another occasion he gave a prophetic exhibition of his talents as military commander. Snow fell heavily during the winter of 1783–4. Shut up indoors with his schoolfellows Napoleon was bored and frustrated. He suggested they should build a snow fortress in the courtyard, divide into two groups and fight a battle with snowballs, besiegers against besieged. The proposal met with enthusiasm. Under his supervision a fortress was built according to the norms of military architecture which attracted sightseers from all over the neighbourhood. Napoleon then appointed himself commander of both sides and for a couple of weeks orchestrated what Bourrienne calls 'a little sham war', until the war became real when the stones mixed with snow caused serious wounds.[25]

He was responsible for worse damage in a midsummer exploit. The monks had given the boys patches of garden to cultivate. Napoleon's was his first territorial conquest. Having forced his two co-proprietors to yield him their shares he enclosed the plot with a 'strong pallisade' and planted trees to shelter it, so re-creating a hideout such as he had enjoyed on the terrace of the *casa* Bonaparte. His motive was not only greed for privacy and possession. Though not brought up to dig the soil Napoleon had a natural taste for gardening; with this pastime, as is well known, he found relief from the tedium and humiliations of Saint Helena.

In his garden at Brienne he retired, it is said, to solve algebraical problems, to feast on Tasso and the works of a great contemporary soldier, the maréchal de Saxe, on Plutarch, and on Ossian, the romantic revelation of the age, which remained through life his favourite reading. There too he could isolate himself from amusements he despised. The celebrations on the feast day of Saint Louis was one of these; dreaming of the liberation of Corsica, Napoleon, the natural republican, held conspicuously aloof from festivities in honour of the French king. The boys had permission that night to let off fireworks; a box of gunpowder accidentally exploded, causing burns, falls, broken limbs. There was a panicked stampede through the gardens; Napoleon, seeing his plot invaded, charged the intruders with a spade, wounding the wounded. Their vengeance, naturally enough, was a harsher punishment than he could ever have suffered at the hands of the monks.[26]

Five years in a French boarding-school had done nothing to tame Napoleon. Yet scenes are recorded that show him in another light, on occasions when he was able to escape the precincts of the college and its forced promiscuity. We have glimpses of Napoleon reading Tasso's *Jerusalem Delivered* in the open country, under a tree, or bathing with Bourrienne in the Aube, which was always ice-cold, where a comrade was drowned and in whose memory they planted a willow tree on the bank. Such picturesque incidents are in counterpoint to the dominant theme: the assembled evidence of Napoleon's life at Brienne goes to show him either violent or meditative, reserved or aggressive, in an alternation of extreme behaviour that is typically Corsican. Corsican, too, was his propensity to vast dreams; his dream to liberate his homeland, successor to Paoli, the dream he had cherished at Autun, if not earlier, and which had haunted Letizia when she carried him in her womb. 'In my mind, Brienne is my country,' he told Montholon, 'it is here that I felt the first impressions of manhood.' Yet all we know about him there recalls his origins.[27]

We are also confronted with a mass of incredible evidence publicized by gullible or unscrupulous writers; no period of Napoleon's life is more encrusted with legend. An indignant letter, quoted *in extenso*, that he is supposed to have written to his father in 1781 is rejected by all serious historians, as is Letizia's scolding reply. Here Napoleon complains savagely of his lack of pocket-money for the *'menus plaisirs'* and exhorts his father in somewhat hectoring language to take him home and teach him a manual trade rather than leave him to be the laughing-stock of his well-off schoolfellows. Not only is the letter out of keeping with Napoleon's proud, stoical disposition, but it is at variance with fact. In accordance with Saint-Germain's ideas of equality, the pupils were not allowed to receive any pocket-money from home. The monks provided it at a fixed low rate according to age. We cannot guess what *'menus plaisirs'* were available, but we can read that much of the pocket-money found its way back to the establishment in fines, to finance the library – there was a tariff for damage to books – and also for neglect of personal appearance, such as a missing button or unkempt hair.[28]

Invention is at work, too, in the story of how the boys insulted Napoleon's parents, calling his mother the 'joyful' Madame Marbeuf, and his father a vulgar *'huissier'* – doorkeeper – not knowing the meaning of the term *'assesseur'*. Napoleon, it has been said, challenged the worst offender, Pougin des Ilets, to a duel, or according to another version simply knocked him unconscious. Incarcerated in punishment, he is supposed to have written a pompous letter of explanation to Marbeuf, quoted in full, complete with date: 8 October 1783. Marbeuf, it is claimed, hurried in person to Brienne to exculpate him. It need hardly be said that the letter, and Marbeuf's visit, are invented; but is there any truth underlying the rest of the tale? Did Balathier de Bragelonne perhaps revenge himself by repeating Corsican gossip? After all, he had been brought up in the entourage of Marbeuf and Madame Varese; he may have known that Marbeuf had dropped her in favour of Letizia; he may even have witnessed her outraged reactions. Many of the boys, moreover, must have seen Napoleon's parents when they visited Brienne in 1782. Did their elaborate dress, and Carlo's over-punctilious manners, suggest that they were dubious parvenus?[29]

If this often-repeated legend may cover some shreds of truth, the same cannot be said for a recently produced tale according to which Napoleon spent his holidays in Marbeuf's castle in Brittany. Marbeuf, presumed to be his father, is said to have lodged him in an attic where he pierced the roof so that he could better enjoy the view. A dormer window known as the *'fenêtre Napoléon'* exists; but nothing in the story is true: Napoleon was not Marbeuf's son; he had no holidays; he never went to Brittany while he was at school.[30]

Rather less incredible, but apparently no less mistaken, is Napoleon's supposed intimacy as a schoolboy with the Loménie de Brienne. Letizia first put the tale about in her less-than-truthful account to Chaptal of her visit to Brienne. Marbeuf, she told him, had recommended her son to the Loménie de Brienne, who invited him to their home and allowed him to ride their horses about their estate. Neither Napoleon nor his schoolfellows mention any such favour, while the historian of the Loménie denies that they even knew of Napoleon's existence. They had used their influence to have a military college located in their village, acted as its patrons and chose the masters (apparently skimping on quality); but they were far from bothering about individual boys. Moreover, there seems no reason why this particularly glamorous and powerful family should have concerned itself with Marbeuf, an old man governing a remote, primitive province, much less with his schoolboy protégé.[31]

The Loménie then cultivated the art of high living with a zest such as sometimes overtakes grand families (though not often the very grandest) towards the end of an epoch, as though fearing their days to be numbered (they were). They had acquired their lands and titles by marriage and purchase no earlier than the previous century. By the time Napoleon went to school their fortunes had been dramatically increased by the marriage of the comte de Brienne to the daughter of a wealthy wine merchant. She 'had ugliness sufficient to make up for her lack of wit', but brought a dowry of 7,000,000 livres. The matchmaker was the count's brother, who climbed the ecclesiastical ladder (as it was hoped Joseph Bonaparte might do) to become archbishop of Toulouse, then of Sens, so that he was able to contribute 'immense revenues' to his family. Such was the power of money in those last years of the Ancien Régime that the parvenu Loménie were thereby raised to a rank 'immediately after that of the royal princes'. In fact their position was better than that of princes, for princes have a boring protocol to observe and duties to perform while the Loménie were able to concentrate on what they most enjoyed.[32]

They began by pulling down the old medieval castle and building a house to their taste. It first appeared to the archbishop in a dream. On waking he summoned an architect – Jean-Louis Fontaine – and ordered him to materialize his vision. As this entailed flattening a mountain top the work progressed slowly and was barely finished before the Revolution put a stop to indulgence in dreams of that kind. The main body of the house was however completed not long before Napoleon arrived at Brienne, and all through his schooldays he had the sight of this sober neo-classical masterpiece overlooking the rather squalid village.[33]

Here was enacted 'a forgotten chapter . . . in the Thousand and One Nights of the French monarchy' in the words of a witness to the 'marvels of existence' of the Loménie. Their house was constantly full of guests who shared their passions for hunting, science, the theatre, public festivals: the fashionable distractions of the day. Napoleon may not have ridden their horses but he must surely have heard the sound of the horn, the cry of the hounds, and glimpsed the hundred or so horsemen galloping through the woods wearing scarlet with sky-blue and gold trimmings or dark green with crimson and silver according to whether the prey was deer or wolf or boar. And surely he saw the illuminations, and heard the music overflowing the house on the nights when everyone danced, the gentry on the floor above, the servants on the one below. It is sad that he who enjoyed acting on table tops could not have witnessed the plays performed by hosts and guests in the private theatre. Nor did he examine the celebrated collection of natural-history 'curiosities', including some stuffed crocodiles, or explore the laboratory equipped with the latest scientific instruments where a distinguished professor gave lectures on electricity which would surely have appealed to him more than the loan of a horse.

But there is no mention of any of this in his recorded sayings, not a word, even, about the high-summer celebrations on the feast days of the Assumption of the Virgin, date of his own birthday, and that of Saint Louis ten days later. The park was then open to the public, which thronged to admire the strolling players, the musicians and dancers and jugglers and tightrope walkers, the itinerant coconut and gingerbread vendors who took possession of the temples and pavilions and kiosks erected for the occasion. The entertainment had a ritual pagan exuberance: on the opening day wild animals were loosed in the park to be chased by hounds to their death in artificial lakes for the delight of the crowd, just as the execution of a man, observes an eyewitness, inaugurated the carnival in ancient Rome. Flamboyant fireworks ushered in the revels of the night, which often lasted till dawn. During the festivities organized in 1781 to honour the duc d'Orléans, garden and park and adjoining woodlands were lit by thousands of lanterns; for the best part of a month the scene was a 'miniature Versailles', writes Bourrienne, who must surely have been allowed a sight of these marvels with masters and schoolfellows after the royal visitor had distributed the prizes. Was Napoleon with him? Or, stern republican, did he stick to his algebra and Plutarch, turning his back on the fireworks filling the sky?[34]

That he was unknown to the Loménie is borne out by the absence of any personal appeal to them in the letters in which he and Letizia pleaded for scholarships for Lucien and Louis, and money for the Salines, in 1787 and 1788, when the archbishop was minister of finance and his brother minister of war.[35] The Loménie were then at the height of their fortunes. Their end was imminent and appalling. The Revolution of course robbed them of their offices. Although the archbishop, described by La Fayette as an 'enlightened liberal', had sworn the civil constitution of the clergy and lost his cardinal's hat in consequence, although he had refused the archbishopric of Paris on the plea that the least of the qualifications required for that dignity was to believe in God, he was none the less put under house arrest in November 1793. He died the following February before he could be taken to the scaffold, after taking poison secretly conveyed to him by Patrault, Napoleon's mathematics master, who had entered the service of the Loménie when the college had been closed some months before. His brother the count also contrived to visit him before he was himself arrested in May and executed along with three nephews he had adopted in the absence of direct heirs, as well as a niece.[36]

But the plain old countess weathered the Terror and lived to be welcomed to the court of Napoleon, whom she alternately called her 'son' and her 'god'. Not, it is said, on account of any favours bestowed by her on him in his schooldays nor by him on her since, but because as an unrepentant royalist she was incapable of addressing him as 'Majesty'. His goodwill to her and other surviving members of her family was a spectacular example of Napoleon's policy of conciliating the pre-revolutionary aristocracy.[37]

Napoleon and the countess owed each other nothing; but it was only human that he should behave to her as though she were his debtor. Human, too, that he should want to acquire her home. This he hoped to arrange when after being crowned emperor he stayed there as her guest for two days in April 1805 on his way to Milan to receive the crown of Italy. The visit seems to have been disappointing, though Wairy, his valet, reports that he kept up a convivial manner. But for

Napoleon, seeing the place for the first time since his schooldays, everything looked unrecognizably small. The school buildings had been so damaged by the Revolution that he gave up his plan of reviving the establishment and instead donated 12,000 francs to the mayor. The Loménie's mansion of course remained desirable, but the countess refused to sell. What could that huge house mean to her, a childless old widow, he demanded? 'Everything,' was her answer. She displeased him, too, when she complained of the familiarity of the peasants who swarmed to greet him; her manner, he concluded, made him realize that certain members of the nobility could never adapt to the common people.

But he slept those two nights in a columned bed draped with blue gold-fringed velvet under a canopy of plumes, the bed reserved for the fat duc d'Orléans who nearly a quarter of a century before had presented him with a prize for mathematics with the words: 'May it bring you happiness.' Or so certain writers maintain.[38]

✦⟨ 8 ⟩✦

END AND BEGINNING:
FATHER AND SON

The future of the scholarship boys at Brienne largely depended on the yearly visit of the inspector – or rather sub-inspector – of the military colleges. Every summer he made a tour of the schools and among other duties selected the brightest scholars to be promoted to the École Royale Militaire in Paris. This magnificent establishment, created at vast expense in 1751, abandoned in 1776 as too luxurious and then reopened, functioned from 1777 as an officers' cadet corps for the pick of the scholars in the provincial colleges together with the sons of nobles who could afford the pension of 2,000 livres. Less able pupils were drafted straight into regiments, where as *'volontaires'* they had to learn their job alongside the common soldiers while waiting for commissions, sometimes for years. Those, on the other hand, who had the brains to enter one of the special services – the navy, the artillery, the engineers – had to study in appropriate training schools, but might also prepare for the same exams in Paris if they had the luck to be placed there.[1]

The sub-inspector Keralio was remembered by Napoleon as a kindly old general, once tutor to the king of Bavaria, who liked to play with the boys after putting them through their tests and dine with his favourites in the refectory. Napoleon, it seems, took his fancy as early as 1782, though he was barely old enough to be admitted to the École Militaire and had spent less than four years in the college, where pupils were expected to stay at least six.[2]

With his encouragement, Napoleon opted for the navy, which could mean a period of training with the fleet at Toulon but did not rule out preparatory studies at the École Militaire. This choice, which he later discarded, is explained by the prestige accruing to the French navy since its performance in the American War of Independence, and – certainly in Napoleon's mind – the possibility of being stationed in the Mediterranean and so playing a part in Corsican affairs. No insular tradition was at work. On the contrary, the Corsicans had distinguished themselves from their Genoese rulers by a distaste for seafaring; outside the Genoese ports, along miles and miles of barely inhabited coastline seaborne trade and even fishing were minimal. But during the oppressed years after the conquest the French had press-ganged into the navy shepherds and peasants who were noted in an official memoir as sailors as good as any others, though an English consul observes that they deserted to Leghorn whenever possible. All the same, some Corsicans did earn fame at sea: Luce de Casabianca, who like Napoleon began life in a military college, ended it heroically on his burning ship, with his eleven-year-old son Giocante, at the battle of Aboukir. They are among the very few Corsicans, apart from Napoleon and Paoli, to have been heard of outside the island.[3]

Napoleon must have made his choice by the time his parents visited him in 1782; a choice that horrified Letizia, who later said that she found the students destined for the navy sleeping in hammocks; but was this strictly true? Even greater doubt overclouds the assertion of Sir William Fraser that Napoleon showed a fellow student at Brienne, an English boy, the future Lord Wenlock, a letter in 'remarkably good English' requesting admission to the British navy, which was eventually filed in the archives of the Admiralty. 'I have not searched for it,' Sir William naïvely adds in 1893, 'for the simple reason that I did not wish so good a story to become prematurely public'; obviously the best way of publicizing it in the circumstances. A memoir, however, from Carlo Bonaparte to the maréchal de Ségur, minister of war, in 1784, leaves no doubt that Napoleon did, for a time, under the influence of Keralio, aim at entering the French navy.[4]

In 1783 he was expecting to be transferred to the École Militaire in Paris or, if not, to the naval training school in Toulon. But Keralio had retired and his recommendation for Napoleon was not followed by his successor, Reynaud des Monts. Had he even made it? The only acceptable evidence comes from Napoleon's words at Saint Helena, and he may have been boasting. A supposed report on Napoleon by Keralio, published by Bourrienne and some earlier writers, is rejected by all serious historians. It certainly seems dubious. One is prepared to believe that Napoleon was under five *pieds* in height, good at mathematics, passable in history and geography but 'not well up in the

ornamental studies or in Latin', and even that he had the makings of
'an excellent sailor'. But the adjoining character sketch – 'obedient,
upright, grateful, conduct very regular' – unconvincing in Bourrienne's English text, is unrecognizable as a portrait in the French.
'*Caractère soumis, doux, honnête, reconnaissant, conduite très regulière*' look
like the words of a forgery (an early one, for the document was
circulating in 1814) intended to correct rumours of schoolboy violence.
Napoleon tried to propagate the same image from Saint Helena.
'Contrary to all the apocryphal histories that have given anecdotes of
his life, Napoleon, at Brienne, was gentle, quiet, conscientious and of a
great sensibility.' This was how Napoleon described himself to his
self-appointed biographer, Las Cases; the story of throwing mattresses
out of windows was kept for Bertrand, a tried friend whom he never
suspected of writing a book.[5]

Only two boys were promoted to Paris by the new inspector in
1783, and there was no question of sending Napoleon to Toulon. The
disappointment was even worse for his father. It was no easy matter
for an impecunious Corsican magistrate to bring up four children in
well-reputed French boarding-schools. He intended taking Maria
Anna (Elisa) to Saint-Cyr at the beginning of the school year of 1784
and on this same journey collect Lucien at Autun and take him to
Brienne on the assumption that he would replace Napoleon as a king's
scholar. Since the regulations forbade two brothers to hold scholarships simultaneously it now looked as though he would have to go on
paying Lucien's fees.[6]

Joseph gave further cause for concern. Having completed four years
education at Autun he was expected to prepare for the priesthood
under the protection of the bishop Marbeuf who, to the great satisfaction of the Bonaparte, had promised him the appointment of *sous-diacre*
with an income of 3,000 livres a year. So far he had been a model
student, much better adapted to his environment than Napoleon. Obedient to the point of timidity, but invariably cheerful, he was on the best
of terms with masters and pupils. Like his father he had a taste for
literature and, studious as Napoleon when a subject really interested
him, was given to browsing on the French classics 'clandestinely'
during the periods of recreation. Though apparently unambitious he
carried off prizes three years running, in 1781, 1782 and 1783, receiving
treasured volumes of Fénélon and Saint-Lambert besides certificates –
'*témoignages de satisfaction*' – in the form of engravings of saints inscribed
with flattering formulae by the abbé Simon, director of studies. A

'*prix d'excellence*' was his reward for an essay on Cornelia's speech when she is holding the urn bearing Pompey's ashes in Corneille's *Mort de Pompée*, a passage he alone had bothered to read. And according to his friend, Jean-Baptiste de Grandchamp, who later became an actor, Joseph had a 'veritable gift' for the stage and triumphed as Aman in the school's production of Racine's *Esther*. At the prize-giving ceremony of 1782 he played the leading role of Dorante in a bowdlerized version of Molière's *Les Fâcheux*.

He ended his studies with a glowing report from the principal: 'no one in the school, physician, rhetorician or philospher, was more talented than he or could do a better translation' (presumably from the Latin). Such qualifications, advantageous in an ecclesiastical career, were unfortunately irrelevant to the one Joseph had chosen; for to everyone's dismay he had suddenly decided to enter the army instead of the Church. He made this known in dramatic style at the prize-giving of 1783 presided over by the prince de Condé. At the end of the ceremony Joseph had the privilege of reciting some verses in his honour. The prince, as a matter of form, asked him what walk of life he would enter, what '*état*'. Whereupon Joseph, amid general consternation, announced 'I want to serve the king.' The prince at least approved and the next day Joseph wrote to tell Napoleon the news. He had decided to enter the artillery, he said, provided Napoleon gave up his plans for the navy. He did; perhaps the only occasion in which Joseph influenced him in a major decision. The letter is unfortunately lost, with others they exchanged; we only know of Napoleon's reactions after he had discussed Joseph's future with his harassed father in June of the following year.[7]

His children were by no means Carlo's only source of anxiety. Misfortune had dogged him ever since he had returned from his glamorous trip with Letizia to Bourbonne-les-Bains and Versailles in September 1782. The Odone heritage, former property of the Jesuits, after three years' earnest solicitation still escaped his grasp. Nothing came of his pleas to the authorities composed with a mixture of pathos and guile that is in itself pathetic. Defrauded by the Jesuits, reduced to 'indigence', father of seven children and unable to give them an education in keeping with their rank, he begs for a lease (no more) on the 'garden of the Milelli', a place most suitable for giving a good example in the cultivation of olive trees, and the little house called La Badina in the rue Malherba, with a cellar where he could stock his wine, which so far he had been unable to keep beyond a year. But his file accumulated in the administrative archives while rivals and enemies tried to wreck the deal and the property remained in the hands of the *subdélégué* Souiris, who no doubt drew a benefit from it.[8]

Sordid domestic squabbles added to his discomfiture. Part of an upper floor of the *casa* Bonaparte, which then probably had three floors above the ground floor, was occupied by a distant relative, Maria Giustina, granddaughter of Carlo's great-great-grandfather, and her husband, a Pozzo di Borgo. The trouble was with Maria Giustina, quarrelsome by nature. She went to law with Carlo when he claimed, obviously unjustly, exclusive use of the main entrance and stairs; but in January 1783 Carlo struck back and had her condemned to pay him a fine for the insults she had hurled at him the previous November. There was worse. Carlo had hung one of his best costumes out of a window to air, a habit still practised by some of the older people in Ajaccio. Maria Giustina poured over it a pot of urine: *'orina'*, the Italian text leaves no room for doubt. This was a kind of accident common enough in Ajaccio until drains were installed in recent years; to limit the damage municipal regulations decreed that receptacles should only be emptied out of windows between 11 p.m. and dawn. Carlo would not have hung out his clothes at night; Maria Giustina had mistaken the time, perhaps on purpose. Carlo went to law. Three hearings were needed, the opinion of an expert, and the unsuccessful efforts of a soldier from the garrison to remove the stains before Maria Giustina, on 17 January 1783, was condemned to pay the cost of the garment. This sorry incident has stuck in the memory of later writers and their readers whereas Carlo's more creditable struggles have been misunderstood or ignored.[9]

While he was warring with his old great-aunt his exploitation of the Salines, undertaken with such optimism, confidently backed by Marbeuf, had run into trouble. In October 1782, soon after his return to the island, the nursery gardener brought at such expense from Tuscany had died of malaria, or in Carlo's words: 'not having taken the necessary precautions, succumbed to the inclemency of the air'. He had been obliged to replace him with a family brought from Avignon, again expensively because skilled workers only emigrated to Corsica for 'considerable profit'. In December 1782 he had duly received an instalment of his subsidy. But the mulberry seeds he had planted that autumn, imported from Italy and France, gave no result; victim of dishonest suppliers, he was unable to produce his quota of seedlings the following year. So he explained at length to Souiris, who inspecting the property on 28 October 1783 reported that there was 'no appear-ance of the execution' of the contract, and 'no vestige of a mulberry plantation'. Carlo's good faith was not questioned; but he was warned that until he fulfilled his engagements subsidies would be withheld.[10]

Carlo was none the less tackling the Salines with a desperate de-termination. He finished draining two thirds of the marsh. Early in 1784 Marbeuf paid a state visit to the site and 'had the pleasure, to the joy and satisfaction of the whole town' of witnessing the sowing of barley on the recuperated land. Meanwhile Carlo, using seed imported from France (but obviously from another merchant) planted between eight and ten thousand mulberry trees which in June 1784 were to be seen standing a *pied* ('*palma*') and a half high, to the approval of an inspector from the *Nobles Douze*.[11]

But the cost had been catastrophic. The draining operations had cost the Bonaparte 29,070 livres, and in Carlo's estimation another 40,000 were needed to complete the job before the autumn rains. This was the subject of a memoir he drafted to the minister of war in 1784: 'father of seven children, having exhausted his resources' he came 'to throw himself at the foot of the throne' to implore compensation.[12]

The fault lay with Bedigis, the official geometer Marbeuf had put in charge of the work in 1779. He might be qualified to direct the *Plan Terrier*, the magnificent land survey of the island devotedly carried on under successive regimes until its completion in 1795 during the British occupation; but he was incapable of draining a small marsh. Under-estimating the task as '*facilissimo*', he accumulated useless expenses while putting about the rumour that the whole project was a mistake. According to Rossi he 'betrayed' Carlo, who only refrained from saying so because he dared not offend a Frenchman. But his motive seems more likely to have been fear of offending Marbeuf, who re-peatedly contributed his own money to the enterprise. Carlo's only resource was to appeal over their heads to the ministers in Paris, in the hope that they might release funds to save the face of the government, if not the fortune of the Bonaparte.[13]

The amount spent – over 29,000 livres – seems less surprising than that Carlo, at whatever risk or sacrifice, was able to spend it. What were the 'resources' he exhausted? The government had provided less than half that sum since he started work on the Salines in 1777. Nothing can have been deducted from his salary of 1,200 livres. The revenues of the Bonaparte from wine and stock-breeding have been estimated at a maximum of 8,000 livres a year. More than a quarter must have been consumed over the past seven years by the Salines. Luciano seems not to have objected. Indeed there is evidence that he collaborated, supervising the work when Carlo was away, while taking good care to make him repay his outgoings. An agricultural investment was presumably something he approved of. He is never said to have complained of the cost of the Salines, though frequently lamenting, after Carlo's death, that his journeys had ruined him. With his narrow peasant's outlook he was apparently unable to grasp that the one activity entailed the other.[14]

In the summer of 1784 it was more than ever necessary for Carlo to throw himself at the foot of the throne, for he had reason to fear that his essential source of finance was drying up. In October 1783, that unlucky month in Carlo's existence, Marbeuf, recently widowed, married a highly born eighteen-year-old French girl by the name of Catherine-Salinguerra-Antoinette Gaillardon de Fenoyl. In March 1784 she was pregnant, as soon became known. Whatever had or had not occurred between Letizia and Marbeuf it was evident that from now on she would cease to be the centre of his affections and the Bonaparte would play a lesser role in his life. Significantly, the last mention of a visit to Cargese in Carlo's 'Livre de Raison' is of sending the children there in February 1783. He and Letizia had not been invited for Christmas; the days when they could use the house as their country residence were over. Marbeuf might still lend himself to the rustic ceremony of the barley sowing; but could he be counted on to cover Carlo's deficit?

Putting on a brave face, Carlo composed a sonnet for the circumstance. Poor value in the original Italian, it is impossible to translate into bearable English. But perhaps Marbeuf was touched by Carlo's clumsy effort to please; for clumsy it was indeed. 'Victorious over envy and death,' he begins, tactlessly reminding Marbeuf that he was old and envied, and continues nine lines on: 'Soon will be seen a charming son, the true image of yourself,' a statement which again one feels could have been more tactfully worded.[15]

The means Carlo resorted to for financing his journey in 1784 leaves little doubt as to his changed relations with Marbeuf. He was reduced to borrowing 600 livres from the military commander of Ajaccio, comte Rosel de Beaumanoir, and the same sum from an aunt Lillina, who obliged him to give her some family silver in security, including a holy-water stoup. Was she ever repaid? Did she return the silver? I have found no other mention of this aunt. At all events Letizia, reduced to poverty after the death of Carlo, still had enough silver to offer to sell to repay her debt to Beaumanoir when he eventually left Corsica, which he refused. He did nothing to reclaim the loan till 1802, when at the age of eighty-eight, exiled in Jersey, deprived of his pension by the Revolution, he appealed to Napoleon, First Consul. 'Send him ten times the sum,' Napoleon is said to have said, 'and strike him off the list of émigrés immediately.'[16]

Carlo left Corsica early in June 1784. He took with him not only the seven-year-old Maria-Anna (Elisa), but also a cousin, a Mademoiselle Casabianca of about the same age, who had also secured a place at Saint-Cyr.[17] The responsibility of looking after them throughout the long, complicated journey by boat and coach or water coach must have weighed heavy; but Carlo doted on his children (an aspect of his character that has been insufficiently emphasized) and one can be sure he was kind to the two little girls. At Autun he stopped to collect Lucien, now a lively boy of nine – 'petulant' – according to one of his masters, and there he heard of Joseph's rash decision from his own lips.[18]

Well-dressed Carlo surely was; but he can no longer have had the 'superb' allure that impressed one of the masters when he first arrived there with Joseph and Napoleon more than five years earlier on his way to Versailles. Carlo was ill, seriously ill, and not the least object of his journey was to consult the celebrated de Lassonne, doctor to the queen. His complaint was exactly what one would expect in a person of his temperament, leading his life; in fact an occupational disease. Over-anxious, over-zealous, over-active, constantly on the move, financially and socially insecure, alternating between need and luxury, skimping and squandering, feasting and starving, he was a natural subject for an ulcer of the stomach, which in the absence of adequate treatment turned to cancer and killed him young. Napoleon, dying of the same malady, gave Antommarchi a tragi-comic picture of his father, afflicted with vomiting and loss of appetite, yet always eager and agitated, rushing from doctor to doctor and credulously gulping down drugs and futile remedies like soft pears – 'poires fondantes' – which were better in Paris than in Corsica.[19]

With the three young children in his care Carlo reached Brienne on 21 June. He lost no time before discussing Joseph's future with Napoleon. Their views are expressed in a letter Napoleon wrote soon afterwards to an unnamed uncle, probably Joseph Fesch, who at twenty-one was finishing his studies at the seminary of Aix, where Joseph Bonaparte should have joined him.

This is the earliest authenticated text of Napoleon's, and it is an astonishing document. Indeed were it not authenticated by serious scholars one might be tempted to regard it at first reading with suspicion, so surprising is its maturity of thought. Both Lucien and Joseph are coldly scrutinized, their characters and capacities appraised; Joseph's future is examined with calculating objectivity. One historian explains the tenor of the letter by supposing it to have been practically dictated by Carlo. True, his opinions are several times cited, yet the voice is not his. After the initial shock one recognizes it as that of Napoleon, general, First Consul and Emperor, the voice that emanates from his innumerable letters, edicts and proclamations, and finally from his will at Saint Helena, the voice that assessed people and situations with an implacable assurance, dispassionate, penetrating and pragmatic. The letter surprises only in being alien to the image of the boy conveyed in anecdotes and historical gossip: isolated, turbulent and aggressive. During all those years for which we have no better sources, Napoleon, beneath his excessive behaviour, had been developing the judgement that was to become his major asset. His mind functioned at fourteen much as it would on his deathbed.

Lucien is dismissed in a few lines. Age: nine. Height: three *pieds*, seven *pouces*, six *lignes*. In the sixth class for Latin. Healthy, fat, lively, scatterbrained; 'one must hope he will turn out well'. Napoleon regards him like an unindulgent schoolmaster. So indeed thought Lucien when his brother received him 'without the least sign of affection . . .'. 'Since then,' he writes, 'I have sometimes thought that he was not very pleased to see a little marmoset of a younger brother . . . entering on the same career as himself.' Napoleon was evidently insensitive to the charm that comes out so potently in Lucien's writings. In Lucien's opinion he was 'naturally very serious' and inspired fear; their unsatisfactory relationship must have dated from those days.

Napoleon probably never much cared for Lucien; but his letter shows as little feeling for Joseph, whom he always held in affection, as is well known. Having quoted the fulsome and irrelevant report of the principal of Autun, he sums up his unsuitability for a military career: not brave enough to face a battle, nor strong enough to endure a campaign; too delicate for the navy. As for the artillery or the engineers, these services demanded more knowledge of mathematics than he possessed or was capable of acquiring, sustained hard work being foreign to his nature. What could he become except a garrison officer, excelling in futile compliments? He would always shine in society; but how would he show up on the battlefield? Did he want to join the infantry so as to do nothing all day? Three quarters of the infantry officers were bad characters. Let him stick to the Church; the bishop of Autun would make sure he got a bishopric and large revenues; what advantages for the family! Some of these reflections were no doubt inspired by Carlo, who is mentioned; but most bear the mark of Napoleon, who in fact had a better grasp of the problem. He had more understanding of Joseph, who wrote to him frequently, whereas he only sent 'two lines' to his father from time to time. And certainly Napoleon was better informed about the conditions of a military career; this was something he could discuss with boys who came from military families, or with the masters, some of whom, like the Berton brothers, had started life in the army. His conclusion was that a final effort should be made to induce Joseph to enter the Church and that if this failed his father should take him back to Corsica, where he might eventually decide to go in for the law.[20]

Carlo apparently stayed only one night at Brienne before hastening on towards the capital to leave the two little girls at Saint-Cyr.[21] After which he set about besieging the authorities with his petitions. Ironically it was the illness of the maréchal de Ségur, not his own, that prevented him presenting his case in person, so that on 30 June he resorted to a pleading letter. Deprived of the honour of paying court to the minister, given his illness, he takes the liberty of sending four memoirs, the purpose of his journey from Corsica, which should be forwarded to the appropriate departments. 'I am father of seven children,' he continues, 'with an eighth on the way'; for to complicate matters further Letizia was pregnant yet again.

The memoirs concerned his sons, the Milelli, the Salines; drafts have survived, passages of which served in the final versions. For Lucien he begs a scholarship at Brienne, where he has already placed him as a boarder, having counted on Napoleon's transfer to the École Militaire in Paris and then to the navy at Toulon. The retirement of Keralio had however altered Napoleon's 'destiny'; now he implores his promotion so that Lucien can take his place as a scholar, as he was unable to go on paying his fees. Carlo was not ignorant of the regulation that forbade two brothers to hold scholarships simultaneously. Indeed he had received a discouraging letter on the subject from the minister in October of the previous year, which also warned him that

Lucien's age might be 'an invincible obstacle'. According to a recent regulation candidates were not accepted after reaching the age of ten. Lucien was born on 21 May 1775, so that he still had a margin of nine months before obtaining a scholarship became imperative. Napoleon, on the other hand, might be required to complete six years' education before leaving Brienne. He had entered the college on 12 May 1779, more than a week before Lucien's birthday; but did six years' education mean six school years, which would not be completed before August 1785? Could Napoleon be moved on before Lucien became too old to qualify for a scholarship? This tormenting calculation was perhaps the reason why Carlo had taken Lucien to Brienne, so that he would be at hand to slip into Napoleon's place the moment a scholarship became possible. The move was not in itself advantageous, for the fees were higher than at Autun: 480 livres a year instead of 360 or 380. Taking him to Brienne was a gamble; but that was how Carlo went through life. The reply to his petition was automatic: two brothers could not benefit from a scholarship at the same time.

The petition for Joseph solicited his entry into the artillery or engineers; precisely the services for which Napoleon had judged him inadequate. It must have been presented after Joseph had somehow convinced his father and brother of his determination to catch up in mathematics, in a correspondence now lost. A letter on the subject from Carlo to the minister is published, with the date 18 July. Enclosing the unsuitable report from the principal of Autun, he has no hesitation in appealing to his 'paternal heart' in favour of a large family eager to serve its king. In reply he was advised to address himself to the inspector-general of the military colleges, the marquis de Timbrune.[22]

In reminding the minister that the promise to give him a lease on the Milelli and La Badina was still unfulfilled, Carlo showed a certain confidence in the wording of his petition. He proposed a rent of 150 livres, which, while considered too low by the minister, was Carlo's method of bargaining for a contract of which he felt fundamentally sure. With some reason: writing to Boucheporn, the *intendant* of Corsica, Ségur admits that even regarding Carlo's request 'in the most unfavourable light', it was 'at least probable' that his rights were founded, so that it behoved the government to treat him with favour. On the other hand, Carlo's memoir concerning the Salines was as dramatic as the circumstances warranted: he had sunk over 29,000 livres in the project, reached the end of his resources; he even lacked the means of staying in Paris for any length of time; he beseeched the minister to make haste in settling the affair.[23]

Most luckily for Carlo, Boucheporn happened then to be in Paris, as well as the geometer Bedigis. His petition, passed on to Calonne, minister of finance, released a flood of correspondence between ministries, *intendant, subdélégué* and geometers that continued from July well into the autumn. Boucheporn was consulted: loyal to his colleagues as much as to Carlo he confirmed that the draining of the Salines was beneficial to public health as well as to agriculture, that Marbeuf had encouraged and subsidized the enterprise, that it had swallowed up Carlo's fortune, that it had to be completed before the autumn rains. In his opinion the work should be taken over by the government, operations of this kind being rarely successful when left to individuals. Bedigis, who knew the terrain, should remain in charge. Consulted, Bedigis, though handicapped by the absence of 'documents and drawings', declared that the reeds should be uprooted from the marsh and estimated the remaining work at 15,000 livres. On 6 September Calonne authorized Boucheporn to have the most urgent work carried out immediately, pending a further investigation. Boucheporn passed on the order to Souiris in Corsica on 11 September. But the day before, Bedigis, treacherous and cornered, had also written to Souiris telling him to undertake only the most indispensable work, the Corsican treasury being short of funds. He maintained his obstructive attitude throughout the autumn, so that Carlo, returning to Corsica with high hopes in mid-August, had to face disappointment yet again.[24]

In the meantime he had carried out the other obligation of his journey by taking the two girls to Saint-Cyr. A letter he wrote to the father of Mlle Casabianca on 28 July from Versailles gives a sharp, surprising glimpse of eighteenth-century living: the coquetry of a seven-year-old girl, the calculations of her elders, the cupidity of the nuns. In keeping with her wishes Carlo had taken Mlle Casabianca to the school in her riding costume, and he had handed over her evening dresses to the mother superior. The girl was presumably put straight into the school uniform; at all events Carlo expected the earrings she was wearing to be returned to him, as well as a silver buckle and her corsage, apparently another item of finery. But the mother superior, approached on the subject a few days later, told him that the jewellery had already been sold as was the custom when a girl came of poor parents, the proceeds being used for her keep. As for the earrings, she had to go on wearing them so as to keep open the piercing of her ears. 'If I had thought of it I would have taken them from her beforehand, but now there's no remedy,' Carlo unfeelingly concludes. He goes on to give an account of the cost of the journey: he had received 300 livres for the girl's travel expenses and she had been given twelve; he owed her father fifty-six. Scrupulous, Carlo was also needy and grasping. The Corsican Estates had not been summoned since 1781, so that Carlo was still a member of the *Nobles Douze*, who advised the *Commissaires du roi* turn by turn for periods of two months with a monthly indemnity of 150 livres. Carlo's period of office was due to begin; he begs Casabianca to find someone to replace him, Giubega, or a certain Rossi: 'That would please me because "*cent écus*" do no harm on one's return from Paris.' Did he expect these friends to do his job for nothing? He still felt close enough to Marbeuf to ask Casabianca to discuss the replacement with him, while wishing him long life and a male child.[25]

Nothing is said of Maria Anna – Elisa – except that she lent Mlle Casabianca a hairnet for the journey. Had she, too, evening gowns in her luggage? The mother superior told Carlo that Mlle Casabianca's would be kept for the theatre, so that it seems that the inmates of Saint-Cyr still enjoyed treats of this kind. Not, perhaps, very often, for when Napoleon, fetching Elisa home from school in 1792, insisted on taking her to the opera in Paris she was so ready to be shocked that she at first kept her eyes tight shut. Thanks to the Revolution her education had not worked out as Carlo expected. She never received the promised dowry of 3,000 livres; only the cost of her journey back to Corsica when the school was suppressed in August 1792. All the same, her years at school were not wasted. The discipline, as much as the learning imposed on Carlo's elder children in their French boarding-schools, gave them a much better preparation for their enormous future responsibilities than they would ever have received at home. Elisa turned out pretentious: 'she had contracted habits of pride and acidity', Napoleon recalls, while Laure d'Abrantès observes that she had 'never known anyone so disagreeably sharp' ('*pointue*'). Yet she was the most respect-worthy of Napoleon's sisters, if not the most attractive: less frivolous than Pauline, though less warm-hearted, loyal when Caroline betrayed, she proved herself a capable ruler of her principalities; in Napoleon's words her activity was 'prodigious' and she corresponded directly with his ministers and quite often opposed their will.[26]

In the course of his crowded weeks in the capital Carlo had apparently been pulling strings to hasten Napoleon's promotion from Brienne. This one gathers from the ceremonious expressions of gratitude in a letter Napoleon wrote to him in mid-September. Like the earlier letter to his uncle, it is somewhat pompous in style. Perhaps the masters at Brienne had a hand in it; but the thought is unmistakably Napoleon's, and the authenticity of the document is unquestioned. 'My dear Father,' it begins, 'Your letter as you can well believe has not given me much pleasure . . .' Napoleon refers to a letter, now lost, in which Carlo told him of his return to Corsica without revisiting Brienne. The decision was no doubt taken on grounds of health, for Napoleon mentions a cure 'at the waters'. The royal doctor had thought of nothing better for Carlo than to prescribe a diet of soft pears and send him back to the Corsican medicinal springs, probably the renowned ferruginous source at Orezza which, while doing nothing for his malady, at least gave him a spell of rest under the chestnut trees in the mountains of his native land.

While Carlo had been trying to organize Joseph's future in Paris, Napoleon had been making inquiries on his behalf at Brienne. Joseph was determined to enter the artillery and now he had persuaded Napoleon to do the same. The lucidity, authority and sense of responsibility in the letter of this fifteen-year-old schoolboy are once again surprising. Joseph, he tells his father, should come to Brienne where they would prepare together for the entrance exam. This would be more convenient than sending him to the artillery school at Metz. Napoleon had discussed his case with the principal, and with father Patrault, who would be happy to give him a crash course in mathematics. He should arrive in November; it would be a 'consolation' for the three brothers to be together at school.

Yet Napoleon's mind and feelings are still fixed on his homeland. He asks his father to send him Boswell's book on Corsica – that paean of praise for the Corsican nationalists and their leader – as well as any histories of the island he could lay hands on. The last words of his letter are messages to his relations – his grandmothers, an uncle, an aunt – in Ajaccio. The sense of responsibility is still apparent: 'I beg you to take care of them'; but the tone is that of an affectionate child.[27]

The letter was written around 13 September, for Napoleon observes: 'the inspector will be here the 15th or 16th at the latest this month; that is to say in three days'. His detached manner of announcing the news and his carefully laid plans for himself and Joseph hardly suggest that he was hoping for anything from the inspector's visit, in spite of the efforts Carlo had been making on his behalf in Paris.[28]

But a surprise was in store: that of being chosen with three schoolfellows for promotion to the École Royale Militaire in Paris. The move took place with little delay: on 30 October, according to Napoleon, they left Brienne, accompanied by a monk. One of his companions was Castres de Vaux who recalls that Napoleon travelled with a stack of notes on the books he had been reading; lacking the 'automatic memory of children' he always recorded his learning. The journey was by coach and water coach; the first night was spent at Arcis-sur-Aube, the second at Nogent-sur-Seine, from whence they proceeded down the river to reach Paris on the evening of the third day. They landed on the left bank in what Napoleon calls 'the Latin country'; but they were allowed no leisure to explore the already celebrated Quartier Latin and were taken straight to the École Militaire in the plain of Grenelle. When Laure d'Abrantès wrote that her uncle found Napoleon wandering bewildered in the ill-frequented arcades of the Palais Royal on the night of his arrival in Paris and took him home to dinner, she was simply – as often – inventing.

A monk accompanied the students from door to door. Tales of Napoleon's visits to Laure's family, to the bishop Marbeuf, to Giacinto Arrighi and to Elisa at Saint-Cyr are no better founded; the cadets were never allowed into town. Napoleon's existence was as cloistered as at Brienne. Yet at first he was not at ease in the École Militaire; the first night, he remembered, was an ordeal: 'the tone was different'. He had entered an unfamiliar world.[29]

Gone was the stuffy but no doubt reassuring provincial atmosphere of the monastery at Brienne; the École Royale Militaire was designed to illustrate the grandeur and glory of monarchical France. Built in the mid eighteenth century by the great architect Gabriel, financed in the reckless manner of the time by Madame de Pompadour, the magnate Pâris-Duverney, a lottery, and a tax on playing-cards, publicized by Beaumarchais, who gave lessons there to harp-playing pupils of the royal family, it is one of the grandest Parisian monuments. Its long facade giving on to the Champs de Mars is ennobled by Corinthian columns supporting a pediment loaded with allegorical figures beneath a quadrilateral dome; the courtyard on the opposite side of the building with its two-storeyed Doric colonnades is more restrained but no less elegant. Inside all is splendour: the decoration, carved, sculpted, painted and gilded, of walls and ceilings, doors and chimneypieces, is a sumptuous framework for the many statues and portraits of military heroes and Le Paon's canvases of victorious battlefields, resounding names in French history: Fribourg, Tournai, Lawfeld, Fontenoy. A flamboyant statue of Louis XV by Lemoine that once stood in the courtyard was destroyed in 1792 by a revolutionary crowd, to be replaced, eventually, by an austere bust of Napoleon surmounting the curving staircase with a gilded bronze balustrade designed by Gabriel with such magnificence that it provoked reproofs for ostentatious extravagance from the *intendant* of the establishment and the minister of war.[30]

Here the fifteen-year-old Corsican schoolboy was flung into the pomp and pride of the century which so far he had only glimpsed, faintly, in the entourage of Marbeuf and the home of the Loménie de Brienne, from afar. This establishment, which would later be dominated by his memory, then represented all he disliked and despised: aristocratic prepotence, conspicuous luxury. It is true that an attempt was made, as in the provincial colleges, to impose equality of status between paying pupils and scholarship boys; but the result was to teach the poor to live richly rather than the rich poorly, as at Brienne. They all wore the same handsome uniform, in blue, with touches of yellow and scarlet on cuffs and revers and silver braiding; they were formed into a single cadet corps organized on military lines, separated into divisions and squads – *peletons* – with cadets as divisional commanders wearing the appropriate insignia. Everyone in the school was noble; but the paying pupils were in the minority: eighty-three in Napoleon's time in a total of two hundred and fifteen. Yet the style was theirs: here they floated along in the environment to which they were born, served and waited on and protected by a host of inferior beings.[31]

The staff in fact outnumbered the students, in accordance with the reckless spending habits of the Ancien Régime. At the summit of the huge pyramid were the governor, Timbrune, the sub-inspector, Reynaud des Monts, Valfort, director of studies, and the commander of the cadet corps, each with his colleagues and subordinates and secretarial staff. A director of buildings had his own underlings. Some thirty professors and a librarian earned salaries of 2,400 livres; religious duties occupied five or six priests, a couple of sacristans, an organist and organ blower, a choir director and choirboys and a chapel sweeper. The riding instructors and their grooms and stable hands constituted another department, as did the doctor, with a salary of 8,000 livres, his assistant surgeons, an apothecary and an infirmary staff of nuns. An armourer and a de-ruster of weapons were attached to military exercises. There were concierges and doorkeepers and guardians of the prison (the form of punishment inflicted), besides a horde of minor specialists such as a clock mender, a gardener, lawn cutter, stove tender, a 'fountain boy', whose health broke down in 1781 through being continually 'in the aqueducts' so that he had to be given a pension, lighters and cleaners of lamps that had to be kept lit in the courtyards except on nights of full moon, a wig-dresser and his assistants, a tailor, several shoemakers and some hundred and fifty servants including a hierarchized kitchen staff of which not the least was a 'fattener of fowls'.[32]

No wonder Napoleon exclaimed to Las Cases: 'We were magnificently fed and served, treated in every way like officers possessed of great wealth, certainly greater than that of most of our families, and far above what many of us would enjoy later on.' There were of course lapses. Vaublanc, inveterate grumbler, recalls how on the very day Monteynard, just appointed minister of war, arrived impromptu for a meal, the salt salmon was rancid and the dried haricot beans old and full of little holes, while the mixture of wine and water known as *abondance* was served in disgustingly dirty pewter mugs. This must have occurred in 1771. After the school was reorganized it was decided, in 1777, to substitute glass and porcelain for pewterware.[33]

For one who, like Napoleon, had started life dining off black Corsican pottery on the days when Letizia had not sent him supperless to bed, the prodigality of the École Militaire was naturally shocking. A memoir he is supposed to have written on the subject and sent to Berton, principal of Brienne, publicized by Bourrienne, has however been dismissed as a fake. But when he came to power he insisted on austere conditions in the military academies, obliging the inmates to groom and shoe their horses and eat out of common mess-tins.[34]

At Saint Helena Napoleon made a point of pouring scorn on the French aristocrats: they were 'the cause of the Revolution', 'the curse of the nation', he told O'Meara, 'imbeciles' who hated all who were not 'hereditary asses' like themselves. Bent on promoting his image as the man of the people, Napoleon was of course expressing only one aspect of his views of a class he had known how to charm and to use. All the same his opinion was genuine. It inspired his guiding creed, '*la carrière ouverte aux talents*' which went far to invigorate French society and usher in the modern era of middle-class supremacy. Like most life-directing ideas it emanated from youthful conditions. Napoleon's attitude was typical of one born on the bottom rung of the aristocracy who knew its privileged members at close quarters and had suffered

their disdain. His reactions were linked to Corsica, where the French
nobility represented the alien oppressor; his years in French schools
confirmed and intensified what he already believed. Much of his contempt for the sons of the great must have dated from his experience
of them at the École Militaire. Needless to say they were not the best
workers: most of them failed their exams. Nor, apparently, were they
very brave. Napoleon is said to have boasted that though small in
body he joined the minor nobles in fist fights with the boys of high
birth and always came out victorious.[35]

Yet anecdotes of conflict are much fewer than at Brienne. Historians
have made much of a supposed feud with Le Picard de Phélippeaux,
relating how he and Napoleon kicked each other under the table when
seated side by side, and how Picot de Peccaduc, placed between them to
keep the peace, complained that he received knocks from them both.
But this, surely, was no more than schoolboy ragging. Later, however,
they became enemies in earnest. Like most of Napoleon's schoolfellows
Phélippeaux emigrated with the Revolution, and, more enterprising
than the average, joined the British and opposed Napoleon's army with
devastating efficacy at Acre, where he died. Yet whether from pride,
admiration of his exploits, Corsican respect for the dead or a genuine
affinity in their schooldays, Napoleon never spoke ill of him. On the
contrary, he told Montholon that Phélippeaux was one of the two
comrades of his youth with whom he had felt most in sympathy. 'By one
of the mysteries of Providence,' he said, both had exercised 'an immense
influence' on his 'destiny'. Phélippeaux had stopped him marching on
Constantinople and so restoring 'the throne of the orient'. His other
friend, Des Mazis, had saved him from suicide.[36]

Alexandre Des Mazis – 'faithful Des Mazis' – was one of the few
human beings Napoleon ever took to spontaneously, without the
prompting of family ties, political contingencies or sexual attraction. A
year older than Napoleon, he had come to the École Militaire from a
provincial college in 1783. Not much is known of him except that he
belonged to a military family of Strasbourg, was royalist, capable but
not brilliant (he failed his artillery exam in 1784), but unusually sensitive and generous. Undisturbed by Napoleon's bizarre personality he
got to know him soon after his arrival. It is said that he instructed
Napoleon in infantry drill; at all events they prepared and sat together
for the artillery exam in August 1785, passed at the same time and
were stationed according to their wish in the same regiment, La Fère,
at Valence.

Their friendship withstood political divergencies, two occasions when Napoleon borrowed money, and a literary reproof from Napoleon when Des Mazis fell in love. 'What strange malady has possessed you?' Napoleon demands in a high-flown imaginary dialogue written, it seems, in 1786. Love, in his opinion, was detrimental to society and to individual happiness; it rendered its victim incapable of reason and of serving society or state. This was composed at Valence, where Napoleon first borrowed money – a small sum – from his friend. The second occasion was in 1795 when the Revolution had flung them apart and they met by dramatic accident in Paris, on a quay of the Seine. Both were acutely concerned for their families. Des Mazis, who had emigrated, had returned disguised as a workman to see his mother. Napoleon, temporarily out of favour and penniless, was frantic with anxiety after an appeal from Letizia, stranded in Marseilles without means of keeping herself and her younger children. Her enemies had no hesitation in saying that she solved the problem by turning her house into a brothel; Napoleon himself feared for the 'honour' of her daughters. He was actually contemplating suicide when he ran into Des Mazis and poured out his story. Des Mazis gave him 30,000 gold livres on the spot and without more ado Napoleon 'ran like a madman' to send it to his mother. Subsequent searches for Des Mazis failed. It was not till Napoleon was ruling France that the friends were reunited, when Napoleon returned the loan multiplied by ten, and besides granting Des Mazis a succession of lucrative appointments.[37]

A journal by Des Mazis was published in 1954: eighteen rather disappointing pages. Trivialities and minor inaccuracies can be excused in the memoirs of an elderly man writing of events long passed (apparently in 1821); but it is hard to see how the episode of the balloon has been included unless the text has been tampered with. Napoleon's schooldays coincided with a period of pioneer ballooning; each flight was a national event. Des Mazis relates how a balloon was to be sent up from the Champ de Mars on a public holiday. Its ascension was for some reason delayed while the cadets of the École Militaire, lining the crowd, waited impatiently under arms. Finally Napoleon strode out of the ranks and slashed its tethering ropes with his sword; the balloon was pierced, collapsed, and Napoleon was severely punished. No more is needed to throw discredit on the journal. An incident of this kind did take place, but on 2 March 1784, eight months before Napoleon entered the school. A crowd was assembled on the Champ de Mars with the cadets in attendance. An enthusiastic Benedictine escaped his monastery to join Blanchard in the ascent; but the balloon was unable to lift two people. While the monk was ejected from the *nacelle* into the arms of military officers, who promptly marched him back to his monastery, an equally enthusiastic cadet, Dupont de Chambon, rushed to take his place. He too was thrown out of the *nacelle* but not before he had wounded Blanchard and burst the balloon. No balloons were sent up during Napoleon's stay at the École Militaire. But the story of his spectacular intervention went around during his lifetime and was not even quashed by his own denial of it at Saint Helena.

One may legitimately wonder how far the rest of Des Mazis' journal is to be trusted. Not that he has anything at all startling to say. That Napoleon was hot-tempered in fencing practice, and impatient of military drill one can easily believe; nor is one surprised to be told that he was bad at writing, keen on history and geography, bored by drawing and dancing lessons and so bored by German that he spent the classes surreptitiously reading Montesquieu, guide and inspirer of Paoli. A voracious reader, severe in morals, taciturn in company, given to solitary musing and dreams of liberating Corsica: these observations are again in line with the conventional portrait of him as a young man. Des Mazis never pierces the surface of his behaviour except, perhaps, when he speaks of his deistic attitude to religion: 'not completely irreligious and even less an atheist, but neither catholic nor protestant'. Beauterne, a somewhat naïve biographer who insists on Napoleon's piety, relates that Des Mazis, whom he knew personally, told him that Napoleon prayed morning and evening in his room before a crucifix of dark wood surmounted by a sprig of box. The anecdote, if true, suggests that he still clung to practices he had learned in Corsica, perhaps from Saveria, the grandmother who prayed for all the family.[38]

The École Militaire had a strong religious bias: catechism, attendance at mass, confirmation, confession and communion were obligatory. On 15 May 1785 Napoleon was confirmed by the archbishop of Paris. Las Cases recounts credibly, that when the archbishop observed that he knew of no saint of his name, Napoleon retorted that more saints existed than days of the year. There was in fact no saint's day in the calendar corresponding with his name until Pope Pius VII, out of 'gallantry' – to use the expression of Las Cases – on signing the Concordat decreed that a legendary saint Neapolus should be honoured on his birthday, an Egyptian martyred by Diocletian. 'Saint Napoleon

ought to be very much obliged to me and do everything in his power
for me in the world to come,' his namesake told O'Meara. 'Poor
fellow, nobody knew him before.' He was not to be known to many
people much longer, for Louis XVIII abolished his cult, thus casting
him back into oblivion.[39]

Las Cases, who had been at the École Militaire a year earlier than
Napoleon, returned there after his death to interview the masters who
had known him. These posthumous judgements must obviously be
considered with caution. Did the professor of history, the eloquent ex-
Jesuit d'Esguille, really predict Napoleon's greatness in reports which
he told Las Cases were still in the school archives but have never come
to light? Des Mazis, describing how Napoleon never missed a chance
of arguing with him about the plight of Corsica, allows one to think
that the professor regarded him more as an oddity than a genius. One
would like to believe that Domairon, the professor of literature,
compared Napoleon's style with 'granite heated in the volcano', an
image that recalls at once Corsica and certain passionate outbursts in
Napoleon's early romantic writings. But did he formulate this judgement while Napoleon was at school? It does, however, seem possible
that Bauer, the ponderous professor of German, when told that
Napoleon was sitting for the artillery examination, exclaimed: 'But
does he know anything?' Informed, in reply, that Napoleon's exam
prospects were good because he was the best mathematician in the
school he is said to have answered: 'Well, I've always heard and
thought that mathematics are for the stupid.'[40]

If not the best, Napoleon was certainly an outstanding student of
mathematics; this his record proves. Entry to the artillery was normally
by two stages: *aspirants* were required to have mastered the first volume
of the *Cours de mathématiques* by the contemporary Bezout; if they
passed the exam they had to spend a year in a school of artillery before
sitting for the second exam on Bezout's next three volumes, after
which, if successful, they received commissions as second lieutenants.
But it was possible for some very gifted boys to skip the intermediate
stage, take an exam on all four volumes of Bezout and go straight into
a regiment with a commission. A few attempted this every year from
the École Militaire. Napoleon set himself to perform the feat, and in a
single year, whereas most students spent two at the school. The candidates were given a cramming course in mathematics in two two-
hour lessons a day. They had distinguished teachers: Louis Monge,
brother of the celebrated Gaspard who accompanied Napoleon to

Egypt, and La Paute d'Agelet, member of the academy of sciences. Until, that is, in May, a few months before the exam, they both made off to sail round the world with La Pérouse. But Napoleon may not have been too put out, for in a shockingly bad poem scribbled in his fourth volume of Bezout he announces that he counts on finishing the course by May.[41]

Every summer an examiner from the artillery school of Metz came to Paris to test candidates: Bezout in person until his death in 1783, and then Laplace, the great astronomer-mathematician of the age. Though gentle in manner he terrorized some students by his mighty reputation, his mere name. It was he who examined Napoleon, standing for the first time in the presence of genius, speaking to one whom he had long admired from a distance that must have seemed impossible to bridge, ever. Later Napoleon was able to make him minister of the interior, senator and count of the Empire. Pommereul, who had taken part in the invasion of Corsica, was also on the board of examiners; since then he had published a caustic but pertinent book on Corsica and another on political and religious oppression in France. Did the name Bonaparte mean anything to him? Probably not. But Napoleon, grateful, made him general, *préfet* (in which capacity he shocked by propagating atheism) of l'Indre et Loire in 1800, councillor of state, baron, and finally *'directeur général de l'imprimerie et de librairie'* (1811), with powers of censorship which he is said to have used with rigour. And Pommereul, grateful, stood by him during the Hundred Days at the cost of being temporarily exiled by Louis XVIII.[42]

Seventeen boys from the École Militaire sat for the artillery exam, hand-picked out of twenty-five. Only four of them were among the fifty-eight successful candidates from various schools. Napoleon was forty-second on the list, immediately behind Phélippeaux, forty-first; Picot de Peccaduc (he who had tried to keep peace between them in the classroom) was thirty-ninth, Des Mazis fifty-sixth, near the bottom. Forty-second: not an exalted position, but achieved in record time and in competition with some of the brightest young men of the kingdom. His wish to enter the regiment La Fère with Des Mazis was granted: his commission as second lieutenant is dated 1 September. This regiment had served in Corsica since the conquest, which was no doubt why Napoleon had expressed a preference for it, hoping to be stationed in his homeland. But in 1785 only two of its twenty companies were on duty in the island; the others were at Valence, where Napoleon was sent with Des Mazis. Here, in the valley of the Rhône, he at least rediscovered the world of vineyards and olive groves and a southern style of living.[43]

Henry d'Estre, one of the more perceptive biographers of Napoleon's youth, observes that Napoleon left school without any real military training, without knowledge even of army regulations. In spite of attempts to modernize the traditional curriculum, his education at Brienne, as in Paris, literary, historical and mathematical, had been essentially abstract. The art and technique of soldiering he had to learn in his regiment and eventually on the battlefield. His situation was analogous to that of the young men from British schools and universities who not so long ago set out, with an excellent understanding of English and classical literature but little else, to administer vast, archaic societies in distant lands. And the value of his education was comparable: a formation of mind and character which he himself esteemed indispensable to a military career. A general was like a ship, he observed; the mind was the sail, the character the keel. At Brienne a real effort was made to mould character in accordance with Spartan precepts, which Napoleon took to readily; in Paris, at the École Militaire, the aim was to turn out officers and gentlemen, to teach students toughened in the provincial colleges how to behave as servants of their king. Napoleon absorbed some of this lore, albeit in spite of himself. He was a very different person when he left. In the next chapter of his life we find him, officer at Valence, enjoying a pleasant social life, flirting simultaneously with a Madame de Colombier and her daughter and at ease with people of varied attainments. During the year spent at the École Militaire his character had expanded and he had begun to develop the charm that became a potent if occasional asset. Was it there that he learned to speak gracefully, an accomplishment usually acquired early on in life? Napoleon was capable of doing so, even if his manners, as Chaptal and others noted, were often rough and rude. John Trevor, the British envoy in Turin, meeting him at the head of the army of Italy, remarks that while he sometimes acted like a 'filibuster' he could also express himself in highly courteous language, with old-fashioned locutions. Was this something he had learned at the École Militaire?[44]

Later, Joseph had no hesitation in assuming credit for Napoleon's entry into the artillery and the enormous consequences of that choice. When Napoleon had to pronounce the fate of the duc d'Enghien, he summoned Joseph to Malmaison to sound his opinion. Joseph, inclined to clemency, thereupon reminded his brother that he owed his entry into the artillery to the encouragement he himself had received from d'Enghien's grandfather, the prince de Condé, when more than twenty years before, at the prize-giving ceremony at Autun, he had declared his wish to join the army. It was unnecessary for him to add that had Napoleon not followed his advice and given up the idea of the navy he would not then be ruling France with power of life and death over a prince of the blood.[45] Curiously enough, this one bold act of Joseph's youth led to nothing, directly, for himself. Napoleon's plans to have him prepared for the artillery were thrown out by his own unexpected move to the École Militaire, and his father never took Joseph to study mathematics at Brienne or at the artillery school at Metz.

Carlo's prescribed cure at the Corsican waters had apparently been a success; he returned home feeling 'fresh and fit' with a complexion 'good for a couple of centuries' so Napoleon told Antommarchi. News of Napoleon's promotion to the École Militaire must have added to his sense of well-being. Did he then set about procuring a scholarship for Lucien? Evidence is lacking. Although Lucien, with a typical disregard for truth, leads us to think that he was granted a scholarship we know that the question was still unsettled when Carlo died. In fact Lucien soon gave up the idea of a military career, though he proved a satisfactory pupil during the two years he spent at Brienne. His talents are praised in some doggerel verse by a schoolfellow called Duval, also an admirer of Napoleon's. His success in the *Exercices publics* of 1784, mentioned by Napoleon, were followed by further distinctions in those of 1785, when appears in a list of boys questioned on the illustrious men of ancient Rome, the Old Testament, French grammar and geography. By then his religious interests must have been uppermost, for a year later he left Brienne on an impulse to enter the Church and joined Joseph Fesch at Aix. But here, too, he stayed only a short time; he disliked study, he admits in his memoirs, and he was bored.[46]

On his return to Ajaccio in 1784 Carlo probably had too many cares and too little money to do much about his sons. All through the autumn letters about the Salines were changing hands, between Boucheporn, the *intendant*, Souiris, the *subdélégué*, Frère, the official geometer charged to plan the work, and Bedigis, trying to restrict it as much as possible. Something was done but not enough. The marsh remained a marsh, so that the family later addressed a tragic plea to Calonne on behalf of eight children, 'innocent victims of the enterprise' which they held responsible for their orphanhood, the 'corrupted air'

Carlo had inhaled when supervising the draining of the land having 'led him to the tomb'. But in 1784 Carlo was still alive and hopeful. In October he received his government subsidy for the last two quarters and started building a house for the gardener, a new one, Jean-Baptiste Daire of Languedoc, who in June had accepted the perilous job of cultivating this ill-starred spot. Completed by Joseph it remained a permanent improvement to the property after the government had cancelled the Bonaparte's contract and all hope of making a fortune out of mulberries had fallen through.[47]

The other venture on which Carlo had pinned his hopes needed quite as much attention. The maréchal de Ségur, minister of war, was favourable to his request for a long lease on the Milelli and the house La Badina; but the rent had to be fixed. Carlo's offer of 150 livres appeared to the minister too low in view of the income received from the Milelli in 1772 and 1773, amounting to between three and four hundred livres; he was evidently not prepared to allow Carlo much profit. Moreover a hundred and ninety olive trees had been grafted since then which would now be in full production. How should the rent be assessed? The minister made the surprising suggestion that it should be decided by public auction in which the Bonaparte would be put in possession of the property at the highest rent offered. Boucheporn however ruled out this proposal, observing that ill-intentioned people, knowing the property would go to Carlo, would push the rent up beyond any fair level. Rossi, referring to the projected auction, relates that public opinion was 'absolutely injurious' to Carlo in the matter of the Odone heritage, so that he was impelled to consult 'all the lawyers in Ajaccio without exception', to prove his rights. Carlo was an obvious target for envy, and as he made his way up in the world he must often have excited the venom of people like the author of the anonymous letter circulated in his youth. Rossi reveals this aspect of his struggle, with the comment that he personally believed in Carlo's 'constant honesty and honourability', as did the lawyers, who were one and all prepared to act for him without fees. Luckily the minister on 5 October accepted Boucheporn's recommendation that the rent should be decided by experts. One was appointed by Souiris, representing the government, the other by Carlo. They must have disagreed, for the following month Carlo sent Souiris a lengthy memoir recapitulating the whole story of his claim since 1779. The rent was finally fixed at 250 livres, but not until a year later, and the Bonaparte were not able to take possession till 9 May 1786. The sumptuous olive groves of the Milelli afforded them a certain security through the following lean years before they were driven out of Corsica; but Carlo was never given credit for a result achieved under the stress of so much frustration.[48]

November 1784 was a time of domestic preoccupations. On the 15th of the month Jerome was born at two in the afternoon and a nurse (presumably a wet-nurse) engaged the same day. Marie, a Sardinian maid, also entered the household that month, and on the 20th Giacomo, a Genoese, the Corsicans being then as now averse to servile employment. Short of money or not, Carlo managed to live in some style. During all this period he had been discharging his functions of assistant judge; in December he appeared several times in court. In January he at last turned his attention to Joseph who had been industriously studying his Bezout in expectation of being taken to Brienne. They left in the New Year. Carlo naturally intended to go on to Paris to stir the ministers to further action in connection with the Milelli and the Salines. There is a note of desperation in the petition he drafted to the minister of war: 'The suppliant, sir, has no other hope except in your justice and protection. He is father of eight children with little fortune and on the point of being no longer able to provide for their education.' He had another motive for his journey: his health had broken down again.[49]

Trouble began at once. Caught in a storm, their ship was driven back to the Corsican coast and could only put into the harbour of Calvi with difficulty. Joseph, writing to his mother and Luciano on 6 January reports that his father was very ill and that they intended to go to Montpellier, a reputed health centre, by way of Toulon. The following day Carlo wrote from Saint-Tropez, which they had reached after a fifteen-hour crossing that he had never hoped to survive. They were leaving the next day for Aix; the expenses of the journey had been 'innumerable'. They were to increase dramatically, for Carlo had to buy himself a carriage to reach his destination. At Aix, where he stopped to visit Joseph Fesch, the eminent doctor Turnatori advised him to consult his colleagues in Montpellier. There at least he and Joseph found friends: Pradier, almoner of the Vermandois regiment formerly stationed in Corsica, whom they met in the street on the very day of their arrival, and Jean Bimar, exploiter of a flourishing coaching business. Madame Permon was also living in the town, daughter of the Stephanopoli de Comnène of Cargese, of Greek and dubious Byzantine origin, now married to a French financier and mother of the future Laure d'Abrantès. Laure relates that her parents rescued Carlo from a 'rather wretched inn' and welcomed him with Joseph Bonaparte and Joseph Fesch to their home. Inaccuracy can here be forgiven since she was only three months old at the time. Her mother did indeed place her house at Carlo's disposal, but he chose to lodge, with Joseph, with a certain Louise Delon where Fesch joined them some days later. Madame Permon was, however, as attentive and generous as Laure affirms; according to Fesch she visited Carlo every day, bringing him her choicest wines.[50]

But the time for such pleasures was over. Persistent vomiting; two or three doctors at his bedside: the abbé Pradier, writing to Luciano on 3 February, could only say that there was still room for hope. But when Joseph Fesch, hurrying from Aix, wrote to Luciano and Letizia on Ash Wednesday, he was able to report that Carlo had experienced a remission from 'horror', and with that irrepressible optimism so few historians have recognized as courage was laughing, 'consoled' and full of hope. He slept well on the night of 7 February, digesting everything without vomiting, so Fesch was assured by the doctor de la Mure. But Fesch attributed the improvement less to the doctor than to holy unction, and the trust he and Carlo had placed in the intercession of the Blessed Virgin. For Carlo, worldly, cynical, author of flippant irreligious ditties, had suddenly recovered the faith of his ancestors: 'he had no sooner seen the coffin open than he was seized with a passion for priests; there were not enough for him in all Montpellier,' Napoleon told Antommarchi. Even dying, Carlo was a slightly comic figure: 'He ended his life so pious that everyone in Montpellier thought him a saint,' Napoleon confided to Gourgaud. Perhaps Fesch was hardly exaggerating when he wrote to Letizia that his end had edified the good Christians of the town and put fear into the hearts of the boastful ('i bravi').[51]

For him, Carlo's conversion was a serious matter and one for rejoicing. He had glimpsed 'the wrath of the Lord', so he wrote to Letizia and Luciano, and seeing death advancing 'with slow steps' he prayed that his will be done, even if this meant that he must suffer more and longer. And Fesch prayed with him, and stayed with him night and day for ten days, and without sleep for the last forty-five hours, urging him to face his destiny with confidence in the Lord's mercy and grace. On Saturday, after a spell of delirium, Carlo made his confession, asking forgiveness in particular for his lack of charity to his fellows. Whom was he thinking of? The two men he had condemned to be broken alive and exposed on the wheel for firing at another and missing him? The twelve-year-old girl he had sent to a 'maison de force' for three years for stealing three silver forks, while her mother who had received them was whipped in public, branded and put in irons for the same length of time? Or, since these terrible sentences were in keeping with the practice of the age, was he not rather remembering those people, unmentioned in any document, whom he had shouldered out of his way in his long hard crawl up the social scale?[52]

Humbled, now, by remorse, in his moments of lucidity he was none the less cheerful and laughing, declaring that he had never been happier in his hours of health and prosperity. Napoleon wrote to assure him that he counted on entering the artillery in August and that Lucien and Elisa were well; news of his illness had gone the round of the family. Time was running out: he dictated a letter to Fesch for Luciano, unfortunately lost, as are those he wrote on the same day to Nicolò Paravisino and Letizia.[53]

Then he relapsed into delirium, much tormented by fear of having forgotten something, over-anxious to the last. Is it true, as asserted by Joseph and repeated by Napoleon and nearly all historians that he had a prophetic hallucination, cried out that he was lost and that not even Napoleon's sword which would conquer Europe could save him from 'the dragon of death'? Fesch says nothing of this in the extremely detailed account of Carlo's last hours that he sent to Luciano and Letizia. On the other hand Joseph is not strictly truthful in his memoirs. He also states that he promised his father on his deathbed not to enter the army. Perhaps he hoped, thereby, to offer posterity a valid reason for not having done so. The fact remains that soon after Carlo's death Joseph wrote home from Aix asking his great-uncle and his mother to decide whether or not he should enter the army, while Fesch discussed with them whether he should go to Brienne, or to the artillery school at Metz, or pursue his original plan of entering the Church or return to Corsica. It can also be noted that Napoleon, describing Luciano's death in 1791, relates that the old man called on him to deliver him 'with his great sword', although Napoleon had not yet displayed any military prowess. On the whole it seems less likely tnat the two men had similar deathbed dreams than that Joseph and Napoleon invented them.[54]

Serenity followed delirium: at half-past two in the morning of 24 February, Carlo, 'without fatigue or anguish', in the words of

Fesch, 'gently rendered his soul to his maker'. His autopsy, signed by four doctors, revealed a tumour at the entrance to the stomach 'of the size of a large potato or an elongated winter pear'; Fesch, who was present, speaks of two tumours, one purulent, the other 'hard as a stone'. Abbé Pradier arranged for his burial in the church of the Franciscans, the 'Pères Cordeliers', which then rated as an honour. Jean Bimar is said to have paid the cost of the funeral. If so he can have paid only part of it, or else lent the money, for Joseph Fesch on his return to Aix sent Luciano an expense account in which one finds 24 livres for the funeral mass and twelve for burial with the Cordeliers. The eighteen noted for a supper – '*cena*' – may have been for the meal following the ceremony; a relatively modest sum because the mourners were few.[55]

Afterwards Madame Permon, 'consoling angel', took Fesch and Joseph Bonaparte into her home. Pretentious and on the make as she appears by contemporary accounts – this descendant of emperors of Byzantium and Trebizond kept a gaming-house in Paris – she gave real proof of Corsican loyalty in time of trouble. The two young men were then much in need of consolation, material as well as emotional. Carlo had lived his last days on credit. The doctors' and apothecary's fees had not yet been presented, Fesch wrote to Luciano and Letizia, and he foresaw they would be exorbitant. The clothes Carlo had bought for Joseph in Toulon at a cost of nearly a hundred livres were unpaid. A certain Meissonnier (perhaps the carriage dealer?) was claiming a debt for 1,598 livres and might go to law. What should be done with Carlo's carriage? Should it be sold on the spot? Or sent to Aix? Or to Ajaccio? Could Madame Permon be counted on to help? Would Letizia write to Marbeuf to tell him of the family's 'calamity and needs'? Fesch hoped he would settle the debts at Autun and Brienne: Lucien's school fees were evidently outstanding. But Fesch affirms that Chabanier, lieutenant-colonel in the Vermandois regiment, had written to Timbrune, his friend and relation, to procure Lucien a scholarship. Marbeuf, he adds, must also be persuaded to activate the claims in connection with the Milelli and the Salines; the family might compose a memoir on the Milelli. So Fesch with devotion and pitiless realism summed up the family's situation on the very day Carlo died.

His own position was critical; but he was prepared to sacrifice himself to the interests of the family, so he explains to Letizia with a mixture of generosity and cupidity that rivalled Carlo's. He had missed an opportunity for ordination by leaving Aix at that time and had overspent his modest scholarship. He would take Joseph to Aix; if he

now decided to enter the Church the bishop Marbeuf might yet give
him the promised stipend of 3,000 lire [*sic*]. The bishop might even be
induced to do something for Lucien. In the meantime he begged that
the 400 lire Carlo had been expecting in Montpellier be sent to him as
quickly as possible: '*subito, subito*'. Carlo died as he had lived in a chaos
of risks and debts and calculations.[56]

It is these that have mainly held the attention of historians, obscuring
his achievements. Very ambitious people invite tragedy, and this is
strikingly true of the Corsicans, who have tended to expand their
ambitions to match the handicap of their inheritance: a poor island,
ruled by foreigners. Sampiero Corso who fought and failed to free
Corsica from Genoa, dying betrayed by his dearest friend; Paoli who
failed to make Corsica an independent nation, dying in his third exile;
Napoleon who saw the world as his domain and ended at Saint Helena:
these are tragic heroes in the Corsican tradition. But the public is
disinclined to see a tragic hero in a scheming, pushing man of law
dying in debt in cheap lodgings. Carlo's story often provokes the
mockery reserved for a small-town bourgeois trying to rise above his
station. All the same, there are societies that applaud such endeavours.

One must admit that Carlo succeeded. Not without an expenditure
of energy that killed him before the age of forty. Not without an
expenditure of cash that often alarmed his family. But there is no
evidence that any of the Bonaparte's property was sold to finance his
ventures; had this happened, Luciano's complaints would certainly be
known. On the contrary, Carlo added to their possessions: the fertile
Milelli, the Salines, which remained productive after the mulberry
planting scheme had fallen through. His desperate struggle to educate
his children is analogous to that of many middle-class Englishmen
striving to bring up theirs in private (public) schools, but using the
methods of his day. Carlo's manipulations were in no way shocking in
eighteenth-century France; indeed compared with expert climbers like
the de Roux, father and son, he appears a mild, rather elegant be-
ginner.[57] For the Bonaparte, it must be admitted, his efforts were
worth while. If ever a man deserved to have such a son as Napoleon it
was he.

He remained a long time concealed in the modest Franciscan church
at Montpellier. When in 1802 the municipality proposed to erect a
monument in his honour Napoleon, First Consul, refused, on the
pretext, which seems heartless, that his father's death had occurred too
long ago to be worth commemorating. Louis Bonaparte had to act

secretly with his brother Joseph to have the corpse disinterred. It was dispatched to Louis by Jean Bimar in May 1803 in a box declared to contain a clock; even after death Carlo was a slightly comic figure. Louis placed his remains in a suitable monument in the park of Saint Leu. But in 1819 they were ejected by the new owner of the property, father of the duc d'Enghien Napoleon had executed, and hidden in a cellar. It was not till 1840, when Napoleon's remains were placed in the Invalides, that room was made for Carlo's in the crypt of the church of Saint-Leu-la-Forêt. Finally, more than a century later, they found a permanent resting place in his native town.[58]

Historians have assumed that Napoleon was deeply distressed by his father's death. But this view is not supported by the available evidence. Des Mazis relates that when the news reached the École Militaire a priest, as was the custom, proposed to offer Napoleon consolation in the quiet of the infirmary, but that he refused, saying he had sufficient strength of spirit to do without being consoled. Was this reaction, which his friend took for stoicism, not rather indifference, or even relief? Certainly the letters Napoleon wrote to Luciano and Letizia after the event are stilted in the extreme. According to a rule of the École Militaire the masters supervised students' letters. They may have been responsible for the pompous style of Napoleon's, yet it is surprising that so little feeling comes through. The words addressed to Luciano, 'The nation, I even dare say, has lost by his death an enlightened and disinterested citizen', ring false when one knows that the only nation that then counted for Napoleon was Corsica, and that he had the greatest contempt for the values of the monarchy Carlo had assumed. His letter to Letizia is particularly frigid: 'I conclude, dear mother, as my grief commands me, begging you to calm your own.' A chatty *post scriptum* gives news of the birth of a son to Marie-Antoinette.[59]

In later years Napoleon spoke of Carlo's death as a liberation. It was even one of the lucky chances of life, so he told Las Cases, and to Montholon and Bertrand he said much the same. Had Carlo lived, Napoleon maintained, he would have been elected to represent the nobility at the Constituent Assembly, or else he would have been guillotined with the Girondins; either way he would have impeded his own career. Napoleon had no time for the insufficiencies and inconsistencies of one who had straddled two eras, but in the inverse order to that inscribed in history. Exalted in his youth by Paoli's revolutionary system, Carlo had to spend the rest of his life bent to the servility needed for making his way under the Ancien Régime. His tragedy was twofold: not to have lived to see the triumph of the principles that had illuminated his youth, nor the triumph of the son for whom he had laboured in the paths of deviousness and humiliation.[60]

Napoleon generously rewarded all who helped and befriended him in his early years, irrespective of their political allegiances and not forgetting their kin: his schoolmasters and schoolfriends, Marbeuf's widow and son and daughter, the maréchal de Ségur who had signed his commission in 1785 and done much for his family, though Carlo had always hoped he would do more, the brother and descendants of the baron Jean-Pierre du Teil, his commanding officer, whom he unsuccessfully tried to save from execution in 1794, and many others; the list is long.[61] It is idle to wonder what he would have done for his father had he lived, since his own life, as he himself observed, might have developed differently. But one may search in vain in his recorded sayings for any recognition of what he owed him. Praise he gives, though always balanced with blame: his father had 'courage and penetration' but became a bigot on his deathbed; he loved liberty 'fanatically' but affected the ridiculous style of politeness of the Ancien Régime; he was 'good' but consumed his patrimony in Pisa; he was enthusiastic for generous and liberal ideas but very attached to the aristocracy and nobility; he was 'a man of pleasure', he liked women, he played the grand seigneur, he made very expensive journeys to Paris. Never a word to acknowledge that he owed his father the education that allowed him to be what he became; never a tribute such as he bestows so copiously on Letizia: 'All that I am, all I have been, I owe to the habits of work I received in my childhood and the good principles given to me by my excellent mother'. But where did he practise the indispensable habits of work? In the loneliness of Brienne, the competitive stress of the École Militaire; not in the little school of Ajaccio playing at Romans and Carthaginians.[62]

'Military genius is a gift from heaven,' he declared; but that gift, to become operative, needs to be directed, canalized. And this is precisely what Napoleon derived from his education: a training of mind and character at his schools, as well as the general culture of the time. And above all the austere discipline of mathematics that enabled him to enter an artillery regiment as second lieutenant at the age of sixteen. The artillery was then the most advanced and efficient branch of the French army. It was reserved for an élite; not those of the highest birth, but the most intelligent, usually young men of rather modest origin, who thereafter lived and worked together in a spirit of egality that in fact prepared them for the Revolution. The innovations introduced by the general and military engineer Gribeauval after the Seven Years' War had made French guns the best in Europe. General Jean du Teil (brother of the executed baron) had written a treatise 'on the use of the new artillery'. The comte de Guibert, he who during the French invasion of Corsica had brilliantly trained the treacherous volunteer legion, had expounded a new theory of warfare in his *Essai général de tactique*, a work that has been esteemed as stimulating in its domain as those of Jean-Jacques Rousseau in his. Napoleon inherited the weapons and the ideas of these leaders of French military thought and practice at the very moment in history when he could make them the instruments of his grand design. This achievement Guibert foresaw. In his glowing introduction he imagines not only a new army, but a society regenerated by a man of genius; a vision that amounts to a prophetic portrait of Napoleon: 'Amidst these men it will be enough for one to rise, and he cannot but do so, some vast genius. He will appropriate the knowledge of all others, create or perfect the political system, place himself at the summit of the mechanism and set it in action.' So wrote Guibert when Napoleon was a three-year-old child.[63]

No such dreams haunted him at the time of his father's death; they came to him, seeping slowly into his consciousness, years later. When he entered the army his ambitions were circumscribed. His education had failed in one respect which Carlo had no doubt counted on: in spite of what Napoleon later said about his schooldays in 1785 he did not feel himself to be French nor a devoted subject of the French king. The child who had excelled in world geography had kept his mind fixed on one point of the globe, the little island where he was born. The adolescent inspired by the deeds of antiquity still looked to Paoli as his hero, imagined his return to Corsica where he would join him as his disciple and right-hand man in founding 'a republic of the Spartans', to use the words of Des Mazis who was convinced that all his great realizations had germinated in his recurrent dream of ruling over an independent Corsica.[64]

Napoleon entered adult life with these attitudes still dominant. His education had not severed him from his emotional dependence on his homeland, and on his mother, focus of his affections. The process, indescribably painful, took seven years. Officer in the French army he contrived to spend more than half that time in Corsica. At home he spontaneously assumed the role of the head of the family: easy-going

Joseph, unpredictable Lucien, narrow-minded Luciano, then an old man crippled with gout, and Louis at the start of life, all became his responsibility. For Letizia, deprived at once of her husband and her admirer, dying within the space of two years, left with eight children and a tarnished reputation, Napoleon was the main hope and support in an existence crowded with difficulties.

His activities were multiple, undertaken with a passionate resolution yet always loaded with disappointment. Whether endeavouring to squeeze compensation from the government for the Salines, to procure scholarships for Lucien and for Louis, to launch Joseph in revolutionary politics, or to engage himself in local politics, to serve Paoli (who disappointed him), to express himself as a writer or take part in an ill-conceived military expedition against Sardinia, he piled failure on failure until he was finally chased from the island with his family by Paoli's partisans. All this had to happen before he was free to look beyond Corsica, to act efficiently, to exploit his gifts, his skills, to love a woman other than Letizia, to become the man known to history.

❦

APPENDIX: FACSIMILE
DOCUMENTS

PASCHALI DE PAOLI

SUPREMO DUCI REGNO CORSICAE

Publicæ felicitatis, secundum Deum, Authori

CAROLUS BONAPARTE

PATRITIUS ADJACENSIS

Bonorum omnium incrementa auguratur

Ulta sunt, eaque tanta, Dux Amplissime, quæ ad nostræ hujus communis Patriæ bonum tua sunt effecta virtute, vix ut ea sperare nostri homines

A 2   po-

Three pages from *Exercitationes accademicae in secundam partem. Ethicae de jur. nat. et gent.* ('Academic Exercises, second part. The ethic of the law of nature and of men')

Dedication

'Pasquale Paoli, supreme chief of the kingdom of Corsica, after God, author of public felicity, by Carlo Buonaparte, patrician of Ajaccio. A general increase of prosperity is foreseen.'

❊(VII)❊

EX PROLEGOMENIS SECUNDÆ PARTIS ETHICÆ

DE JUR. NAT. ET GENT.

 1. Isciplina de jur. nat., et Gent. est scientia practica. 2. Ejus obiectum est homo socialis. 3. Finis vero est felicitas hominis. 4. Est necessaria, et utilissima ad vitam socialem: 5. Et fundamentum, et fons omnium Legum civilium. 6. Ejus principium *essendi* est ipsius Dei voluntas. 7. *Cognoscendi* vero est ipsa hominis ratio cui Deus suam voluntatem patefecit. Quæ vero sint illa principia, quibus veluti luminibus ratio hominis jus natura cognoscit, inferius definiemus.

EX LIB. I. SECUNDÆ PARTIS ETHICÆ.

DE JUR. NAT. ET GENT.

Hᴀᴇc *dogmata in antecessum stabilimus*. 1. Existit Deus qui omnia curat. 2. Omnis causa rationem habens, ob aliquem finem agit, quo posset so sit felix. 3. Homo est rationis particeps. 4. Et liber. 5. Natura ipsa ducitur ad sibi procurandam felicitatem. 6. Et est factus ad societatem. 7. Homo, qui nunc est, est miser. 8. Felicitas hominis consistit in perfectione suæ naturæ, idest intellectus, voluntatis, et corporis. 9. Hæc autem perfectio est totum id, quod est vere bonum. 10. Hoc bonum st

A 4   sit

'*From Prolegomena to Ethic, second part*

Of the law of nature and of nations
1. The science of the law of nature and of nations is a practical science. 2. Its subject is man living in society. 3. But its aim is the happiness of man. 4. It is necessary and most useful to life in society. 5. It is at once the basis and source of all civil law. 6. The principle of its existence resides in the will of God Himself. 7. But the principle of the knowledge of it is to be found in the reason of man, to whom God has revealed His will. We will define, below, what are these principles which like rays of light aid human reason to know the law of nature.

From Book I of the second part of Ethic: On the law of nature and of nations
We affirm in advance the following principles. 1. A God exists who controls all things. 2. Each thing acts according to reason to attain an object so as to achieve happiness. 3. Man is endowed with reason. 4. He is free. 5. Nature herself leads him to procure his own happiness. 6. And he is made to live in society. 7. Man in his present state is unhappy. 8. The happiness of man consists in the perfection of his nature, that is to say of his intelligence, his will and his body. 9. Perfection is all that which is truly good . . .'

)※(X.)※(

idem: 2. Nec potentiam Dei, et potentiam creatu-
rarum. 3: In Deo, et in homine esse veram liberta-
tem.

Interea defendimus 1. Statum Revelationis esse
homini omnium optimum. 2. Statum civilem esse
meliorem statu naturali temperato. 3. Hunc demum
meliorem esse statu merè naturali. 4. Et universum
genus humanum numquam extitisse in statu merè naturali in se spectato : 5. Nec existere posse. 6. Demum omnes homines esse naturaliter æquales.

De jure necessitatis.

1. Summa necessitas non dat jus ad pejerandum,
2. Neque ad violandum præcepta, quæ a Theologis
negativa vocantur. 3. Summa necessitas ad incolumi-
tatem præferri potest aliquando necessitati ad hone-
statem; si incolumitas virtute, et justitia obtineri
possit. 4. Aliquando etiam dat jus in membra sui
corporis, 5. Non tamen in propriam vitam, 6. Neque in Venerem illicitam. 7. Potest tamen dare jus in
vitam aliorum, 8. Et in res, 9. Non tamen dat jus
Regi timenti periculum ab altero Rege, occupandi
loca, arces, et urbes alterius Principis inviti, qui
utrique bellanti est finitimus. 10. Etiamsi periculum
sit certum.

EX

'None the less we maintain: 1. That the state of revelation is the best of all things for man. 2. That the civil state is better than the improved state of nature. 3. That this last is better than the pure state of nature. 4. That the universal human species has never existed in the pure state of nature. 5. Nor can it so exist. 6. Finally we assert that all men are naturally equal.' (Translation of first paragraph only.)

fino all' età di anni dodeci fui
educato dai Gesuiti che in quel
tempo esistevano, e mostrai una
propensione grandissima per la
Poesia. si potranno leggere in
margine riportati qualche sonetto,
e canzoni dedicati per il più
al Dio d'amore che infiamma
l'incauta Gioventù, allorquando
non si mette in guardia contro
le sue ingannevoli lusinghe.

La mia prima passione amorosa
fu per una Forcioli, e quantunque
ella fosse senza nascita, senza
bellezza, e d'una età sproporzio-
nata, tuttavia il mio cuore non
conosceva altre fiamme che
le sue, e senza la mano forte
dei miei fj che vedevano con
l'occhij della ragione, mi sarei
precipitato in un matrimonio che
avrebbe in appresso fatto la di-
sgrazia dei miei giorni, ed im-
pedita la fortuna della nostra
famiglia.

Facsimiles of three pages from the memoirs of Carlo Bonaparte, *Raggionamento Istorico, o siano memorie domestiche della famiglia di Buonaparte di Ajaccio in Corsica scritte da me Carlo di Buonaparte quondam Giuseppe l'anno mille e settecento ottanta* ('Historical relation or domestic memoirs of the family Buonaparte of Ajacciò in Corsica written by me Carlo di Buonaparte son of the late Giuseppe in the year seventeen eighty') M S from the Archives Napoléon, now in Archives Nationales (400 A P, 115).

'Until the age of twelve I was educated by the Jesuits who existed [in Ajaccio] at that time, and I showed a marked inclination to poetry. One can read in the margin some sonnets and songs mostly dedicated to the God of love who inflames incautious young people when they are not armed against his false seductions.*

'My first amorous passion was for a Forcioli, and though she was without breeding or beauty and of a corresponding age none the less my heart knew no other flame than for her, and without the strong hand of my uncles, who saw with the eyes of reason, I would have flung myself into a marriage that would later have brought me unhappiness and handicapped the fortune of our family.'

* These poems are not included in the existing manuscript.

Questa deve essere una buona
lezzione per gli miei Discen-
denti, che non devono giammai
lasciarsi condurre da una cieca
passione, ma consultarsi con
quelli che vedono con occhij
indifferenti, cosa peraltro dif-
cilissima a mettersi in pratica,
perche disse il Poeta = che se
raggion conosce, subito amor non è.

Dopo varij contrasti, e varie vi-
cende inseparabili da un' amor
contrastato, finalmente cedei
alla raggione, e consentij a prender
per mia sposa Letizzia Ramolino
Giovina dotata di una vera bellezza, e di costumi morigerati, e
ciò segui di 3. Giugno 1764 ——
un' anno circa dopo la morte ——
di mio Padre.

ecco il mio Istromento dotale
" Sia al nome del Sig.re Iddio &.
" vedi Registro di scritture pag. 34.
" per atti del Dott.e Pietro Franc.o Costa

'This should be a good lesson for my descendants, who should never allow themselves to be led by blind passion, but take the advice of those who see with impartial eyes; something very difficult to put into practice, because as the poet says: "If love knows reason it promptly disappears."

'After various disputes and incidents inseparable from thwarted love, I finally submitted to reason and agreed to take for my wife Letizia Ramolino, a young girl of real beauty and irreproachable morals, and this happened on 3 June 1764, about a year after my father's death . . . '

Contratti li sponsali sud.i, e con-
sumato il matrimonio Dopo alcuni
mesi partij per Roma a motivo
di proseguire lo studio delle leggi,
e lasciai mia moglie gravida d'
una figlia che morì.

Dimorai in Roma per lo spazio
di circa Due anni, verso la fine
dei quali infiammato dall'amor
della Patria, che allora travagliava
per scuotere il giogo dei Genovesi,
e sulle notizie della nova ereg-
zione dell' Università in Corti,
presi il partito di ripatriare,
e fu allora che connobbi il sig.r
Pasquale De Paoli allora Generale
del Regno di Corsica, il quale
mi ricevette con tant'amorevo-
lezza che io mi decisi a segui-
tare gli miei studij in quella
Capitale che in quel tempo fioriva
nelle armi, e nelle lettere.

Dopo qualche tempo ritirai appresso
di me la sig.ra Letizia mia

'The said marriage contracted and consummated after some months I departed to Rome for the purpose of studying law, and I left my wife pregnant with a daughter who died.

'I stayed in Rome the space of about two years, after which, inflamed with love of my country which was then struggling to throw off the yoke of the Genoese, and learning of the foundation of a university in Corte, I made the decision to return. It was then that I met Signor Pasquale de Paoli, General of the kingdom of Corsica, who received me with such kindness that I made up my mind to pursue my studies in the capital which at that period was flourishing in the arts of arms and of letters . . .'

✤○✤

NOTES

Full details of published sources referred to in abbreviated form are given in the Select Critical Bibliography (pp. 267–85), in the section indicated in brackets; further details of manuscript sources are given in the first section of the bibliography.

ABBREVIATIONS

AN	Archives Nationales
SHAT	Service Historique de l'Armée de Terre
BN	Bibliothèque Nationale
PRO	Public Record Office
FO	Foreign Office
ADCS	Archives Départementales de la Corse du Sud
ACA	Archives Communales d'Ajaccio
ACC	Archives Communales de Corte
BSSHNC	*Bulletin de la Société des Sciences Historiques et Naturelles de la Corse*
AHRF	*Annales Historiques de la Révolution Française*
EC	*Études Corses*
REC	*Revue d'Études Corses*
CH	*Corse Historique*
c.	*carton*
l.	*liasse*
r.	*registre*
t.	*tome*

1. BIRTH OF THE AVENGER

1. Dress, weapons: Boswell (*A, 1, d*), pp. 182–3; 'Mémoires . . . par un officier . . . de Picardie . . .' (*A, 1, d*), p. 204; Arrighi (*A, 2, d*), pp. 46–54. Chestnut flour, then a common substitute for cereals was made after the harvesting of the chestnuts in

November. I am indebted to Mlle C. Rocchi, who remembers how her father carried the infants of his family on mules in the years after the First World War.

2. Clemente: Boswell (*A*, *1*, *d*), p. 224.

3. Rossi (*A*, *1*, *b*), vol. XI, pp. 345–7; see also chapter 2, n. 50, below.

4. '. . . resolution of a Roman': Boswell (*A*, *1*, *d*), p. 119. Anti-Genoese rebellion: see Rossi (*A*, *1*, *b*), vols. VIII–XII; 'Journal des opérations . . .', SHAT, Mr. 248/1; Dumouriez (*A*, *1*, *b*), vol. I, pp. 85–139, Guibert (*A*, *1*, *b*), Ettori (*A*, *2*, *a*), and chapter 2 below.

5. Jean-Jacques Rousseau, *Du contrat social* (1762; Paris, Garnier, 1962), p. 269.

6. Despot: Rossi (*A*, *1*, *b*), vol. XI, p. 87; 'properly limited': Boswell (*A*, *1*, *d*), p. 162; constitution: ibid., pp. 144–58, Carrington (*A*, *2*, *b*).

7. Style of antiquity; austerity, 'avoiding every kind of luxury': Boswell (*A*, *1*, *d*), pp. 293; see also pp. 302–4, 332; gazette, university: ibid., pp. 196–7, 357–8, see also chapter 2 below.

8. Home-manufactured weapons, salvaged cannon: Boswell (*A*, *1*, *d*), pp. 184–5. Boswell as seen by Corsicans: Rossi (*A*, *1*, *b*), vol. XI, pp. 215–17; see also Carrington, 'Boswell seen through Corsican eyes' (*A*, *2*, *b*).

9. 'Roman slaves', 'inanimate objects': Paoli, letter to Agostinorso, 30 Aug. 1768, *BSSHNC*, 1893, pp. 304–6; 'true basis of sovereignty': Paoli's proclamation to nation, 29 Aug. 1768; Rossi *(A*, *1*, *b)*, vol. XI, pp. 359–62. Doctrine of legitimacy expressed in Traité de Versailles concluded between France and Genoa, 15 May 1768: Villat *(A*, *2*, *c)*, vol. I, pp. 5–8. Text of treaty, ibid., vol. II, pp. 423–8.

10. Declaration at national *consulta*, Sept. 1768: Rossi (*A*, *1*, *b*), vol. XI, p. 368.

11. Rousseau to Claude-Aglancier de Saint-Germain (retired army officer), 26 Feb. 1770: *Rousseau* (*A*, *1*, *c*), letter 6673 *bis*, pp. 272–95. Rousseau had convinced himself that Choiseul had invaded Corsica purposely to prevent him writing a constitution for the patriots. He had been invited to do so by Matteo Buttafoco (collaborator of Paoli, whom he later betrayed); it is uncertain how far Paoli approved the scheme: see Boswell (*A*, *1*, *d*), pp. 361–6. Rousseau however later sketched a 'Projet de Constitution pour la Corse', which remained unknown to the Corsicans and others until its publication, 1861, by Streckeisen-Moultou (*A*, *2*, *b*); see also Dedeck-Hery (*A*, *2*, *b*).

12. Boswell's *Account* . . . appeared 18 Feb. 1768: see Pottle (*A*, *2*, *b*), p. 354; the invasion of the Corsican interior began at the end of July. '. . . fanaticized the English': Paoli, letter to Casabianca, 15 June 1768, *BSSHNC*, 1893, p. 274. Lord Holland: quoted Pottle, op. cit., p. 395. Arms and money sent by Boswell and his fans: see ibid., pp. 396–7. Their action was illegal, for a government proclamation of 1763 forbade British subjects to aid the rebels. The British government however sent the Corsicans secret aid: see McErlean (*A*, *2*, *b*).

13. '*Cette canaille*', ball at Opera: Dumouriez (*A*, *1*, *b*), vol. I, p. 92. Clemente Paoli: Boswell (*A*, *1*, *d*), pp. 223–4; guerrilla tactics: 'Mémoires . . . par un officier . . . de Picardie . . .' (*A*, *1*, *d*), pp. 204–5. 'The Corsicans loved liberty . . .': Dumouriez, op. cit., p. 98.

14. '*Patria e Libertà*': Pommereul (*A*, *1*, *d*), vol. II, p. 270. Artillery officer in the Corsican campaign, he makes some astute observations on Paoli's regime. He was also author of *Recherches sur l'origine de l'esclavage religieux et politique en France* (1781). In 1785 he was one of the examiners in Napoleon's passing-out

exam from the École Royale Militaire to the artillery: see chapter 8, n. 42, below. Napoleon appointed him councillor of state, 1810, and head of the imperial censorship, 1811: see *Nouvelle biographie générale* (Paris, 1863). 'Liberty . . .': Dumouriez (*A, 1, b*), vol. I, p. 132; see also ibid., p. 133: 'The Corsicans are full of courage and that resignation that ennobles man.'

15. 'For us it is a matter of indifference . . .': quoted, without reference, by Thrasher (*D, 1*), p. 138. French reinforcements: 'Journal des opérations . . .', SHAT, Mr. 248/1. Corsican mobilization, *consulta*, March 1769: Rossi (*A, 1, b*), vol. XI, p. 398; French troops 22,000, Paoli's theoretically 30–35,000: Pommereul (*A, 1, d*), vol. II, p. 292; Paoli could only count on 4,000: Bettinelli (*A, 1, c*), p. 304. Corsicans without bayonettes: Dumouriez (*A, 1, b*), vol. I, p. 103. French use of bayonettes: Pommereul, op. cit., p. 302; Guibert (*A, 1, b*), p. 38; on Guibert, see chapters 2 and 8 below.

16. Both Rossi (*A, 1, b*), vol. XII, pp. 13–17, and Renucci (*A, 1, b*), vol. I, pp. 89–90, maintain that Paoli posted troops at the end of the bridge with orders to fire on anyone, including Corsicans, seeking to cross it: see chapter 2 below. 500–600 killed: Guibert (*A, 1, b*); 'a great carnage': 'Journal des opérations . . .', SHAT, Mr. 248/1; Voltaire: Voltaire (*A, 1, b*), p. 1553; 'consternation': Pommereul (*A, 1, d*), vol. II, pp. 300–303.

17. Renucci (*A, 1, b*), vol. I, pp. 96–8. Until the end of this chapter the story of the Bonaparte follows the traditions recorded by Rossi and Renucci, and diffused by the Bonaparte family, which are repeated by later historians; an analysis of the sources, and alternative versions, is given in chapter 2 below.

18. In 1763 an unsuccessful attempt was made by Corsicans to seize the citadel of Ajaccio: Rossi (*A, 1, b*), vol. XI, pp. 91–5; in 1765 a crowd of citizens acclaimed Paoli just outside the town: ibid., pp. 206–7; in 1766 two singers were arrested for singing pro-nationalist songs – one of them was executed: Versini (*D, 2, a*), pp. 50–51.

19. Letizia's resolution: Rossi (*A, 1, b*), vol. XII, pp. 28–9; retreat to Monte Rotondo: Renucci (*A, 1, b*), vol. I, p. 96. Letizia prepared to give birth in a cave: Napoleon to Bertrand: Bertrand (*C, 2*), vol II, p. 418. See chapter 2 below.

20. Renucci *(A, 1, b)*, vol. I, pp. 96–8; character of de Vaux: Dumouriez *(A, 1, b)*, vol. I, pp. 115–16.

21. Birth of Napoleon: see Las Cases *(C, 2)*, vol. I, p. 91; Gourgaud *(C, 2)*, vol. II, p. 71; Antommarchi *(C, 2)*, vol. I, p. 275. H. Lee reports in *Life of the Emperor Napoleon* (London, 1834), pp. 5–6, that Letizia told him, when he visited her in her old age in Rome, that 'she was just able to reach her house and throw herself on a sofa in the parlour' before giving birth, and that Carlo was then in Porto Vecchio with the intention of accompanying Paoli to England, but returned in compliance with the 'expostulations' of Luciano; see chapter 2 below. Her doctor, J. Héreau, in *Napoléon à Sainte-Hélène* (Paris, 1829), pp. 27–8, reports that the birth was painless. Comet seen from Ajaccio: Rossi *(A, 1, b)*, pp. 27–8.

2 BIRTH OF NAPOLEON BONAPARTE

1. C. Bonaparte, memoirs: AN, 400 AP, 115.
2. C. Bonaparte, ibid. The Forcioli were none the less a respected family in Ajaccio

of Italian origin. I have found no evidence to support the assertion in Larrey (*D*, *2*, *b*), vol. I, p. 20, that an attempt was made to marry Carlo to a wealthy Mlle Alberti of Antibes, whose parents refused on account of his youth.

3. Letizia's dotal act: AN, AE I, *c*. 11–12, no. 17. Giovan' Andrea Ramolino, mentioned in the document as her uncle, was her grandfather's brother (*c*. 1694–1765): see family tree in A N, 400 A P, 114. A *'lenza'* (in French *'canne'*) measured 1.71–2.98 metres. Dowries in eighteenth-century Corsica: see Arrighi (*A, 2, d*), p. 233.

4. A register of landed property declared by the citizens of Ajaccio, 1775, A C A, H H, *c*. 2, *r*. 4, shows that Luciano and Carlo owned, jointly, more than 80 *'giornate di zappera'* of vines, including those brought by Letizia's dowry, besides 10 *'bacinate'* of uncultivated but potentially fertile land in the marshy area known as the Saline (Salines) – see chapters 4–8 below – and 10 *'mezzinate'* of other land, some of it owned jointly with other families. Luciano also possessed extensive properties, including pastures and olive groves, in the territory of Alata in the hills above Ajaccio, some of it in partnership with other owners, among whom his niece, Isabella, wife of Ludovico Ornano. Saveria, Carlo's widowed mother, had 20 *giornate* . . . of vines, while Nicolò Paravisino possessed 51 *giornate* . . ., some of which had come to him with the dowry of Carlo's sister, Geltrude: see declaration of dowry, 1 Dec. 1768, A N, 400 A P, 114. Four Ramolino are listed as owning between them 85 *giornate* . . . of vines, and a rather small extent of other land: register in A C A, *ubi supra*; Letizia's maternal grandmother, widow of Giuseppe Maria Pietrasanta, owned 30 *giornate* . . . jointly with her daughter, Maria Anna Benielli: ibid. That nearly all the land is described as of poor or bad quality is because the declarations were required for tax purposes. A *giornata di zappera* represented the extent of a vineyard that could be hoed by a man in a day, which varied according to the quality of the soil from 1·5 to over 2 *ares*; an *are* equalled 100 square metres. A *bacinata* represented the surface that could be sown with a *bacino* of grain (7–10 litres), which varied according to the soil from 3·01 to 4·04 *ares*; a *mezzinata* equalled 6 *bacinate*: Monti (*A, 2, d*). Peraldi owned 320 *giornate* . . . of vines besides large areas of other agricultural land: register in A C A, *ubi supra*. Bacciochi: see S H A T, Mr. 1099.

5. Carlo's only brother, Sebastiano, died 24 Nov. 1760, his father, Giuseppe Maria, 13 Dec. 1763: A C A, G G, *c*. 6, *r*. 10. Geltrude married, 25 June 1763, Nicolò Paravisino: ibid., nephew of Carlo's mother, Maria Saveria Paravisino. The name, of Italian origin, was also written Paravisini Paravicino, Paravicini, Pallavicino, Pallavicini. Law relative to girl's dowries and right to inheritance: *Statuti* . . . (*A, 1, e*), *capitolo* XLIV, pp. 63–4. Napoleone married Maria Rosa Bozzi, 4 Nov. 1743: A C A, G G, *c*. 6, *r*. 9. His trading activities: Maestrati, *CH*, 1962, no. 5–6.

6. Supposed objection to marriage: see Chuquet, vol. 1, p. 52; the author suggests that Paoli intervened to arrange it, as does Marcaggi (*D, 3*), p. 31, who points out that Paoli's aim was to attract the pro-Genoese Bonaparte, Ramolino and Paravisino to his cause. See also Cesari Rocca, *Le Nid* . . . (*E*), p. 94. Letizia's father, Giovan' Geronimo Ramolino (1723–55, see A C A, G G, *c*. 6, *r*. 8), was appointed by the Genoese Republic, 7 Dec. 1743, captain of the infantry and cavalry of the city of Ajaccio, and by the marquis de Cursay, administering Corsica on behalf of Genoa, 23 May 1750 'chancellor of the jurisdiction of Bocognano': A N, 400 A P,

114. Giuseppe Maria Pietrasanta, b. 1705 (ACA, GG, *c.* 5, *r.* 5), d. 1773 (see chapter 5, n. 26, below), was Letizia's maternal grandfather: see letters to him from Letizia's father, AN, 400 AP, 115, and Rossi (*A, 1, b*), vol. XII, p. 28. Carlo and Letizia sign their letters to him '*profiglio*' and '*profiglia*', 'grandson' and 'granddaughter'. They however address him: '*Sig. Pro avo*', and this has led a classifier of the Archives Napoléon, prior to their entry to AN, to define him, mistakenly, as 'great-grandfather'. '*Pro avo*' should not in this context be translated as 'great-grandfather'; the '*pro*' should be regarded as an abbreviation of '*padrone*', a term of respect, but written without the customary tilde which, be it noted, is used by Luciano Bonaparte in addressing Pietrasanta in a letter, 16 March 1767, in the correct abbreviated form, '*prõne*': AN, 400 AP, 115. Cession of fortress of Ajaccio: Rossi, op. cit., vol. XI, p. 168. In Dec. 1768 Pietrasanta took up his post as councillor in the Conseil Supérieur in Bastia: ADCS, 1 B, 1. Supreme tribunal in Corsica, created by the French government in anticipation of the conquest, it was composed of six French and four Corsican councillors: ADCS, A, 1; see also Villat (*D, 3*), vol. I, p. 88.

7. Giuseppe Maria Bonaparte, supported by forty families of Ajaccio, represented the city at a *consulta* in Corte, 14 Jan. 1749; 17 Feb. he welcomed de Cursay to Ajaccio with his brother-in-law, Paravisino, French consul: Rossi (*A, 1, b*), vol. IX, pp. 178, 197. The post of consul was taken over by his son, Nicolò, Geltrude's husband, who already held it in 1761: ibid., vol. XI, p. 19; see also 'Lettera anonima . . .', Coll. Santini. Luciano's pro-Genoese sympathies, recalled by Napoleon: Bertrand (*C, 2*), vol. II, p. 218; Antommarchi (*C, 2*), vol. I, p. 275; studied in Genoa: ADCS, 3 E, 734, see chapter 3, n. 29, below; see also Versini (*D, 2, a*), p. 56.

8. The will of Giovan' Andrea Ramolino, by which he constituted Letizia's dowry, 28 Aug. 1761, included safeguards against an unsuitable marriage: she was not to marry before the age of eighteen; her choice of husband was to be approved by her uncle, the priest Francesco Maria Ramolino; in case of disagreement between uncle and niece the matter was to be arbitrated by the father superior of the Jesuits in Ajaccio: see Maestrati (*E*), *CH*, no. 7, 1962. I have found no evidence that the Ramolino invoked any of these clauses to obstruct Letizia's marriage to Carlo Bonaparte; on the contrary, the stipulation regarding age was overlooked.

9. See register of accommodation in Ajaccio for billeting French troops: ACA, EE, *l.* 4, undated. It may have been compiled in 1740 when Maillebois, bringing four battalions to Ajaccio, was unable to accommodate them in the citadel and had to commandeer billets in monasteries and private houses: see Louis Campi (*A, 2, e*), p. 15. The supposition that the document refers to this arrival of French troops is supported by the name of the street where the *casa* Bonaparte was situated: Contrada del Vicario Forcioli. Street names in Ajaccio changed frequently; at the time of Napoleon's birth this street was known as Strada Malerba: ACA, BB, 37; it is now the rue Saint-Charles. The register in ACA, *ubi supra*, describes the *casa* Bonaparte as consisting of two flats, one above the other, each with a living-room, bedroom and kitchen. The house of Gio' Agostino Ramolino, Letizia's paternal grandfather, is also described as comprising two flats, each with a bedroom and living-room. Situated near the Oratorio di San Carlo (ibid.), it can be identified as the house in the Contrada di San Carlo where Letizia's dotal act was

executed: see A N, A E 1, c. 11–12, no. 17. Both houses must also have had ground-floor rooms used for storage of agricultural produce.

10. Documents relative to origins of Ramolino: A C A, A A, l. 7. Cesari Rocca, *Le Nid* . . . (*E*), p. 175, considers that no serious historian could be duped by these documents, which arouse distrust by their appearance, content and style. They include a copy, dated 1553, of a request to the Genoese Senate, dated 1490, by *Il Magnifico Messer Ramolino gentiluomo fiorentino del Magnifico Messer Abramo Comte di Coll'Alto* for a concession of land in the city of Ajaccio, which was founded that year, and a copy of a letter patent, dated 1524, from the Genoese senate conferring nobility on *Nicolaum Ramolineum . . . nobilem fiorentinum*. The latter quotes a reference to a notice in the 'Libro Grosso' (register of municipal edicts, A C A, B B, c. 7) on p. 5, which is however now missing from the volume with all pages to p. 33 (renumbered p. 1). On p. 36 (renumbered p. 3) is a mention of a concession of land to Gabrile Ramolino, 2 Feb. 1490, signed by the chancellor Fabro Sorba, which appears to be an interpolation and a fake: Fabro Sorba was active in 1598 (see 'Libro Grosso', op. cit.), and signed differently. Cesari Rocca, op. cit., p. 175, cites as the sole authentic evidence concerning the first Ramolino in Corsica a document in Archivio di Stato (Genoa), Corsica, Supplicatione, f. 20, in which Morgante Ramolino, soldier in the service of the Office of Saint George (a Genoese mercantile institution that administered Corsica, with interruptions, from 1453 to 1562), applies for the post of commander of a watchtower on the coast near Ajaccio. Letizia's father however compiled a genealogy tracing the family to a Venetian count of Coll'Alto of the ninth century; see Beaucour (*E*), pp. 264–5. The genealogist Valynseele (*E*), p. 117, rejects this affiliation, but Beaucour, op. cit., accepts it, as do Larrey (*D, 2, b*), vol. I, p. 4, and Masson (*D, 3*), pp. 11–12. The Ramolino did not, apparently, solicit noble status from the French monarchy (see chapter 3 below). When Napoleon created André Ramolino (1767–1831, Letizia's first cousin, son of her uncle Bernadino) count of the empire, 11 June 1815, it was in recognition of his fidelity, not his supposed noble ancestry: see Beaucour, op. cit., p. 294. André, dying without issue, appointed as his heir his nephew Napoléon Levie, who in 1837 obtained official permission to use the name Levie-Ramolino. His application to Napoleon III for the title of comte de Coll'Alto in 1861 was refused on the grounds that it was not transmissible through the female line; it was however granted in 1870 to Nicolas Ramolino, member of a branch of the family that had split from that of Letizia in the early seventeenth century: see Beaucour, op. cit., pp. 326–30. Bosc, A C A, p. 51, suggests that the documents in A C A, B B, c. 7, were assembled by this Nicolas Ramolino in view of his application.

11. Francesco Il Mauro settled in Ajaccio c. 1500: see Cesari Rocca, *Le Nid* . . . (*E*), who traces his life from Genoese archives, pp. 253–4 and identifies his father as Giovanni Buonaparte, employed in Bastia by Tommasino Campofregoso (temporary Milanese ruler of Corsica), c. 1479–83: ibid., pp. 248–9. Caraffa (*E*), p. 63, has found evidence of Bonaparte in Bonifacio (Genoese fortress town in southern Corsica), 1238–9, but it is not known if they were ancestors of those who settled in Ajaccio. Written indifferently Bonaparte or Buonaparte, their name appears in the municipal records of Ajaccio from 1572 with a mention of Geronimo Bonaparte, grandson of Francesco Il Mauro: A C A, A A, l. 1; man of law active 1560–97: Cesari Rocca, op. cit., pp. 259–78. In 1596 (erroneously dated 1575 by Bosc,

ACA, p. 105) Agostino and another Francesco Buonaparte (*sic*), are listed among the *anziani* (city councillors) participating in the election of a commander ('*capitano*') and the '*pacificatori*' (arbitrators in local disputes) of the city: 'Libro Grosso', ACA, BB, *c.* 7, p. 33 (renumbered p. 1). Thereafter the Bonaparte exercised the function of *anziani* through five successive generations to (and including) Carlo's father: ACA, AA and BB. The recognition of kinship by the Buonaparte of Florence, 1759, was no more than an adoption, unsupported by any authentic documents linking the Buonaparte of Tuscany with those of Sarzana: Valynseele (*E*), pp. 26–7. Carlo and, later, Joseph Bonaparte vainly sought to obtain such proof: see chapter 6, nn. 6, 7, below.

12. The pages recording baptisms, 1741–60, being now missing from the municipal register of Ajaccio, the birth dates of Carlo and Letizia have been subject to discussion: see Larrey (*D, 2, b*), vol. I, pp. 9–16. Carlo's memoirs, AN, 400 AP, 115, establish his birth on 27 March 1746; this date is confirmed by an extract made in 1808 from the municipal register (then apparently intact) for the 'État civil impérial', AN, AE 1, *c.* 11–12, no. 4, *pièce* 1. Carlo was baptized Carlo Maria, 29 March: ibid. Letizia's birth date is less certain. In a census of Corsica made in 1770, Carlo, in accordance with a Corsican custom still operative, gave his age as that of his next birthday, i.e. twenty-five, and Letizia as twenty-two, so that one may conclude she was born in 1749: AN, Q^i 298^6. Iung (*C, 1*), vol. I, p. 7, states that she was born 24 Aug. 1749. Joseph Bonaparte also believed she was born in 1749: see his marriage act of 1794 in AN, AE 1, *c.* 11–12, no. 7, *pièce* 4, in which he states that she was then forty-five. The year 1749 is accepted in preference to others proposed, by Larrey, op. cit., p. 16, and some other biographers. But the family tree in AN, 400 AP, 115, gives 1750, as does Beaucour (*E*), p. 254, and the *Encyclopédie Larousse*, 1972. The 'État civil' in AN, AE 1, *c.* 11–12, no. 4, *pièce* 2, raises a problem unexamined by any of these authorities: the extract cited from the municipal register of Ajaccio records the birth, 13 Jan., and the baptism, 15 Jan. 1745, of Maria Letizia Ramolino. The most likely explanation is that this entry refers to a child who died in infancy (this cannot however be verified, for the records of burials, 1739–59, are missing), and that Letizia, born some years later, was given the same name, in accordance with a practice very common in Corsica. One may suppose that the clerk employed to make the extract, having found what he took to be Letizia's baptismal act, did not trouble to look further, or that the following pages were then missing. Some doubt nevertheless subsists that is not clarified by statements attributed to Letizia in 'Souvenirs . . .', dictated to her lady-in-waiting Rose Mellini, 1836 (*C, 1*), published in Larrey, op. cit., pp. 528–32, in which she presents herself in the different circumstances of her life as younger than she could possibly have been: thirteen at the time of her marriage, thirty-two at the death of her husband in 1785 (and so only eleven when she married); but these memoirs of her old age contain too many obvious errors to inspire confidence.

13. Letizia 'ravishing', 'one of the prettiest women . . .', severity of her physiognomy, soul in her expression: d'Abrantès (*C, 3*), vol. I, *t.* 2, p. 76; see also Colchen (*C, 3*), pp. 329–30, and chapter 5, below.

14. Letizia Bonaparte: 'Souvenirs . . .' (*C, 1*); 'a man of tall stature . . .': Colchen

(*C, 3*), p. 329; Iung (*C, 1*), vol. I, p. 27; Chardon in Peignot (*B, 1*), vol. II, p. 135; cf. Fontenay, (*B, 1*), pp. 4–5.

15. Dotal act, see n. 3 above.
16. C. Bonaparte, memoirs: A N, 400 A P, 115.
17. Marriage acts of Giuseppe Maria and of Napoleone Bonaparte: A C A, G G, *c*. 6, *r*. 9; of Geltrude: ibid., *r*. 10.
18. Lamotte (*D, 2, a*); municipal register, marriage acts 1764–6: A C A, G G, *c*. 6, *r*. 10; see p. 132, verso. At the bottom of this page one reads, in a writing that is not that of Carlo Bonaparte: '*vu et paraphé ne varietur*', signed with indecipherable initials. The words, some being in French, must have been added after the French conquest of 1769. The record of the marriage presents various anomalies: the date, '1764 *primo giugno*', is placed above the text in the middle of the page, whereas elsewhere in this register only the month is placed in this position, above all the marriages celebrated during that month, while the date of each marriage is included in the text. The names of the two people concerned, Carlo and Letizia, do not appear in the margin to the text, as in the other marriage acts; no abbreviations are used, which are frequent in the other acts. Clearly this entry is not the work of someone habitually entrusted with the task. One cannot suppose that it was inserted in a regular manner because the entry had been accidentally omitted when the marriage took place in 1764; nor can one suppose that a marriage taking place in the cathedral would not have been entered in the register at the time of the event. A copy of this act, with translation into French, exists in the 'État civil impérial', A N, A E 1, *c*. 11–12, no. 4, *pièce* 3.
19. An official French report by Chévrier, A N, K 1225, no. 21, gives evidence of cohabitation after an engagement ceremony in which a priest blessed the ring in the home of the bride. The tradition of 'customary' non-religious unions is described, with a wealth of archival evidence, in Marin-Muracciole (*A, 2, d*), pp. 279–311. Such unions took place in remote rural areas until recent years.
20. The original of the permit, and other documents Carlo sent to the heraldist d'Hozier de Serigny, have disappeared. They are known to us by an inventory of them which was returned to Carlo: A N, A E, 1, *c*. 13. no. 1, *pièce* 4. The date of the permit, 2 June 1764 (ibid.), invalidates the marriage act in A C A of 1 June (see above). It seems possible that the permit was authentic and that Carlo preferred to send it rather than a copy of a faked marriage act which, supposing it already existed, would have had to be authenticated by a local magistrate. The discordance of dates can be attributed to Carlo's carelessness when writing the supposed marriage act. The absence of sound evidence for the date of the marriage is reflected in the work of historians, few of whom however comment on the difficulty or offer references for the dates they advance: Iung (*D, 3*), vol. I, p. 33, gives 2 June 1764, referring to d'Hozier (see above), Larrey (*D, 2 b*), vol. I, pp. 23–4, accepts this date after discussion, followed by Chuquet (*D. 3*), vol. I, p. 45, while Coston (*D, 3*), vol. I, p. 6, no. 3, states that the marriage took place in 1767 without reference (a date that could be supported by the position of the entry of the marriage act in A C A) as does Rémusat (*C, 3*), vol. I, p. 127. Masson (*D, 3*), avoids the issue; Cesari Rocca, *Le Nid . . . (E)*, p. 94, surprisingly gives 7 May 1764, without reference, although he was familiar with the Corsican archives; Marcaggi (*D, 3*), p. 29, gives 1 June 1764 with reference to ACA.

21. Letizia's dotal act, see n.3 above, contains the clause that 'in case of restitution, which God forbid' Carlo and Luciano undertook to return the dowry intact. Disputes concerning dowries: see Marin-Muracciole (*A, 2, d*).

22. Anti-religious verses: Antommarchi (*C, 2*), vol. I, p. 259; Las Cases (*C, 2*), vol. I, p. 85; poetic talent: C. Bonaparte, memoirs, AN, 400 AP, 115; Iung (*C, 1*), vol. I, p. 27.

23. Bertrand (*C, 2*), vol. I, p. 177; Las Cases (*C, 2*), vol. I, p. 647.

24. Marcaggi (*D, 3*), p. 36, believes that Carlo went to Rome to pursue a lawsuit against the Jesuits in connection with an inheritance of property (a plausible supposition, see chapter 5, n. 24, below, but unsupported by any references or evidence); Masson (*D, 3*), p. 14, denies the journey; Stirling (*D, 2, b*), p. 28, asserts, fancifully, that Paoli entrusted Carlo with a mission to the Pope. I am much indebted to Professor Saitta for researches relative to Carlo's activities in Rome, made under his supervision, with negative results.

25. Letter from Celli to Pietrasanta in the collection of the Frasseto family, summarized by Marcaggi (*D, 3*), p. 36, n. 1; see also Cesari Rocca, *Le Nid . . . (E)*, p. 144. Cesari Rocca also asserts, ibid., p. 143, referring to a letter from Antoine Franceschi to the comte de Cardi in the collection of Paul Alfonsi, that Carlo on his return to Bastia lodged with the Franceschi, relatives of Paoli, and took the opportunity to seduce their servant, who died nine months later giving birth to a child strongly resembling Carlo, whom she none the less never named. These revelations, published 1902 (Marcaggi) and 1905 (Cesari Rocca), after the major works on Napoleon's youth by Masson (1895) and Chuquet (1897–9), shook Carlo's reputation, already undermined by the personal bias of Iung, in *Bonaparte et son temps . . . (1880–1881) (D, 3)*, without however discrediting his role as a Corsican patriot. Though Napoleon recalled that he was 'inclined to love women' – Bertrand (*C, 2*), vol. II, p. 137 – I have found no evidence of love-affairs subsequent to those cited above.

26. 'Lettera anonima . . .', Coll. Santini. The document is a copy of a text made by two people whose calligraphy belongs to the period; presumably the text was circulated in several copies in a campaign to destroy the reputation of Carlo and his family. One of the copyists gives his name: Marc' Ariotto Benielli; he was probably related both to Carlo and Letizia. The material was apparently collected from Corsicans in Italy, such as the Costa and their friends in Leghorn, Celli, Saliceti and others in Rome, besides Count Rivarola, to whom Carlo supposedly wrote four letters, dated 16 Sept. (two letters), 20 and 24 Sept. 1765. Quoted *in extenso*, written in Carlo's characteristic lively, humorous style, they appear authentic.

27. Uncle in Prato: letter to Rivarola, 16 Sept. 1765. Canon Filippo Buonaparte: see chapter 3, n. 18, and chapter 6, nn. 5, 6, and 7, below.

28. Carlo's letter to Rivarola of 16 Sept. describes the entry into Florence of the Grand-duke Leopold and the Duchess, and their banquet in the Palazzo Pitti accompanied by Count and Countess Francis of Thurn. These events took place 13 Sept.: 'Archivio Stato di Firenze, Archivio de LL' I. R. Corte, no. 3519 *bis*, Funzioni di Corte dal 1765 al 1790, vol. I, *cc*. 3 ff.; researches kindly undertaken by Signora Artom in conjunction with the British Institute, Florence. Carlo describes these events as taking place the day before he wrote, i.e. 15 Sept.; the

discordance of dates may be due to an error of the copyist or to a carelessness not infrequent in Carlo's writing. His debts and departure from Rome: letters to Rivarola 20 and 24 Sept.,' 'Lettera anonima . . .', Coll. Santini.

29. There is no evidence that the Florentine Buonaparte were ever granted a title: see Lumbroso (*E*), p. 4.

30. According to the 'Lettera anonima . . .' Coll. Santini, Carlo, on returning to Bastia stayed with Gio' Lucca Poggi until he was thrown out of his house, borrowed money from his own servant so as to play billiards with army officers in a low tavern, and sponged on some distinguished Corsicans (Gio. Battista Baciocchi and Giacinto Piozzi) just returned from France, making use of his kinship with the French consul (Nicolò Paravisino). He sent his servant ahead of him to Ajaccio, where he was badly received by Luciano in a poorly furnished house and had to squat on bags of flour by a public mill in the cellar. Luciano refused to repay the sum Carlo owed him. Carlo eventually sent him back to Italy, unpaid, while he himself settled in Corte.

31. See Carlo's memoirs, A N, 400 A P, 115.

32. Ristori to Paoli's government, Furiani, 1 Nov. 1765: A D C S, Gouvernement Corse, 6. Boswell reached Paoli 21 Oct. 1765 nine days after landing in Cap Corse, at Sollacaro, where he was presiding over the *Sindicato*, a court of appeal: see Pottle (*A, 2, b*), pp. 243–61, 523.

33. Marbeuf to Carlo Bonaparte, Bastia, 5 Nov. 1765: A N, 400 A P, 115. A copious correspondence between Marbeuf and Paoli is preserved in S H A T, A^i 3638, A^i 3658.

34. Carlo Bonaparte to Paoli, 16 Dec. 1765: A D C S, Gouvernement Corse, 6.

35. University: C. Bonaparte, memoirs, A N, 400 A P, 115. See Antonetti (*A, 2, b*); Rossi (*A, 1, b*), vol. XI, pp. 170–74. Curriculum: circular letter of Paoli and Supreme Council of State, 25 Nov. 1764; Tommaseo (*D, 1*), pp. 64–6; university qualifications required for notaries: Rossi, op. cit., p. 244; indoctrination of students with principles of Corsican nation, contents of monks' libraries: Pommereul (*A, 1, d*), vol. II, pp. 69–71. See also Boswell (*A, 1, d*), pp. 196–7, 357–8.

36. Marcaggi (*D, 3*), p. 33, first gave precise evidence of Carlo's university activities, quoting documents in the Coll. Frasseto: a register of studies showing that he enrolled in the rector's course in ethics in Dec. 1765; some verses he composed in honour of St Gregory, patron of the university, whose feast day was celebrated 4 May 1766, and the title of his 'academic exercises', a copy of which is preserved in the Coll. Flori. Notes on criminal procedure: *Libro di Pratica criminale (A, 1, a)*.

37. Most historians believe that a son called Napoleon was born and died 1765, and a daughter called Maria Anna, in Corte, 1767. The authority generally quoted, Brotonne (*E*), p. 13, gives no references. No confirmation of these births is to be found in the municipal registers of Corte or Ajaccio; but as only baptisms, and not births, are recorded, the children could have died before they were baptized. The supposition that the eldest child was a boy is contradicted by Carlo's memoirs; see above. Iung (*D, 3*), vol. I, p. 34, confuses the girl supposedly born in Corte, 1767, with Maria Anna, b. 14 July 1771, in Ajaccio, d. 23 Nov. that same year (A C A, G G, *c.* 7, *r.* 12), wrongly dating her baptism with Napoleon's, 4 Sept. 1769. Letizia in her 'Souvenirs . . .' (*C, 1*), recalls that she had thirteen children, three of whom died in infancy and two at birth, and it seems

not impossible that two of them were born in 1765 and 1767: Napoleon, however, maintained that he was Letizia's third child of the thirteen: Gourgaud (C,
2), vol. II, p. 71.

38. Luciano Bonaparte to Pietrasanta, 16 March 1767: AN, 400 AP, 115.

39. Geltrude, b. 1741 (ACA, GG, c. 6, r. 9), married her cousin Nicolò Luigi
Paravisino 1763 (see n. 5 above), French consul in Ajaccio: see n. 7 above. Her
dowry was restituted 4 July 1766: Maestrati (E), CH, no. 5–6, 1962. A joint
declaration of her dowry by Geltrude and her husband, 1 Dec. 1768, states that
their separation lasted two years: AN, 400 AP, 114. They are registered as
living together in Ajaccio in a census of 1770: AN, Qⁱ. Renucci (A, 1, b), vol. I,
p. 96, is responsible for the story that Nicolò Paravisino took part in the retreat
to Monte Rotondo and the delegation to de Vaux.

40. See chapter 3 below.

41. The 'Lettera anonima . . .', Coll. Santini, states that Carlo first lodged in Corte
with doctor Rossi; Pommereul (A, 1, d), vol. II, p. 69, notes that a large house
belonging to the Rossi had been taken over by the university. The Bonaparte
family was received on arrival into the house of Giovan' Tommaseo Arrighi,
Letizia's uncle: Larrey (D, 2, b), vol. I, p. 25, presumably through his marriage to
Maria Biadelli: see Du Casse (D, 2, d), vol. I, p. 5. House seven times burned:
Bertrand (C, 2), vol. III, p. 81. Joseph recalls that he was born there: Du Casse, op.
cit., p. 45–6; his baptismal certificate, and the death certificate of Napoleone
Bonaparte are in the municipal registar of Corte: ACC.

42. Four examples of Joseph's baptismal act exist, all written in Latin: 1. The original
entry in the municipal register of Corte, in which it is stated that he was born
7 Jan. 1768 and baptized the following day 'Joseph Nabulion'. 2. A copy of 1,
without significant variations, in the municipal register of Ajaccio, on the page
for the entries of 1775, ACA, GG, c. 7, r. 16, in which the name is again given as
'Joseph Nabulion'. This entry is written in the hand of Carlo Bonaparte; presumably he thought that a record of Joseph's birth should be registered in the
town where he then resided. It is presented as a copy of the original, without any
attempt to falsify or deceive. 3. A copy of 1, dated 19 July 1782, authenticated by
Augustin Andriani, magistrate in Corte, preserved in SHAT, Dossier Napoléon
Ier, p. 8. The differences in wording from example 1 are insignificant except for
the omission of the name 'Joseph'. This may be due to carelessness, of which
there are other signs – the word 'septingentesimo' is omitted from the date – or else
to a Corsican custom of using only the second of two Christian names. 4. A copy
of 1, without significant variations, except that the name is given as 'Joseph
Napoléon' in the 'État civil impérial' made to order of Napoleon, dated Corte, 5
July 1806: AN, AE i, c. 11–12, no. 7, pièce 1. The supposed mystery concerning
the birth dates of Joseph and Napoleon stems from the erroneous deductions of
historians, beginning with Iung (D, 3), vol. 1, pp. 35–50, who, not having seen
examples 1 and 2, believed example 3 to be an exact copy of the original. He
supports his thesis that Napoleon was the elder brother with the following
arguments. In May 1794 Joseph, then in Toulon, required a copy of his baptismal
act for his forthcoming marriage, and being unable to obtain such a document
because Corsica was then controlled by Britain, found four Corsicans to testify
that he was born in Ajaccio and was twenty-five years old, as features in his

marriage act: AN, AE 1, *c.* 11–12, no. 7, *pièce* 4. Iung also observes that Napoleon produced a baptismal act for his marriage to Josephine stating that he was born 5 Feb. 1768 (in the copy of his marriage act in the 'État civil impérial', AN, AE 1, *c.* 11–12, no. 5, *pièce* 1, the date of his birth is omitted). These facts are to be explained as follows: the testimony of Joseph's Corsican acquaintances was not strictly accurate and was merely designed to identify him as Corsican-born, major and unmarried; Napoleon confessed that he used a copy of Joseph's baptismal act for his own marriage: Bertrand (*C, 2*), vol. II, p. 262 (it must have been example 3, but the date of the birth was inaccurately copied). It has also been said that Joseph must have been born after the French conquest of Corsica in 1769 because his name appears in example 2 as 'Joseph', not 'Giuseppe'; this is to disregard the fact that this document, like example 1, is written in Latin, not in Italian as was then the custom in Corsica, as pointed out by Bosc (ACA), p. 254. Chuquet (*D, 3*), vol. I, pp. 65–6, being acquainted only with examples 2 and 3, suggests that the name Joseph in example 2 was added after the French conquest in memory of a son born in 1765 and baptized Joseph who was still living in 1768 but died soon afterwards. All these arguments are disposed of by examination of Joseph's baptismal act in the communal archives of Corte, and the two examples of Napoleon's baptismal act in Ajaccio: ACA, GG, *c.* 7, *r.* 12, and ADCS, 2 E (duplicate register deposited in the Juridiction Royale in accordance with the regulations of the French administration). Iung, loc. cit., however, disregards the indisputable authenticity of Napoleon's baptismal acts. He argues that Carlo Bonaparte falsified documents to make Napoleon appear the younger of the two brothers in order to ensure his entry in 1779 to the military school of Brienne, restricted to children not over ten: op. cit., p. 50. But in fact the minister of war was prepared to accept either of the two brothers, as appears in a letter, 19 July 1778, from the minister of war, the prince de Montbarey, to Marbeuf, quoted in Montzey (*B, 4, a*), vol. I, p. 246. It has also been suggested that Carlo's object in falsifying the documents was to ensure that Napoleon, the more promising of the two sons, would benefit by the advantages of being born French, after the conquest; this is to forget that all Corsicans, whenever born, became French subjects after the signing of the Traité de Versailles, 15 May 1768. For analyses and bibliographies of these aberrations of scholarship see Masson (*D, 3*), pp. 16–20, and Norward Young (*B, 4, b*), pp. 49–60. It must be noted that Carlo Bonaparte gives the correct dates of the births of Joseph and Napoleon in his memoirs, AN, 400 AP, 115, and in his 'Livre de Raison', BN, p. 27, but that the former only recently became available to the public, and the latter not until 1965, when the MS was acquired by the BN.

43. Napoleon, name in Greek legend: Armoises (*D, 3*), p. 16. Written also Napoleone, Nebulione, Nabuleone, the name was of ancient Genoese origin and appears in Corsica at least from the sixteenth century. The Bonaparte were connected with a Napoleone dalle Vie, of Levie in southern Corsica, ennobled by Henri II of France for military valour, through his wife, and through a descendant who married a Colonna Bozzi and so brought the name into a family with which the Bonaparte several times intermarried: see Cesari Rocca, *Le Nid . . .* (*E*), pp. 117–19; Maestrati (*E*). Carlo's grandfather, Sebastiano Bonaparte, b. 29 Sept.

1683, had as godfather the Genoese '*commissario*' of Ajaccio, Napoleone Lomellino, when he was baptized 27 April 1684: ACA, GG, *c. 5, r.* 4. Napoleon mistakenly believed that his name had been given to the second son in his family for several generations in memory of a connection with a celebrated Italian warrior, Napoleon des Ursins (Orsini): Las Cases (*C, 2*), vol. I, p. 80. Joseph believed the name had entered the family through a connection with Napoleon Zomellini (*sic*), commander of the Genoese galleys in the sixteenth century: Joseph Bonaparte (*C, 1*), vol. I, p. 42.

44. Joseph's godparents: see baptismal act, n. 42 above. Their son Giacinto (1748–1819) added 'de Casanova' to his name to distinguish his lineage from another branch of the family. In 1774 he married Maria Antonietta Benielli, daughter of Letizia's maternal aunt. Deputy to the court of France for the Corsican Estates, 1781, he may have used his influence to aid Napoleon, then at school (see chapter 8, n. 28, below), who subsequently nominated him *préfet* of the *département* of the Liamone in Corsica (1796–1811), then of the unified *département* of Corsica (1811–14) and baron of the empire. His son, Jean-Thomas (1778–1853), outstanding in the Napoleonic wars, was created duc de Padoue, 1808: Du Casse (*D, 2, d*), vol. 1, pp. 7–8 ff., Albertini et Rivollet (*F*), pp. 130–41. The circumstances that impelled the Bonaparte to leave the Arrighi's house are related by a descendant, Mme Arrighi Castadot, in a letter to François Flori, Brussels, 15 Nov. 1954, Coll. Flori. The 'Lettera anonima . . .', Coll. Santini, states that Carlo met Maria Gaffori when lodging with Dr Rossi. The Arrighi and Gaffori houses can still be seen, little changed; the dramatic siege of the latter is commemorated in a bas-relief on the statue of General Gaffori, murdered 1753.

45. The mistaken idea that Carlo was secretary of state derives from the unreliable memoirs of Lucien Bonaparte: Iung (*C, 1*), vol. I, p. 27. It has gained some support from his signature on a letter of marque delivered by Paoli to Captain Lazaro Costa, 19 Nov. 1768: ADCS, Gouvernement Corse, 32. Rossi's realistic account of Carlo's functions is contradicted by his citation of the speech attributed to Carlo at the *consulta* of May 1768: (*A, 1, b*), vol. XI, pp. 345–7; see below. Masson (*D, 3*), p. 14, while ignoring the speech, concludes that Carlo was 'an influential member of the assembly'. This is an error: members of the *consulta* had to be over twenty-five, and the member for Corte in May 1768 was Francesco Gaffori, son of the murdered general: ADCS, Gouvernement Corse, 27; see also Carrington (*A, 2, b*). Carlo's activities in Ajaccio: 'Correspondance . . .' (*A, 1, c*), letters of 11 Sept. and 23 Oct. 1767, *BSSHNC*, pp. 482, 576–7.

46. Pommereul (*A, 1, d*), vol. II, p. 240, comments on Paoli's elevating influence on young men. Boswell (*A, 1, d*), 'highest ideal', p. 328, advice on marriage, pp. 305–8, manners, pp. 300, 343, 291–4, dazzling conversation, p. 332. Boswell stayed with Paoli at Sollacaro 21–9 Oct. 1765, reached Corte 31 Oct., and was probably in Bastia 9–20 Nov.: Pottle (*A, 2, b*), Carrington, *Rivista* (*A, 2, b*). See also Bettinelli (*A, 1, c*).

47. Carlo's expenditure in Corte: Nasica (*D, 3*), p. 12. Letizia's card-playing with Paoli: Larrey (*D, 2, b*), vol. I, p. 397, quoting Lucien Bonaparte; Paoli's admiration of Geltrude: Bertrand (*C, 2*), vol. I, p. 176. Boswell (*A, 1, d*) on Paoli's austerity, p. 293; stayed in house of Colonna (d'Istria), p. 294; 'much decayed'

like its owners', let in wind and rain, p. 352; Paoli's dress, p. 291. Pommereul (*A, 1, d*), vol. II, p. 241, describes Paoli's lifestyle in Corte from contemporary hearsay, which is confirmed by archival sources; receipts in official accounts, ADCS, Gouvernement Corse, 39, reveal that Paoli's provisions cost 400 lire a month and double that sum in exceptional circumstances, that he had nine servants with salaries totalling 230 lire a month, and that he imported large quantities of chocolate from Italy, besides furniture.

48. 'Less beautiful than solid': Pommereul (*A, 1, d*), vol. I, p. 90; the armchairs were intended for meetings of the executive supreme Council of State: ibid., vol. II, p. 103; reactions to thrones: Rossi (*A, 1, b*), vol. XI, pp. 88–9, 240–41; looting of palace: Dumouriez (*A, 1, b*), vol. I, p. 125; 'horrible village': Pommereul, op. cit., p. 6; Carlo's praise of Corte: memoirs, AN, 400 AP, 115.

49. Shipwreck, Tunisian envoy: Pommereul (*A, 1, d*), vol. II, p. 111, Renucci (*A, 1, b*), vol. I, p. 74. Letizia's success recalled by Napoleon: Las Cases (*C, 2*), vol. 1, p. 87. Larrey (*D, 2, b*), vol. I, p. 28, asserts that her rivals at the reception accused her of 'coquetry and avarice' and that their jealousy was at the origin of criticisms later made against her in contemporary pamphlets. After the looting of the palace de Vaux offered the tiger to the duc de Choiseul, who refused it: Villat (*A, 2, c*), vol. I, p. 110.

50. Carlo '. . . passionately attached': Rossi (*A, 1, b*), vol. XI, p. 346. The speech was first published by Cambiaggi (*A, 1, b*), vol. IV, pp. 163–4; it was reprinted, without significant variations, by Nasica (*D, 3*), pp. 374–6, with a translation into French, pp. 13–17. Rossi (1754–1820) compiled his chronicle from 1778 and donated the MS to the Bibliothèque Royale: see Letteron's introduction to Rossi (*A, 1, b*), vol. I (*BSSHNC*, 1906), pp. vi–xiv. Thirteen of Rossi's seventeen volumes are published in *BSSHNC*, 1895–1906, not in chronological order; vol. XI, which includes the speech attributed to Carlo, pp. 345–7, was published 1902. Rossi alone quotes the oath taken after the speech, ibid., p. 347; it is attributed to Carlo after Ponte Novo by Cesari Rocca, *Le Nid . . .* (*E*), p. 99, and to Paoli by Chuquet (*D, 3*), vol. I, p. 53, who nevertheless believes Carlo to have been the author of the speech: ibid. Napoleon's quotation from the speech in paraphrase: Montholon (*C, 2*), vol. II, p. 16; accurately word for word: Las Cases (*C, 2*), vol. I, p. 87; 'laudable custom of professors': Cambiaggi, loc. cit.; speeches by fathers Mariani and Leonardo: Renucci (*A, 1, b*), vol. I, pp. 77–9.

51. Napoleon studied Corsican history for the writing of his 'Lettres sur la Corse à Monsieur l'abbé Raynal', an incomplete history in MS in the Fonds Libri, published in Masson et Biagi, *Napoléon inconnu . . .*, pp. 395–445. Cambiaggi's history is not, however, among the works on Corsica belonging to Napoleon found in the Fonds Libri, Masson (*D, 3*), pp. 174–5, nor is it listed among those Napoleon ordered on 20 July 1786 from Paul Borde, bookseller in Geneva; but he also asked Borde to send him any other works he had on Corsica, so it is not impossible that he received Cambiaggi: Masson, ibid., pp. 144–5. Napoleon creator of his own legend at Saint Helena: see in particular Albert Soboul, 'Le héros, la légende et l'histoire', *La Pensée*, 1969, n. 143.

52. Carlo 'friend of liberty': J. Bonaparte (*C, 1*), vol. I, p. 25; Napoleon, in Las Cases (*C, 2*), vol. I, p. 566. Corsicans excluded from posts of authority by Genoese: see Guerrini-Graziani, *Gênes et la Corse* (Bastia, 1984), pp. 72–3;

Antonetti (*A, 2, a*), p. 278. '. . . the best model': Boswell (*A, 1, d*), p. 161. Notables in Paoli's regime: see Arrighi (*A, 2, a*); Carrington, 'Paoli et sa "constitution"' (*A, 2, b*); C. Bonaparte, memoirs, AN, 400 AP, 115.

53. Royal Corse: Albertini et Rivollet (*E*), pp. 61–5. Buttafoco's treachery: Rossi (*A, 1, b*), vol. XI, pp. 363–8. Guibert, major-general in the Corsican war, author of a brief account of its last phase (*A, 1, b*), later wrote the magnificent *Essai général de tactique* (*F*), see chapter 8 below.

54. Increase in paid troops: Rossi (*A, 1, b*), vol. XI, p. 350. Rolls of volunteers: ADCS, Gouvernement Corse, 44. Letter from Paoli, Olmeta, 28 Aug. 1768, to Octave Colonna d'Istria: copy of unpublished text in Coll. Santini. Larrey (*D, 2, b*), vol. I, p. 40, followed by other historians, asserts that Carlo commanded the volunteers of the *pieve* (district) of Talavo; but the document in ADCS, *ubi supra*, does not mention any district in connection with the group of volunteers in which he enrolled, and it seems unlikely that he was associated with the *pieve* of Talavo (or Talabo), far from Ajaccio in the central southern mountains. Possibly he has been confused with Napoleon, who in 1792 was elected officer of the volunteers of Tallano, a different *pieve* in southern Corsica: Masson (*D, 3*), pp. 273–92. Letter from Paoli to the *intendant* of the mint, Murato, 12 Jan. 1769; ADCS, Gouvernement Corse, 21, confirmed by entry, 14 Jan. 1769 in 'Libro magistrale de conti pubblici': ADCS, Gouvernement Corse, 39. Larrey, op. cit., pp. 40–41, maintains that Carlo was present at the battles of Borgo and Ponte Novo; Masson (*D, 3*), states that he was ADC to Paoli at Borgo. Chuquet (*D, 3*), vol. I, p. 54, asserts that Carlo tried to rally the army after Ponte Novo.

55. Paoli never at the head of his troops: Pommereul (*A, 1, d*), vol. II, p. 243; Rossi (*A, 1, b*), vol. XII, p. 32, confirmed by 'Journal des opérations . . .', SHAT, Mr. 248/1. Lacked military ability: Dumouriez (*A, 1, b*), vol. I, p. 132; Pommereul, op. cit., p. 244. Letter from Paoli, 28 Aug. 1768, see n. 54 above.

56. The Bonaparte women's participation in the war was in keeping with Corsican custom: Faustina Gaffori's role in the defence of Corte was celebrated, see above; women took an active part in the pro-Napoleonic rebellion in the Fiumorbo in 1816: see 'Mémoires du Commandant Bernard Poli', EC, no. 6, 1955. Geltrude's heroism: Iung (*C, 1*), vol. 1, p. 70. Letizia's exploits: ibid., p. 68; Beauterne, quoting her lady-in-waiting, Mme de Bressieux (*D, 3*), p. 25; Las Cases (*C, 2*), vol. I, p. 87; Bertrand (*D, 3*), vol. II, p. 418; see also Rossi (*A, 1, b*), vol. XII, pp. 28–9. Letizia's letter to Pietrasanta, Corte, 13 March 1769: AN, 400 AP, 115.

57. Letter from Paoli to Carli, Rostino, 9 May 1768: ADCS, Gouvernement Corse, 21. French and Corsican versions of the battle: see chapter 1, n. 16 above (this bibliography is not exhaustive). An analysis of the collected evidence of the battle, including Paoli's letter, is in preparation by a Corsican historian.

58. Carlo Bonaparte's memoirs, AN, 400 AP, 115, here quoted, discredit the various and incompatible accounts of his actions after Ponte Novo hitherto published. Napoleon told Las Cases (*C, 2*), vol. I, p. 82, that his father wanted to share Paoli's exile but was dissuaded by Luciano, as is repeated by Coston (*D, 3*), vol. I, p. 5, and Chuquet (*D, 3*), vol. I, p. 55. This version of events presupposes that Carlo had already returned to Ajaccio before he thought of joining Paoli, whereas his memoirs, *ubi supra*, clearly state that he stayed with Paoli till he embarked and then, following Paoli's injunctions, returned to Corte to rejoin

members of his family and take them to Ajaccio. They cannot have made the journey before the latter half of June, seeing that Paoli embarked from Porto Vecchio on 13 June. Bartel (*D, 3*), p. 20, however, quoting the journal of a maréchal d'Audeux in the Coll. Mirtil (but not mentioned in Mirtil's *Napoléon d'Ajaccio* (*D, 3*) states that Carlo Bonaparte had returned to Ajaccio 25 May 1769; but Bartel is an unreliable writer, given to misquoting dates and misinterpreting documents. Joseph Bonaparte, denying reflections attributed to Napoleon in Bourrienne's *Mémoires* (*B, 2, a*), see chapter 7 below, asserts that his father remained faithful to Paoli 'to the last moment': *Bourrienne et ses erreurs . . .'* (*B, 2, a*), vol. I, p. 238. Carlo's loyalty to successive protecters: Rossi (*A, 1, b*), vol. XIII, p. 84.

59. The relation of Renucci (*A, 1, b*), vol. I, pp. 96–7, of the retreat to Monte Rotondo, the encampment in a cave and the delegation to de Vaux, see chapter *1* above, accepted by Nasica (*D, 3*), pp. 20–21, and by Masson (*D, 3*), pp. 15–16, questioned by Chuquet (*D, 3*), vol. I, p. 54, is incompatible with Carlo's narrative in his memoirs, AN, 400 AP, 115 (having made his submission to de Vaux he could not then have accompanied Paoli), although Larrey (*D, 2, b*) tries to reconcile the two. Much of Renucci's story seems to be legend; but it is not impossible that the Bonaparte, perhaps with other patriots, took the route to Ajaccio over the mountains, starting up the valley of the Restonica in the direction of Monte Rotondo, and then turning north over the plateau d'Alzo to enter the Niolo. A rock shelter known as the Grotte des Réfugiés in the valley of the Restonica may have served as a camping place and have supported the story, known to Napoleon, that Letizia was prepared to give birth to her child in a cave: Bertrand (*C, 2*), vol. II, p. 418. D'Abrantès (*C, 3*), vol. I, *t.* 2. p. 118, reports that Letizia recalled an exhausting retreat to Monte Rotondo with some leading patriot families but not, significantly, that Carlo took part in a delegation to de Vaux. Rossi (*A, 1, b*), vol. XII, pp. 28–9, relates that after Ponte Novo Pietrasanta offered Letizia a safe-conduct to Bastia, but that she chose to stay with her husband, that they accompanied Clemente Paoli into the Niolo to raise reinforcements and, having failed, proceeded to the west coast where Clemente organized a brief resistance to French troops before re-crossing the island to join Pasquale at Porto Vecchio. This version is preferred by Chuquet, op. cit., pp. 54–5, and Cesari Rocca, *Le Nid . . . (E)*, pp. 100–102. Nasica (*D, 3*), pp. 21–2 combines it with Renucci's. It is not really likely that Carlo, after crossing the Niolo, accompanied Clemente to Porto Vecchio, for he says nothing of such a journey in his memoirs, but states that he joined his family in Corte after leaving Paoli. Mme Des Armoises (*D, 3*), p. 11, using reminiscences from a great-niece of Nicolò Paravisino, relates that towards the end of the war Letizia entrusted Joseph to Geltruda, who took refuge with the child in the house of a kinsman of her husband's in the Niolo, and that Carlo and Letizia, after 'an interminable detour' collected them on their way back to Ajaccio. A house in Lozzi, in the Niolo, is remembered as one where Letizia stayed. The story of Letizia's perilous fording of the Liamon, Nasica, op. cit., pp. 22–3, may be based on fact: 'Journal des opérations . . .', SHAT, Mr. 248/1, reports violent storms, with snow, on 15 June.

60. Napoleon's birth: see chapter 1, n. 21, above. Letizia denied story of carpet:

Larrey (*D, 2, b*), vol. II, p. 425. Caterina: Antommarchi (*C, 2*), vol. I, pp. 251, 275; comet seen from Saint Helena: ibid., vol. II, p. 74.

3. STRUGGLES AND TRIALS OF A CORSICAN FAMILY

1. Napoleon to Paoli, Auxonne, 12 June 1789, first published Coston (*D, 3*), vol. II, pp. 87–8; the original has disappeared: see Masson (*D, 3*), p. 202.

2. Zampaglino, already condemned to death by default by Paoli's severe justice for murdering a French officer in 1766: ADCS, Gouvernement Corse, 169, escaped to Tuscany via Sardinia after the French conquest and joined Paoli in England: Rossi (*A, 1, b*), vol. XII, pp. 51, 138, 315. He was killed in June 1796 participating in a revolt against the Anglo-Corsican kingdom: PRO, FO, 20/11, Elliot to Portland, 26 June 1796, dispatch 108. One of his sons aided Napoleon to be elected lieutenant-colonel of a battalion of volunteers for the districts of Ajaccio and Tallano, 2 April 1792, by forcibly obliging an official supervisor to lodge in the *casa* Bonaparte: Masson (*D, 3*), pp. 284–5. The Bonelli of Bocognano were related to the Bonaparte through the marriage, 1708, of Carlo's grandfather, Sebastiano, to a Tusoli of that village: see Maestrati (*E*), *EC*, no. 5–6, 1962. Domenico Leca: Rossi, op. cit., pp. 29, 51, 133.

3. Use of altars: Pommereul (*A, 1, d*), vol. I, p. 21; 'more like bandits': de Vaux, memoir, AN, K 1226, no. 4. Franciscans: P. André-Marie (*A, 2, c*), pp. 7–8; see also 'Mémoires . . . par un officier . . . de Picardie . . .' (*A, 1, d*); Jaussin (*A, 1, d*); Gaudin (*A, 1, d*).

4. Groups of resistants: Rossi (*A, 1, b*), vol. XII, p. 136; Anfosi: ADCS, 13 B, 6, 1 Aug. 1769; executions: ADCS, ibid.; '*pazienza*': Jaussin (*A, 1, d*), vol. I, pp. 104–5; 'Mémoires . . . par un officier . . . de Picardie . . .' (*A, 1, d*), p. 206. Corsican collaborators with French: see Casanova et Rovere (*A, 2, c*), pp. 122–5.

5. Napoleon on conquered peoples: Bertrand (*C, 2*), vol. II, p. 218; bandits, 'terrible village', cousins: ibid., see also n. 2 above. Attitudes of Luciano and Carlo: Bertrand, ibid., pp. 218, 142–3.

6. Carlo's fidelity to Paoli: C. Bonaparte, memoirs, AN, 400 AP, 115; see also chapter 2, n. 58, above; chapter 7, n. 7, below.

7. Vow of fidelity to Louis XV: 'Prestation de serment de la ville et faubourg d'Ajaccio', 18 April 1769, ADCS, 1 C, 503. Letter from Carlo to Pietrasanta, 8 July 1769, AN, 400 AP, 115.

8. Marbeuf, career: see chapter 4, n. 8, below. Carlo's song is cited by Nasica (*D, 3*), p. 29, who learnt it from a M. Ramolino (presumably Letizia's cousin André), who assured him that it became very popular.

9. Genoese towns in Corsica: see Kolodny (*A, 2, e*); populations: census of 1770, AN, Q^i 298^6; Bastia 5,286 inhabitants, Ajaccio 3,907 inhabitants. The bishops of Mariana, Aleria and Nebbio, the seats of whose dioceses were in unhealthy coastal areas, habitually resided in Bastia where, according to a sixteenth-century chronicler 'one lived well, as in wealthy towns': Filippini, 'Chronique . . .' (1559–94), translated by Letteron, *BSSHNC*, 1890, nos. 109–12, p. 304; see also Antonetti in *Bastia, regards sur son passé* (*A, 2, e*), pp. 41–114. Ajaccio was founded by the Genoese in 1490–92 to replace a city dating from Roman times in a less healthy

site a little to the south: see J. Campi, *Notes et documents* . . . (*A, 2, e*); L. Campi, (*A, 2, e*). Pommereul (*A, 1, d*), vol. I, pp. 85–6.

10. Cathedral: J. Campi, *Édifices religieux* . . . (*A, 2, e*); Marcaggi (*A, 2, e*); Arman (*A, 2, e*). The cathedral having been built between 1582 and 1593 to the order of Pope Gregory XIII, it was assumed that it was designed by Giacomo della Porta, architect to that Pope, a supposition doubted by Marcaggi, op. cit., and dismissed as 'mere drawing-room talk' by Arman, op. cit., p. 16. Corpses, smells: Chaume (*A, 2, e*); see also Versini (*A, 2, e*) and (*D, 2, a*) *passim*. Napoleon's comment: Bertrand (*C, 2*), vol. III, p. 79.

11. Bonaparte's life-style: Bertrand (*C, 2*), vol. III, p. 64; 'sordid avarice': 'Éclair cisse- ment sur la localité d'Ajaccio . . .', S H A T, Mr. 1099 and A N, K 1225, no. 3.

12. Luciano appointed archdeacon: A N, 400 A P, 115; see chapter 6, n. 30, below. Carlo's letter to Pietrasanta: A N, 400 A P, 115. The '*Ordonnance Civile*' was the French civil code which the government tried to impose in Corsica in place of that included in the Genoese *Statuti civili e criminali* (*A, 1, e*); the Corsicans, however, protested at the Assembly of Estates, Sept. 1770, and secured the partial use of the old civil code: 'Procès-verbal . . . des États . . . 1770', p. 10, 'Procès-verbal . . . des États . . . 1772', p. 42 (*A, 1, e*).

13. See A D C S, 2 B, 241.

14. Of the four Corsicans nominated to the Conseil Supérieur in Sept. 1768 only one, Jean-Lucas Poggi, already possessed the required qualifications: Villat (*A, 2, c*), vol. I, p. 88. He must have been the Gio' Lucca Poggi whose hospitality Carlo is said to have abused on his return to Bastia from his first Italian journey: see chapter 2, n. 30, above.

15. Doctorates given to innkeepers: Versini, quoting G. Cuvier, 1810 (*D, 2, a*), p. 26. There is no record of any studies undertaken at the university by Carlo Bona- parte. On 27 Nov. 1769 he appeared before the chancellor, Giovan' Lorenzo Meazzuoli, and swore 'hand on heart' that he had adequately studied the subject: 'Archivio di Stato, Pisa. Archivio Vecchio dell'Università di Pisa, filza 115: dottorati degli anni 1768–69', n. 758. He was examined 29 Nov. with Dr Vannuchi among the examiners and Dr Gio' Batta' Buonaparte among the witnesses: 'Archivio Arcivescovile di Pisa dell'anno 1769, no. 4 del mese di novembre'. On 30 Nov. he received his doctorate with an oration from Van- nucchi. He is described as '*Il Sig. Carlo quondam Sig. Giuseppe Buonaparte Nobile Patrizio Fiorentino Samniniatese e di Ajaccio*': ibid. and 'Registro dell'archivio antico', *sezione* D II, *registro* 8, no. 600: references communicated to François Flori by Ersilio Michel. The text of Vannucchi's oration is in A N, 400 A P, 115, and quoted in the memoirs of C. Bonaparte: ibid. Doctorates given to 15 Buonaparte of San Miniato, as well as to Carlo and Joseph Bonaparte of Ajaccio: Masson (*D, 3*), p. 24, n. 1. Supposed subject of C. Bonaparte's supposed thesis: Garnier (*D, 2, d*), p. 51, quoted by Versini (*D, 2, a*), p. 26.

16. Jacopo Buonaparte was the supposed author of *Ragguaglio storico di tutto l'occorso, giorno per giorno, nel sacco di Roma del'anno 1527*, published under his name, because the M S was found among his papers, Cologne, 1756. On a handsome memorial erected for him in the cathedral of San Miniato at the expense of Napoleon III he is described as '*Jacobo Bonaparte Philosopho Poetae Historico*'. Cesari Rocca, *Le Nid* . . . (*E*), p. 165, n. 2, however, believes that the author of this work was more

probably Luigi Guicciardini. Napoleon's march on Rome: see Las Cases (*C, 2*), vol. I, p. 79.

17. The seventeenth-century jurist Niccolò Buonaparte of San Miniato, see Lumbroso, *I Bonaparte dell'Isola* . . . (*E*), p. 6, should not be confused with Niccolò Buonaparte of Florence, uncle of Jacopo and author of a dramatic comedy *La Vedova*, produced in Florence 1568, published 1592: see Lumbroso, loc. cit., Cesari Rocca (*E*), p. 164.

18. The authorization of the archbishop of Pisa, 30 Nov. 1769, was not, curiously enough, submitted by Carlo and Luciano in their application for recognition of nobility, granted by the Conseil Supérieur, 13 Sept. 1771, ADCS, 1 B, 20; but it was included among the documents produced by Carlo to prove Napoleon's nobility and submitted, March 1779, to the royal heraldist d'Hozier de Serigny, AN, AE 1, *c.* 13, no. 1, *pièce* 4, see chapter 6, n. 20, below.

19. C. Bonaparte's registration as lawyer, 11 Dec. 1769: ADCS, 1 B, 6.

20. The Buonaparte of Florence died out in 1570: Lumbroso, *I Bonaparte dell'Isola* (*E*), p. 5, or in 1620: Sforza (*E*), p. 239. Lumbroso, loc. cit., maintains that a Captain Nicolò Buonaparte, a banished Ghibelline, moved to San Miniato, then a dependency of the emperor, in 1265; but this is unproved. Stefani, minister to Napoleon III, in an official report (E), concludes that the name, meaning 'good party' was adopted by various unrelated families in Florence, Sienna, Ascoli, Lucca and San Miniato during the struggle between Guelphs and Ghibellines. Cesari Rocca, *Le Nid* . . . (*E*), pp. 221–2, adheres to this thesis and believes that unrelated families bearing the same name adopted the same coat of arms in the mistaken belief that they had a common origin; see also Sforza, op. cit., pp. 239–52. Masson, however (*D, 3*), pp. 2–3, inclines to attribute a common origin to the Buonaparte (in Bonaparte) of Florence, San Miniato and Sarzana (and therefore Corsica) on the grounds that they had the same coat of arms. It may, however, be noted that the arms of the Tuscan Buonaparte are not identical with those of the Bonaparte of Ajaccio: see chapter 6, n. 22, below.

21. Montholon: Montholon (*C, 2*), vol. II, p. 16.

22. Letizia dreaded paying servants' wages: letter to Joseph Bonaparte, 1788, quoted by Masson (*D, 3*), pp. 169–70, from the Coll. Levie Ramolino. Census 1770: AN, Q^i 298^6. Wages: C. Bonaparte, 'Livre de Raison', BN, p. 25; he notes the engagement of two female servants in 1782, a cook at 6 and another at 4 livres a month.

23. Napoleon to his father, Brienne, 12–13 Sept. 1784: published in Masson (*D, 3*), pp. 86–7; noted, with summary, AN, 400 AP, 139; see chapter 8, n. 27, below.

24. Camilla gives Napoleon delicacies: Marchand (*C, 2*), vol. I, p. 67; 'paid him a cult': Antommarchi (*C, 2*), vol. I, p. 348; welcomes him in Ajaccio: Marchand, op. cit., vol. II, p. 272; Lavalette (*C, 3*), vol. I, p. 337; visits Paris: Antommarchi, loc. cit.; Bertrand (*C, 2*), vol. I, p. 42; Méneval (*C, 3*), vol. I, p. 379, Las Cases (*C, 2*), vol. II, p. 137; Napoleon's gifts, Letizia's opposition: Antommarchi, op. cit., vol. I, p. 349; see also Larrey (*D, 2, b*), vol. I, pp. 416–17; Barbaud (*A, 2, e*), pp. 15–20; Faustina in Paris: Poli, 'Mémoires . . .', *EC*, no. 3, 1954; 'Guerre du Fiumorbo', ibid., no. 4, 1954, and nos. 5, 6, 1955.

25. Geltrude reconciled with her husband: see chapter 2, n. 39, above; 'a second mother': J. Bonaparte (*C, 1*), vol. I, p. 31.

26. Saveria indulgent, pious, Carlo indulgent, Letizia too busy to go to church: Letizia Bonaparte, 'Souvenirs . . .', in Larrey (D, 2, b), vol. II, pp. 528–30.

27. Angela Maria Fesch, née Pietrasanta (c. 1725–c. 1790): see Beaucour (E), p. 275. Her defence of Letizia, expensive clothes: letter from Luciano to Pietrasanta, 16 March 1767, AN, 400 AP, 115; see chapter 2 above. François Fesch, son of a Swiss banker: Melito (C, 3), vol. II, p. 33; certified by burgomaster and consul of Basle, 29 March 1779, as belonging to a family distiguished for several generations in the magistrature, army and letters: AN, 400 AP, 113. Admitted as second lieutenant of the Swiss regiment of Seedorf, 5 March 1748, promoted lieutenant, 8 Oct. 1751, certified as having served in the Swiss regiment of Bocard, 4 Sept. 1761, ibid. An undated letter from the mother of Angela Maria, asks her husband's authorization for the marriage of her daughter to François Fesch, described as 'a man of accomplishments'; she is able to give her a dowry of 4,000 livres, ibid. They married 1757: Beaucour, loc. cit. François Fesch resigns from army: Maestrati (E), CH, no. 7. Conversion, attitude of Bonaparte, of Saveria, choice of career for son: Bertrand (C, 2), vol. II, p. 316. Made will in favour of his son Joseph, 2 Jan. 1770, the dispositions of which were refused by his family in Basle on account of his conversion: AN, 400 AP, 113. Luciano, in his letter to Pietrasanta, 16 March 1767, AN, 400 AP, 115, states that he was fully occupied exploiting his wife's properties and in litigation with an employee. He was buried 5 Jan. 1770, 'aged about fifty': ACA, GG, c. 6. r. II. Description of Joseph Fesch: Iung (C, 1), vol. I, p. 12.

28. Napoleon, in Elba, spoke to his valet Marchand of a grandmother who walked with a stick 'bent like an old fairy', whom he mimicked, with Pauline, behind her back. The grandmother complained to Letizia, who smacked Pauline 'because it is easier to pull up skirts than undo breeches', while Napoleon escaped punishment. But the next day Letizia told him to change his clothes because he had been 'invited to dine with the governor', and while he was dressing, 'like a cat watching a mouse' she sprang into his room and whipped him: Marchand (C, 2), vol. I, p. 67. Masson, who had access to Marchand's MS before its publication in 1952 (Marchand, ibid., xv–xvi), quoting the incident in Masson (D, 3), pp. 38–9, observes that since Pauline was not born till 1780 it must have occurred when Napoleon, on leave from his regiment, returned to Ajaccio in 1786 for the first time since he went to school in mainland France in 1778. He would then have been of an age to be invited to dine with the 'governor', presumably of the citadel of Ajaccio, for Napoleon told Marchand that he was pleased to 'go to dine with the officers': Marchand, loc. cit. The 'governor' cannot have been Marbeuf, who died 20 Sept., about five days after Napoleon's arrival in Corsica: see Masson (D, 3), pp. 17, 153. Masson concludes that Letizia knew how to make herself respected by her children, whatever their age: op. cit., pp. 38–9. His readiness to believe what Napoleon said twenty-eight years after the supposed incident is nevertheless surprising, for it is stretching credulity to suppose that Letizia would presume to whip her son, an adult and an officer, or that Napoleon, precociously serious at that period of his life, would join the six-year-old Pauline in playing such a prank. But Masson had not the advantage of knowing Bertrand's *Cahiers*, published 1949–59, which contain another and

much more credible version of the whipping incident: Napoleon, as a child, laughing when serving mass, performing his role without reverence. The following day Letizia told him to change his clothes because his uncle had invited him to lunch in the country to eat cherries; while he was dressing she sprang on him and whipped him: Bertrand (*C, 2*), vol. II, p. 137. This story is probably true, whereas the one Napoleon told Marchand was deformed by lapse of memory or deliberately, to make a good tale. Such a prank was perhaps played by Pauline and one of the younger children, and there is no reason to doubt that they had a grandmother crippled with rheumatism. The supposition that it was Angela Maria Fesch is supported by Jerome's baptismal act, 16 Nov. 1784, in which it is stated that his godmother, widow of Fesch, declared she was unable to sign, '*non poter scrivere*': ACA, GG, *c*. 8, *r*. 25. Had she been illiterate the expression, common in the documents of the period, would have been '*non sapere scrivere*'.

29. Overcrowding in notables' homes: Chaume (*A, 1, d*). Joseph Bonaparte (*C, 1*), vol. I, p. 42, indicates the site of the Bonaparte's first home and asserts that Napoleon's birthplace came to the family in a dowry from the Bozzi. He oversimplifies a complicated sequence of events that has never been completely elucidated. Maestrati (*E*), *CH*, no. 5–6, notes the marriage, 1703, of Giuseppe Bonaparte to Maria Bozzi and quotes her dowry, which included a house in Ajaccio, from the register of the notary Costa. Barbaud (*A, 2, e*), quotes from the register of the same notary the dowry of Maria Rosa Bozzi, 2 Nov. 1743, on her marriage to Napoleone Bonaparte. It consisted of the lower part (only) of her father's house in the 'Contrada della di Malerba': the lower floor and the cellar (ground floor). She and her father were to have common use of the entrance, where her father was to have the right to tether the animals which worked the mill (in the cellar?). The presence of a mill on the ground floor of a notable's house in Ajaccio was not exceptional: the author of 'Lettera anonima . . .', Coll. Santini, states that the servant Carlo Bonaparte sent to Ajaccio had to sit on a sack of corn brought by a client to the mill. Maria Rosa had come into possession of the whole house (presumably by inheritance) when in 1766 she exchanged it for a vineyard in the Saline belonging to Luciano, who thereby prevented it from leaving the family with the dowry of Maria Rosa's daughter Isabella (see chapter 2 above). The act was signed before a notary in the house of Saveria, Carlo's widowed mother, in the Contrada . . . Lazaro Rossi: AN, 400 AP, 112. Luciano's 'grandiose expenses', listed in the act, were taken into consideration in the exchange. The house is described as situated in the Contrada della di Malerba, overlooking, to the back, the *casetta* of the Ponte (see chapter 4 below), touching the public street on two sides (that is being on the corner of the Contrada . . . Malerba and the Strada del Pevero) and adjoining on one side the house of Luciano Bonaparte. The latter must have been the house the Bonaparte acquired from the Bozzi by marriage in 1703 (see above), the original *casa* Bozzi having been divided vertically (as is the custom in Corsica, so as to allow each owner his entrance to the street). In 1737 Luciano had received from his uncle Antonio (acting on behalf of his deceased father Sebastiano), the lower flat of the *casa* Bonaparte, consisting of a *sala*, two bedrooms and a kitchen (the two bedrooms must have been made into one by the time the house was

described in a municipal register, 1740?, see chapter 2, n. 9, above), together with a bedroom bought by Antonio from Gio' Battista Bozzi, presumably in the adjoining house which the Bozzi then owned and inhabited, and a portion of a vineyard in the Salini (which Luciano later gave Maria Rosa Bozzi in exchange for her house); these donations were to enable Luciano to undertake ecclesiastical studies in Genoa at the Collegio del Bene, which required a deposit of 1,500 lire: ADCS, 3 E, 734, acts of 23 Oct., 22, 23 Nov. 1737; see also Versini (*D, 3*), p. 56, n.i. The *casa* Bonaparte is described as being in the Strada di San Carlo, the name to which it later reverted and which it has retained; see chapter 2, n. 9, above.

30. Letter from C. Bonaparte to Pietrasanta, 27 April 1770: AN, 400 AP, 115. It is in many points obscure. He had apparently returned from a journey by sea: 'At last after so many storms I am in the calm and in port'; is this fact or image? He may have been away for over three months, for his name is absent from the court register of Ajaccio, 8 Jan.–7 May 1770: ADCS, 2 B, 241. He cannot have been staying in Bastia, where Pietrasanta resided, for he writes: 'I think you have received my letter of the last month'; but he must have called there, for he begs Pietrasanta to forward – 'embark' – his trunk (heavy luggage then normally travelled between the two towns by sea). He writes of being 'arrested' on his arrival: perhaps he was detained for quarantine by the port authorities; cf. letter to Pietrasanta, 7 Dec. 1771, in which he mentions his 'arrest' by the commissioner of the port: AN, 400 AP, 115. Had he again been to Italy, and was this the cause of Luciano's ill humour?

31. Lawsuit between Bonaparte and Ornano: 31 May, 25 June 1770, ADCS, 2 B, 241, 14 Feb. 1771, ADCS, 2 B, 243; continuation: see chapter 4 below. See AN, 400 AP, 112; also Mirtil (*D, 3*), pp. 21–37. Luciano to Pietrasanta, 17 Aug. 1770: AN, 400 AP, 115.

32. Directeur des Domaines *v.* Beau, 23 July 1770: ADCS, 2 B, 241.

33. Elisabetta Tassy and Jean-Baptiste Feretti, 23 Dec. 1770–25 Feb. 1771: ADCS, 2, B, 8.

34. Post of '*assesseur*' created in royal jurisdictions of Corsica: ADCS, A 16, Code Corse, vol. II, pp. 247–9. Giubega: see chapter 4, n. 3, below. Letters from Carlo to Pietrasanta, 10 April, 3 July, 9 Sept. (Cuneo an obstacle), 14 Sept. (advance news of nomination as *assesseur*), 11 Oct. (Orto '*coglione*', etc.): AN, 400 AP, 115.

35. Carlo Bonaparte, official nomination as *assesseur*, Versailles, 10 May 1771, registered by Conseil Supérieur 22 Nov. 1771: ADCS, 1 B, 2: see also C. Bonaparte, memoirs, AN, 400 AP, 115. Salaries: Pommereul (*A, 1, d*), vol. II, p. 219; the *assesseurs* were required to work eight hours a day in summer and six in winter: ibid., p. 220. A request from the Corsican Estates that Corsican magistrates should receive the same salaries as the French was dismissed by the King: 'Procès-verbal ... des États ... 1777' (*A, 1, e*), p. 254. Prestige of post of *assesseur* regarded as a means of winning government favour: Colchen (*C, 3*), p. 329. Carlo's debt to Marbeuf: Rossi (*A, 1, b*), vol. XIII, p. 84.

36. Recognition of nobility; election to Estates: see chapter 4 below. Delay in receiving commission, 15 June 1772: ADCS, 2 B, 3. By then Guillaume Louis Armand had succeeded Cuneo as judge, 30 April 1772, while Paul Baptiste Cataneo had been appointed *procureur du roi* for the jurisdiction of Ajaccio, on 15 June 1772: ibid.

4. THE TRIUMPHS OF A CORSICAN FAMILY

1. Correspondence between C. Bonaparte and Marbeuf, Nov. 1765: see chapter 2, n. 33, above. On leave since Aug. 1769, Marbeuf was appointed commander-in-chief in Corsica 1 April 1770: ADCS, 1 B, 2; he reached the island 7 May: see Villat (*A, 2,* c), vol. I, p. 171. Luciano evidently knew how to conceal his dislike of the French when family interests were at stake; unwilling to meet Marbeuf, he was won over when they met accidentally: Bertrand (*C, 2*), vol. II, pp. 142–3; this occasion must have been before the baptism of Napoleon.

2. Baptismal act of Napoleon and Maria Anna (b. 14 July 1771– d. 23 Nov. 1771): ACA, GG, *c.* 7, *r.* 12 (at present exhibited in Town Hall, Ajaccio); another copy exists in ADCS, 2 E, 2 (duplicate of parish register from 1770); birth and death of Maria Anna, ibid. They both had as godfather Lorenzo Giubega; Geltrude Paravisino was godmother to Napoleon, Anna Ternano godmother to Maria Anna. Luciano Bonaparte to Pietrasanta, 24 July 1771: AN, 400 AP, 115. Baptism of Lucien and Elisa: see chapter 6, n. 30, below.

3. Lorenzo Giubega, elected to Estates, 1770, for nobility of Calvi: Villat (*A, 2, c*), vol. II, p. 460; installed as secretary of Estates, 1 May 1772: 'Procès-verbal . . . des États . . . 1772' (*A, 1, e*), pp. 10–11; salary: Rossi (*A, i, b*), vol. XII, p. 158. Qualities: Roux (*A, 1, c*), p. 102. Letter from Carlo: published in Chuquet (*D, 3*), vol. I, p. 358. Having enjoyed the confidence and prodigality of the French government, he was eclipsed during the Revolution, quarrelled with Paoli and retired to Calvi where his family gave refuge to the Bonaparte in their flight from Corsica in June 1793: see Masson (*D, 3*), p. 347.

4. Baptism of Napoleon, in Luciano to Pietrasanta, 24 July 1771 (AN, 400 AP, 115): '*Questa* [*Maria Anna*] *s'e battezzata con l'assistenza del signor Giubega e nel medesimo tempo si battezzo o siasi suppli alla ceremonia della chiesa per Napoleone . . .*'; cf. baptismal act (ACA, GG, *c.* 7, *r.* 12): '*si sono adoprate le sacre ceremonie e precie sopra di Napoleone . . . al quale gli fu data l'acqua in casa di licenza dal molto Riverendo Luciano Bonaparte . . .*' The words '*di licenza*' are omitted in the copy in ADCS 2 E, 2; cf. baptismal act of Luciano and Maria Anna (Lucien and Elisa) Bonaparte, 4 Sept. 1779: ACA, GG, *c.* 8, *r.* 20: '*io sotto-scritto arciprete Luciano ho supplito alle sacre ceremonie avendo avuta l'acqua in casa colla licenza di Monsig. Vescovo . . .*'. Baptismal act of Luigi (Louis) Bonaparte: ACA, GG, *c.* 8, *r.* 19.

5. Luciano to Pietrasanta, 17 Aug. 1771; Carlo Bonaparte to Pietrasanta, 25 Aug. 1771: AN, 400 AP, 115. The expression Carlo uses to describe Marbeuf's visit suggests that it was intimate and unceremonious: '*fatte la veglia*'/'*faire la veillée*', a custom still practised in Corsican villages, means sitting up late with guests; 'to the envy and anger of our rivals': '*invidia e dispiacere ai nostri emuli*'.

6. Napoleon in Las Cases (*C, 2*), vol. I, p. 84. Evidence is lacking to show whether Marbeuf knew Letizia before the outbreak of hostilities in the summer of 1768, but during the war any meeting between them was virtually impossible. Allegations of meetings, in Bartel (*D, 3*), pp. 45–7, which betray an astonishing ignorance of Corsican geography and conditions, are adequately disposed of by Flori (*D, 2, b*); Marbeuf's occupations in Nov. 1768 are known from 'Journal des opérations . . .' SHAT, Mr. 248/1. Bartel, op. cit., p. 43, also offers as evidence a supposed conversation between Napoleon and Gaspard Monge during their

voyage back from Egypt, in which Napoleon is said to have wondered if he inherited his military talent from Marbeuf, but concluded that, 'treating the problem as a scientific question', he was Carlo's son. The source given is Monge's 'Mémoires', but as no memoirs by Monge have been published the story cannot be checked; Bartel did, however, have access to the Monge family papers: op. cit., p. 10. But the story is unconvincing; Napoleon, of all people, knew that Marbeuf lacked military talent.

7. Colchen (*C, 3*), pp. 329–30, Rémusat (*C, 3*), vol. I, p. 127, Chaptal (*B, 2, b*), p. 174, de Romain (*C, 3*), vol. I, pp. 106–7; veiled allusion in de Créquy (*C, 3*), vol. VII, pp. 120–22.

8. Louis-Charles-René comte (later marquis) de Marbeuf (1712–86), *maréchal-de-camp*, 1762, was appointed gentleman-in-waiting to Stanislas Leczinsky, duc de Lorraine, former king of Poland and father-in-law to Louis XV. In 1764 he was sent to Corsica as commander of the French garrison troops. Passed over in favour of the marquis de Chauvelin to command the invasion force in 1768, he was promoted lieutenant-general in October of that year and provisional commander of French troops in Corsica in December, only to be superseded by de Vaux in April 1769, whom he, however, replaced as commander-in-chief from April 1770 (see n. 1 above). He remained in Corsica till his death in 1786, playing an essentially administrative role; in 1778 he was rewarded with a grant of land and the title of marquis (see chapter 5, n. 20, below): see Chuquet (*D, 3*), vol. I, pp. 368–9. Powers: see Casanova et Rovere, Bordes, Carrington (all *A, 2, c*). Marriage contract with Éléonore Julie de Guémadeuc, widow of the comte de Guyon, 29 May 1752: E. P., 'Napoléon et la Bretagne et Marbeuf', *Le Fureteur Breton, mai/juin – juillet*, 1921; her prayers: Roux (*A, 1, c*), p. 80. After her death in 1783 he married in Oct. of that year Catherine Salinguerra Antoinette Gaillardon de Fenoyl (b. 1765) who bore him a daughter, 24 Dec. 1784, and a son, 26 May 1786, before his own death, 20 Sept. 1786: see Villat (*A, 2, c*), vol. II, pp. 29–30, and chapter 7 below.

9. Mme Varese, French lovers, Paoli: Dumouriez (*A, 1, b*), vol. I, p. 111; age, dressing, Cleopatra: 'Mémoires . . . par un officier . . . de Picardie . . .' (*A, 1, d*), pp. 49–53; see also Colchen (*C, 3*), p. 330, Roux (*A, 1, c*), pp. 126–7. Marbeuf and Mme Chardon: Lauzun (*C, 3*), pp. 82–92.

10. Mme Varese, informer: 'Mémoires . . . par un officier . . . de Picardie . . .' (*A, 1, d*), p. 54; Carlo's service as informer to Paoli: see chapter 2, n. 45, above; to Marbeuf: see chapter 6 below.

11. Rivalry between Marbeuf, de Vaux, Colla de Pradine, Narbonne: see Villat (*A, 2, c*), vol. I, pp. 171, 286–91, 313–46 and chapter 5 below.

12. Napoleon maintained that Marbeuf protected his father because he was 'in the front line of his partisans' and not because of his 'supposed love' of his mother: Montholon (*C, 2*), vol. II, p. 18. Corsicans seen by French: Jaussin (*A, i, d*), vol. I, p. 105; 'Mémoires . . . par un officier . . . de Picardie . . .' (*A, 1, d*), p. 207; Gaudin (*A, 1, d*), pp. 170–71; inhabitants of Ajaccio, anonymous memoir: S H A T, Mr. 1099; depressed officers: Roux (*A, 1, c*), pp. 143–4, 169.

13. At the *consulta* summoned by Paoli in Corte, 27–9 May 1793, that marked his break with the Convention, the Bonaparte brothers, then in the opposing, Republican faction, were stigmatized as 'born in the slough of despotism, nour-

ished and brought up under the eyes and at the expense of a luxurious pasha who then commanded this island': Proceedings of *consulta* in Corte, 27–9 May 1793 ... (*A, 1, e*) p. 395. Missionaires: Jaussin (*A, 1, d*), vol. I, p. 31, Olivesi (*A, 2, e*); Marbeuf is also said to have lodged in a large neighouring house overlooking the sea that became the residence of Sir Gilbert Elliot, viceroy of the Anglo-Corsican kingdom. Theatre: Rossi (*A, i, b*), vol. XIII, p. 14, 'Deux députations ...': (*A, 1, e*), p. 9; see chapter 5 below. Pavilion: 'Mémoires ... par un officier ... de Picardie ...' (*A, 1, d*), p. 51; 'pleasure ground': Boswell (*A, i, d*), p. 373.

14. Boswell on Marbeuf: Boswell (*A, 1, d*), pp. 366–7. Carlo, 'too fond of pleasure', connoisseur of food and wine: Antommarchi (*C, 2*), vol. I, p. 353, p. 258, cf. Gourgaud (*C, 2*), vol. I, p. 473; women: Bertrand (*C, 2*), vol. II, p. 137. Loyalty: Rossi (*A, 1, b*), vol. XIII, pp. 84–5.

15. Judgements of Letizia vary between the loyal attitude of Larrey (*D, 2, b*), who avoids discussing her relationship to Marbeuf; the unproved accusations of Bartel (*D, 3*); the passionate defence of Marthe Arrighi de Casanova (*D, 2, b*); and the savage condemnations of such pamphleteers as Goldsmith: see chapter 8, n. 37, below.

16. Aim of French government: de Vaux, 'Mémoire' AN, K 1226, no. 4. Concessions of crown lands: see Pomponi (*A, 2, d*). Royal edict creating order of nobility, April 1770: ADCS, 1 B 2, and ADCS, A 16, Code Corse, vol. II, pp. 79–92. Acts of recognition: ADCS, 1 B, 20, 21, 22. See also Cesari Rocca, *Armorial* ... (*E*), who, including different branches of certain families, lists 161 families with descriptions and illustrations of their coats of arms, without naming individuals except the small number who received titles. Acts of recognition of Pietri and Ortoli: ADCS, 1 B, 22; Ortoli of Olmiccia: Patin de la Fizelière (*A, 1, e*).

17. Letters to Pietrasanta from C. Bonaparte, 3 March, 25 Aug. 1771, from L. Bonaparte, 17 Aug. 1771 (complains of Carlo): AN, 400 AP, 115.

18. Act of recognition of nobility of Bonaparte: ADCS, 1 B, 20; AN, 400 AP, 112; published in Versini (*D, 2, a*), pp. 193–5. Letters to Pietrasanta from C. Bonaparte, 18 Sept. 1771, from L. Bonaparte, 19 Sept. 1771: AN, 400 AP, 115. Writing to Pietrasanta 11 Oct. 1771 (AN, 400 AP, 115), Carlo begs him to make Luciano pay for the copies of the act he has ordered. The connection with the Lomellino is substantiated by the fact that Napoleone Lomellino stood godfather to Luciano's father, Sebastiano, 1684: see chapter 2, n. 43 above. 'Lettera anonima ...', Coll. Santini, states that the Bonaparte were farmers for the Lomellino; evidence of blood relationship is lacking. The Cuneo were ennobled 9 April 1771; the earliest document cited in their act of recognition is dated 1585: ADCS, 1 B, 20.

19. Volumes submitted by Colonna d'Istria and Gentile, acts of recognition: ADCS, 1 B, 20, 21. Matteo Buttafoco, act of recognition: ADCS, 1 B, 20; he received various favours from the government and was created count 1781: Cesari Rocca, 'Armorial ...' (*E*), p. xxix; see chapter 6, n. 12, below. Many of the new nobles were descendants of the '*caporali*', local leaders who assumed hereditary privileges after the collapse of the feudal families: Bertrand (*C, 2*), vol. III, p. 81. Bernadino Delfino (or Delfini) claimed to possess a collection of authentic ancient documents; denounced by a client, Giacomo Antonio Filippini, Nov. 1786, he escaped

before his house at Carogna de Casacconi was searched, 30 Nov., by the police. Witnesses described his documents, which were written in black and red ink on small pieces of parchment and usually mentioned the Office of San Giorgio, and a 'catalogue' of noble families, in Latin, bearing the arms of the Genoese Republic: ADCS, 1 B, 62, 83. Demartini (E), asserts that the Malaspina of Belgodere possess a MS which may be this 'catalogue': an inventory made in 1454 by the Office of San Giorgio (which had assumed administration of the island the preceding year) of more than 100 noble Corsican families, most of which were ennobled by the French monarchy. The document, of doubtful authenticity, is in error concerning the Bonaparte, the branch of the family that settled in Ajaccio not being heard of before 1497: see chapter 2, n. 11, above. Delfino 'bandito fugitivo': see Carrington (A, 2, d).

20. The first document cited by the Bonaparte in their act of recognition, see n. 18 above, is an order from the Office of San Giorgio, 1536, in response to a request from Geronimo Bonaparte and other municipal officers to prohibit Corsicans (as distinct from Genoese colonists) from residing in Ajaccio. The second, dated 1554, is an unspecified request from Geronimo on behalf of the municipal officers to the Genoese senate. Neither can be verified, the earliest record in the municipal archives (ACA, AA, l. 1) being dated 1562, and the earliest reference in the Libro Grosso (ACA, BB, c. 7), 1596. Geronimo is not mentioned in the archives before 1572, when he appears as spokesman of the city to the Genoese senate, one of his requests being for the edification of a cathedral: ACA, AA, l. 1. In 1577 he appears again as spokesman, making the same request as that cited in the document of 1536 in the Bonaparte's act of recognition, with the same municipal officers (and one other): ibid. The document of 1536 therefore appears as a fake modelled on the authentic document of 1577, the Bonaparte, in their anxiety to prove their noble status for over 200 years, being unwilling to quote the authentic document of 1572 as the earliest they could produce. Pinoteau (E) dismisses the documents of 1536 and 1554 as fraudulent (Les Bonaparte avant 1789, pp. 6–7, Vingt-cinq ans . . ., p. 224), pointing out that according to archival sources Geronimo Bonaparte was a man of law active 1560–85; see also Cesari Rocca, Le Nid . . . (E), pp. 270–78. Evidence for his legal career in Corsica, 1560–97 exists in ADCS, Civile Governatore. Copies of documents of 1536 and 1554 (AN, 400 AP, 114) form part of a collection of family papers, the subsequent documents being copies of notarial acts bearing no relation to this book. Geronimo Bonaparte's request relative to a cathedral in the Archives Napoléon is longer and more elaborate than that in ACA, l. 1, as though Carlo and Luciano had embroidered on the subject. The copies of these documents, in Italian, are accompanied by French translations made by an annotator of the Archives Napoléon prior to their cession to AN. The translation of the 1554 document is dated 22 août 1572, although the date given in the Italian text, MDLIIII die XXII agosto, cannot be read as other than 1554. Was the annotator of the Archives Napoléon acquainted with the authentic document of 1572, and seeking to shield the Bonaparte from accusations of fraud? Carlo, no doubt wary of the experienced eye of the royal heraldist, omitted the documents of 1536 and 1554 from the genealogy he submitted for Napoleon in 1779: AN, AE

1, *c.* 13, no. 1, *pièce* 4, replacing them with others later in date: see chapter 6, n. 20, below. Pinoteau gives a comparative table of documents submitted in 1771 and 1779: (*E*), *Le Dossier nobiliaire* . . ., pp. 34–6, and *Vingt-cinq ans* . . ., pp. 267–9. Claims submitted to the Conseil Supérieur were examined by two councillors, one Corsican, one French; that of the Bonaparte (see n. 18 above) was examined by Stefanini and Baude, it being no doubt considered improper that Pietrasanta, a relation, should participate in the task. It seems unlikely that his influence did more than expedite the procedure.

21. Carlo and Joseph Bonaparte, efforts to trace Tuscan ancestors: see chapter 6, nn. 6, 7, below.

22. The various suppositions about Napoleon's ancestry are summarized by Cesari Rocca, *Le Nid* . . . (*E*), Pinoteau and Valynseele (*E*). Napoleon regarded them with suitable disdain, though he so often spoke of his relationship to the Italian Buonaparte that one may wonder whether he was not secretly proud of these possible connections: Las Cases, vol. I, pp. 81–3, Antommarchi, vol. I, pp. 155–60, Bertrand, vol. I, pp. 43–4 (all *C, 2*).

23. Napoleon's descent from the Comnenos emperors of Byzantium and Trebizond was put about by Laure d'Abrantès and her family. Her mother was a Stephanopoli, a family that had settled in Corsica in 1676 with a group of Maniot Greeks, refugees from the Turks, who believed themselves to be descended from the Comnenos emperors, so that Louis XVI was induced to grant Demetrius, Laure's uncle, the title of Prince Comnènes, 1782: *Précis historique de la maison impériale des Comnènes* . . . (Amsterdam, 1784); Cesari Rocca, *Le Nid* . . . (*E*), pp. 207–10. Laure d'Abrantès maintains in her *Mémoires* . . . (*C, 3*), vol. I, *t.* i, pp. 29–30, that a son of Constantine Comnenos, leader of the original colony in Corsica, called Calomeros, meaning 'good party', was sent on a mission to Tuscany, settled there and later returned to Corsica under the name of Bonaparte. Napoleon ridiculed the pretensions of the Stephanopoli no less than their attempt to link him to their genealogy: Bertrand (*C, 2*), vol. I, p. 45, vol. II, p. 136.

24. 'Old kings of the north': Las Cases (*C, 2*), vol. I, p. 80; Napoleon related through Malaspina to the Brunswick and so to the English royal family: Bertrand (*C, 2*), vol. II, p. 250; to the Bourbon through the Medici: ibid. 'Man in the iron mask', presumed brother of Louis XIV, imprisoned in Marseilles, supposed to have escaped, married the daughter of his gaoler called Bompart, reached Corsica and changed his name to Bonaparte: Las Cases, vol. II, pp. 19–20, Bertrand, vol. II, p. 249 (both *C, 2*).

25. George Sand, *Un Hiver à Majorque* (Paris, 1841), pp. 96–7, maintains that a register in a Dominican monastery in Palma mentions a family called Bonpar, 1276, that the name was changed to Bonapart, and that a Hugo Bonapart was sent from Mallorca to Corsica, 1441, as regent for Martin king of Aragon (who in fact had a claim to the sovereignty of the island granted by the Pope, 1284). The Mallorcan thesis is seriously examined by Roux (*D, 3*), pp. 309–11, who concludes that a family by the name of Bonaparte existed in Mallorca.

26. Napoleon, 'My titles . . .': Bertrand (*C, 2*), vol. I, p. 44; 'Permit me to be . . .', ibid., vol. II, p. 249. 'The house of Bonaparte . . .': *Moniteur Universel*, 14 July 1805. Clovis: Bertrand, op. cit., vol. I, p. 44.

27. Origin of name: Cesari Rocca, *Le Nid* . . . (*E*), pp. 221–3, Stefani (*E*), see

chapter 3, n. 20, above. In 1802, the scholar Bernucci, on behalf of the inhabitants of Sarzana, who wished to raise a monument to Napoleon, proposed an affiliation linking a Bonapart-Pax, living in Sarzana *c.* 1270, with the Bonaparte of Ajaccio: Cesari Rocca, op. cit., pp. 196–8, Caraffa (*E*), pp. 29–30. These researches were further developed in 1856 by L. Passerini (*E*), see also Cesari Rocca, op. cit., p. 212, and re-presented in an official report, 1859 (*E*) by Stefani, minister to Napoleon III, who, while rejecting a common origin for the various families named Buonaparte in different Italian towns, accepts Passerini's thesis of a descent of the Buonaparte of Florence, linked with those of San Miniato, Sarzana and Ajaccio, from a family of Lombard counts, the Kadolingi, and provides a genealogy tracing their ascendance to a common ancestor, a Count Tedix living in the tenth century; see also Cesari Rocca, who is unconvinced: op. cit., pp. 212–17.

28. Descent from Charlemagne: Cesari Rocca, *Le Nid* . . . (*E*), pp. 236–41.

29. Bonaparte of Sarzana: Cesari Rocca, *Le Nid* . . . (*E*), pp. 225–32. Condottieri: Bertrand (*C, 2*), vol. II, p. 419; 'little gentlemen adventurers': ibid., vol. I, p. 44.

30. Regulations for assembly of Estates: ADCS, A 16, Code Corse, vol. II, pp. 64–78. The electoral system, apparently equitable, in fact gave a controlling voice to the nobles. The primary electoral assemblies were those of the sixty-five *pievi*, each containing several communes. The people permitted to take part in these assemblies were: the *pievan* (senior priest of the *pieve*), the municipal officers (the *podestat*) and two '*pères du commun*' of each commune, and all the nobles of the *pieve*. The assembly elected one noble and one representative of the Third Estate to the assembly of the province; the *pievan* being a member of that assembly by right. The provincial assemblies then elected, from their members, a number of representatives of the three orders proportionate to the populations of each province, in all 18 *pievans*, and 23 members of the nobility and of the Third Estate, one of each to every thousand households. The province of Ajaccio, with 8 *pievi*, returned 3 *pievans*, 5 nobles and 5 commoners to the Estates. See Code Corse, *ubi supra:* Colombani, Carrington, 'Les Pozzo di Borgo . . . ', 'The Corsican Estates . . .' (all *A, 2, c*).

31. C. Bonaparte's election: assembly of *pieve*, assembly of province: ADCS, 1 C, 541, 546. Letter to Pietrasanta, 11 Oct. 1771: AN, 400 AP, 115. See also Carrington, 'Les Pozzo di Borgo . . .' (*A, 2, c*). Carlo's election in the provincial assembly apparently took place without difficulty, for none is mentioned in the document, *ubi supra.*

32. Interventions of *commissaires du roi* in elections: see Bordes, Carrington (both *A, 2, c*).

33. Narbonne, kinship with Sampiero Corso, local costume, ball at Bocognano, criticism of Marbeuf: Rossi (*A, 1, b*), vol. XII, pp. 193–4; Boswell's costume, Boswell (*A, 1, d*), p. 317. Napoleon compares Marbeuf and Narbonne, who was 'of a superior reputation and breeding': Las Cases (*C, 2*), vol. I, p. 83; weakness of Marbeuf: 'Mémoires . . . par un officier . . . de Picardie . . .' (*A, 1, d*), pp. 52–5.

34. Luciano to Pietrasanta, 8 April 1772: AN, 400 AP, 115. Celebration of mass: 'Procès-verbal . . . des États . . . 1772' (*A, 1, e*), p. 8; wall hangings: 'Procès-verbal . . . des États . . . 1775' (*A, 1, e*), p. 254.

35. Illusion of liberty: Matteo Buttafoco, 'Mémoire . . .', AN, K 1228, no. 5. Limits of powers: see n. 31, 32 above. Taxation: Memoirs, Versailles, 16 April, 9 July 1770: ADCS, 1 C, 549. The principal form of taxation, known as the 'subvention territorial', in accordance with the doctrines of the physiocrats, was imposed not on persons but on land. From 1778 it was levied in kind: see Colombani, Casanova and Rovere, Carrington, 'The Corsican Estates . . .' (all *A, 2, c*).

36. See 'Procès-verbal . . . des États . . . 1772' (*A, 1, e*). Election of *Nobles Douze*, terms of office, ibid., pp. 131–4; expense allowances of deputies to Estates: ibid., p. 157. Expense allowances of *Nobles Douze*: ADCS, 1 A, 16, Code Corse, vol. II, p. 78. Bastia nearly as expensive as Paris: Greslaie in Villat (*A. 1. d*), vol. II, p. 481.

37. See Mirtil (*D, 3*), pp. 28–39. Evidence of witnesses: ADCS, 2 B, 218.

38. Luciano to Pietrasanta, 'fatal epoque', 31 March 1773; 'crucified', 'orphans', 'little stars' (was Luciano thinking, consciously or not, of the two stars in the Bonaparte's coat of arms? See chapter 6, n. 22, below), 'die in peace', 3 April 1773; 'master-stroke of vengeance', insults, 'foreign sky', 20 June 1773: AN, 400 AP, 115. Carlo to Pietrasanta, 8 July 1773; draft of memoir, undated, but evidently of 1774, addressed to Marbeuf, unnamed, but styled 'Eccelenza': ibid. Defence of forty-seven pages, seen by Mirtil but now inaccessible: Mirtil (*D, 3*), p. 38. Notarial act of agreement between Luciano and Isabella, signed in the presence of Marbeuf, 12 Sept 1773: AN, 400 AP, 114.

39. Terrace: C. Bonaparte, 'Livre de Raison', BN, p. 29. In the nineteenth-century the Bonaparte bought two small rooms in an adjoining house at the end of the gallery, mistakenly shown to tourists as the bedrooms of Joseph and Napoleon. Enlargement of house: see Carrington (*A, 2, e*). In the inventory drawn up by Letizia, 1 June 1798, the house is described as having 'four storeys including the ground floor': ADCS, 4 L, 56; published in *EC*, 1956, no. 12, with the reference ADCS, 4 L, 15 (superseded inventory).

5. THE WAY TO THE THRONE

1. See 'Mémoires . . . par un officier . . . de Picardie . . .', who witnessed the rebellion and repression (*A, 1, d*), pp. 40–44; Roux, another contemporary (*A, 1, c*), pp. 118–19, Russian ships, ibid., p. 105; trials: Flori (*A, 2, c*); prisoners in Toulon: Emmanuelli et Zonza (*A, 2, c*). Summaries: Rossi (*A, 1, b*), vol. XII, pp. 304–10, Narbonne's proposal, ibid., p. 310; Renucci, who doubts Clemente's complicity and blackens Sionville (*A, 1, b*), vol. I, pp. 134–44; Villat (*A, 2, c*), vol. I, pp. 307–12; Casanova et Rovere (*A, 2, c*), pp. 149–61. Pasquale Paoli, though harbouring a plan to free Corsica from France, denied any participation in the revolt.

2. Sionville burnt in effigy in Sartene: report of Corsican agent to Brame, British consul in Genoa, 23 Nov. 1789: PRO, FO, 28, Genoa, I, see Bibliography, PRO, Carrington, (*A, 2, e*), p. 154. According to Rossi (*A, 1, b*), vol. XIV, pp. 57–8, Sionville merely overheard a reveller suggest throwing him into a bonfire and died at home soon afterwards of fever brought on by distress. Defranceschi (*A, 2, c*), p. 36, maintains that the judge Vidau was burnt in effigy in Sartene, 23 Aug. 1789, and that Sionville, affected by the sight, died afterwards.

3. 'Nouvelle Corse', Masson et Biagi, *Napoléon inconnu* . . . (*D, 3*), MS xxxv, pp. 381–9. Undated, it would appear to have been written in 1789, perhaps when Napoleon was in Corsica in Sept., see Masson (*D, 3*), p. 213), when feeling against Sionville was running high (see above, n. 2), and before the integration of Corsica to France on equal terms, 30 Nov., and the application of the new constitution had palliated Corsican grievances: Defranceschi (*A, 2, c*), pp. 42–4. The obvious influence of Bernardin de Saint Pierre's *Paul et Virginie* (Paris, 1788), leaves no doubt that the 'Nouvelle' was written after that date. Napoleon apparently read Ossian at school at Brienne in the translation of Le Tourneur (Paris, 1777): see chapter 7, n. 26, below. He read Rousseau when doing garrison service with his regiment, 1786–91, at Valence and Auxonne: see P. C. Healey, *Rousseau et Napoléon* (Paris, 1957). Joseph on his arrival in Ajaccio, 1787: *Mémoires* . . . (*C, 1,*), vol. I, p. 32. Influences in 'Nouvelle': Healey (*B, 4, b*), p. 42; his notice, though brief, is much to be preferred to Christopher Frayling, *Napoleon Wrote Fiction* (Salisbury, 1972), in which the literary analysis is superficial and the translation, otherwise adequate, discredited by the absurd title: 'New Corsica'. It may be noted that Napoleon also wrote a fragmentary tale entitled 'Le Comte d'Essex: Nouvelle Anglaise' (Masson et Biagi, op. cit., MS xix), which Frayling ignores. Reminiscences of the revolt of 1774 are frequent in 'Nouvelle Corse': it was started by sixty men; forty men were captured by the French, though not all were executed as Napoleon's narrator asserts (see above); the tales of killing, rape and hanging reflect memories of real events. Nothing concerning Gorgona however relates to fact except that a Benedictine monastery existed there in the Middle Ages which owned churches and lands in Corsica: see Arrighi and Olivesi (*A, 2, a*), pp. 162–4. Corsican code of honour and justice, duty to spirits of murdered dead: see J. Busquet, *Le Droit de la vendetta et les paci Corses* (Paris, 1920); Carrington, *Granite Island* (London, 1971).

4. Stendhal, *Vie de Napoléon* (Paris, 1876), p. 13.

5. Giacominetta: Antommarchi (*C, 2*), vol. I, p. 180; Letizia Bonaparte (*C, 1*).

6. Joseph bullied: Antommarchi (*C, 2*), vol. I, p. 352; Beating, Saveria, Napoleon's fortitude: d'Abrantès (*C, 3*), vol. I, t. 1, p. 35. Carlo pampered children: Letizia Bonaparte (*C, 1*) 'too fond of pleasure': Antommarchi (*C, 2*), vol. I, p. 353; Letizia's masculine nature: ibid, p. 276. O'Meara (*C, 2*), vol. II, p. 100; mother head of family: Letizia Bonaparte, op. cit.

7. Letizia's tenderness 'severe': Antommarchi (*C, 2*), vol. I, p. 353. Drove Napoleon to church: Roederer (*C, 3*), p. 188; punished for misbehaving in church: Bertrand (*C, 2*), vol. II, p. 137; for stealing fruit: Antommarchi, loc. cit., d'Abrantès (*C, 3*), vol. I, t. 1, p. 35; for laughing at crippled grandmother: Marchand (*C2*), vol. I, p. 67 (see chapter 3, n. 28, above). Napoleon's tribute to Letizia: Montholon (*C, 2*), vol. I, p. 321; O'Meara (*C, 2*), p. 100; Letizia inculcated truthfulness: Antommarchi, loc. cit.; Napoleon an habitual liar: Rémusat (*C. 3*), vol. I, p. 105, O'Meara (*C, 2*), 1888 edn, vol. II, p. 52.

8. Napoleon ate garrison bread: Letizia Bonaparte (*C, 1*); Letizia attached importance to appearances: Bertrand (*C, 2*), vol. II, pp. 137, 315; dry bread for punishment: d'Abrantès (*C, 3*), vol. I, t. 1, p. 36; sent to bed without supper: Bertrand, op. cit., p. 315; sent to spy on father, deceived by Letizia: ibid., p. 137; see chapter 3, n. 28, above.

9. Letizia's dotal act: AN, AE 1, c. 11–12, no. 17; see chapter 2 above. The case

was heard 9 March and Giovanni Ramolino's property sold 4 May 1775; the
quarrel was not settled till 21 Nov. 1776 when Ramolino was condemned to pay
the Bonaparte the price of an ox: ADCS, 2 B, 245, 246; see also Mirtil (*D, 3*), pp.
77–80. Conflict between André Ramolino and Camilla Ilari: chapter 3, n. 24,
above.

10. De Pradine's sympathy with *narbonisti*: Rossi (*A, 1, b*), vol. XII, pp. 315–16, 337;
welcome for Narbonne, jeers for Marbeuf: ibid., pp. 337–63; 'Procès-verbal . . .
des États . . . 1775' (*A, 1, e*). The offence to Petriconi features among the bishop's
complaints of Marbeuf to the King: Rossa (*A, 1, b*), vol. XIII, p. 12; see also 'La
députation des États de 1775 à la Cour . . .' in Letteron, 'Deux députations . . .'
(*A, 1, e*), p. 7. Estimates of Marbeuf and Narbonne: 'Mémoires . . . d'un officier
. . . de Picardie . . .' (*A, 1, d*), pp. 52–3, 75–83; departure of Narbonne: ibid., p.
84, Roux (*A, 1, c*), p. 145. Deputies to court: Letteron, op. cit., pp. ix–xi.

11. 'La députation . . .' (in Letteron, 'Deux députations . . .') gives a detailed account
of the mission with publication *in extenso* of the relevant documents, found by
Letteron in AN, K 1227, several of which have disappeared from this series
and have not to my knowledge been found elsewhere, such as the bishop's
speech, his twenty-nine complaints of Marbeuf, and his sixty-three petitions to
the King: Letteron (*A, 1, e*), pp. 1–10, 31–60. Rossi (*A, 1, b*), vol. XIII, pp. 8–
15, 19–26, gives a summary of the bishop's speech, twenty (only) of his complaints of Marbeuf, and thirty (only) petitions to the King. Letizia's request for
her aunt: see Larrey (*D, 2, b*), vol. I, pp. 95–6.

12. The royal reply granting the amnesty is given in the summary of the proceedings
of the Estates in Rossi (*A, 1, b*), vol. XIII, pp. 64–194. Identical versions, in
French, of Benedetti's conversations with Paoli are included in Letteron, 'Deux
députations . . .' (*A, 1, e*), pp. 12–24, and Rossi, op. cit., pp. 31–46; this text was
found by Letteron in AN, K 1227, from which it is now missing, and inserted
by him in Rossi's chronicle to replace Rossi's Italian version: see Letteron's note
in Rossi, op. cit., p. 31. Benedetti's meeting with Paoli, placed in the context of
Paoli's intellectual–social life: Colonna (*D, 1*), p. 128. *Lettres de cachet*: Rossi, op.
cit., pp. 68–9; Benedetti ennobled: Cesari Rocca, *Armorial . . . (E)*, pp. 9–10.
The text of the Latin inscription on the tablet in honour of Marbeuf, mentioned
by Rossi, op. cit., p. 88, and in 'Procès-verbal . . . des États . . . 1777' (*A, 1, e*)
p. 407, is given in Letteron, op. cit., pp. xxiv–xxv, and Renucci (*A, 1, b*), vol. I,
pp. 175–6; destroyed during the French Revolution, it was replaced by a tablet
bearing an inscription hostile to Marbeuf, in its turn destroyed during the Anglo-
Corsican Kingdom: Letteron, loc. cit.

13. Rossi's estimate of Carlo's qualifications (*A, 1, b*), vol. XIII, pp. 84–5; de Roux's:
Roux (*A, 1, c*), p. 188; see also chapter 6 below. Elections, support of Pozzo di
Borgo: C. A. Pozzo di Borgo, unpublished memoirs, cited in Carrington (*A, 2,
c*). C. Bonaparte elected deputy to court: 'Procès-verbal . . . des États . . . 1777'
(*A, 1, e*), p. 178. Votes 'bought . . .': Roux, op. cit., p. 180. Concession of land at
Verdana, 12 Sept. 1781, with perpetual rent of 30 livres a year: ADCS, 1 C, 195,
see also Carrington, op. cit. Concessions of crown lands, favours, titles: see
Pomponi (*A, 2, d*) and chapter 6, n. 12, below. Pozzo di Borgo and Napoleon:
see Pierre Ordioni, *Pozzo de Borgo . . .* (Paris, 1935).

14. Circular specifying rules for admission of scholars: ADCS, 1 C, 182. Provincial

military colleges: see chapter 7, n. 10, below. The deputation from the Corsican Estates of 1775 requested that six places should be reserved for the sons of poor Corsican nobles, not necessarily officers in the French army, in the two military colleges then existing: Letteron, 'Deux députations . . .' (*A, 1, e*), pp. 48–9. The principle of admittance was accepted: Rossi (*A, 1, b*), vol. XIII, p. 67, but it does not seem that a specific number of places was reserved in the twelve military colleges available from 1776. Records of twenty-one applications for Corsican boys, 1776–90, of which five were apparently accepted as well as Napoleon, can be seen in ADCS, 1 C, 184. The names of eight other successful Corsican candidates appear in Chuquet (*D, 3*), vol. I, p. 21, and Masson (*D, 3*), p. 45, so that one may suppose that fourteen Corsicans won places over a period of as many years. Much of the correspondence concerning Napoleon's application is known only from secondhand sources. Masson, op. cit., p. 43, mentions, without date or reference, Carlo's certificate of indigence endorsed by Annibal Folacci and Pietro Colonna d'Ornano; letters from Montbarey, minister of war, dated 19 July and 28 Oct. 1788, in reply to two letters of solicitation on behalf of Napoleon from Marbeuf, see Montzey (*B, 4, a*), vol. I, p. 246. Napoleon's nomination, 31 Dec. 1778, communicated to Boucheporn by Montbarey in a letter dated 30 Jan. 1779 is preserved in ADCS, 1 C, 184, together with drafts of a reply to Montbarey, Bastia, 16 Feb. 1779, and of a letter, 17 Feb., informing Carlo Bonaparte, then in Paris, of Napoleon's nomination. Great names to recommend candidates, Marbeuf's recommendations: Chuquet, op. cit., p. 81; Balathier de Bragelonne: see chapter 7, n. 6, below.

15. Yves-Alexandre de Marbeuf (1734–99) was a nephew of the comte de Marbeuf, and not his brother as stated in various books of reference, an error rectified by Villat (*A, 2, c*), vol. I, p. 179, referring to C. Monternot, *Yves-Alexandre de Marbeuf* (Lyon, 1911). Appointed bishop of Autun 1767, he obtained the direction of the '*feuille des bénéfices*' and became member of the King's council; Jan. 1788 he was appointed archbishop of Lyons, being succeeded in Autun by Talleyrand. See also chapter 6 below.

16. Napoleon eats garrison bread, draws soldiers on walls, dresses up as soldier: Letizia Bonaparte (*C, 1*). Stays out in storm: Letizia to comtesse d'Orsay, quoted Bartel (*D, 3*), p. 36.

17. Failure of Joseph Bonaparte and Aurele Varese to pursue ecclesiastical careers: see chapter 6, n. 11, below, and for Joseph, chapter 8. Joseph Fesch: see chapter 6 below.

18. Napoleon's gratitude to educators: see chapters 7 and 8 below. Expulsion of Jesuits: S.-B. Casanova, *Histoire de l'Église Corse*, 4 vols. (Ajaccio–Bastia, 1931–8), vol. IV, p. 396; requests for seminaries, colleges, university: see *procès-verbaux* of Corsican Estates (*A, 1, e*), *passim*. Government discourages education: 'Procès-verbal . . . des États . . . 1777' (*A, 1, e*), p. 164. Napoleon and Joseph at school in Ajaccio: Joseph Bonaparte (*C, 1*), pp. 40–41.

19. Greek colonists, Cargese: see M. R. Comnène Stefanopoli and Theodora Stephanopoli de Comnène (both *A, 2, e*). Genealogical pretensions of Stephanopoli: see chapter 4, n. 23, above; Napoleon to Bertrand: Bertrand (*C, 2*), vol. II, p. 136.

20. Marbeuf granted property and marquisate 17 June 1778: ADCS, 1, B, 3; disputes: ADCS, 1 C, 81–4; see also M. R. Comnène Stephanopoli (*A, 2, e*). Marbeuf's house destroyed 1796: ibid., (1919), p. 189; T. Stephanopoli (*A, 2, e*), plan of house, p. 36. Carlo and Letizia visit: see C. Bonaparte, 'Livre de Raison', *BN*, pp. 1, 17, 33, Colchen (*C, 3*), p. 330. Letizia did not hesitate to take or send her children to Cargese: see letters from Marbeuf to Captain Georges Stephanopoli, leader of the Greek colony, 25 Sept. and 6 Oct. 1778, referring to her request for a lodging for her daughter, who can only have been the year-old Elisa, published in T. Stephanopoli de Comnène (*A, 2, e*), pp. 132–3.

21. Marbeuf and Letizia: Colchen (*C, 3*), pp. 329–30; Letizia's shyness: d'Abrantès (*C, 3*), vol. I, *t.* 1, p. 32, *t.* 2, pp. 76–7. De Roux, letters to his father, 16 June, 11, 18, 25 July 1778: Roux (*A, 1, c*), pp. 201, 204, 206. Louis Marbeuf's son: Colchen, loc. cit. Family resemblance: d'Abrantès, op. cit., *t.* i, p. 383. Baptism of Louis: 24 Sept. 1778: ACA, GG, *c.* 8, *r.* 19. The oratory of San Gerolamo, dated 1581, belonged to the oldest religious fraternity of the town, by that name, which at an early date fused with that of Saint Jean Baptiste. It can still be seen in the street known as rue Roi de Rome: Santini (*A, 2, e*). Marbeuf's marriage, birth of son, death: see chapter 4, n. 8, above. Louis fails to obtain scholarship: see chapter 7, n. 35, below.

22. Carlo Bonaparte's claim to the 'Étang des Salines', 27 June 1776, enclosing copy of an act of donation, 1584, authenticated by 3 notaries, in Sept. 1775, and a document dated 1597 in which Geronimo Buonaparte claims compensation for damage done by trespass to his property at the Saline where he had built a tower at great expense, authenticated by Judge Armand, 17 May 1775: ADCS, 1 C, 65. Letters from the ministry of finance, Versailles, geometers in Corsica, the *subdélégué, intendant* and his secretaries and C. Bonaparte: ibid. The map in the Genoese archives is communicated by the Institut d'Études Corse, Université Pascal Paoli, Corte.

23. Memoir from C. Bonaparte to the *côntroleur général*, Calonne, 1 April 1776, in which he relates damage to property at Salines by French troops and proposes to re-drain it: memoir, undated, in which he describes his first unsuccessful attempt to drain the Salines according to plans of Vuillier, with labour of troops and encouragement of Marbeuf: AN, 400 AP, 112. His possession of the Salines officially confirmed, with grant of 6,000 livres: 'Procès-verbal . . . des États . . . 1777' (*A, 1, e*), p. 306. Government scheme for cultivating mulberries: see chapter 6 below.

24. Drafts of memoirs of C. Bonaparte concerning his claim to heritage of Pietro Odone, with genealogy: AN, 400 AP, 112. Correspondence between minister of war and *intendant* in Corsica: AN, K 1229, *l.* 5; see in particular two communications from Ségur to Boucheporn, 13 Aug. 1784, in which he recapitulates Carlo's claim to a long lease strongly encouraged by Marbeuf; see also chapters 6, 7 and 8 below. Carlo Maria Bonaparte's reputation in 'Lettera anonima . . .' Coll. Santini, see chapter 2 above; his activities as merchant: Maestrati (*E*), *CH*, 5–6, pp. 46–7. Procuring of copy of Odone's will: ADCS, 2 B, 85, no. 514.

25. Visit to Cargese: Colchen (*C, 3*), p. 330. Departure for France 12 Dec. 1778: C. Bonaparte, 'Livre de Raison', BN, p. 30; 15 Dec.: Napoleon Bonaparte,

'Époques de ma vie', text written before 1788, published in Masson (D, 3), p. 17. Napoleon's account of journey: Bertrand (C, 3), vol. III, p. 69. Carriage road only from Corte to Bastia: see Villat (A, 2, c), vol. II, p. 267. Bertrand quotes Napoleon as saying that they slept 'the first day' in Bastia in a bad inn; but either he or Napoleon made a slip, for they could not have reached Bastia in a day and would have slept the first night at Bocognano where the inn was no doubt rudimentary (their relations, the Tusoli, lived in the upper, outlying hamlet of Poggiola). Napoleon's memory was unreliable, for he said he left Corsica 'in August or September': Bertrand, loc. cit. M. Arrighi de Casanova (D, 2, b), is unconvincing in her attempt to prove that they left Ajaccio 17 Dec. 1778, and that Ristori was therefore lying.

26. Jean-Baptiste Ristori, unconnected with the man of the same name who served Paoli (see chapter 2 above), b. 1727, was then a captain in the Régiment Provincial Corse; he obtained the Croix de Saint Louis six years later and after an undistinguished career was appointed by Napoleon (who cannot have known of his aspersions on his mother) commander of the fortress of Bastia: see Flori (D, 2, b) and Arrighi de Casanova (D, 2, b) pp. 70–4. His letter of 16 Dec. 1778 in the Coll. Flori has been misdated by several writers in the belief that the date in the text, '16 xbre' means the 16th of the tenth month (i.e. October), whereas the use of 'Xbre' for December (as of '9bre' for November) is prevalent in manuscripts of the period. Bartel publishes the letter in a misleading article, 'Une énigme autour de la naissance de Napoléon', Le Figaro Littéraire, 1 May 1954, with the date 18 Oct. 1778, and refers to it again unconvincingly in La Jeunesse de Napoléon (D, 3), p. 41. The tradition of the blessing of the children by Lazarists is repeated by Stirling (D, 2, b), p. 45, as well as by Bartel (D, 3), p. 51, both of whom suppose it took place in Ajaccio, whereas the only foundation of the order in Corsica was in Bastia: S.-B. Casanova, Histoire de l'Église Corse, 4 vols. (Ajaccio–Bastia, 1931–8), vol IV, p. 396. Pietrasanta's death is mentioned in the notice of the appointment of his successor, Ant. Nicolas-Joubert de l'Hyberderie, to the Conseil Supérieur, 30 Dec. 1773: see Villat (A, 2, c), vol. II, p. 447. His health had been failing since 1771, to judge by a less than tactful letter from Luciano, 27 Nov. 1771, who had sent Joseph Fesch to stay with him, in which he sympathizes with his illness and expresses the hope that Joseph would not thereby be made an orphan a second time: letter 27 Nov. 1771, AN, 400 AP, 115.

27. 'Brilliancy' of Marbeuf's reception: Boswell (A, 1, d), pp. 366–7; Marbeuf's entertaining during sessions of Estates: Roux (A, 1, c), p. 83.

6. EFFORTS AND REWARDS

1. Gourgaud (C, 2), vol. II, p. 345, cf. Lucien Bonaparte (C, 1), p. 11: 'The continental education of my two older brothers, and my own, and the mission of my father in Paris had rendered us entirely French . . .'.

2. Bertrand (C, 2), vol. III, p. 70. Villefranche was in fact then in the comté of Nice.

3. Visit to Florence: Las Cases (C, 2), vol. 1, p. 83; Antommarchi (C, 2), vol. I, p. 252. Biagi ascertained that the grand-duke was absent from Florence between 30 Aug. 1778 and 23 March 1779: Florentine State Archives, 'Registre delle funzioni di corte dal 1765 al 1790' (Cartellino verde, no. 610), see Masson (D, 3), p. 50, n.i.

4. Distinguished Florentine Buonaparte: Corsini (E), p. 14; related to Medici: see chapter 4, n. 24, above; no title: Lumbroso (E), p. 5. Florentine line extinct 1570 or 1620, see chapter 3, n. 20, above.

5. Distinguished Buonaparte of San Miniato: see chapter 3, nn. 15, 16, above. Death of Giovan' Battista Buonaparte: Sforza (E), p. 241, n. 3. Letizia's comments: letter to Lucien Bonaparte, Rome, 1826, quoted Larrey (D, 2, b), vol. II, p. 318. Sforza, loc. cit., however, maintains that the Canon Filippo was Giovan' Battista's brother and therefore an authentic Buonaparte in the male line. Legacy from Moccio Giuseppe: Sforza, op. cit., p. 242; C. Bonaparte, 'Livre de Raison', BN, p. 110.

6. Luciano visits Canon Filippo: Letizia, letter to Lucien Bonaparte, quoted Larrey (D, 2, b), vol. II, p. 318. Filippo Buonaparte to Carlo, 22 April 1778: AN, 400 AP, 114. Joseph Bonaparte no doubt refers to this journey when he states that his father visited the grand-duke after he had been elected deputy for the nobility, but not on his way to Versailles: J. Bonaparte (C, 1), vol. I, p. 26. Letizia refers to a visit by Carlo to Filippo Buonaparte at an unspecified moment before this journey to Versailles but without mention of the grand-duke: letter to Lucien, loc. cit. One may conclude that Carlo did not visit Florence again on his way to Versailles, and that the reception by the grand-duke, with Napoleon present, and the introduction to the Queen, are embellishments added by Joseph and Napoleon. Undoubtedly Carlo was interested in proving his noble Italian ancestry at this period; the Archives Napoléon include his correspondence on this subject, 1776–1780, with Landinello, an erudite of Sarzana: AN, 400 AP, 114.

7. Joseph went to Tuscany early in 1787, to study law in Pisa, re-learn Italian and inquire into family affairs: J. Bonaparte (C, 1), vol. I, pp. 33–4. He took a doctorate at the university of Pisa and returned to Corsica where he was registered as lawyer by the Conseil Supérieur, 17 May 1788: ADCS, 1 B, 16, 269. During this stay in Italy he wrote to Canon Filippo Buonaparte proposing a visit to San Miniato and received a chilling reply, 10 Dec. 1787: 'I regret, in the circumstances, being unable to offer you my house or my person, and having no title to advise, direct or enlighten you, or to serve you in your wishes, aims or intentions . . .', AN, 400 AP, 114. In 1789 Joseph returned to Pisa – a journey ignored by Masson (D, 3), p. 180, but established by Sforza (E), p. 250 – and undertook genealogical researches. He also decided to travel to Florence to obtain from the grand-duke recognition of the family's Tuscan nobility that would give him the right to the Order of Santo Stefano. He would travel there from Pisa in the company of the cardinal and marquise Loménie de Brienne (the latter was the widow of a brother of the cardinal who had died in 1743; according to Masson, op. cit., p. 61, n.i, she remarried, 1748, an Englishman, Mr Grant; perhaps she still used her title or Joseph preferred to use it): letter from Joseph to Joseph Fesch, Luciano and Letizia Bonaparte, Pisa, 4 May 1789: AN, 400 AP, 114. Joseph's request, discovered by Biagi: Archives of Pisa, Order of Santo Stefano, filza 80 'Secondo le suppliche e informazioni dell'anno 1789', nos. 111, 220, published by Masson, op. cit., pp. 181–3, was turned down, 10 Sept. 1789, on the grounds that he was a foreigner, ibid. He nevertheless obtained from the comte de Durfort, French ambassador, permission, 11 June 1789, to enter the 'casinos' (clubs) of the nobility: AN, 400 AP, 114. Joseph probably visited Sarzana, and he corresponded

with Gio. Ant. Vivaldi, notary and archivist of that town, April–Oct. 1789, in a vain attempt to obtain proof of the affiliation of the Bonaparte of Sarzana with the Buonaparte of Tuscany: see A N, 400 A P, 114; Sforza (E), pp. 250–51; Cesari Rocca, *Le Nid* . . . (E), pp. 184–90.

8. 'Musty old records': O'Meara (1822) (C, 2), p. 401. Napoleon's reception by Canon Filippo: Las Cases (C, 2), vol. I, p. 81; Antommarchi (C, 2), vol. I, p. 155. Bonaventura Bonaparte, already beatified: see Cesari Rocca, *Le Nid* . . . (E), pp. 167–9, who maintains that Bonaparte was only his first name and that he belonged to the Ghisleri family and lived in the thirteenth-century. Order of Santo Stefano given to canon: Las Cases, loc. cit.; Cesari Rocca, loc. cit. The Pope raised the question of canonizing Bonaventura when he crowned Napoleon, who discouraged him: Las Cases, loc. cit. Napoleon told Las Cases, op. cit., p. 82, that the canon made him his heir and that he donated the legacy to a charitable foundation; but the legacy is denied by Sforza (E), p. 241. With the death of the canon in 1799 the Buonaparte of San Miniato became extinct: Lumbroso (E), p. 7.

9. Masson (D, 3), p. 50, implies that they passed through Aix-en-Provence to leave Joseph Fesch at the seminary, whereas he was not with them and did not win his scholarship till June 1779; see below. The date of arrival at Autun is given by Napoleon in 'Époques de ma vie', published by Masson, ibid., p. 17.

10. Augustodunum, schools, gladiatorial training: Joan Liversidge, *Everyday Life in the Roman Empire* (London, NY, 1976), pp. 79, 86. History of college: A N, M 81. The Jesuits erected the existing buildings, 1709–12; in 1786 the college was in charge of Oratorian monks at the request of the bishop Marbeuf: see Fontenay, *Autun et ses monuments* (Paris, 1884), p. 469; Gaunet (B, 1), pp. 9–13. 'French Eton': Vincent Cronin, *Napoleon* (London, 1971), p. 27; only thirty boarders: Grandchamp in Beaune (B, 1), p. 158.

11. The bishop of Autun, brother of Marbeuf (see chapter 5, n. 15, above) was in Paris in Jan. 1779: Rossi (A, 1, b), vol. XIII, p. 85. Appointment promised to Joseph: Bertrand (C, 2), vol. III, p. 70; see chapter 8 below. Aurele Varese, first appointed 'sous-diacre': see Pourcenaux (B, 1), p. 5, became 'grand-vicaire' of Autun 'to his own astonishment': letter from abbé Chardon to abbé Forien: Peignot (B, 1), pp. 134–9. His manifesto: 'Rapport fait au Comité du Salut Public (D, 2, d), Paris, July 1793. Carlo Bonaparte 'un superbe homme': Peignot, op. cit., p. 135, Fontenay, op. cit., pp. 4–5.

12. Concessions of crown lands (usually on long or perpetual leases): see Pomponi (A, 2, d); titles: Cesari Rocca, *Armorial* . . . (E), pp. xxix–xxx. Matteo Buttafoco, concession of fishing rights and land, 1776: ADCS, 1 B, 3; title of count, 1781: Cesari Rocca, op. cit., p. xxix, or 1771 or 1776: see Masson (D, 3), p. 215; Giuseppe Maria Casabianca, concession of land, title of viscount, 1776: ADCS, 1 B, 3; Georges Stephanopoli, concession of La Confina, 17 June 1778: ADCS, 1 B, 3; Marbeuf, concession of land at Cargese with marquisate, 17 June 1778: ADCS, 1 B, 3, see chapter 5, n. 20, above. Pietro Paolo Colonna de Cesari Rocca, election to Estates but not as deputy to court: 'Procès-verbal . . . des États . . . de Corse . . . 1773' (A, 1, e), pp. 6, 97; 'Procès-verbal . . . des États . . . de Corse . . . 1781' (A, 1, e), pp. 6, 94–5. Petition for ninety-nine-year lease, 1773, for lease and marquisate, 1785, lease for twenty-five years granted May 1785: ADCS, 1 C, 102. His request for a marquisate was perhaps judged excessive although his family

claimed an ancient title to nobility, confirmed by the Count Palatine, 1720: Cesari Rocca, op. cit., p. 72. In 1784 Louis XVI however conceded the title of count to another member of the family (Roch François Colonna de Cesari Rocca): Cesari Rocca, op. cit., p. 72, and p. xxx. Mulberry plantation: see below and chapter 8. Pietro Paolo aided by de Roux: Roux (*A, 1, c*), p. 186; manoeuvres of de Roux for their own advancement: ibid., pp. 11, 29, 58, 163–209.

13. Joseph Bonaparte (*C, 1*), vol. I, p. 26, is probably mistaken in thinking his father obtained Elisa's scholarship during his first journey to Paris; but he may have prepared the ground. She was apparently accepted 24 Nov. 1782; see below.

14. Santini's election: Rossi (*A, i, b*), vol. XIII, p. 83, 'sunk in debt': memoir from *directeur des finances*, 16 April 1779, granting the deputies' request that 6,000 livres from the royal purse, already promised, should be doubled, 12,000 livres being the sum usually allowed. This extra 6,000 livres was granted in consideration of their good conduct, the bishop receiving 2,500, C. Bonaparte, 2,000, Casabianca, 1,500: S H A T, Dossier Napoléon Ier. De Roux's estimate of Santini: Roux (*A, i, c*), p. 188.

15. See Albertini et Rivollet (*F*), pp. 207–24, and below.

16. Instructions to deputies, their performance: Rossi (*A, 1, b*), vol. XIII, pp. 83–5, 146; Casabianca, bishop Marbeuf: ibid., p. 146; Letizia Bonaparte, letter to her mother March 1779: AN, 400 AP, 115; see below. Napoleon's version of Carlo's role: Montholon (*C, 2*), vol. II, p. 18; Napoleon mistakenly told Montholon that his father was a member of the Assembly of Notables (1787), thus making his story even more incredible. Date and circumstances of Narbonne's departure from Corsica: 'Mémoires . . . par un officier de Picardie . . .' (*A, 1, d*), p. 84; Roux (*A, 1, c*), pp. 136, 145. De Roux's estimate of Carlo Bonaparte: ibid., p. 188; his own tactics with Marbeuf: *passim*.

17. See 'Processo verbale della deputazione degli Stati di Corsica al Corte del 1785', in 'Deux députations . . .' (*A, 1, e*), pp. 94–145. Monteynard appointed governor-general in 1772: ADCS, 1 B, 2. Expenses of attending court: see letter from comte Charles de Villeneuve-Bargemon to his father, 17 Feb. 1788, in 'Lettres d'un officier de l'Ancien Régime. Les honneurs de la cour', *Carnet de la Sabretache* (Paris, Sept.–Oct. 1920, no. 267), pp. 257–80. His presentation cost him *c.* 1,200 livres, Carlo Bonaparte's salary for a year. Interior of Versailles: see Jacques Levron, *La Vie quotidienne à la cour de Versailles . . .* (Paris, 1965); Nancy Mitford (*B, 5*).

18. Dates of Carlo's reception by King and his departure, see n. 21 below. Claim to Odone heritage, memoir to Calonne, recalling steps taken in 1779: AN, 400 AP, 112. Sightseeing of 1785 deputation, gardens, fountains: 'Processo verbale . . .' in 'Deux députations . . .' (*A, 1, e*), pp. 94–105; Mitford (*B, 5*), p. 93, Levron, *A la cour de Versailles . . .* (Paris, 1965), p. 62. Carlo '*un homme de plaisir*': Gourgaud (*C, 2*), vol. I, p. 473; '*enclin à aimer les femmes*': Bertrand (*C, 2*), vol. II, p. 137; addicted to gambling, see chapter 4 above; gambling at Versailles: Mitford, op. cit., pp. 56–7; Levron, op. cit., p. 84; François Bluche, *La vie quotidienne de la noblesse française au XVIIIe siècle* (Paris, 1973), p. 88; Norvins (*B, 2, c*), vol. I, p. 65.

19. Draft of letter to C. Bonaparte from office of *intendant*, Bastia, 16 Feb. 1779: ADCS, 1 C, 184.

20. Inventory of acts submitted to d'Hozier: AN, AE, 1, *c*. 13, no. 1, *pièce* 4. Dubious acts produced 1771: see chapter 4, n. 20 above. The documents concerning

Geronimo Bonaparte submitted 1779 date from the period 1562–97, during which he is recorded as active as man of law: ADCS, Civile Governatore (C 34, 54, 66, 78, 103, 144, 148), and state, ascertainably, that he was the son of Gabriel and a municipal councillor of Ajaccio, 1597, with the title of *magnifico* (which was in fact given to all the *anziani*): ACA, BB, *c.* 7, 'Libro Grosso', p. 9. Gabriel and Francesco Il Mauro: see chapter 2, n. 11, above. Recognition of kinship from Tuscan Buonaparte: see chapter 2, n. 11, above; patent from archbishop of Pisa: see chapter 3, n. 18, above. Pinoteau gives a comparative table of documents submitted 1771 and 1779: *Dossier nobiliaire . . . (E)*, pp. 34–6, and *Vingt-cinq ans . . . (C)* pp. 267–9. Marriage certificate: chapter 2, n. 18, above.

21. D'Hozier's questions, 8 March 1779, with Carlo's replies which include the date, 10 March, of his reception by the King: AN, AE 1, *c.* 13, no. 1, *pièce* 1.

22. Coloured representation of arms: AN, AE 1, *c.* 13, no. 1, *pièce* 2. Carlo's description: inventory of acts submitted to d'Hozier: AN, AE 1, *c.* 13, no. 1, *pièce* 4. See also Cesari Rocca (E), *Armorial . . .*, p. 13. Embellishments in taste of day; arms not adopted till 1759? Resemblance to arms of Tuscan Bonaparte: Pinoteau (E), *Le Dossier nobiliaire . . .*, pp. 6–7, *Vingt-cinq ans. . .*, pp. 238–9. Acquisition of *casa* Bonaparte: see chapter 3, n. 29, above. Arms above door, displaced, damaged, recuperated: Bosc, ACA, pp. 325–6. Arms of Bonaparte of San Miniato: Corsini (E) frontispiece; of Florence: ibid., pp. 12–14; not in Bargello: ibid., p. 14. House in Florence 'a monument': Antommarchi (C, 2), vol. I, p. 155; destroyed: Corsini, op. cit., pp. 10–11.

23. C. Bonaparte, letter to d'Hozier, 15 March 1779: AN, AE 1, *c.* 13, no. 1, *pièce* 3. D'Hozier, certificate of Napoleon's nobility, 8 March 1779: SHAT, Dossier Napoléon Ier; published in Pinoteau, *Vingt-cinq ans . . . (E)*, p. 252. By a decree of 1760 d'Hozier was to be paid 200 livres per certificate by the École Royale Militaire: see Hennet (B, 4, a), p. 36. The fee was evidently subsequently reduced; on 25 Nov. 1777 he received 12,000 livres for 130 certificates for students at the college La Flèche: AN, MM 670; on 19 May 1784 he requested from the École Royale Militaire a yearly salary of 12,000 livres for certificates for all students in the military colleges: AN, MM 676. Presents to heraldists, to d'Hozier: Bluche, *La Vie quotidienne de la noblesse française au XVIIIe siècle* (Paris, 1973), p. 15. Villeneuve-Bargemon spent 90 livres entertaining the heraldist Chérin and his colleague: 'Lettres d'un officier de l'Ancien Régime. Les honneurs de la cour', *Carnet de la Sabretache* (Paris, Sept.–Oct. 1920), p. 277. Prince de Montbarey, minister of war, Versailles, 28 March 1779, to C. Bonaparte, Hôtel Hambourg, Rue Jacob, Paris: SHAT, Dossier Napoléon Ier.

24. Differing specifications of the trousseau for Brienne are given in the school's prospectus of 1776 in *Almanach de la ville . . . de Troyes* (B, 2, a), p. 139, and Prévost (B, 2, a), pp. 191–3. The colleges thereafter provided clothes and such necessities as pens, ink, mathematical and musical instruments as well as pocket money (see chapter 6 below): ibid., p. 192. Cost of Joseph's school clothes: C. Bonaparte, 'Livre de Raison', p. 55, see also p. 43.

25. Joseph and Napoleon at Autun: letter from abbé Chardon to abbé Forien, Peignot (B, 1), pp. 134–8, quoted Fontenay (B, 1), pp. 4–5; Grandchamp, in Beaune (B, 1), p. 160 (his evidence, given at the age of eighty-six, and the authenticity of the text, are open to question). Childhood memories, see chapter

3 above; 'laden with chains': Napoleon Bonaparte, fragment, *c.* 1786, published in Masson et Biagi, *Napoléon inconnu* . . . (*D, 3*), pp. 5–6; 'Brienne is my country': Montholon (*C, 2*), vol. II, p. 19; 'more Champenois than Corsican', Gourgand (*C, 2*), vol. II, p. 170.

26. A note at the end of the inventory of documents submitted by C. Bonaparte to d'Hozier, written by Armand, commissioner for the royal lottery, states that he collected the documents from d'Hozier in accordance with a request from C. Bonaparte written from Brienne, 25 April 1779: AN, AE, 1, *c.* 13, no. 1, *pièce* 4. Fontenay, who discovered the accounts register of the college in the municipal archives of Autun, publishes the note relative to Napoleon (*B, 1*), p. 4. Leave-taking: Joseph Bonaparte (*C, 1*), vol. 1, p. 26. Napoleon put in charge of Champeaux; Chardon in Peignot (*B, 1*), p. 136; Fontenay (*B, 1*), p. 5. Napoleon's recollections: Bertrand (*C, 2*), vol. III, p. 70; Napoleon, 'Époques de ma vie', in Masson (*D, 3*), p. 17. Masson's evidence on Hemey d'Auberive's journey with Napoleon rests on a note by Tourneux, editor of *Merceriana ou notes inédites de Mercier Saint-Léger* (Paris, 1893), pp. 91–2, and Napoleon's subsequent offer to d'Auberive of the bishoprics of Digne and Agen, which he refused: see Masson, op. cit., p. 54. The issue is further complicated by a document quoted by Bourrienne (*B, 2, a*), vol. I, p. 19, supposedly written by Berton, vice-principal of Brienne, stating that Napoleon entered the college 23 April 1779, aged 9 years, 8 months, 5 days. The document is suspect because Napoleon's age was then 9 years, 8 months, 9 days; moreover the documents of Brienne disappeared during the French Revolution and were searched for in vain by the French government after Napoleon's death: see Chuquet (*D, 3*), vol. I, p. 400, and Berton had not yet been appointed to the college: ibid. If however the document is authentic (written by Berton after his appointment), it must refer to the date on which Carlo registered his son as pupil rather than that when Napoleon actually arrived.

27. C. Bonaparte at Estates: 'Procès-verbal . . . des États . . . 1779' (*A, 1, e*), pp. 6, 10–11. Abbatucci: Rossi (*A, i, b*), vol. XIII, pp. 164–9; Renucci (*A, 1, b*), vol. I, pp. 161–6; Albertini et Rivollet (*F*), pp. 171–6; he was rehabilitated after revision of his trial, 1787, and was appointed general, 1796, in the army of Italy: ibid.

28. The royal decision to offer scholarships at the seminary of Aix-en-Provence was announced at the Estates of 1775 and 1777: 'Procès-verbal . . . des États . . . 1775', p. 112; 'Procès-verbal . . . des États . . . 1777', pp. 161–3 (both *A, i, e*). Twenty young Corsicans were to be chosen from the five dioceses by the bishops in concert with the *commissaires du roi*; three candidates were to be proposed in each assembly of the *pievi* equipped with certificates of good conduct from the bishop and parish priest and confirmed by the municipal officers; the assemblies of the provinces would then make a choice from among these candidates. Evidence is lacking as to whether this elaborate procedure had been carried out when, on 22 June 1779, the Estates elected ten out of twenty candidates proposed by the five bishops (four from each diocese), among them Joseph Fesch: 'Procès-verbal . . . des États . . . 1779' (*A, 1, e*), pp. 265–9. Letizia is perhaps referring to an inspector from the municipality in her letter to her mother: AN, 400 AP, 115.

29. Letizia's letter to her mother, March 1779: AN, 400 AP, 115. Gratification: see

n. 14 above. Boswell and Thérèse Le Vasseur: see Pottle (*A, 2, 6*), p. 277. Letter from Ristori to de Pradine, 17 Aug. 1779: Coll. Flori, quoted by Bartel, *Figaro Littéraire*, 1 March 1954, and paraphrased in Bartel, *La jeunesse . . .* (*D, 3*), p. 41, with the erroneous date 27 Sept. See also M. Arrighi de Casanova (*D, 2, b*), pp. 95–100. Letizia's 'fundamental ignorance': Bartel, op. cit., p. 45. Renaud de Greslaie in Villat (*A, 2, c*), vol. II, p. 482–3. Letizia Bonaparte (*C, 1*). Pauline her favourite: Montholon (*C, 2*), vol. II, p. 17. Paternity of Louis, see chapter 4 above.

30. Baptism of Lucien and Maria-Anne (Elisa), 4 Sept. 1779 '*in casa*': ACA, GG, *c.* 8, *r.* 20. C. Bonaparte in his 'Livre de Raison', BN, p. 27 notes that Lucien was baptized 4 Sept. 1776 and 'Marianne' (Elisa) 4 Sept. 1779; though the date for Lucien's baptism seems more probable it must be an error, for the register in ACA makes no mention of it and unmistakably records the double baptism on 4 Sept. 1779. Luciano's reception as archdeacon at the cathedral of Ajaccio, 3 Sept. 1779: AN, 400 AP, 115. Threw out Fesch on his deathbed: Las Cases (*C, 2*), vol. I, p. 85.

31. Birth of Pauline: C. Bonaparte, 'Livre de Raison', BN, p. 27; baptism (as Paola Maria): ACA, GG, *c.* 8, *r.* 21; nurse engaged: C. Bonaparte, op. cit., p. 25.

32. Expenditure on house: C. Bonaparte, 'Livre de Raison', BN, p. 29; the marble chimneypiece arrived with other items from Genoa, Oct. 1780, followed by 435 livres' worth of velvet sent by Giubega from Bastia and paid for 20 Jan. 1781: ibid., pp. 17–18. For the vicissitudes of the *casa* Bonaparte see Barbaud (*A, 2, e*); David (*A, 2, e*); Carrington, 'The Casa Bonaparte in Ajaccio' (*A, 2, e*). Letizia's bedroom: Bertrand (*C, 2*), vol. 1, p. 42. Inventory: ADCS, 4 L, 56, published in Tomi (*D, 2, d*). Card-parties: Colchen (*C, 3*), p. 334.

33. Library: inventory, ADCS, 4 L, 56, published in Tomi (*D, 2,* d); works belonging to C. Bonaparte in Fesch Museum, Ajaccio, from the Legs Fesch. Boswell: see Ettori (*D, 1*); see also chapter 8 below.

34. Inventory of clothes: C. Bonaparte, 'Livre de Raison', BN, p. 112; 'cerise jacket . . .': n. 50 below; payments to wig-dresser: C. Bonaparte, op. cit., p. 1; shoes: ibid., p. 33. Visit to Cargese, 12 Dec. 1780–31 Jan. 1781: ibid., p. 1. Entry of 1 Jan. 1781; ibid., p. 36. The cows were entrusted to a Greek of Cargese on a traditional fifty-fifty profit-sharing arrangement.

35. Expenditure in France: C. Bonaparte, 'Livre de Raison', BN, p. 30. Payments to servants, labourers: ibid., *passim*; loan from 'Zia Angela Maria' accepted and repaid: ibid., p. 1. The term '*zia*', meaning aunt, can also be used to designate a respected older woman. Loan from '*zia*' (aunt) Lillina: see chapter 8 below. Luciano ruined by Carlo's journeys: Antommarchi (*C, 2*), vol. I, p. 276. Yield of Bonaparte's properties: Versini (*D, 2, a*), pp. 94–5. Carlo received 1,000 écus from the Estates, and 4,000 francs royal bounty: 'Livre de Raison', BN, p. 30. Gratifications: 'Procès-verbal . . . des États . . . 1779' (*A, i, e*), pp. 10–11.

36. Carlo took with him from Corsica '100 gold louis': C. Bonaparte, 'Livre de Raison', BN, p. 30 (a louis was worth 24 livres); school fees for Joseph and Napoleon: ibid., p. 43. Bishop's promise to Joseph: Bertrand (*C, 2*), vol. III, p. 70. Joseph's school fees for a year, with extras, 834 livres; without extras, 360 livres: C. Bonaparte, op. cit., p. 55; or 380 livres a year without extras: see Fontenay (*B, i*), p. 7. Carlo states that he paid 123 livres for Napoleon's fees for four months at Autun: C. Bonaparte, op. cit., p. 43; but a receipt found in the

municipal archives of Autun records a payment of 111 livres, 12 sols, 8 deniers for Napoleon's pension for 3 months and 20 days: Fontenay, op. cit., pp. 3–4. Was this sum a rectification obtained by Carlo?

37. Lucien's journey with Fesch: Iung (C, 1), vol. I, pp. 11–16. The Estates of 1781 sat 1–27 June: 'Procès-verbal ... des États ... 1781' (A, i, e); C. Bonaparte was a member: ibid., p. 6. Abbé F (correspondent of Abbé Chardon of Autun) states that he taught 'the good and petulant Lucien during 20–22 months', Peignot (B, 1), p. 138, n. 2, a period that would correspond with the time between his arrival in the autumn of 1782 and June 1784, when it is known that Carlo took him to Brienne: see chapter 8 below. Harold de Fontenay, Autun et ses monuments (Paris, 1884), p. 468, Gaunet (B, 1), p. 12, and Pourcenoux (B, 1), p. 6, agree that Lucien reached Autun Nov. 1782. Lucien's statement that he spent a year at Autun is an obvious untruth: Iung, op. cit., p. 16. Bishop Marbeuf, Talleyrand, see chapter 5, n. 15, above. Fesch's biographers believe that he left Corsica for Aix in 1781: Colombani (D, 2, c), p. 8; Lyonnet (D, 2, c), vol. I, pp. 22–4, 'between the ages of 17 and 18' (he was born 3 Jan. 1763: AN, 400 AP, 113); a certificate from the superior of the seminar dated 19 May 1785 states that he had spent five years there, which suggests that he entered in 1780: ibid.

38. Legacy from Giuseppe Moccio: C. Bonaparte, 'Livre de Raison', BN, pp. 110–11; Letizia Bonaparte, letter to Lucien, Rome, 1826, see n. 3 above.

39. Copy of letter from Gautier, secretary to intendant, to secretary of Marbeuf, 11 Sept. 1779: AN, 400 AP, 112. The documents in this series reveal the progress of the Bonaparte's claim to the Odone heritage from Carlo's first presentation of his case 1779 to the Bonaparte's entry into possession of the properties May 1786. A genealogical tree showing their relationship to Paolo Francesco Odone is included. See in particular: drafts of memoirs from C. Bonaparte to Souiris 23 Nov. 1784 stating that he first presented his claim to Montbarey 1779; that Montbarey had given him hope of satisfaction, undated; that his object being to avoid a lawsuit he requests only a long lease on the Milelli and La Badina, undated. See also correspondence between Ségur, minister of war and intendant, 1784–86: AN, K 1229, l. v. For sequel see chapter 8 below.

40. The canning factory existed 1968–73: see Janine Renucci, Corse traditionnelle et Corse nouvelle (Lyon, 1974), p. 361. Government scheme for silk industry, mulberry plantations, Giubega's proposal, proposal of Arena, near Bastia: 'Procès-verbal ... des États ... 1779' (A, i, e), pp. 166–8.

41. Carlo Bonaparte's draining operations resumed 30 Aug. 1779: memoir from C. Bonaparte to Calonne, undated: AN, 400 AP, 112. Payments of subsidy recommended by Bedigis: ADCS, 1 C, 65; C. Bonaparte's estimate of cost: ibid.

42. Requests to Estates from C. Bonaparte and Colonna: 'Procès-verbal ... des États ... 1781' (A, i, e), pp. 218–19; memoir from C. Bonaparte, ibid., pp. 246– 7. Aid from Marbeuf: ibid., and memoir to Calonne, see n. 41 above. Tuscan gardener, Bacini, engaged 19 Sept. 1780: C. Bonaparte, 'Livre de Raison', BN, p. 2. Giubega's request presented and partly satisfied: 'Procès-verbal ... des États ... 1781', op. cit., pp. 217, 244–5. Acceptance of requests of Bonaparte and Cesari Rocca: ibid., pp. 247, 248. C. Bonaparte elected to Nobles Douze: ibid., p. 97.

43. Departure to Cargese, 15 Aug. 1781, wig-dresser paid, clothes sent to Ajaccio, table: C. Bonaparte, 'Livre de Raison', BN, p. 1.

44. Subsidy received 11 Nov. 1781: ADCS, I C, 65. Tuscan gardener, Geronimo Bambini of Santa-Maria di Caffagio, dependency of Prato: C. Bonaparte, 'Livre de Raison', BN, p. 54.

45. Payment to wig-dresser, visit to Cargese May 1782: C. Bonaparte, 'Livre de Raison', BN, p. 3.

46. Inspection of Salines, 15 May 1782: ADCS, I C, 26. Contract (draft), ibid., and AN, 400 AP, 112, and AN, K 1229, *l.* v, no. 1; published in Versini (*D, 2, a*), pp. 196–8.

47. According to Pommereul (*A, i, d*), vol. I, p. 65, mulberry trees were hitherto unknown in Corsica. Nevertheless John Stewart, British agent sent to Corsica in 1768 by Lord Shelburne, reported that silk of good quality could be produced there: McErlean (*A, 2, b*), p. 181. Attempt to promote silk industry under Restoration: Antoine Albitreccia, *La Corse, son évolution au XIXe siècle et au début du XXe siècle* (Paris, 1942), p. 77.

48. Departure for Bourbonne-les-Bains: C. Bonaparte, 'Livre de Raison', BN, p. 30. Birth of Maria Annunziata: ACA, GG, *c.* 8, *r.* 23. Value of waters: Dr Baudry, *Traité des eaux minérales de Bourbonne-les-Bains* (Dijon, 1736), quoted Versini (*D, 2, a*), p. 87. Health-giving waters in Corsica: see chapter 6 below Duc de Fitz-James: Bluche, *La Vie quotidienne de la noblesse française au XVIIIe siècle* (Paris, 1973), p. 18; Diderot: quoted Versini, loc. cit.; return to Ajaccio: C. Bonaparte, op. cit., p. 113.

49. Debts for journey 1784: see chapter 8 below. Grandchamp: Beaune (*B, i*), p. 161. Fees for Lucien outstanding on Carlo's death: see chapter 8 below.

50. Letizia at Brienne: Montholon (*C, 2*), vol. II, p. 18, Las Cases (*C, 2*), vol. I, p. 87; C. Bonaparte at Brienne: Bertrand (*C, 2*), vol. II, p. 136; affability: Rossi (*A, i, b*), vol. XIII, p. 146.

51. Chaptal: (*C, 3*), pp. 175–6. Conclusive evidence for this journey became available only with the acquisition of C. Bonaparte's 'Livre de Raison' by the Bibliothèque Nationale in 1965; in consequence it is overlooked by earlier historians of Napoleon's youth, including Chuquet (*D, 3*), and doubted by Masson (*D, 3*), who distrusts Chaptal, perhaps not without reason, for his memoirs contain certain inaccuracies and he may have distorted Letizia's confidences, see chapter 7 below.

52. Letizia admired in Paris: Las Cases (*C, 2*), vol. I, p. 87.

53. Entrance certificate for Marie-Anna Bonaparte, 24 Nov. 1782: Archives des Yvelines, I F, 95; published in Pinoteau, *Vingt-cinq ans . . .* (*E*), pp. 253–4. Corsican girls were admitted by royal decree 13 April 1777: ADCS, A 18, Code Corse, vol. IV, pp. 149–53. Qualifications: Lavallée (*B, 5*), pp. 319–22. Simplification of proofs of nobility: Code Corse, loc. cit.; military qualifications waived: ADCS, I C, 550. The Estates of 1775 had requested 'at least three places' for girls at Saint Cyr: 'Deux députations . . .' (*A, i, e*), p. 49, but evidently more were granted: see Lavallée, op. cit., pp. 351–8, who names six Corsican girls in 1792, and chapter 8 below.

54. Foundation, curriculum, regulations, père La Chaise, dowry: Lavallée (*B, 5*), pp. 40–46, 139–45, Mitford (*B, 5*), pp. 149–54, 'civilized piety', ibid., p. 150. Theatricals, reforms: Lavallée, op. cit., pp. 72–102, Mitford, op. cit., pp. 154–73. Horace Walpole (*B, 5*), vol. V, no. 1194, 17 Sept. 1769, pp. 189–93.

55. Letizia sees Marie-Antoinette: see Martineau (*D, 2, b*), p. 31. 'Presented' nobles: Bluche, *La Vie quotidienne de la noblesse française au XVIIIe siècle* (Paris, 1973), p. 329, Levron, *La Vie quotidienne à la cour de Versailles* . . . (Paris, 1965), p. 145; possibilities of entering Versailles: Levron, op. cit., pp. 29, 94–9, 147, Mitford (*B, 5*), p. 88. Joseph Barry, *Passion and Politics. A Biography of Versailles* (New York, 1972); see French edn, *Versailles. Passions et politiques* (Paris, 1987), pp. 197, 209, 280.

7. FORMATION OF A HERO

1. Letizia: Chaptal (*C, 3*), pp. 175–6. Montholon (*C, 2*), vol. II, p. 17. Bourrienne (*B, 2, a*), vol. I, p. 4 (English edn, 1885); vol. I, p. 4 (French edn, 1829). Quotations are hereinafter given from the English edition followed by references to their equivalents in the French edition in brackets.

2. The memoirs of C.H. (*B, 2, a*), published in London in 1797 and in French translation the same year, ring true. Attributed to Cumming of Craigmillar, whose father served Prince Xavier of Saxony: Cronin, *Napoleon* (London, 1971), p. 453. Bourrienne became Napoleon's secretary and councillor of state before being disgraced for treasonable corruption; his untrustworthy memoirs were ghosted by Maxime de Villemarest: Cronin, op. cit., p. 442; N.-J.-C.-P. Bonaparte, *Napoléon et ses détracteurs* . . . (Paris, 1887), pp. 107–10; *Bourrienne et ses erreurs* . . . (*B, 2, a*). His souvenirs of Brienne contain various obvious inaccuracies, and borrow from C. H. and *Traits caractéristiques* . . ., yet they betray a close observation of Napoleon. Their friendship is confirmed by the anonymous, plausible *Traits caractéristiques* . . . (*B, 2, a*), p. 18, and by the fourth schoolboy witness, de Castres (*B, 2, a*), but the authenticity of the latter text, discovered on a bookstall in 1905, is open to question.

3. 'piercing . . . glance': Bourrienne (*B, 2, a*), vol. I, p. 6 (p. 32). Boswell (*A, i, d*), p. 291.

4. Sallow skin: Bourrienne (*B, 2, a*), vol. I, p. 6 (p. 32); olive oil: Castres (*B, 2, a*), p. 9. Name ridiculed at Autun: Grandchamp, in Beaune (*B, 1*), p. 161; '*paille au nez*': Las Cases (*C, 2*), vol. I, p. 92; ice: Bertrand (*C, 2*), vol. III, p. 70.

5. There were thirty boarders at Autun: Beaune (*B, 1*), p. 158, 150 at Brienne in 1779; C.H. (*B, 2, a*), p. 14. Norwood Young (*B, 4, b*), p. 104. Reactions to teasing, to attacks: Bourrienne (*B, 2, a*), vol. I, p. 7 (p. 33); C.H., loc. cit.; *Traits caractéristiques* . . . (*B, 2, a*), p. 23.

6. Vicomte Élie (or Éloi)-Charles Balathier de Bragelonne was son of the *lieutenant du roi* at Bastia who had taken a Corsican wife. Born 1771, he had as godparents Marbeuf and Mme Varese. He entered Brienne 1782; in the *exercices publics* . . . of 1783 he was questioned in German, the New Testament and modern geography, in those of 1785 he took part in performances of dancing, music and singing and the exercise of arms. Expelled in 1786, he emigrated with the Revolution, served in the army of prince de Condé, and returned to Corsica 1794 to engage in the forces of the Anglo-Corsican kingdom; subsequently he served in the army of the Cisalpine Republic and became general in 1811. Chuquet (*D, 3*), vol. I, pp. 116, 387; *Traits caractéristiques* . . . (*B, 2, a*), pp. 25–6 (reception by Napoleon); *Exercices publics* . . . 1783, 1785 (*B, 2, a*); Albertini et Rivollet (*F*), pp. 188–92.

7. Portrait of Choiseul: Antommarchi (*C*, *2*), vol. I, p. 252. Napoleon blames father: Bourrienne (*B*, *2*, *a*), vol. I, p. 7 (p. 32); refuted by J. Bonaparte in *Bourrienne et ses erreurs* . . . (*B*, *2*, *a*), p. 238. Bourrienne, loc. cit., relates that the masters criticized Paoli, by pre-arrangement, when dining at the principal's table to which Napoleon had been invited according to a custom by which the pupils were given this privilege in turn. Chuquet (*D*, *3*), vol. I, p. 384, denies that the principal had a separate table; but a small panelled room in the remaining building of the school is shown as the professors' refectory, and it may well have been there that Napoleon was invited and made his pronouncement.

8. Parker (*B*, *2*, *a*), p. 12 Paoli 'his god': *Traits caractéristiques* . . . (*B*, *2*, *a*), p. 24; dream of succeeding him: ibid., p. 30. Caricature reproduced by Chuquet (*D*, *3*), vol. I, p. 261, who believes it to be the work of a student at the École Militaire in Paris.

9. Memories of Corsica, everything better, scent: Las Cases (*C*, *2*), vol. I, pp. 647–8, Montholon (*C*, *2*), vol. I, p. 297, Antommarchi (*C*, *2*), vol. I, p. 131–2, 'strokes of fire': ibid., p. 154. Indulgent father, scolding mother: ibid., p. 353, Letizia Bonaparte (*C*, *1*); Camilla Ilari: Antommarchi, op. cit., p. 348; Caterina, ibid., p. 251.

10. École Royale Militaire, colleges, regulations 1776: Montzey (*B*, *4*, *a*), vol. I, pp. 219–21, Hennet (*B*, *4*, *a*), pp. 73–84; two colleges were subsequently added to the original ten, including La Flèche, founded 1603, which had a high academic standard and continued to prepare some students for the magistrature and Church: Hennet, op. cit., p. 137. Egality: Hennet, ibid., p. 83, Babeau (*F*), vol. II, p. 67. Foreigners accepted: C. H. (*B*, *2*, *a*), p. 12.

11. Punishments: Hennet (*B*, *4*, *a*), p. 91, Vaublanc (*B*, *3*), vol. I, pp. 31–2. Napoleon punished: Las Cases (*C*, *2*), vol. I, p. 92, Petit (*B*, *2*, *a*), p. 23. Patrault, tall, red-faced: Las Cases, loc. cit., p. 95; 'rather ordinary': Bourrienne (*B*, *2*, *a*), vol. I, p. 34 (edn 1829).

12. Saint-Germain (*B*, *4*, *a*), p. 153; curriculum: Hennet (*B*, *4*, *a*), pp. 89–90. Inspection of colleges, 1787: Montzey (*B*, *4*, *a*), vol. I, pp. 243–5; inspection of Brienne, 1785: Prévost (*B*, *2*, *a*), p. 205. Funds lacking for good teachers: Bourrienne (*B*, *2*, *a*), vol. I, p. 8 (p. 35); teachers appointed by Loménie de Brienne: *Almanach* . . . *de Troyes*, 1776 (*B*, *2*, *a*), p. 114. Locked in cells: Prévost, op. cit., p. 192. Homosexuality: Chuquet (*D*, *3*), vol. I, p. 113, and 'Souvenirs d'un cadet de Brienne', anonymous text, 1787, published in Chuquet, op. cit., pp. 405–12. Religious observance perfunctory: Chuquet, op. cit., p. 114.

13. Professors, classes: Prévost (*B*, *2*, *a*), p. 197, Chuquet (*D*, *3*), vol. I, pp. 108–13, 381–2. Patrault: see n. 36 below. Napoleon consulted Dupuy in 1789 on his 'Lettres sur la Corse . . .' and as First Consul appointed him librarian at Malmaison; see his letters to Napoleon, 1789, with detailed criticism of his text: Masson (*D*, *3*), pp. 204–10; appointment: ibid., pp. 62–3. L. Berton 'too hard', rude songs: Chaptal (*B*, *2*, *b*), pp. 181–2. Pichegru, pupil of Patrault, and nephew of nurse in the infirmary, gave Napoleon help in mathematics while employed in the college before entering the army, 1780: O'Meara (*C*, *2*), vol. I, p. 240, Masson, op. cit., pp. 63–4. General commanding the army of the Rhine, he subsequently deserted to the prince de Condé and in 1803 was implicated in Cadoudal's attempt on the life of Napoleon.

14. No home holidays, regulations of 1776: Hennet (*B*, *4*, *a*), p. 87; yearly break:

Almanach . . . de Troyes, 1776 (*B, 2, a*), p. 140. Walks encouraged: Hennet, op. cit., p. 89. Founded 1627, the monastery became a secondary school in 1744; exensive buildings added in 1776, when it became a military college, were destroyed during the Revolution, the college being suppressed 1793: Prévost (*B, 2, a*), pp. 190, 239, 241–2.

15. Cells, timetable, diet: Prévost (*B, 2, a*), pp. 196–7; these details, derived from the departmental archives of Aube, are also displayed in the Musée Napoléon Ier in the remains of the monastic building at Brienne. Also exhibited there is the menu for Epiphany (*'les Rois'*) on the flyleaf of Napoleon's atlas: '. . . *on a eu du poulet du gateau et des choux fleurs de la salade aux beteraves, au desert des echaudés de gimbes et des marons à l'ecole royal militaire le 6 janvier'*. The spelling is uncorrected, the abominable handwriting is unmistakably Napoleon's.

16. Parker (*B, 2, a*), p. 13; Napoleon's severe morality at Brienne, at the École Militaire in Paris: *Traits caractéristiques . . .* (*B, 2, a*), pp. 23, 33; 'pedagogue': C.H. (*B, 2, a*), p. 14. Aloofness to sex after leaving school: Bertrand (*C, 2*), vol. II, p. 67. His first sexual experience seems to have been with a prostitute he picked up in the arcades of the Palais Royal when on leave in Paris from his regiment, 1787, to judge by his own account, 'Rencontre au Palais Royal', a fragment of youthful writing: published in Masson et Biagi, *Napoléon inconnu . . .* (*D, 3*), pp. 21–3.

17. Prize giving is denied by Chuquet and Masson; but the programme of the *Exercices publics . . .*, 9–14 Sept. 1780 (*B, 2, a*), p. 51 removes any doubt on the subject: 'At the end of the last sessions, the prizes will be distributed to the pupils who have been most successful in their classes and different exercises.' See also Bourgeois (*B, 2, c*), prize giving followed by theatrical performance: p. 301. Napoleon in *Exercices publics . . .* 1780 (*B, 2, a*), pp. 20, 36, 46; *Exercices publics . . .* 1782 (*B, 2, a*), pp. 16, 39, 51; on the title-page is written in ink: *'histoire, géometrie, géographie, Buonaparte'*; *Exercices publics . . .* 1783 (*B, 2, a*), p. 71; under 'De Buonaparte' is added in ink *'empereur des français'*. A manuscript note on the cover mentions that he also took part in *'les exercices d'escrime en fait d'armes et tirer au mur et faire assaut'* but this is not confirmed by the printed text where he is noted only for mathematics. Bourrienne asserts that he and Napoleon were awarded the prize for mathematics in 1783 by the duc d'Orléans and Mme de Montesson: (*B, 2, a*), vol. I, p. 8 (p. 37); but in fact their visit to Brienne and awarding of prizes took place in 1781, for which year the printed programme is lacking, though it was seen by Bourgeois: op. cit., p. 300. The prizes were awarded in 1783, possibly to Bourrienne and Napoleon, by Mgr Rouille d'Orfeauil: *Exercices . . .* 1783, loc. cit. The story that Napoleon insulted d'Orfeuil because he opposed his entry to the École Royal Militaire in Paris and that L. Berton went to Paris to exculpate Napoleon before the King can be dismissed as legend: see Masson (*D, 3*), p. 79, Chuquet (*D, 3*), vol. I, p. 126. I have found no evidence on the circumstances in which Napoleon was awarded, on 26 May 1783, the *Histoire de Scipion l'Africain*, exhibited in the Musée Napoléon Ier at Brienne. The *exercices publics* of 1783 took place 15–19 Sept.: *ubi supra*.

18. Geometry 'the sublime abstract . . .': Napoleon to Narbonne in Villemain (*B, 4, b*), vol. I, p. 146. Napoleon to Bertrand: Bertrand (*C, 2*), vol. II, p. 216. The three professors of mathematics received salaries of 1,600 livres each compared

with 1,200 livres for the professors of history, geography and Latin: Prévost (*B,* *2, a*), p. 197. C. Bonaparte's 1,000 volumes: see chapter 6, n. 3, above. Napoleon's aptitude for mathematics in Corsica, nuns, plank shelter, watermill: Letizia Bonaparte (*C, 1*).

19. Patrault 'a great mathematician': Gourgaud (*C, 2*), vol. I, p. 362. Letizia on Patrault: see chapter 6, n. 51, above. Castres (*B, 2, a*), p. 14; Bourrienne (*B, 2, a*), vol. I, p. 8 (p. 35). Napoleon and Laplace: see Kline (*B, 4, b*), p. 243.

20. Letizia whipped Napoleon to church: see chapter 5, n. 7, above, lost faith at school: see n. 23 below. Ideas on God and religion: Las Cases (*C, 2*), vol. I, p. 689; see also Adrien Dansette, *Napoléon, pensées politiques et sociales* . . . (Paris, 1969), pp. 137–72, 240.

21. Teaching not limited to Latin: *Almanach* . . . *de Troyes* (*B, 2, a*), p. 139; value of history: *Exercices publics* . . . 1783 (*B, 2, a*), p. 8; programme of ancient history: ibid., p. 21. Plutarch: Hennet (*B, 4, a*), p. 91. Greek not taught: Prévost (*B, 2, a*), p. 199; Latin authors: *Exercices publics* . . . 1780, 1782; mythology: *Exercices publics* . . . 1783 (*B, 2, a*); Napoleon fascinated by classical history: Villemain (*B, 4, b*), vol. I, pp. 145–58; averse to Latin: Bourrienne (*B, 2, a*), vol. I, p. 6 (p. 31), C.H. (*B, 2, a*), p. 15; library: ibid., pp. 17–18; reading concealed: ibid., p. 20. Acting on table tops: Castres (*B, 2, a*), p. 8; they may also have acted Corneille, one of Napoleon's favourite authors, who was studied at Brienne: Prévost (*B, 2, a*), p. 200; see Villemain, op. cit., p. 157; Healey (*B, 4, b*), pp. 17–18, 93–4.

22. Although Bossuet was also studied at Brienne – Prévost (*B, 2, a*), p. 200 – it seems that Napoleon did not discover his *Discours sur l'histoire universelle,* for him an inspiration, until later, when stationed at Valence: Villemain (*B, 4, b*), vol. I, pp. 157–8. Napoleon readily compared his conquests with those of Caesar and Alexander, his other preferred hero: see Bouineau (*B, 4, b*). He identified himself with Caesar when, leaving for Elba, he asked Caulaincourt not to take steps for Marie-Louise to join him: 'Caesar can be satisfied to be a citizen! It might distress his young wife to be no more than Caesar's wife': Bouineau, op. cit., p. 351, n. 254, quoting Caulaincourt, *Mémoires,* 3 vols. (Paris, 1933), vol. III, p. 376. Caesar 'competing with himself': Plutarch, *Fall of the Roman Republic,* trans. R. Warner (London, 1958), p. 265. Comet: see Antommarchi (*C, 2*), vol. II, p. 74.

23. Vaublanc (*B, 3*), vol. I, p. 30. Antiquity, French Revolution: Parker, Jehasse, Bouineau (all *B, 4, b*); 'born republican': *Traits caractéristiques* . . . (*B, 2, a*), p. 24. Faith shaken: Bertrand (*C, 2*), vol. I, p. 286, Las Cases (*C, 2*), vol. II, p. 195. First communion: Prévost (*B, 2, a*), p. 199; kindness to priest, to whom he gave a pension of 1,000 livres: Chuquet (*D, 3*), vol. I, p. 152; prayer book: AN, 400 AP, 1.

24. 'Sombre and morose': Las Cases (*C, 2*), vol. I, p. 92; quarrels, austerity: *Traits caractéristiques* . . . (*B, 2, a*), p. 23; feared: Iung (*C, 1*), vol. I, p. 25. Enjoyed supremacy: Antommarchi (*C, 2*), vol. I, p. 252; mattresses: Bertrand (*C, 2*), vol. I, p. 286, who states that Napoleon later appointed the baited monk director of the lycée 'of the Rhine' (Bas-Rhin? Alsace?). The monk may well have been the principal, L. Berton, whom Napoleon appointed director of a lycée at Reims: Chaptal (*B, 2, b*), p. 182, Bertrand having mistaken Reims for Rhin.

25. Bourrienne's account of the snow battle (*B, 2, a*), vol. I, p. 4 (pp. 25–6), is apparently borrowed from C.H. (*B, 2, a*), pp. 23–4, and *Traits caractéristiques* . . . (*B, 2, a*), pp. 28–9; see also Assier (*B, 2, a*), p. 15.

26. Garden: C.H. (*B, 2, a*), p. 19. Studied algebra: *Traits caractéristiques* . . . (*B, 2, a*), p. 27. Reading: Petit (*B, 2, a*); if he is to be trusted Napoleon must have had access to the translation of Ossian by Le Tourneur (Paris, 1777); Fête of Saint Louis: *Traits caractéristiques* . . ., op. cit., p. 20, C.H., op. cit., pp. 26–9.

27. Read Tasso: Gourgaud (*C, 2*), vol. I, p. 533. Bathing in river: Assier (*B, 2, a*), p. 13; Bourrienne, in account of revisiting Brienne during campaign of 1814 (*B, 2, a*), 1829 edn, vol. IX, pp. 358–9. River bathing, though evidently hazardous, was advocated in the original regulations for the colleges: Montzey (*B, 4, a*), vol. I, p. 219, Hennet (*B, 4, a*), p. 88, Montholon (*C, 2*), vol. II, p. 18.

28. Napoleon's supposed letter to father, 5 April 1781: see fanciful publication by comte d'Og – Charles Dangeais, comte d'Oguereau – who claims to have been with Napoleon at Brienne: (*B, 2, a*), pp. 22–3; also quoted by Coston (*D, 3*), vol. I, pp. 35–6, Iung (*D, 3*), vol. I, p. 84. Several of Letizia's biographers (but not Larrey) quote Letizia's supposed reply, with varying dates: see Stirling (*D, 2, b*), p. 48, Martineau (*D, 2, b*), p. 32. Napoleon's need for pocket money is denied by Prévost (*B, 2, a*), p. 192, who states that the pupils received 20–40 sous a month according to age; Castres (*B, 2, a*), p. 11, specifies 8–10 sous a week; fines, ibid. C.H. (*B, 2, a*), states, certainly in error, that Napoleon received money from Marbeuf, which he spent on his garden.

29. Insults to Napoleon's parents: d'Og (*B, 2, a*), p. 19, Petit (*B, 2, a*); Letizia 'joyful, Mme Marbeuf': ibid., 32–3. Duel, Napoleon's supposed letter to Marbeuf, his intervention: d'Og, op. cit., pp. 30–38; also quoted by Coston (*D, 3*), vol. I, p. 52, Iung (*D, 3*), vol. I, p. 92. Other apocryphal anecdotes are exposed in *Traits caractéristiques* . . . (*B, 2, a*), pp. viii–xiii, Castres (*B, 2, a*), p. 10; see also Chuquet (*D, 3*), vol. I, pp. 114–15, Masson (*D, 3*), pp. 57–8, n. 3.

30. Bartel (*D, 3*), pp. 43–4, propagates the story of Napoleon's holidays in Marbeuf's castle, deriving from local tradition and denied by E. Martin: see E. P., 'Napoléon, la Bretagne et Marbeuf', *Le Fureteur Breton, mai-juin-juillet* and *août-septembre-octobre*, 1921.

31. Letizia to Chaptal: Chaptal (*B, 2, b*), p. 176. Bourgeois, historian of the comtes de Brienne (*B, 2, c*), denies that Napoleon received favours from the Loménie at school, or was known to the count (minister of war 24 Sept. 1787–28 Sept. 1788), pp. 271–2.

32. Ascension of Loménie: Bourgeois (*B, 2, c*), pp. 90–104; plain countess, dowry: Norvins (*B, 2, c*), vol. I, p. 137; family, rank, revenues: Norvins, ibid., pp. 99–102.

33. Archbishop's dream; the remodelling of the landscape and laying out of the gardens took thirty-two years; the house was erected 1770–77, but a pair of gatehouses were not finished until 1788: Bourgeois (*B, 2, c*), pp. 141–7, Babeau (*B, 2, c*), pp. 7–8. Norvins (*B, 2, c*), vol. I, p. 98, however, relates that the 'unlimited generosity' of the Loménie changed the poverty-stricken appearance of the village.

34. 'Thousand and One Nights', 'marvels of existence', hunting, entertainments scientific experiments: Norvins (*B, 2, c*), vol. I, pp. 100–108; hunting, theatre,: Bourgeois (*B, 2, c*), p. 149; natural history curiosities, laboratory: Babeau (*B, 2, c*), pp. 9–10. Fête for duc d'Orléans, 1781: Bourgeois, op. cit., p. 300, Assier (*B, 2, a*), p. 13; 'miniature Versailles': Bourrienne (*B, 2, a*), vol. I, p. 8 (p. 37),

(Bourrienne misdates the duke's visit to 1783). Chuquet (*D, 3*), vol. I, p. 147, states, without giving his source, that Napoleon visited the park with his schoolfellows on the feast day of Saint Louis, and that the guardian noted his unusual name.

35. No indication of personal intimacy or reminder of Napoleon's schooldays appear in the appeals made by Letizia and Napoleon to the comte de Brienne when he held office; see letter from Letizia, 18 June 1788, in which, with heartless determination, she solicits a scholarship in a military college for Louis, although he has passed the prescribed age, encouraged by a 'ray of hope' following the death, two days before, of Jean-Grégoire Benielli (who must have been a relative), who had been granted a scholarship which she esteemed might now be filled by Louis: SHAT, Dossier Napoléon Ier. In a memoir (undated) to the count on the subject of the Salines she appeals to him as a protector not of her family but of justice: AN, K 1229, *l*. v, no. 20. Only a vague reference to the count's goodwill, not suggesting personal acquaintance, appears in Napoleon's letter soliciting a scholarship for Lucien at the seminar at Aix: quoted Iung (*C, 1*), pp. 28–9. Joseph alone attempted, with small success, to make use of a possible family connection with the Loménie: see chapter 6, n. 7, above.

36. Archbishop's career, arrest (9 Nov. 1793), death (19 Feb. 1794): Bourgeois (*B, 2, c*), pp. 119–31; 'enlightened liberal': La Fayette in letter to George Washington, quoted Bernard Fäy, *Louis XVI ou la fin d'un monde* (Paris, 1955); see Joseph Barry, *Passion and Politics: a Biography of Versailles* (New York, 1972), p. 310; refused archbishopric: Gaston duc de Levis, *Souvenirs et Portraits, 1780–1789* (Paris, 1813), see Barry, op. cit., p. 309; poison conveyed by Patrault who had entered the archbishop's service after the suppression of the college of Brienne, 1793: Las Cases (*C, 2*), vol. I, p. 94; having revolutionary sympathies he tried unsuccessfully to save the archbishop by a personal appeal to Danton: ibid. In 1796 Napoleon gave him employment in the army of Italy; he made a fortune, squandered it, and ended his life on a pension from Napoleon: see Masson (*D, 3*), p. 62. Adoption of Loménie nephews: Norvins (*B, 2, c*), vol. I, pp. 119–20; execution with count and niece, 10 May 1794: Bourgeois, (*B, 2, c*), pp. 175–6, Masson, op. cit., p. 61, n. 1; a brother of Norvins married a survivor, the widow of Charles, one of the nephews: Masson, ibid., Norvins, op. cit., vol. III, p. 118.

37. Countess and Napoleon: Norvins (*B, 2, c*), vol. III, p. 117; she had recovered her property after the Terror without Napoleon's aid. Napoleon's favours to surviving Loménie: Masson (*D, 3*), p. 81.

38. Visit to Brienne, 3–4 April 1805; peasants, countess: Bertrand (*C, 2*), vol. II, p. 138; see also Gourgand (*C, 2*), vol. I, p. 533, Norvins (*B, 2, c*), vol. III, pp. 117–20; Wairy (*C, 3*), p. 220. Countess refuses to sell; Napoleon abandons project for reviving college, gift to mayor: Norvins, loc. cit. He bequeathed 200,000 francs to be distributed to the inhabitants in compensation for their sufferings in the war: Jean-Pierre Babelon, Susanne d'Huart, *Napoleon's Last Will and Testament* (New York, 1977), p. 88. Furnishing of room reserved for d'Orléans: Norvins, op. cit., vol. I, p. 104. 'May it bring you happiness': Assier (*B, 2, a*), p. 13. Chuquet (*D, 3*), vol. I, p. 125, attributes the words to Mme de Montesson. The Château de Brienne is now a departmental psychiatric hospital. The Paris residence of the Loménie, the Hôtel de Brienne, rue Saint Dominique, was bought by Lucien Bonaparte, who sold it to Letizia; it is now the Ministry of War.

8. END AND BEGINNING: FATHER AND SON

1. Inspection of military colleges (the chief inspector was the governor of the École Royale Militaire, who remained in Paris, then the marquis de Timbrune-Valence): Chuquet (*D, 3*), vol. I, pp. 90–93, Masson (*D, 3*), pp. 102–3. Fee for École Militaire, 2,000 livres per year: Montzey (*B, 4, a*), vol. I, p. 282; 2,000 livres per term: Hennet (*B, 4, a*) p. 95. Cadet corps, entry to army, '*volontaires*', special services: Montzey, op. cit., vol. I, pp. 233–6, Hennet, op. cit., pp. 95–101; Babeau (*F*), vol. II, pp. 6–18, 45–50, 88–99, 103–4.

2. In his recollections of Brienne communicated to Las Cases, Napoleon maintains that Keralio recommended him for the École Militaire in Paris although he had barely reached the required age, because he discerned in him 'a spark' worth encouraging, that he died soon afterwards but that his successor carried out his recommendation the following year: Las Cases (*C, 2*), vol. I, p. 96. The age limits for entry to the École Militaire were fourteen to sixteen: Montzey (*B, 4, a*), vol. I, p. 234; the lower limit was reduced to thirteen in 1782: Hennet (*B, 4, a*), p. 97, n. 3; students were expected to spend six years at Brienne: Chuquet (*D, 3*), vol. I, pp. 371–2. Napoleon's recollections were inaccurate: he had to wait till 1784 to enter the École Militaire (see below), and Keralio retired 16 May 1783 and died 1788: Chuquet, op. cit., vol. I, p. 137.

3. Corsicans in navy: Chuquet (*D, 3*), vol. I, p. 136; conscripts and deserters: Consul Collet to Lord Weymouth, Genoa, 21 March 1780, PRO, FO, 28 Genoa, I, see Bibliography, PRO, Carrington, p. 152.

4. Sleeping in hammocks; Letizia also deplored that in the navy Napoleon would have to fight simultaneously water and fire: Campbell (*B, 2, b*), p. 277, see also Pichot (*B, 2, b*), p. 131. Fraser (*B, 2, b*), pp. 5–6. C. Bonaparte, memoir to maréchal de Ségur, draft, June 1784, states that Napoleon was destined by Keralio to the École Royal Militaire and the navy in Toulon, and solicits a place for him in the navy: AN, 400 AP, 115; Iung (*D, 3*), vol. I, pp. 101–2 publishes a letter from C. Bonaparte to the minister, undated, on the same subject, using similar phrases, with the false reference: Archives de la Guerre; see below. Naval training centres existed also at Brest and Rochefort: Montzey (*B, 4, a*), vol. I, p. 288–319.

5. Supposed report by Keralio: Bourrienne (*B, 2, a*), vol. I, p. 9 (vol. I, p. 38); the date, 1784, is obviously false if Keralio is the supposed author. Chuquet (*D, 3*), vol. I, p. 142, believes the text to have been attributed to Reynaud des Monts, and in spite of the concordance of the date rejects the supposition. Bourrienne, loc. cit., asserts that the text is a genuine extract from a register of the ministry of war, stolen in 1794 and bought from a bookseller by Louis Bonaparte in 1806. Previous writers had quoted it: the author of *Premières années de Buonaparte* (London, undated), and J.-B. Salgues, *Mémoires pour servir à l'histoire de la France sous le gouvernement de Napoléon Bonaparte* (Paris, 1814) who claimed to have taken it from *Annales de l'Europe*, 1814; but Chuquet, op. cit., vol. I, p. 377, failed to find it there; see also Masson (*D, 3*), p. 88, n.i. Napoleon's self-portrait: Las Cases (*C, 2*), vol. I, p. 92; mattresses: see chapter 7, n. 24, above.

6. Only two promotions in 1783: Chuquet (*D, 3*), vol. I, p. 116. Two brothers not eligible for scholarships simultaneously: see n. 22 below.

7. Living promised to Joseph by Bishop Marbeuf: see chapter 6, n. 11, above.

Character: Chardon to Forien in Peignot (*B, 1*), vol. II, pp. 137–8; read 'clandestinely': Pourcenoux (*B, 1*); prizes, certificates: Fontenay (*B, 1*), p. 9. Mort de Pompée, essay: Nabonne (*B, 1*), p. 16; acting: Grandchamp in Beaune (*B, 1*), p. 162; *Les Fâcheux*: Pourcenoux, Nabonne, loc. cit.; Fontenay, op. cit., p. 10, publishes the school's cast of the play, which seems unrelated to Molière's. Principal's report: quoted by Napoleon in letter to uncle, June 1784, see below; Joseph decides to enter army; persuades Napoleon to give up navy and enter artillery with him: J. Bonaparte (*C, 1*), vol. I, p. 27, referring to his letter (subsequently lost with other correspondence between them): ibid., p. 32, n. 2. Napoleon, letter on Joseph: see n. 20 below.

8. C. Bonaparte, drafts of memoirs, undated, to Souiris, *subdélégué* and administrator of the former property of the Jesuits: AN, 400 AP, 112. Hostility of rivals, see below.

9. Lawsuit with Maria Giustina: ACA, FF, *c*. 5, *r*. 30; see also Cesari Rocca (*E*), *Le Nid . . .*, p. 131, Versini (*D, 2, a*), p. 86.

10. Death of gardener, family engaged from Avignon: C. Bonaparte, memoir to Souiris, 25 Oct. 1782, AN, 400 AP, 112; receipt of subsidy, 8 Dec. 1782, 1,862 livres, 10 sous: ibid.; inspection by Souiris 28 Oct. 1783, gardener died from not taking the 'necessary precautions', imported seeds unproductive: ADCS, IC, 26.

11. Two thirds of marsh drained, Marbeuf's visit: C. Bonaparte, draft of memoir to minister (of war?), undated, June–July 1784: AN, 400 AP, 112. Inspection by Michel-Angelo Colonna d'Ornano of *Nobles Douze*, 21 June 1784 (Carlo had already left Corsica, ibid.): ADCS, 1 C, 26.

12. Cost of drainage, sum required to complete work: C. Bonaparte, draft of memoir, undated, to minister of finance; see also draft of memoir June–July 1784, cf. n. 11, above: AN, 400 AP, 112, and draft of letter from Boucheporn to ministry of finance, 27 July 1784: ADCS, 1 C, 65.

13. Carlo betrayed by director of Plan Terrier, '*facilissimo*': Rossi (*A, i, b*), vol. XIII, pp. 275–6; aid from Marbeuf: chapter 5, nn. 23, 24, above, memoir presented in Paris 1784, see n. 11 above.

14. Carlo received a subsidy of 6,000 livres in 1777: see chapter 5, n. 23, above; his contract of July 1782 provided 5,500 livres plus 600 livres a year for a gardener's wages: see chapter 6, n. 46, above. In fact the Tuscan gardener's wages amounted to 70 livres a month: C. Bonaparte, memoir, 25 July 1782, see n. 10, above. Estimate of Bonaparte's revenues: Versini (*D, 2, a*), p. 95 (maximal and approximate). Luciano supervises work at Salines, 1782, reclaims expenses: C. Bonaparte, 'Livre de Raison', BN, p. 113; letter from C. Bonaparte to *intendant*, 1 June 1784, informing him that Luciano would be in charge of the Salines during his absence: ADCS, C, 26.

15. Marbeuf's marriage: see chapter 4, n.8, above. His first child, a daughter, was born 24 Dec. 1784. Children's visit to Cargese: C. Bonaparte, 'Livre de Raison', BN, inner top cover. It is quite possible that the children stayed not with Marbeuf but in some humbler home. Sonnet, C. Bonaparte, ibid., p. 3; see French translation in Versini (*D, 2, a*), p. 133.

16. See letter from Beaumanoir to Napoleon published in Chuquet (*D, 3*), vol. I, pp. 367–8; another version is given by Coston (*D, 3*), vol. I, pp. 39–40, n.i, in

which Beaumanoir describes the circumstances in which Letizia proposed to repay the loan; Napoleon's reactions: ibid., p. 41; see also Versini (*D, 2, a*), p. 104. Loan from aunt Lillina: C. Bonaparte, 'Livre de Raison', BN, p. 1. I have not identified this relation.

17. Carlo takes Maria Anna (Elisa) to Saint-Cyr: see Napoleon's letter to uncle, below. Lavallée (*B, 5*), p. 273, notes her admission 22 June 1784; but an erroneous date – 1787 – is given in a register of pupils when the school was suppressed, 1792, quoted ibid., pp. 351–8. The register includes six girls from Corsica besides Elisa: Balathier (sister of Napoleon's schoolfellow Balathier de Bragelonne?), Buttafoco, Cataneo, de Morlax, Vareze (Varese?), Casabianca, admitted 1784. She accompanied Elisa with Carlo, see below; Elisa describes her as a cousin in a letter to Letizia, 1786, quoted Masson (*D, 3*), pp. 132–3. Masson, ibid., p. 82, see n. 1, suggests that Carlo also conducted a Mlle Colonna, but I have found no trace of her in his correspondence or in documentation connected with Saint-Cyr.

18. Carlo pampered his children: Letizia Bonaparte (*C, 1*); Lucien 'petulant': abbé Forien in Peignot (*B, 1*), vol. II, p. 138, n. 2; he states that he taught Lucien for 20–22 months, which suggests he entered the school in the autumn of 1782: see chapter 6, n. 37, above. He reached Brienne on 21 June; see below; lines from him to Fesch, published in Iung (*C, 1*), vol. I, p. 23, from Brienne, stating he had arrived three days before, should obviously be dated 25 June, instead of 25 July: see n. 20 below.

19. Carlo's 'superb allure': see chapter 6, n. 11, above; visits Paris for health: J. Bonaparte (*C, 1*), vol. I, p. 28, who mistakes the name of the doctor, de Lassonne, for 'de la Sonde': see Versini (*D, 2, a*), p. 108. Napoleon on his father's illness: Antommarchi (*C, 2*), vol. I, p. 257.

20. Napoleon, in his letter to '*Mon cher oncle*' states that his father had reached Brienne with Lucien 'on the 21st' (June 1784) on his way to Saint-Cyr with Maria-Anna and another young lady. Originally in the Coll. Levie-Ramolino this document was inherited by count Lucien Biadelli. The text, copied from the original, is in the Archives Napoléon, AN, 400 AP, 137; and is published in Du Casse, *Supplément de la correspondence de Napoléon Ier* (Paris, 1887), pp. 50–55; in Iung (*C, 1*), vol. I, p. 24, with the date 25 July 1784 and the false reference Archives Guerre, and in Masson (*D, 3*), pp. 83–5, with the suggested date 25 June, which is convincing, for a note from Lucien added to the end of the letter states that he had arrived at Brienne three days before. A reference to Luciano in the text rules him out as addressee. Masson, loc. cit., doubts that it was written to Fesch because of its respectful tone; but Chuquet (*D, 3*), vol. I, p. 133, assumes it was addressed to him. This seems to me probable because Fesch was concerned by Joseph's proposed ecclesiastical career and already had a keen sense of responsibility; see below. One may also note the absence of any messages to relations in Corsica, which abound in a subsequent letter from Napoleon to his father after he had returned there in Sept., see below, and which one would expect to find had he been writing to an uncle in the island, such as Nicolò Paravisino (Paraviccini) as suggested by Masson, op. cit., p. 85, n.i. Napoleon also states that his father arrived at Brienne 'with Luciano and the two young ladies you have seen'; he must refer to Maria-Anna and Mlle Casabianca and to a

visit Carlo paid to Fesch at Aix on the way, for he would hardly have used these words had he been writing to an uncle in Corsica. Carlo's influence is several times apparent in the letter: e.g.: 'As my dear father observes . . .'; but I cannot agree with Norwood Young (*B, 4, b*), p. 106, that it is paramount. Lucien's meeting with Napoleon: Iung (*C, 1*), vol. I, pp. 24–5.

21. Maria-Anna is registered as entering Saint-Cyr 22 June 1784, see n. 17 above; but the date may be questioned for it is hard to see how Carlo could have covered the distance from Brienne in a day.

22. C. Bonaparte to the maréchal de Ségur, minister of war, 30 June 1784: AN, K 1229, *l*. v, no. 2; now in AN, AE 1, *c*, 13, *no. 32*. The drafts of memoirs by C. Bonaparte to the minister of war exist in the Archives Napoléon: AN, 400 AP, 115. The earliest, dated in his hand April 1784, written before he left Corsica, begs for a scholarship for Lucien, still at Autun, to replace Napoleon who would have been transferred to Paris but for the retirement of Keralio; the navy is not mentioned. The second, undated, evidently composed after his visit to Brienne, begs for a scholarship for Lucien, whom he has moved to Brienne to replace Napoleon, selected by Keralio for the École Militaire in Paris and 'the navy in the *département* of Toulon'. He solicits a place for him at Toulon, and for Joseph (not mentioned in the earlier memoir) a place either in the engineers or artillery. Joseph had presumably convinced his father and brother of his ability to qualify for these services, while Napoleon, in the interests of Joseph's career, was apparently willing to renounce his possible place at the École Militaire and go straight to Toulon, in spite of Joseph's suggestion in the summer of the previous year that they should enter the artillery together. There is no evidence that either memoir was sent as drafted; on the other hand phrases from both are included in two letters to the minister of war published in Iung (*D, 3*). The first, undated, ibid., vol. I, pp. 101–2, with a false reference to Archives Guerre, but which seems genuine, solicits a scholarship for Lucien, already at Brienne, in place of Napoleon whose 'destiny' has been changed by the retirement of Keralio, who had recommended him for the École Militaire in Paris and for Toulon. The minister notes at the top of the page: '*Faire la réponse ordinaire, s'il y a lieu*', and a marginal note states that the request is not admissible while Napoleon is still at Brienne. The second letter, ibid., pp. 103–4, and Iung (*C, 1*), vol. I, pp. 21–2, dated 18 July 1784, with the same false reference, pleads for Joseph's entry to the artillery or engineers (without mention of Lucien), enclosing the report of the principal of Autun, and ending with an appeal to the minister's 'paternal heart'. A note above the text states that Carlo should consult Timbrune. The letter from the minister of war to Carlo relative to Lucien's non-eligibility for a scholarship, and his age, 17 Oct. 1783, is published in Chuquet (*D, 3*), vol. I, p. 375, without reference. It mentions a recent edict concerning the age of candidates, 26 July 1783, of which a copy exists in ADCS, 1 C, 182. Fees at Brienne: *Almanach . . . de Troyes* (*B, 2, a*); at Autun, chapter 6, n. 36, above.

23. Ségur to Boucheporn, lease of Milelli and Badina, Carlo's rights, Paris, 13 Aug. 1784: AN, 400 AP, 112. C. Bonaparte, draft of memoir, undated, expense of Salines, lacks means to stay in Paris: ibid, see n. 12 above.

24. Letters from Boucheporn to ministry of finance, Paris, 27 July 1784; Bedigis to

Boucheporn, Paris, 3 Aug. 1784; Calonne to Boucheporn, Paris, 6 Sept. 1784, Boucheporn to Souiris, Paris, 11 Sept. 1784, Bedigis to Souiris, Paris, 10 Sept. 1784, *et seq.*: ADCS, 1 C, 65.

25. C. Bonaparte, letter to Lieut. Comm. Casabianca, Bastia, from Versailles, 28 July 1784: AN, 400 AP, 115. Member of the *Nobles Douze*, chapter 6, n. 42, above; neither Giubega nor Rossi was a member (see 'Procès-verbal . . . des États . . . 1781' (*A, i, e*), p. 97), so that Carlo cannot have been proposing to exchange his period of office for theirs; duties and indemnity: see chapter 4, n. 36, above.

26. Closing of Saint-Cyr: Lavallée (*B, 5*), pp. 270–300; Napoleon takes Elisa to opera: Bertrand (*C, 2*), vol. I, p. 285. Elisa's character: Montholon (*C, 2*), vol. II, p. 468, d'Abrantès (*C, 3*), vol. I, *t,* 2, p. 77; capacities as ruler, 'prodigious activity': Antommarchi (*C, 2*), vol. I, p. 415.

27. Napoleon's letter to his father, 12 or 13 Sept. 1784, from the Fonds Braccini, is noted with summary in the Archives Napoléon: AN, 400 AP, 139; published in Masson (*D, 3*), pp. 86–7; previously published with variations in wording Coston (*D, 3*), vol. I, p. 44; Nasica (*D, 3*), p. 72; Iung (*D, 3*), vol. I, pp. 105–7, with the false reference 'Archives de la guerre' The mistaken date, 1783, proposed in the Archives Napoléon, *ubi supra*, given by Coston, loc. cit., and some other writers is disposed of by Masson, op. cit., pp. 85–6, n. 3, who justifiably concludes that any date other than 1784 'leads to fiction'. The relations Napoleon remembers in his letter (see chapter 3, n. 23, above) include Carlo's mother, Letizia's mother, Letizia's cousin, wife of Giacinto Arrighi, Carlo's sister and her husband Nicolò Paravisino (Paraviccini); this last mention makes it most improbable that Napoleon's previous letter was addressed to him as suggested by Masson; see n. 20 above.

28. Chuquet (*D, 3*), vol. I, pp. 137–8, maintains that Giacinto Arrighi (married to Letizia's cousin, Maria-Antonietta Benielli, see chapter 2, n. 44, above), intervened for Napoleon with the minister of war at Carlo's request. Elected by the Corsican Estates of 1781, deputy to court for the Third Estates ('Procès-verbal . . . des États . . . 1781' (*A, i, e*), p.100), he was then in Paris and obtained a place in a military college for his own son thanks to Col. Rossi, kinsman of his wife: Rossi (*A, i, b*), vol. XIII, p. 279. Did Arrighi and Rossi aid Napoleon? Chuquet does not quote his source.

29. Order for Napoleon's admission to École Royale Militaire signed by Louis XVI and maréchal de Ségur, minister of war, 22 Oct. 1784: AN, 400 AP, 1. Date of departure: Napoleon Bonaparte, 'Époques de ma vie', published Masson (*D, 3*), p. 17. Different, earlier dates have been given: Castres (*B, 2, a*), p. 12, gives 17 Oct. Napoleon's notes: ibid., p. 8. Journey, arrival, first night: Bertrand (*C, 2*), vol. III, p. 70; see also Bartel (*D, 3*), pp. 97–104, from research in Musée Postal, an exception to the prevailing carelessness of his work. Napoleon in Palais Royal: D'Abrantès (*C, 3*), vol. I, *t.* i, pp. 53–6; cadets not allowed into town: Castres, op. cit., p. 10, Masson, op. cit., 131–3; anecdotes of Napoleon's supposed visits in Paris: ibid.

30. École Royale Militaire; foundation, appearance: see Laulan, *L'École Militaire. Le Monument* . . . (*B, 3*); balustrade: ibid., pp. 76–7; financed with lottery, tax on playing cards: Castres (*B, 2, e*), p. 16, Montzey, vol. 1, pp. 184, 192.

31. Only paying pupils had to spend 400 livres on equipment on entering school: Hennet (*B, 4, a*), p. 95. Uniform, simplified 1780, renewed twice yearly: A N, M M 660; see also Chuquet (*D, 3*), vol. I, p. 190. Equality, cadet corps: Hennet, op. cit., pp. 95, 101. A similar military organization existed at Brienne (perhaps only for the older boys): see Castres (*B, 2, a*), p. 10; C.H. (*B, 2, a*), pp. 21–2, who states that Napoleon was elected captain, degraded by hostile schoolfellows, then reinstated; C. Bonaparte, who states that Napoleon was head of his '*pluton*' ('*peleton*') : draft of memoir to minister of war, June–July 1784, A N, 400 A P, 115; see also his letter, undated, published in Iung (*D, 3*), vol. I, pp. 101–2; cf. n. 22 above. Numbers of paying and scholarship students: Masson (*D, 3*), pp. 115–16.

32. Staff of École Militaire; only a selection is here given of the details to be found in A N, M M 670–76; see also Castres (*B, 2, a*), p. 17; Chuquet (*D, 3*), vol. I, pp. 194–204, 413–15; Masson (*D, 3*), pp. 102–15.

33. Las Cases (*C, 2*), vol. I, pp. 678–9; Vaublanc (*B, 3*), vol. I, pp. 85–6 (Monteynard was appointed minister of war Jan. 1771). Pewter replaced by porcelain and glass, decision 10 Sept. 1777: A N, M M 670.

34. Black pottery: see chapter 3, n. 11, above. Apocryphal memoir: Bourrienne (*B, 2, a*), vol. I. pp. 43–4; uncritically repeated by later writers, see Masson (*D, 3*), p. 95, n.i. Austere conditions in Napoleon's military academies: Las Cases (*C, 2*), vol. I, pp. 678–80; d'Estre (*D, 3*), p. 24.

35. O'Meara (*C, 2*), vol. I, pp. 102–3; paying pupils fail exams: Masson (*D, 3*), p. 115, who ascertains that only fifteen to twenty-nine out of eighty-three paying pupils obtained commissions. Fights: see Chuquet (*D, 3*), vol. I, pp. 260–61.

36. Phélippeaux, quarrels with Napoleon, Picot de Peccaduc: Chuquet (*D, 3*), vol. I, pp. 231–2; Phélippeaux's subsequent career: see Masson (*D, 3*), pp. 118–19. Napoleon on Phélippeaux and Des Mazis: Montholon (*C, 2*), vol. II, p. 415.

37. 'Faithful Des Mazis': Las Cases (*C, 2*), vol. I, p. 241; failed exam, 1784: Chuquet (*D, 3*), p. 223. Napoléon Bonaparte; 'Dialogue sur l'amour'; published Masson et Biagi, *Napoléon, manuscrits inédits* . . . (*D, 3*), M S XLIX, pp. 523–30; borrows at Valence: Bertrand (*C, 2*), vol. II, p. 67; meeting in Paris: Montholon (*C, 2*), vol. II, pp. 413–14. Gossip about Letizia: Rémusat (*C, 3*), vol. I, p. 128, gives a polite version; the pamphleteer Lewis Goldsmith, *Secret History of the Cabinet of Bonaparte* . . . (London, 1810), p. 12, asserts that Letizia and her daughters were thrown out of Corsica, 1793, for keeping 'a house of accommodation in which every species of vice was encouraged'; see also *Memoirs of Bonaparte* (London, 1810–11?) describing brothel in Marseilles kept by Letizia, a 'most notorious prostitute', quoted in Alan Palmer, 'Napoleon's Earliest English Biographers', in *Essays by Divers Hands* (Royal Society of Literature, 1986), vol. XLIV, pp. 89–90. Des Mazis emigrated 1792, solicited an amnesty 1802, was appointed '*administrateur du mobilier national*' (later '*impérial*') and finally chamberlain, 1812: see Masson (*D, 3*), p. 117, Chuquet (*D, 3*), vol. I, p. 423; Napoleon also gave appointments to Des Mazis' relations: ibid.

38. 'Cahiers d'Alexandre des Mazis' in Bartel (*D, 3*), pp. 253–65; see Laulan 'Que valent les "Cahiers" de Des Mazis?' (*B, 3*). Balloon incident: 'Cahiers . . .' op. cit., p. 259; true version: G. Tissandier, *Histoire des ballons et des aeronautes célèbres, 1783–1800*, 2 vols. (Paris, 1887), vol. I, p. 62; legend corrected by Castres (*B, 2, a*), p. 16, and *Traits caractéristiques* . . . (*B, 2, a*), pp. 38–43, denied by Napoleon: Las Cases (*C, 2*), vol. II, p. 429.

39. Napoleon's religion: 'Cahiers . . .' in Bartel (*D, 3*), p. 259; Beauterne (*D, 3*), p. 130. Confirmation, Pope's 'gallantry': Las Cases (*C, 2*), vol. I, p. 95; 'Saint Neapolus (Neapolo)': *The Book of Saints* (New York, 1947), p. 433, *Dictionnaire historique des saints* . . ., (Paris, 1964), p. 281. O'Meara (*C, 2*), vol. II, p. 246.

40. Opinions of professors: Las Cases (*C, 2*), vol. I, pp. 97–8; d'Esguille, ex-Jesuit, argues with Napoleon: 'Cahiers . . .', in Bartel (*D, 3*), p. 258. Domairon was author of several books including *Principes généraux des belles-lettres à l'usage des cadets-gentilshommes de l'École Royale Militaire* of which 200 copies were bought for the school library, 8 March 1784: A N, M M 671. He too was an ex-Jesuit; he was later well rewarded by Napoleon: Masson (*D, 3*), p. 106.

41. Qualifications for commissions in artillery regiments; exams: Chuquet (*D, 3*), vol. I, pp. 215–25. Monge and d'Agelet join La Pérouse: A N, M M 627; see also Chuquet, op. cit., p. 223; Napoleon's poem: ibid., p. 226.

42. Laplace: Chuquet (*D, 3*), vol. I, pp. 227–9; Pommereul: see *Nouvelle Biographie Générale* (Paris, 1863) and chapter 1, n. 14 above.

43. Exam entries; results: Chuquet (*D, 3*), vol. I, pp. 223–5. The complete list of successful candidates is published in Coston (*D, 3*), vol. III p. 52. A school-leaving report, quoted by Iung (*D, 3*), vol. I, p. 125, and others, deriving from the comte d'Og (Charles Dangeais) (*B, 2, a*), p. 63, is apocryphal: '*Napoléon Bonaparte, né en Corse. Reservé et studieux; préfère l'étude à toute espèce d'amusements; . . . très-appliqué aux sciences abstraites; . . . capricieux, hautain . . . ambitieux et aspirant à tout: ce jeune homme est digne qu'on le protège.*' All reports on Napoleon in École Militaire have disappeared, including that attributed to de l'Esguille: '*Corse de la nation et de caractère; il ira loin si les circonstances le favorisent*': Masson (*D, 3*), p. 105. Commission of second-lieutenant in artillery regiment La Fère, signed by Louis XVI and the maréchal de Ségur, Saint-Cloud, 1 September 1785: A N, 400 A P, I. Detachments of Regiment La Fère in Corsica since 1774: see Villat (*A, 2, c*), vol. II, pp. 476–7, and at Valence: D'Estre (*D, 3*), p. 32, n. 1.

44. Lack of military training; worldly education at École Militaire: see D'Estre (*D, 3*), pp. 21–4; a general like a ship: maréchal Gouvion Saint-Cyr, *Mémoires pour servir à l'histoire militaire sous le Directoire, le Consulat et l'Empire*, vol. III (Paris, 1812), pp. 48–9, quoted D'Estre, op. cit., p. 25. Napoleon at Valence: Coston (*D, 3*), vol. I, pp. 77–96, is particularly rich in detail. Rough manners: Rémusat (*C, 3*), vol. I, pp. 103–4, Chaptal (*B, 2, b*), pp. 321–2; 'filibuster', graceful old-fashioned speech: John Trevor, dispatches 28 April, 21 May 1796; P R O, F O, 67 Sardinia; see Bibliography, P R O, Carrington, p. 28.

45. J. Bonaparte (*C, 1*), vol. I, pp. 97–8.

46. Cure at Corsican waters: see Napoleon's letter to his father, 12–13 Sept., n. 27 above; '*Il était frais, dispos, avait un teint à braver deux siècles*': Antommarchi (*C, 2*), vol. I, p. 257. Lucien untruthfully asserts that when he left Autun his father had 'obtained a second place' for him at Brienne: Iung (*C, 1*), vol. I, p. 16; verses by Duval, 1800, published in Chuquet (*D, 3*), vol. I, p. 132. Lucien's success in *Exercices publics* in 1784, Napoleon's letter to his father, *ubi supra*; the programme for the *exercices* of that year is missing; programme of *Exercices*, 1785 (*B, 2, a*); Lucien leaves Brienne, joins Fesch, is soon bored: Iung, op. cit., vol. I, p. 28.

47. Correspondence concerning Salines: A N, 400 A P, 112; A N, K 1229, *l.* v, nos. 1–9; A D C S, 1 C, 65. Plea to Calonne, 1785, draft, in name of Letizia, apparently

written by Joseph: A N, 400 A P, 112. Boucheporn sends subsidy, 6,512 livres, 25 Oct. 1784, ibid. Daire engaged by contract June 1784: ibid.; gardener's house begun Oct. 1784, completed Oct. 1785: C. Bonaparte, 'Livre de Raison', B N, p. 99, in hand of Joseph. The contract for the mulberry plantation was cancelled by decision of the Corsican Estates with that of Cesari Rocca at Porto Vecchio, 30 June 1785: 'Procès-verbal . . . des États . . . 1785' (*A, 1, e*), pp. 430–37; letter from ministry of finance to *intendant*, implementing recommendation of Estates, 31 Jan. 1786: A D C S, 1 C, 26. See also official recapitulatory report on mulberry plantations, 1788, ibid., stating that the Bonaparte's plantation contained only 23,219 trees instead of the required 50,000; that they had spent 7,895 livres on the plantation including 1,285 livres for the gardener's wages, and that the agreed subsidy of 8,500 livres would be paid in full. Though the Bonaparte came out of the affair with a profit of over 700 livres – cf. Versini (*D, 2, a*), p. 117 – they repeatedly claimed compensation over the next six years: see A N, 400 A P, 112, A N, 400 A P, 137; A D C S, 1 C, 26; A N, K 1229, *l. v*. The *c.* 29,000 livres they had spent partially draining the marsh were however irrecoverable; but the expense was not a dead loss, for they cultivated fruit trees other than mulberries as well as barley and garden produce on the recuperated land: see sources cited above and C. Bonaparte, 'Livre de Raison', B N, p. 90.

48. Ségur to Boucheporn on rent of Milelli, 13 Aug. 1784; copies in A N, 400 A P, 112 and A N, K 1229, *l. v*, nos. 6, 7; reply from Boucheporn rejecting project of auction, 15 Aug. 1784: A N, K 1229, *l. v*, no. 7 *bis*. Rossi, auction, opposition to Carlo: Rossi (*A, 1, b*), vol. XIII, pp. 272–4, Ségur to Boucheporn, 5 Oct. 1784: A N, 400 A P, 112; C. Bonaparte to Souiris, 25 Nov. 1784: ibid.; 99 year lease on Milelli and La Badina at 250 livres, 5 Nov. 1785, Bonaparte take possession 9 May 1796: ibid. and A D C S, 5 H, 5, no. 31.

49. Birth of Jerome: C. Bonaparte, 'Livre de Raison', B N, p. 27; A C A, G G, *c.* 8, *r.* 25; nurse, Sardinian maid, Genoese servant: C. Bonaparte, op. cit., pp. 56–7; C. Bonaparte attendance in court: A D C S, 2 B, 31; Joseph studies Bezout: J. Bonaparte (*C, 1*), vol. I, p. 28. C. Bonaparte, draft of petition to Ségur: A N, 400 A P, 112.

50. Fesch was informed of Carlo's illness before he left Corsica: see his letter to Luciano, Aix, 1 Jan. 1785: A N, 400 A P, 113. Joseph to Luciano and Letizia, Calvi, 6 Jan. 1785; C. Bonaparte to Luciano and Letizia, Saint-Tropez, 7 Jan. 1785: A N, 400 A P, 115. Carlo's passage through Aix: Fesch to Luciano, Aix, 11 Jan, 1785: A N, 400 A P, 113. Arrival in Montpellier, meeting with Pradier: Carlo and Joseph to Luciano and Letizia, Montpellier, 14 Jan. 1785; A N, 400 A P, 115. Journey, advice of Turnatori: J. Bonaparte (*C, 1*), vol. I, pp. 27–8; see also Grasset-Morel (*D, 2, a*), pp. 176–80. Régiment Vermandois in Corsica, 1780–84: Villat (*A, 2, c*), vol. II, p. 477. Stephanopoli de Comnène; see chapter 4, n. 23, above; Laure d'Abrantès: Abrantès (*C, 3*), vol. I, *t.i*, p. 62. Fesch to Luciano and Letizia, '*giorni delle ceneri*': A N, 400 A P, 113.

51. Pradier to Luciano: A N, 400 A P, 115. Joseph Fesch to Luciano and Letizia, '*giorno delle ceneri*': A N, 400 A P, 113. Fesch speaks of two doctors and mentions only one, de la Mure, ibid.; Joseph names three, de la Mure, Sabatier, Barthes: Bonaparte (C, 1), vol. I, p. 29. Napoleon in Antommarchi: Antommarchi (*C, 2*), vol. I, p. 259, in Gourgaud: Gourgaud (*C, 2*), vol. I, p. 473. Carlo's edifying end: Fesch to Letizia, 25 Feb. 1785: A N, 400 A P, 113.

52. Carlo faces death, confession: Fesch to Luciano and Letizia, 25 Feb. 1785: AN, 400 AP, 113. Fesch stays with him night and day: Fesch to Letizia, 25 Feb., ibid. Carlo's sentences: ADCS, 2 B, 14; 1 B, 77; 2 B, 20; cf. Versini (*D, 3*), pp. 92–3; the *procurateur du roi*, considering the mother's sentence insufficient, appealed to the Conseil Supérieur, which increased it to nine years' hard labour: ibid., p. 94.

53. Carlo's letters to Luciano, Paravisino, Letizia, letter from Napoleon (none of which have come to light): Fesch to Luciano and Letizia, 25 Feb. 1785, AN, 400 AP, 113; Carlo cheerful: ibid.

54. Carlo's delirium: Fesch to Luciano and Letizia, 25 Feb. 1785, AN, 400 AP, 113; his hallucination: J. Bonaparte (*C, 1*), vol. I, p. 29, Antommarchi (*C, 2*), vol. I, p. 259. Plans for Joseph's career: J. Bonaparte to Luciano and Letizia, Aix, 4 March 1785 (erroneously dated by Joseph 4 Feb.): AN, 400 AP, 115; Fesch to Luciano and Letizia, 25 Feb. 1785: *ubi supra*. Luciano's death-bed hallucination: Bertrand (*C, 2*), vol. II, p. 316.

55. Carlo's death: Fesch to Letizia, 25 Feb. 1785, to Luciano and Letizia, 25 Feb. 1785: AN, 400 AP, 113. Autopsy: AN, 400 AP, 115; published Masson (*D, 3*), pp. 375–7, Versini (*D, 2, a*), pp. 199–201. Fesch's version; Fesch to Letizia, 25 Feb. 1785, *ubi supra*. Death certificate: AN, 400 AP, 115. Funeral: see Grasset-Morel (*D, 2, a*), p. 182; expenses: Fesch, expense account sent to Luciano, Aix, March 1785, AN, 400 AP, 113.

56. Mme Permon, 'consoling angel': J. Bonaparte (*C, 1*), vol. I, p. 29. Family debts and problems: Fesch, letter to Luciano and Letizia, and to Letizia, 25 Feb. 1785, AN, 400 AP, 113. Marbeuf, in a rather brief letter of condolence to Luciano, 16 March 1785, assures him he will do what he can for Carlo's sons: AN, 400 AP, 115; evidence of practical help is however lacking. Nor is there evidence that he wrote a separate letter to Letizia. The expense account sent by Fesch to Luciano from Aix, March 1785, AN, 400 AP, 113, notes doctors' and apothecary's fees amounting to over 250 livres, and 49 livres for salaries to day and night nurses. The cost of Carlo's illness and funeral, added to Joseph's and Fesch's stay in Montpellier, with the purchase of appropriate clothes and their travelling expenses between Montpellier and Aix, totals 1,008 livres.

57. Carlo also increased the family property by purchase; 17 Sept. 1777 he added to the extent of the vineyard of Vitolu by buying land for 80 livres: AN, 400 AP, 114. De Roux, scheming father and son: see chapter 6, n. 12, above.

58. Napoleon refuses monument: Las Cases (*C, 2*), vol. I, pp. 84–5. Transfer of Carlo's remains to Saint-Leu: Grasset-Morel (*D, 2, a*), pp. 182–3, see also Chuquet (*D, 3*), vol. I, p. 213. His remains were placed in the Chapelle Impériale in Ajaccio (built to order of Napoleon III), 5 May 1951, where also lie those of Letizia, Joseph Fesch and other members of the family: *Les Guides Bleus, Corse, Île d'Elbe, Sardaigne* (Hachette, 1968), p. 181.

59. Napoleon's reactions to his father's death: Des Mazis in Bartel (*D, 3*), p. 259; letters to Luciano and Letizia, 28 March 1785: AN, 400 AP, 137, published in Masson (*D, 3*), pp. 126–7; the rule for supervision of students' letters, 28 July 1755, was no doubt still in force: AN, MM 658.

60. Napoleon liberated by death of father: Las Cases (*C, 2*), vol. I, p. 566, Montholon (*C, 2*), vol. II, p. 16, Bertrand (*C, 2*), vol. I, p. 178.

61. Napoleon rewards schoolmasters at Brienne: see chapter 7, nn. 24, 36, above, at École Militaire: Chuquet (*D. 3*), vol. I, pp. 199, 202. He gave Mme de Marbeuf an income of 15,000 livres (1809), created her '*baronne*' (1813), encouraged her son's military career, making him a.d.c. (1808), captain, baron (1809), colonel (1811), and gave her daughter a dowry; see Masson (*D, 3*), pp. 46–7. In 1800 he rescued Ségur from penury and allocated him a suitable pension: Chuquet, op. cit., vol. I, pp. 179–80. Attempt to save Baron Gen. J.-P. du Teil, advancement for son, grandson remembered in will: Baron J. du Teil (*F*), pp. 205–22.

62. Napoleon's opinions of his father: Antommarchi (*C, 2*), vol. I, pp. 258–9, Montholon (*C, 2*), vol. II, p. 16; Bertrand (*C, 2*), vol. I, p. 178, Las Cases (*C, 2*), vol. I, p. 566, Gourgaud (*C, 2*), vol. I, p. 473, vol. II, p. 166; of Letizia: Montholon, op. cit., vol. I, p. 321, cf. O.Meara (*C, 2*), vol. I, p. 100. School in Ajaccio: see chapter 3, n. 18, above.

63. 'Military genius . . .': Montholon (*C, 2*), vol. II, p. 240. French artillery: Babeau (*F*), vol. II, p. 88, Rouquerol (*F*), p. 77; see also Du Teil, Guibert, Wilkinson, (all *F*), Guibert's prophecy: Guibert, op. cit., p. xix.

❖(}❖

SELECTED CRITICAL
BIBLIOGRAPHY

In books hitherto written on the childhood and adolescence of Napoleon, sources of very unequal value have been strung together to make a story. The following bibliography represents an attempt to relate sources to the themes of the narrative and to distinguish them according to their authenticity and reliability.

MANUSCRIPT SOURCES

Private Collections
Archives Napoléon
Collection François Flori
Collection Général Pascal Santini
Collection Pozzo di Borgo
Archives
Archives Nationales, Paris (AN)
Services Historiques de l'Armée de Terre, Château de Vincennes, Paris (SHAT)
Bibliothèque Nationale, Paris (BN)
Public Record Office, London (PRO)
Archives Départementales de la Corse du Sud, Ajaccio (ADCS)
Archives Communales d'Ajaccio (ACA)
Archives Communales de Corte (ACC)
Institut d'Études Corses, Université Pascal Paoli, Corte

PRINTED SOURCES
A. The Bonaparte in Corsica, their life and environment

1. Texts contemporary or nearly contemporary with events related in this book
   a. Original works
   b. Historiography and biography
   c. Correspondence
   d. 'Accounts' of Corsica
   e. Official documents

2. Later works
   a. General histories of Corsica
   b. Regime of Pasquale Paoli
   c. Regime of French monarchy
   d. Customs and social conditions
   e. Localities

B. The Bonaparte at school

1. Joseph, Napoleon and Lucien at Autun
2. Napoleon and Lucien at Brienne
   a. Napoleon at school
   b. Letizia's reactions; Napoleon and the navy
   c. Napoleon and the Loménie de Brienne
3. Napoleon at the École Royale Militaire, Paris
4. Napoleon's education as a whole
   a. Military education
   b. Intellectual education
5. Maria-Anna (Elisa) at Saint-Cyr

C. Memoirs

1. Memoirs by members of Napoleon's family
2. Memoirs from Saint Helena
3. Memoirs by contemporaries of Napoleon

D. Biography

1. Pasquale Paoli
2. Napoleon's family, friends and dependants
   a. Carlo Bonaparte
   b. Letizia Bonaparte
   c. Joseph Fesch
   d. Various
3. Napoleon in his youth

E. Genealogy

F. Military History

Abbreviations

AN	Archives Nationales
BN	Bibliothèque Nationale
BSSHNC	Bulletin de la Société des Sciences Historiques et Naturelles de la Corse
AHRF	Annales Historiques de la Révolution Française
EC	Études Corses
REC	Revue d'Études Corses
CH	Corse Historique
c.	carton

MANUSCRIPT SOURCES
A. Private Collections

Archives Napoléon
Access to unpublished or unexploited manuscript sources has been my pretext for writing this book. The collection of HIH the Prince Napoleon has been of the first importance, and I am extremely grateful to the Prince and Princess for allowing me to consult these documents before their cession to the Archives Nationales, where they are available to the public only on microfilm. Part of the collection is formed by the Fonds Braccini, a collection of family papers saved by a friend when the Maison Bonaparte was ransacked in 1793. Invaluable for any close study of the childhood of Napoleon, they contain more material than could be used in a book of this scope. My role has been to point a way for others to explore.

Collection Flori
I am indebted to the rich collection of the late François Flori for access to interesting controversial letters by J.-B. Ristori, notes relative to Carlo Bonaparte's doctorate at the university of Pisa, his 'academic essay' published in 1766; see section A, 1, below.

Collection Santini
General Pascal Santini has generously communicated to me an important letter by Pasquale Paoli and a remarkable anonymous contemporary letter by detractors of Carlo Bonaparte: 'Lettera anonima contenente tutte l'eroiche virtu, azzioni, ed imprese del Signor Carlo Bonaparte cittadino infame della città d'Ajaccio in Corsica dell'anno di sua dimora in Roma 1764', 1766.

Collection Pozzo di Borgo
I owe my thanks to J. M. P. McErlean, professor of history at York University, Toronto, who has kindly communicated to me the text of the unpublished memoirs of Charles-André Pozzo di Borgo in the collection of his family.

B. Archives

Archives Nationales, Paris (AN)
The *Archives Napoléon* (see above) fill the series 400 AP, 1–220.
The *Fonds Braccini*, contained in 400 AP, 112–115, includes items of vital concern to this book, such as correspondence relative to the Bonaparte's claim to nobility, the succession of the Milelli and the exploitation of the Salines, unpublished letters by Carlo, Letizia, Luciano and Joseph Bonaparte and Joseph Fesch, and Carlo Bonaparte's memoirs: 'Raggionamento istorico, o siano memorie domestiche della famiglia di Buonaparte di Ajaccio in Corsica scritte da me Carlo di Buonaparte quondam Giuseppe l'anno mille e settecento ottanto': 400 AP, 115. Youthful letters by Napoleon are to be found in 400 AP, 137.
    The following series have also been consulted:
AE 1, c. 11–12, 'État civil', compiled from 1806, giving copies of baptismal and marriage certificates of the Bonaparte and Letizia's dotal act.

A E 1, *c.* 13, no. 1, correspondence between Carlo Bonaparte and d'Hozier de Serigny relative to proof of nobility required for Napoleon's admission to a military college. K 1225–1229, under heading *Monuments Historiques.* Contains interesting official memoirs on Corsica, 1769–89, documents relating to the proposed amnesty of Paoli, K 1227, and letters in connection with the Bonaparte's claim to the Milelli and exploitation of the Salines, K 1229.

Q^i 298, censuses of Corsican population.

M 81, documents concerning the college of Autun.

MM 656–683, documents concerning the École Royale Militaire, Paris.

Services Historiques de l'Armée de Terre, Château de Vincennes (SHAT)

Dossier Napoléon Ier: of capital importance.

Mémoires Historiques: contain a wealth of material on Corsica. Of particular relevance to this book: 'Journal des opérations de l'armée du Roy en Corse commencé le 20 juin 1768 au moment de l'embarquement de la division commandée par M. de Grand Maison, maréchal de camp, 1771': Mr. 248/1.

'Eclaircissement sur la localité d'Ajaccio et de ses environs': Mr. 1099 (another copy exists in AN, K 1225, no. 3).

Also consulted, in *Archives Historiques* (another important source for Corsican history): correspondence between Paoli and Marbeuf, in A^i 3638, A^i 3658.

Bibliothèque Nationale, Paris (BN)

Charles Bonaparte, 'Livre de Raison', *Cabinet des manuscrits, nouvelles acquisitions françaises (1958–1968), no. 15764.* Commonplace book from 1780, noting agricultural and domestic accounts, family events, etc.

Public Record Office, London (PRO)

The volume and importance of Corsican material in the series *Foreign Office, General Correspondence*, is indicated in Dorothy Carrington, *Sources de l'Histoire de la Corse au Public Record Office (Londres) avec 38 lettres inédites de Pasquale Paoli* (Ajaccio, 1983). More than 2,200 documents relative to Corsica are analysed from the series: Foreign Office 20 Corsica, 28 Genoa, 67 Sardinia, 79 Tuscany.

Archives Départementales de la Corse du Sud (ADCS)

The cardinal source for Corsican history from the sixteenth century to the present day. The following series have provided material:

Civile Governatore, Genoese administration 1548–1757.

Gouvernement Corse, 1753–1769, Corsican rebellion; regime of Pasquale Paoli.

A, *Actes du Pouvoir Souverain*, decrees of French monarchy, including the *Code Corse*, A 15–A 23, royal edicts 1768–1790.

1 B, *Conseil Supérieur*, proceedings of supreme tribunal under the French monarchy.

2–12 B, *Juridictions Royales*, provincial courts.

13 B, *Prévôté*, military justice.

1 C, *Intendance*, civil administration.

2 C, *Insinuation par entier*, official register of notarial acts.

2 E, *Registres Paroissiaux*, parish registers.

3 E, *Enregistrement*, register of notarial acts.

H, religious orders in Corsica.

J, documents privately donated to archives. Contains original text of Corsican constitution written and signed by Pasquale Paoli in minutes of *consulta* at Corte 16–18 Nov. 1755: 7 J, I.

4 L, *Administration du Département du Liamone*. 4 L, 56 contains an inventory, dated *10 prairial, 1' An 6*, of Bonaparte property lost since 1793.

Due to revisions of the inventory progressively made since 1970, certain references in articles to documents in ADCS may not correspond with their present classification.

Archives Communales d' Ajaccio (ACA)
An indispensable source for local history offering much information about the Bonaparte from 1572. A useful inventory exists to series prior to the French Revolution: C. Bosc, *Ville d' Ajaccio. Inventaire sommaire des Archives Communales antérieures à 1790 par Célestin Bosc, archiviste communale* (Draguignan, 1896).

Series consulted:
AA, municipal affairs.
BB, municipal administration; *c.* 7 consists of the 'Libro Grosso', a register of municipal edicts 1596–1674. The volume originally covered a longer period, pages being missing at the beginning and end.
GG, religious affairs, social assistance; *c.* 5–*c.* 38 give marriage, death and baptismal certificates, with interruptions, 1612–1797.
EE, maritime and military affairs.
FF, justice, litigation, police.
HH, agriculture, industry, commerce, markets, supplies.

Archives Communales de Corte (ACC)
Repeated errors in historiography could have been avoided by consultation of these archives which contain the death certificate of Napoleon's great-uncle, Napoleone, 1767, and the baptismal certificate of his brother Joseph, 1768.

Institut d' Études Corses, Corte (IEC)
Of particular use in this collection of photocopies of private archives has been the Collection Levie-Ramolino.

References to manuscript documents consulted are given in the notes according to the archival classification.

PRINTED SOURCES

The following books and articles have directly contributed to this book. General works on the eighteenth century, and full-length biographies, and studies of Napoleon are not included, though those relevant to particular points in my text are cited in notes. Very long titles are shortened, generally in accordance with the usage of the Bibliothèque Nationale.

A. THE BONAPARTE IN CORSICA, THEIR LIFE AND ENVIRONMENT

1. Texts contemporary or nearly contemporary with events related in this book

Evidence of exceptional value on the Bonaparte before as well as after they achieved fame.

a. Original works

Carolus Bonaparte (*sic*), *Exercitationes accademicae in secundam partem. Ethicae de jur., nat., et gent.* (Corte, 1766). In Latin.

Libro di prattica criminale, transcription du course de procédure criminelle pris par un étudiant de l'Université de Corte, 1768 (Association Franciscorsa, Bastia, 1980).

b. Historiography and biography

Giovacchini Cambiaggi, *Istoria del regno di Corsica* ..., 4 vols. (Florence, 1770–72). The Bonaparte were too obscure to attract the attention of this Italian churchman when he compiled his history.

Ambrogio Rossi, 'Osservazioni storiche sopra la Corsica ...', history of Corsica to 1814 in 17 vols. (vol. 18 remains unfinished), of which 13, covering the years 1705–1814, are published in *BSSHNC*, 1895–1906, ed. Abbé Letteron. Vols. consulted: vol. IX, 1745–52 (1900, nos. 229–33); vol. X, 1752–60 (1900, nos. 237–40); vol. XI, 1761–9 (1902, nos. 260–65); vol. XII, 1769–75 (1895, nos. 173–6); vol. XIII, 1776–88 (1896, nos. 181–5). The work of a scholarly churchman, supported by original documents. Writing from 1778 to his death, 1820, protected by Napoleon, to whom he may have been related, Rossi shows himself an ardent partisan of the Bonaparte. Though his account of their Corsican activities cannot be rejected wholesale, it certainly contributed to their legend.

Francesco-Ottaviano Renucci, *Storia della Corsica*, 2 vols. (Bastia, 1833–4). Less scholarly than Rossi, Renucci, who met Napoleon during the campaign of Italy, is equally enthusiastic, though he tells a different and no doubt legendary story of the Bonaparte's adventures in 1769.

Charles-François du Perier Dumouriez, *La Vie et les mémoires du général Dumouriez*, 4 vols. (Paris, 1822–3). Vol. I contains a vivid first-hand account of the French invasion, not without respect for the Corsicans.

Comte Jacques-Antoine-Hippolyte de Guibert, 'Opérations militaires de la réduction de la Corse du Ier au 25 mai 1769', ed. Letteron, in 'Pontenuovo', *BSSHNC*, 1913, nos. 352–4. Factual account of the Corsican defeat by a future master of military strategy.

Chevalier de Lenchères, 'Journal des campagnes de 1768 et 1769 en Corse ...', *BSSHNC*, 1889, nos. 103–6.

Voltaire, *Précis du siècle de Louis XV* (2nd ed., 1769), chapter LX, a dramatic picture of Corsican heroism (edn used Oeuvres historiques, Paris, 1968).

Tommaso Nasica, *Mémoires sur l'enfance et la jeunesse de Napoléon jusqu'à l'âge de vingt-trois ans, précédés d'une notice historique sur son père* ..., ed. abbé Nasica (Paris, 1852). Written 1821–9 with an admiration that allows for legend.

c. Correspondence

Two sets of letters written before 1779 offer unflattering portraits of Carlo and

Letizia Bonaparte by their contemporaries. 'Correspondance de M. Jadart, commissaire des guerres en Corse, avec le comte de Marbeuf . . ., 1767–1769', *BSSHNC*, 1882, 1883; see 1882, nos. 16–19.

Christine Roux, *Les Makis de la résistance Corse 1772–1778* (Paris, 1984). Unindulgent letters about French and Corsicans, including the Bonaparte, by Alexandre Louis Gabriel Roux de Laric, scheming, disdainful French officer unwillingly stationed in the island.

Saverio Bettinelli, 'Observations sur M. de Paoli écrites à Madame de l'Hôpital par le Révérend Père Bettinelli, Jésuite, *BSSHNC*, 1881, no. 11. Interesting report on Paoli on his arrival in Italy in June 1769.

Jean-Jacques Rousseau, admirer of Paoli and the Corsicans, see *Du contrat social* (1762), was outraged by the French invasion: see letter of 26 Feb. 1770 to C.-A. de Saint-Germain in *Correspondance complète de Jean-Jacques Rousseau*, ed. R. A. Leigh (Geneva/Oxford, 1965–   ), vol. XXXVII (1981).

d. Accounts of Corsica
Political developments drew many foreigners to eighteenth-century Corsica, the French as conquerors, the British as sympathetic observers. Their discovery of this little-known island produced numerous 'accounts', in which history, geography, and political and military commentary are juxataposed with description of local customs and scenery and the relation of personal experiences. The following are a selection that have contributed to this book.

Louis-Armand Jaussin, ancien apothicaire des armées, *Mémoires militaires, historiques et politiques sur les principaux évènements arrivés dans l'isle et royaume de Corse . . .* (Lausanne, 1769; a previous edition was published in 1758).

James Boswell, *An Account of Corsica, the Journal of a Tour to that Island and Memoirs of Pascal Paoli* (London, 1768). Visiting Corsica on the advice of Rousseau, Boswell was warmly welcomed by Paoli and has left a memorable if somewhat idealized portrait of the Corsicans and their leader forging their national independence.

Baron François-René-Jean de Pommereul, *Histoire de l'Isle de Corse*, 2 vols. (Berne, 1779). Artillery officer in the French army, caustic and sceptical but alive to the Enlightenment, he makes some penetrating observations on Paoli and his countrymen.

'Mémoires historiques sur la Corse par un officier du régiment de Picardie, 1774–1777', *BSSHNC*, 1889, nos. 100–102.

Renaud de la Greslaie (Grelaye, Grelée), inspector of forests in Corsica from 1776, 'Voyage de Paris en Corse', published in Villat, *La Corse de 1768–1789* (A, 2, c, below), vol. II, appendix VII, from MS in Bibliothèque Municipale de Dijon (Fonds Baudet, 271, no. 1231, MS Dépt., *t*. v, 1889).

Jacques-Maurice abbé Gaudin, *Voyage en Corse et vue politique sur l'amélioration de cette isle . . .* (Paris, 1787; edn used, Marseille, 1978).

e. Official documents
Statuti civili e criminali di Corsica, ed. G. C. Gregorj (Lyon, 1843). Genoese legal code applied to Corsica.

Proceedings of Corsican Estates, ed. A. de Morati and abbé Letteron, *BSSHNC*, 1896–1906. Texts consulted: 'Procès-verbal de l'Assemblée Générale des États de

Corse tenue à Bastia le Ier mai 1772 et jours suivants' (1896, nos. 188–192); 'Procès-verbal . . . des États . . . 1773' (1896, nos. 188–92); 'Procès-verbal . . . des États . . . 1775' (1899, nos. 219–26); 'Procès-verbal . . . des États . . . 1777' (1899, nos. 219–26); 'Procès-verbal . . . des États . . . 1779' (1901, nos. 251–2, 1903, nos. 269–70); 'Procès-verbal . . . des États . . . 1781' (1904, nos. 283–5); 'Procès-verbal . . . des États . . . 1785' (1906, nos. 296–303).

Record of deputations of Corsican Estates to court of Versailles, ed. Letteron, 'Deux députations des États de Corse à la Cour de France', *BSSHNC*, 1912, nos. 337–9: 'La députation des États de Corse de 1775 à la Cour de France', pp. 1–96; 'Processo Verbale della Deputazione degli Stati di Corsica alla Corte del 1785', pp. 97–145.

Patin de la Fizelière, 'Mémoire sur la province et juridiction de Sartene ou de la Rooca', *CH*, 1963, no. 9–10. Original in AN, K 1228, no. 39.

Proceedings of *consulta* in Corte, 27–9 May 1793, ed. Letteron in 'Documents pour servir à l'histoire de la Corse pendant la Révolution française', *BSSHNC*, 1890, nos. 115–18.

2. *Later works*

a. *General histories of Corsica*

Paul Arrighi, et Antoine Olivesi, eds., *Histoire de la Corse* (Toulouse, 1986), with contributions by Eugène Bonifay, René Emmanuelli, François-Xavier Emmanuelli, Fernand Ettori, Roger Grosjean, Jean Jehasse, Laurence Jehasse, Antoine Olivesi, Huguette Taviani-Carozzi.

Pierre Antonetti, *Histoire de la Corse* (Paris, 1973).

Francis Pomponi, *Histoire de la Corse* (Paris, 1979).

b. *Regime of Pasquale Paoli*

Dorothy Carrington, 'The Corsican constitution of Pasquale Paoli (1755–1769)', *English Historical Review*, 1973, no. 348. Dorothy Carrington, 'Paoli et sa "Constitution"', *AHRF*, 1974, no. 21. Dorothy Carrington, 'Le texte original de la constitution de Pasquale Paoli', *BSSHNC*, 1976, nos. 619–20, original Italian text with French translation and commentary.

Pierre Antonetti, 'L'Université de Pascal Paoli', *Corse-Matin* (Nice), 9–10 Nov., 17 Dec. 1981.

J. M. P. McErlean, 'Paoli et la Corse en juillet–août 1768. Rapports de deux agents britanniques', *EC*, 1982, nos. 18–19.

Fernand Ettori, 'La Révolution de Corse (1729–1769)', Arrighi et Olivesi, eds., *Histoire de la Corse* (A, 2, a).

Jean-Baptiste Marchini, *Pascal Paoli et l'État Corse . . .* (ADECEC, Cervioni, 1986).
    For biographical works on Paoli see D, 1, below.
    Concerning Jean-Jacques Rousseau and Corsica:

M. G. Streckeisen-Moultou, *Jean-Jacques Rousseau, oeuvres et correspondence inédites* (Paris, 1861). First publication of Rousseau 'Projet de Constitution pour la Corse', with relevant correspondence.

Ernestine Dedeck-Hery, *Jean-Jacques Rousseau et le projet de constitution pour la Corse* (Philadelphia, 1932).

Concerning James Boswell and Corsica:
Frederick A. Pottle, *James Boswell, The Earlier Years, 1740–1769* (London, 1966). Illuminating account of Boswell's Corsican adventure.
Dorothy Carrington, 'Boswell seen through Corsican eyes', *Rivista* (London), Jan.–June 1976, nos. 250, 251, 252. Boswell misunderstood by Rossi and the Corsicans, used by Paoli.

c. Regime of French monarchy
Louis Villat, *La Corse de 1768 à 1769*, 2 vols. (Besançon, 1925).
Francois-Xavier Emmanuelli, Claudine et Simon-Pierre Zonza, 'Déportation – colonisation – francisation: la Corse dans les archives des intendants de Provence', *BSSHNC*, 1969, no. 593.
Thad. E. Hall, *France and the Eighteenth-Century Corsican Question* (New York, 1971).
Maurice Bordes, 'La Corse pays d'États', *AHRF*, 1974, no. 218.
François Flori, *Le Procès des Niolins, 1774* (Bastia, 1975).
P. André-Marie, o f m (Claude Valleix), *Éléments d'un procès* (Bastia, 1975).
José Colombani, *Aux origines de la Corse française. Politique et institutions* (Ajaccio, 1978).
Antoine Casanova et Ange Rovere, *Peuple corse, révolution et nation française* (Paris, 1979).
Jean Defranceschi, *La Corse française (30 novembre 1789 – 15 juin 1794)* (Paris, 1980).
Dorothy Carrington, 'Les Pozzo di Borgo et les Bonaparte (jusqu'en 1793) d'après les mémoires manuscrits de Charles-André Pozzo di Borgo', in *Problèmes d'histoire de la Corse* . . . (*Actes du Colloque d'Ajaccio, 29 oct. 1969*) (Paris, 1971).
Dorothy Carrington, 'The Corsican Estates, 1770–1789', *Annali della Facoltà di Scienze Politiche a.a. 1982–1983, Università di Perugia* (Rimini).

d. Customs and social conditions
Madeleine-Rose Marin-Muracciole, *L'Honneur des femmes en Corse du XIIIe siècle à nos jours* (Paris, 1964).
Paul Arrighi, *La Vie quotidienne en Corse au XVIIIe siècle* (Paris, 1970).
Francis Pomponi, 'La politique domaniale sous l'Ancien Régime', *AHRF*, 1974, no. 218.
Antoine-Dominique Monti, *Essai sur les anciennes unités de mesure utilisées en Corse avant l'adoption du système métrique* (Cervioni, 1982).
Xavier Versini, *En Corse: vieilles affaires et procès oubliés* (Melun, 1972).
Dorothy Carrington, 'Sur les inégalités sociales en Corse rurale au XVIIIe siècle', *AHRF*, (1985, no. 260).

e. Localities
Alex Arman, *Notre-Dame d'Ajaccio, archéologie, histoire et légendes* (Paris, 1844).
Louis Campi, *La Citadelle d'Ajaccio* (Ajaccio, 1893).
Lieut.-Col. J. Campi, *Notes et documents sur la ville d'Ajaccio, 1492–1789* (Ajaccio, 1901).
Lieut.-Col. J. Campi, *Édifices religieux d'Ajaccio* (Ajaccio, 1914).
M. R. Comnène Stefanopoli, 'Une colonie grecque en Corse', *BSSHNC*, 1918, nos. 385–9, 393–6, 1919, nos. 405–8.

Charles Barbaud, 'La maison Bonaparte. Historique', *Revue des Études Napoléoniennes,* juillet-août, 1924.

Yeramiel Kolodny, *La Géographie urbaine de la Corse* (Paris, 1962).

Jean-Baptiste Marcaggi, *La cathédrale d'Ajaccio* (Ajaccio, 1930).

Xavier Versini, *Ajaccio, mon village* (Compiègne, 1974).

Theodora Stephanopoli de Comnène, *La Fondation de Cargese* (Marseille, 1975).

Yvan David, *Le Musée National de la Maison Bonaparte* (Paris, 1976).

Dorothy Carrington, 'The *casa* Bonaparte in Ajaccio', *Connoisseur,* Aug. 1979.

Thion de la Chaume, 'Mémoire médico-topographique sur la ville d'Ajaccio en 1792', ed. P. Gherardi, *BSSHNC,* 1981, no. 638.

Pascal-P. Santini, 'Les confréries d'Ajaccio', *BSSHNC,* 1983, no. 645.

P. Simi, A. Amadei, J. Magdeleine, J.-C. Ottaviani, P. Antonetti, A. Rovere, F. Beretti, A. Agosto, *Bastia, regards sur son passé* (Paris, 1983).

Jean-Marc Olivesi, 'Le couvent et l'église des missionnaires à Bastia', *BSSHNC,* 1986, no. 650.

B. THE BONAPARTE AT SCHOOL

1. Joseph, Napoleon and Lucien at Autun

Étienne-Gabriel Peignot (pseud.), *Choix de testamens anciens et modernes . . .,* 2 vols. (Paris, 1829). Contains informative letters on the Bonaparte brothers by their masters at Autun.

Henri Beaune, 'Un condisciple de Napoléon Ier au College d'Autun', *Annuaire de la Société Philotechnique* (1868). Recollections of eighty-six-year-old Jean-Baptiste de Grandchamp, schoolfellow of Joseph and Napoleon. Of doubtful accuracy.

Harold de Fontenay, *Napoléon, Joseph et Lucien Bonaparte au Collège d'Autun en Bourgoyne* (Paris, 1869). Informative and well documented.

Anatole de Charmasse, *Les Jésuites au Collége d'Autun, 1618–1763* (Autun, Paris, 1884).

Ch.C. Gaunet, *Le Collège d'Autun sous les Jésuites (1618–1763) et après eux* (Autun, 1940).

Bernard Nabonne, *Joseph Bonaparte. Le roi philosophe* (Paris, 1949). Underlines Joseph's accomplishments at school.

M. Pourcenaux, 'Les trois frères Bonaparte au Collège d'Autun', *Souvenir Napoléonien* (1981, no. 319).

2. Napoleon and Lucien at Brienne

a. Napoleon at School

Almanach de la ville et du diocese de Troyes (Troyes, 1776), contains valuable extracts of the prospectus of the newly founded college.

Exercices publics des élèves de l'École Royale Militaire de Brienne-le-Château (four publications, Troyes, 1780, 1782, 1783, 1785).

C.H., Some Account of the Early Years of Buonaparte at the Military School of Brienne; and of His Conduct at the Commencement of the French Revolution, by Mr C.H., one of his Schoolfellows (London, 1787). The most convincing souvenirs published by a fellow student of Napoleon's, by an English boy tentatively identified as Cumming of Craigmillar (see Vincent Cronin, *Napoleon* (London, 1971). Translated by Bourgoing, *Quelques notes sur les premières années de Bonaparte* (Paris, an VI).

Traits caractéristiques de la jeunesse de Bonaparte et réfutation des différentes anecdotes qui ont été publiées à ce sujet, par un de ses camarades à l'École Militaire de Brienne et de Paris (Leipzig, 1802). Plausible memoirs of anonymous schoolfellow.

Charles Dangeais, comte d'Oguerau, *Mémoires historiques et inédites sur la vie politique et privée de l'empereur Napoléon, depuis son entrée à l'école de Brienne jusqu'à son départ pour l'Égypte par le Cte. Charles d'Og* (Paris, 1822). Misleading; mostly fiction.

Louis-Antoine Fauvelet de Bourrienne, *Mémoires de M. de Bourrienne . . . sur Napoléon . . .*, 10 vols. (Paris, 1829; English edn, London 1885). These memoirs by a disloyal intimate of Napoleon's, ghosted by Maxime de Villemarest, have come in for much criticism. Yet the account of his schooldays at Brienne, if it reports unreliable anecdotes and exaggerates his friendship with Napoleon, seems to carry germs of truth.

Bourrienne et ses erreurs volontaires et involontaires . . ., 2 vols. (Paris, 1830). Bourrienne's deficiencies exposed and corrected by a team of Napoleon's upholders, including the comte de Survilliers (Joseph Bonaparte).

A.-N. Petit, *Napoléon à Brienne* (Troyes, 1839). This unpretentious account by a schoolmaster is not without misleading errors.

Alexandre Assier, *Napoléon Ier à l'École Militaire de Brienne . . .* (Paris, 1874).

Henri-Alexandre-Léopold de Castres de Vaux, 'Souvenirs de Brienne, *1780–1784*', ed. F. Puaux, *Revue de Paris, jan.-fév.* 1905. Contains some intriguing details, but the authenticity of the text, picked up on a bookstall, is open to question.

Abbé Arthur Prévost. 'Le collège et les premiers maîtres de Napoléon: les Minimes de Brienne', *Mémoires de la Société Académique . . . du département de l'Aube*, 1915 (t.LXXIX de la coll. t.III, 3me série). Valuable work based on archival sources.

Harold T. Parker, 'The formation of Napoleon's personality: an exploratory essay', *French Historical Studies*, 1971–2, vol. 7, essay 1.

b. Letizia's reactions; Napoleon and the navy

Major-General Sir Neil Campbell, ed. Neil Campbell Maclachan, *Napoleon at Fontainebleau and Elba . . .* (Paris, 1869).

Amadée Pichot, *Napoléon à l'île d'Elbe . . .* (Paris, 1875).

Comte Jean-Antoine-Claude Chaptal, ed. vicomte A. Chaptal, *Mes souvenirs sur Napoléon . . .* (Paris, 1893).

Sir William Augustus Fraser, *Hic et Ubique . . .* (London, 1893).

c. Napoleon and the Loménie de Brienne

M. Bourgeois, *Histoire des comtes de Brienne . . .* (Troyes, 1848).

Jacques Margret de Montbreton de Norvins, *Souvenirs d'un historien de Napoléon . . .*, 3 vols. (Paris, 1896–7). Brilliant account of the glamorous, doomed Loménie de Brienne by one connected with the family.

Albert Babeau, *Le Château de Brienne* (Paris, 1877).

3. Napoleon at the École Royale Militaire, Paris

While there is no lack of information about this celebrated establishment, descriptive evidence of Napoleon's stay here, apart from his own recollections, is limited to the brief accounts of de Castres de Vaux and the author of *Traits caractéristiques . . .*

(already cited, *B, 2, a*) and the unconvincing 'Cahiers d'Alexandre Des Mazis' published by Paul Bartel in *La Jeunesse inédite de Napoléon*, see D, 3, below. This short text provided by a member of the author's family contains too many obvious errors to inspire confidence; see Robert Laulan, 'Que valent les "Cahiers" de Des Mazis?', *Revue de l'Institut Napoléon*, 1956, no. 59.

Disgruntled memories of the school some years earlier, following sombre complaints of the Collège La Flèche, are provided by comte Vincent-Marie Viennot de Vaublanc, *Souvenirs par le Cte de Vaublanc*, 2 vols. (Paris, 1890).

Robert Laulan, *L'École Militaire. Le monument, 1751–1788* (Paris, 1950).

Robert Laulan, 'La discipline à l'École Militaire de Paris (1753–1788)', *Information historique*, 1955, nos. 4, 5.

4. Napoleon's education as a whole

a. Military education

Comte Claude-Louis de Saint-Germain, *Mémoires* . . . (Amsterdam, 1779).

Charles de Montzey, *Institutions d'éducation militaire jusqu'en 1789*, 2 vols. (Paris, 1866– 7).

Léon Hennet, *Les Compagnies de cadets-gentilshommes et les collèges militaires* (Paris, 1889).

J. Colin, *L'Éducation militaire de Napoléon* (Paris, 1900). See also 'Military History' (F, below).

b. Intellectual education

Abel-François Villemain, *Souvenirs contemporains d'histoire et de littérature*, 2 vols. (Paris, 1854–5). Vol. I reports comte Louis de Narbonne's conversations with Napoleon on mathematics and antiquity.

Norwood Young, *The Growth of Napoleon, a Study in Environment* (London, 1910).

Harold Talbot Parker, *The Cult of Antiquity and the French Revolutionaries* (Chicago, 1937).

F. G. Healey, *The Literary Culture of Napoleon* (Geneva/Paris, 1959).

Jean Jehasse, 'Napoléon, Bossuet et le mythe antique', *Cahiers d'Histoire*, 1971, t.XVI, nos. 3–4.

Morris Kline, *Mathematics in Western Culture* (USA, 1953, London, edn used, 1954; Harmondsworth, 1972).

Jacques Bouineau, *Les Toges du pouvoir, ou la révolution de droit antique, 1789–1799*, preface G. Godechot (Toulouse, 1985).

5. Maria Anna (Elisa) at Saint-Cyr

Théophile Lavallée, *Histoire de la Maison Royale de Saint-Cyr (1686–1793)* (Paris, 1853).

Horace Walpole, in a letter of 17 Sept. 1769 to George Montagu gives a charming picture of the young ladies at work and play: *The Letters of Horace Walpole . . .*, ed. P. Cunningham, 9 vols. (London, 1891), vol. V, no. 1194.

Nancy Mitford, *The Sun King* (London, 1966). A perceptive account of the founding and development of the school.

C. MEMOIRS

It need hardly be said that memoirs are unsatisfactory source material. This is particularly true of those concerning Napoleon. Nearly all are heavily coloured by the feelings and interests of their authors, and strongly biased for or against their subject. The memoirs written, dictated or inspired by Napoleon, and members of his family are no exception: the Bonaparte participated in the creation of what they considered to be a suitable image of themselves.

1. Memoirs by members of Napoleon's family

The memoirs of Carlo Bonaparte (see A N – p. 269 above) written for the edification of his descendants, though leaving much unsaid, seem closer to truth than most of what the members of his family wrote or allowed to be written about themselves.

Letizia Bonaparte, 'Souvenirs de Madame Mère dictés par elle-même dans les derniers temps de sa vie', published in H. Larrey, *Madame Mère* . . ., 2 vols. (Paris, 1892, see D, 2, b, below), vol. II. pp. 528–30. This brief text dictated to her lady-in-waiting Rosa Mellini towards the end of 1836 misrepresents facts to extol her husband but gives some precious pictures of intimate family life.

Joseph Bonaparte, *Mémoires et correspondance politique et militaire du roi Joseph*, ed. A. du Casse, 10 vols. (Paris, 1853–4; edn used, Paris, 1855). Generally considered reliable; but when writing of his youth and origins Joseph has more respect for his family than for fact.

Lucien Bonaparte, *Mémoires de Lucien Bonaparte, prince de Canino. Écrits par lui-meme*, 1 vol. (London, 1835). Less misleading than the following:

Général Théodore Iung, *Th. Iung, Lucien Bonaparte et ses mémoires, 1775–1840, d'après les papiers déposés aux Archives Étrangères et d'autres documents inédits*, 3 vols. (Paris, 1882–3). Untrustworthy memoirs arranged by an untrustworthy writer; but Lucien's colourful portraits of his family, in which he does justice to his father, deserve attention.

2. Memoirs from Saint Helena

The memoirs of Napoleon's companions in exile are subject to multiple distortions resulting from Napoleon's attitude to their authors and theirs to him, as well as their individual temperaments and their concern for their positions and potential public. It is well known that Napoleon used his memorialists to build up a legend of himself as the popular leader sprung from the people, the idealistic liberal statesman. When speaking of his youth his position is however fluctuating: he alternately applauds his father as a champion of liberty and blames him as an irresponsible pleasure-seeker, and while proclaiming his contempt for noble lineage, dwells on his family's distinguished Tuscan origins. With Las Cases, his self-appointed official biographer, the tone of his confidences is less spontaneous than with his other fellow-exiles, especially Bertrand, whom he did not suspect of keeping a journal, and O'Meara, himself given to downright expression. The company of his fellow-countryman Antommarchi stimulated affectionate recollections of Corsica.

Comte Marie-Joseph-Emmanuel-Dieudonné de Las Cases, *Mémorial de Saint-Hélène ou journal où se trouve consigné . . . tout ce qu'a dit et fait Napoléon . . . du 20 juin 1815 au 25 novembre 1816*, 8 vols. (Paris, 1823), edn used, ed. M. Dunan, 2 vols. (Paris, 1951).

Barry E. O'Meara, *Napoleon in Exile; or a Voice from St Helena . . .*, (London, 1822; with additions, London, 1888).

François Antommarchi, *Mémoires du docteur F. Antommarchi ou les derniers moments de Napoléon*, 2 vols. (Paris, 1825).

J. Héreau, *Napoléon à Sainte-Hélène . . .* (Paris, 1829).

Comte Charles-François-Tristan de Montholon, *Récits de la captivité de l'Empereur Napoléon à Sainte-Hélène . . .*, 2 vols. (Paris, 1847).

Baron général Gaspard Gourgaud, *Sainte-Hélène, journal inédit de 1815 à 1818 . . .*, 2 vols. (Paris, 1889).

Comte Louis-Joseph-Narcisse Marchand, *Mémoires de Marchand, premier valet de chambre et exécuteur testamentaire de l'empereur . . .*, ed. J. Bourguignon, 2 vols. (Paris, 1952, 1955).

Comte général Henri-Gratien Bertrand, *Général Bertrand . . . Cahiers de Sainte-Hélène*, 3 vols. (Paris, vol. I, 1951; vol. II, 1959; vol. III, 1949).

3. Memoirs by contemporaries of Napoleon

The following are noted not for their intrinsic value but because they have in varying degrees contributed material to this book.

Comte Jean-Victor Colchen, in Hugues de Montbas, 'Robespierre et les Bonaparte vus par le comte Colchen', *Revue des Deux Mondes*, 15 Sept. 1952. Secretary to the *intendant* Boucheporn, Colchen recalls his experience of Corsica in 1778 in unpretentious memoirs, written 1811–12, offering observations on the Bonaparte that seem to be those of an impartial witness.

Armand-Louis de Gontaut, duc de Lauzun, *Mémoires de M. le duc de Lauzun* (Paris, 1882).

Comte colonel Félix de Romain, *Souvenirs d'un officier royaliste . . .*, 3 vols. (Paris, 1824–9). Hostile observations on Napoleon.

Laure, duchesse d'Abrantès, *Mémoires de Mme. la duchesse d'Abrantès . . .*, 18 vols. (Paris, 1835); edn used, 12 t. in 6 vols. (Paris, 1831–5). Lively fictitious accounts of blood relationship with Napoleon and his intimacy with her family in his student days; but her descriptions of Letizia, to whom she was lady-in-waiting, ring true.

Comte Antoine-Marie Chamans de Lavalette, *Mémoires et souvenirs du comte Lavalette . . .*, 2 vols. (Paris, 1831).

Renée-C.-Victoire de Froulay, marquise de Créquy, *Souvenirs de la marquise de Créquy de 1740 a 1800*, 7 vols. (Paris, 1834–5). Includes a notorious sly dig at Letizia.

Comte André-François Miot de Melito, *Mémoires du comte de Melito . . .*, 3 vols. (Paris, 1858); edn used, 3 vols. (Paris, 1880).

Claire-Elizabeth-Jeanne Gravier de Vergennes, comtesse de Rémusat, *Mémoires de Madame de Rémusat*, ed. P. de Rémusat, 3 vols. (Paris, 1880). Denigrates Napoleon and his family in attempt to ingratiate herself with the Bourbons.

Baron Claude-François de Méneval, *Mémoires pour servir à l'histoire de Napoléon Ier*, 3 vols. (Paris, 1831).

Comte Pierre-Louis Roederer, *Mémoires sur la Révolution, le Consulat et l'Empire*, ed. Aubry (Paris, 1942).

Constant Wairy, *Mémoires intimes de Napoléon par Constant son valet de chambre*, ed. Dernelle (Paris, 1967).
Memoirs of Chaptal and Norvins, see B, 2, b, above.
Louis-Antoine Fauvelet de Bourrienne, *Mémoires* . . ., see B, 2, a, above.

D. BIOGRAPHY

1. Pasquale Paoli

Paoli's reputation has been considerably damaged by unscholarly panegyric works published in the last century. A complete, impartial biography based on the original sources remains to be written. In the meantime the following works can be cited, all of which emphasize the scope and quality of his culture.
Saverio Bettinelli, 'Observations sur M. de Paoli . . .', see A, 1, c.
Abbé Letteron, 'Pascal Paoli avant son élévation au Généralat . . .', *BSSHNC*, 1913, nos. 358–60. Quotes important letters.
Dominique Colonna, *Le Vrai Visage de Pascal Paoli en Angleterre* (Nice, 1969).
Peter Adam Thrasher, *Pasquale Paoli, an Enlightened Hero, 1725–1807* (London, 1970).
Fernand Ettori, 'La formation intellectuelle de Paoli (1725–1755)', *AHRF*, 1974, no. 218.
René Emmanuelli, *Vie de Pascal Paoli*, Lumio, 1978.

For the institutions and historiography of his regime see A, 1, b and A, 2, b, above. A complete edition of his correspondence is in preparation; the most important existing collections of his letters are in *BSSHNC*, 1881–1931, and N. Tommaseo, *Lettere di Pasquale de' Paoli* (Florence, 1846).

2. Napoleon's family, friends and dependants

a. Carlo Bonaparte

Carlo, generally underrated by historians, has had to wait till 1977 for a full-length biography; but interesting studies of his life and death had already been published, as follows:
M. Grasset-Morel, *Les Bonaparte à Montpellier* (Montpellier, 1900).
Pierre Lamotte, 'L'acte de mariage de Charles Bonaparte', *REC*, 1961, no. 3, an investigation of first-rate importance.
Charles Salvo, 'Charles de Bonaparte . . .', *BSSHNC*, 1961, no. 559, contains inaccuracies, but commendably impartial.
Louis H. Escuret, *Charles Bonaparte à Montpellier* (Montpellier, 1964).
Xavier Versini, *M. de Buonaparte ou le livre inachevé* (Paris, 1977). Sympathetic account based on research in contemporary Corsican documents; includes a translation of the major part of Carlo Bonaparte's 'Livre de de Raison', see BN – p. 270 above.

b. Letizia Bonaparte

Letizia is the subject of a detailed biography by Baron Hippolyte Larrey, *Madame Mère (Napoleonis Mater)* . . ., 2 vols. (Paris, 1892). In spite of an unscholarly approach this work has not been surpassed by later writers.
Clara Tschudi, *Napoleon's Mother* (London, 1900).
Clement Shaw, *Letizia Bonaparte* . . . (London, 1928).
François Duhourçau, *La mère de Napoléon* (Paris, 1921).

Lydia Peretti, *Letizia Bonaparte* (Paris, 1922).

A. Augustin Thierry, *Madame Mère* (Paris, 1939).

Monica Stirling, *A Pride of Lions* . . . (London, 1961).

Gilbert Martineau, *Madame Mère* (Paris, 1980).

Alain Decaux, *Letizia mère de l'empereur* (Paris, 1983).

A controversial question is disposed of in François Flori's illuminating 'Le père de Napoléon: une fausse énigme', *Le Petit Echo de la Corse*, 1954.

Marthe Arrighi de Casanova makes a spirited but sometimes misleading defence of Letizia in *Letizia mère de Napoléon a été calomniée* (Brussels, 1954).

c. Joseph Fesch

Neither of the following lives of Letizia's half-brother, the Cardinal Fesch, a wealthy, worldly collector and patron of the arts, does justice to the subject.

Mgr Jean-Paul-François Lyonnet, *Le Cardinal Fesch* . . ., 2 vols. (Paris, 1841).

Hélène Colombani, *Le Cardinal Fesch* (Paris, 1979).

d. Various

Albert Du Casse, *Le Général Arrighi de Casanova, duc de Padoue* . . . (Paris, 1986). Furnishes information on the links between the Bonaparte and their Arrighi cousins of Corte.

Arthur Chuquet, 'Le parrain de Napoléon', *Nouvelle Revue*, Paris, 15 *juillet/1 août* 1908). Study of Lorenzo Giubega, not altogether free from traditional suppositions.

Arthur Chuquet, 'La nourrice de Napoléon', *Séances et travaux de l'Académie des Sciences Morales et Politiques*, Comte rendu, Paris, 1910, t. CLXXIV. Study of Camilla Ilari.

Pierre Tomi, 'Les biens de la famille Bonaparte', *EC*, 1956, no. 12. Based on archival sources; corrects some widespread notions about the poverty of the Bonaparte.

Jean-Paul Garnier, *L'Extraordinaire Destin des Bonaparte*, Paris, 1968. Offers intriguing detail concerning Carlo Bonaparte.

The numerous biographies of Napoleon's brothers and sisters are outside the scope of this book; for Joseph at school see B, 1, above. The following publication deserves mention as a surprising self-revelation of Letizia's cousin, Aurele Varese, who in the context of this book appears as an insignificant young ecclesiastic.

Aurele Varese, *Rapport sur la Corse fait au Comité de Salut Public de la Convention National et au Conseil exécutif provisoire, par Aurele Varese, député de la Société des Amis de la Liberté et de l'Égalité de Bastia* (*juillet* 1793).

3. Napoleon in his youth

Many books of very unequal quality have been written about Napoleon's childhood and adolescence. The standard works on the subject, by Coston, Masson, Chuquet and Marcaggi, all written before 1903, have aged. Others, by Iung and Bartel, are misleading; nearly all are flawed to some degree by partiality, preconceptions, uncritical use of sources and insufficient study of archival material. Two works of modern times, however, by Mirtil and Versini (see D, 2, a, above), are exceptional in throwing new light on the Bonaparte in Corsica by documentary research.

Baron François-Gilbert Coston, *Biographie des premières années de Napoléon Bonaparte* . . . *avec un appendice renfermant des documents ou inédits ou peu connus* . . .,

2 vols. (Paris/Valence, 1840). Can be faulted today, but the seriousness of this work is not in question. Particularly informative about Napoleon's stay as an artillery officer in Valence.

Robert-Ant. chevalier de Beauterne, *L'Enfance de Napoléon depuis sa naissance jusqu'à sa sortie de l'École Militaire* (Paris, 1846).

Tommaso Nasica, *Mémoires sur l'enfance et la jeunesse de Napoléon* . . . (see A, i, b, above). Written 1821–9, the biography closest in time to its subject but not the most instructive.

General Théodore Iung, *Bonaparte et son temps (1769–1799) d'après des documents inédits*, 3 vols. (Paris, 1880–81). Publishes some important documents, but mistakes dates, gives numerous inexact quotations and references and is responsible for the false enigma concerning the birth dates of Joseph and Napoleon, and the widespread underestimation of Carlo Bonaparte.

Frédéric Masson et Guido Biagi, *Napoléon inconnu: papiers inédits (1786–1793) publiés par Frédéric Masson et Guido Biagi, accompagnés de notes sur la jeunesse de Napoléon (1769– 1793) par Frédéric Masson*, 2 vols. (Paris, 1895). Extremely valuable publication of the Fonds Libri, a collection of youthful writings and notes by Napoleon, with biographical narrative by Masson. Most of Napoleon's writings are republished with the title: Frédéric Masson et Guido Biagi, *Napoléon, Manuscrits inédits, 1786–1791* (Paris, 1969, edn used).

Masson's biographical notes are published as a separate book: *Napoléon dans sa jeunesse (1769–1793)* (Paris, 1907; new edition, Paris, 1969, edn used). Work based on scholarly investigation of available sources, with scrupulous references, though Corsican material is neglected. In spite of some blind spots still a valid guide.

Arthur Chuquet, *La Jeunesse de Napoléon*, 3 vols. (Paris, 1897–9). The product of very wide scholarship, with some attention to Corsican material, but without references. Alone in his generation the author makes a case for Carlo Bonaparte.

Madame Olivier Des Armoises, *Avant la gloire: Napoléon enfant* . . . (Paris, 1898). Acquires interest from evidence, accurate or not, supplied by a great-niece of Carlo Bonaparte's brother-in-law, Nicolò Paravisino.

J.-B. Marcaggi, *La Genèse de Napoléon* . . . (Paris, 1902). Exceptional value is given to this work by the author's knowledge of Corsica and consultation of local documents, some no longer accessible.

Lorenzo de Bradi, *La Vraie Figure de Bonaparte en Corse* (Paris, 1946). Creates a convincing picture of the Bonaparte in Corsica without recourse to scholarship.

Henry d'Estre, *Bonaparte, les années obscures (1769–1795)* (Paris, 1942). Perceptive; concentrates on the military aspect of the subject.

Marcel Mirtil, *Napoléon d'Ajaccio* (Paris, 1947). Meticulous research in Corsican legal records produces an altogether new and often surprising picture of the Bonaparte during the infancy of Napoleon.

Paul Bartel, *La Jeunesse inédite de Napoléon, d'après de nombreux documents* (Paris, 1954). Confusing, seldom inspires confidence. Misquotes dates, betrays ignorance of Corsican history and geography; refers to unidentified memoirs by Gaspard Monge and publishes unconvincing memoirs by Des Mazis.

Georges Roux, *Monsieur de Buonaparte* (Paris, 1964).

Baron Thiry, *Les Années de jeunesse de Napoléon Bonaparte* (Paris, 1975).

E. GENEALOGY

Précis historique de la maison impériale des Comnènes (Amsterdam, 1784, reprinted 1969). Traditional story of the Stephanopoli de Comnène, who emigrated to Corsica from Greece in 1676 and claimed descent from the emperors of Byzantium and Trebizond. Laure d'Abrantès also claimed that they were ancestors of the Bonaparte, a pretension that is not echoed in this work, written when the Bonaparte were still obscure, to celebrate the granting of the title of prince by Louis XVI to Demetrius Comnène.

The following is a selective list from the very numerous works on the genealogy of the Bonaparte that have aided the writing of this book.

M. Foissy, avocat, *La Famille Bonaparte depuis 1264* (Paris, 1830).

Luigi Passerini, 'Della origine della famiglia Bonaparte, dimonstrata con documenti . . .', *Archivio Storico Italiano*, nuova serie, vols. III, IV, 1956.

Frédéric de Stefani, *Sur les origines des Bonaparte, rapport à M. le ministre de l'instruction et des cultes de l'Empire français* (Turin, 1859).

Philippe de Caraffa, *La Vérité sur l'origine de nos Bonaparte* (Bastia, 1869). Throws light on the first Bonaparte in Corsica.

Comte P.-P.-R. Colonna de Cesari Rocca, *L'Armorial Corse* (Paris, 1892).

Léonce de Brotonne, *Les Bonaparte et leurs alliances* (Paris, 1833).

Giovanni Sforza, introduction to 'Undici lettere giovanili di Giuseppe Bonaparte', in Baron Alberto Lumbroso, *Miscellanea Napoleonica* (series I–VI, 1895–9), series VI, 1899.

Comte P.-P.-R. Colonna de Cesari Rocca, *Le Nid de l'aigle: Napoléon, sa patrie, son foyer, sa race, d'après des documents inédits* (Paris, 1905). Comprises revised text of valuable genealogical study first published as *La Vérité sur les Bonaparte avant Napoléon* (Paris, 1899), together with important historical material.

Baron Alberto Lumbroso, *I Bonaparte dell'isola e i Buonaparte del continente*, first published in *Archivio Storico di Corsica*, Jan.–March 1933 (Leghorn, 1933).

Joseph Valynseele, *Le Sang des Bonaparte* (Paris, 1954).

Léon Maestrati, 'La généalogie des Bonaparte de Corse', *CH*, 1962, nos. 5–6, 7. Interesting detailed study, regrettably without references.

Andrea Corsini, *I Bonaparte a Firenze* (Florence, 1961).

Baron Hervé Pinoteau, *Les Bonaparte avant 1789* (Braga, 1962).

Baron Hervé Pinoteau, *Le Dossier nobiliaire et héraldique des Bonaparte* (Braga, 1966). The above two valuable studies are published, revised, in Pinoteau, *Vingt-cinq ans d'études dynastiques* (Paris, 1982).

Fernand Beaucour, 'La famille maternelle de Napoléon Ier: Les Ramolino et leur généalogie . . .', *Bulletin historique de la Société du Château Impérial de Pont-de-Briques*, 1974, nos. 8, 9, 10.

François Démartini, 'Les Bonaparte', *Annales de généalogie et d'héraldique*, 1985, nos. 1, 2, 3.

François Démartini, work in preparation, partly consulted in MS: 'Blasons et filiations des principales familles corses'.

F. MILITARY HISTORY

(See also Napoleon's 'Military Education', B, 4, a, above.)

Comte Jacques-Antoine-Hippolyte de Guibert, *Essai général de tactique précédé d'un discours sue l'état actuel de la politique et de la science militaire en Europe*, 2 t. in 1 vol. (London, 1772). Revolutionary work on military strategy prefaced by prophetic portrait of a military leader who was to be incarnated by Napoleon.

Albert Babeau, *La Vie militaire sous l'Ancien Régime*, 2 vols. (Paris, 1890).

Baron Joseph du Teil, *Une Famille militaire au XVIIIe siècle* (Paris, 1896).

G. Rouquerol, *L'Artillerie au début des guerres de la Révolution* (Paris, 1898).

Spenser Wilkinson, *The French Army before Napoleon* (Oxford, 1915).

Colonel J. Reval, *Histoire de l'armée française* (Paris, 1929).

P.-L. Albertini et G. Rivollet, *La Corse militaire. Ses généraux. Monarchie. Révolution. Ier Empire* (Paris, 1959). Summarizes the careers of fifty-five Corsican generals, without Napoleon, too illustrious to be included.

References to printed works consulted are given in the Notes with the name of the author followed by the code classification of the above bibliography.